WORKS ISSUED BY
THE HAKLUYT SOCIETY

Series Editors
Gloria Clifton
Joyce Lorimer

THE ARCTIC WHALING JOURNALS
OF WILLIAM SCORESBY THE YOUNGER
VOLUME III
THE VOYAGES OF 1817, 1818 AND 1820

THIRD SERIES
NO. 21
(Issued for 2009)

Donations

The Hakluyt Society gratefully acknowledges donors in 2008. The Society thinks it appropriate that the generosity of donors should be recorded not only in its Annual Report, but also in the book which these donations have helped to make possible. Donations and legacies, and, for British members, Gift Aid, are a valuable supplement to the Society's subscription income which rarely matches the steadily increasing cost of producing our books to the high standard we seek to maintain. The officers of the Society, and the editors and series editors of our books, receive no remuneration and are proud to continue the endeavour which Richard Hakluyt himself inspired, and which we have maintained for 162 years – the endeavour to record, to understand and to interpret the means by which, for better or worse, the different regions and different peoples of the world have become connected with one another.

Mr Edward Alsip
Mr Robert C. Baron
Mr Greg and Mrs Astrid Bear
Mr M. Schermer Blum
Dr John Bockstoce
Mr Bruce Bogert
Dr Norman Fiering
Mr Paul Garber
Dr Martin L. Greene
Professor William Harris

Mr Warren Heckrotte
Mr Paul Herrup
Dr Ross MacPhee
Ms Maureen O'Donnell
Mr Thomas Peckham
Mr Werner Schuele
Professor Paul Seaver
Mr Kenneth J. Siple
Dr Edward L. Widmer
Mr Thomas Winter

The Hakluyt Society is particularly grateful to the Gladys Krieble Delmas Foundation of New York which made a substantial grant to the American Friends of the Hakluyt Society as a contribution to the cost of publishing this volume. Dr David Stam's advice in this matter is much appreciated. The President and Council of the Society wish also to thank the American Friends and in particular Dr Ross McPhee and Dr Edward L. Widmer, the outgoing and present Presidents of that organization, for their continuing support and financial assistance.

Model of the *Baffin*.
Constructed by Stanley Hogarth of Bradford from the original plans in Whitby Museum, the model (SCO97) was presented to the Museum by the Chapman Trust in 1957, to mark the centenary of William Scoresby's death. Photo courtesy of Whitby Museum.

THE
ARCTIC WHALING JOURNALS
OF
WILLIAM SCORESBY THE YOUNGER

VOLUME III
THE VOYAGES OF 1817, 1818 AND 1820

Edited by
C. IAN JACKSON

With an Appendix by
FRED M. WALKER

Published by
Ashgate
for
THE HAKLUYT SOCIETY
LONDON
2009

Published for The Hakluyt Society by

Ashgate Publishing Limited
Wey Court East
Union Road
Farnham
Surrey GU9 7PT
England

Ashgate Publishing Company
Suite 420
101 Cherry Street
Burlington
VT 05401-4405
USA

Ashgate website: http://www.ashgate.com

British Library Cataloguing in Publication Data
Scoresby, William, 1789–1857.
The Arctic whaling journals of William Scoresby the younger.
Vol. 3, The voyages of 1817, 1818, 1820. – (Hakluyt Society. Third series ; v. 21)
1. Scoresby, William, 1789–1857 – Diaries. 2. Whaling – Arctic regions.
3. Arctic regions – Description and travel.
I. Title II. Series III. Jackson, C. Ian. IV. Hakluyt Society.
919.8'04–dc22

Library of Congress Cataloging in Publication Data
LCCN: 2004445100

ISBN 978-0-904180-95-4

Typeset by Waveney Typesetters, Wymondham, Norfolk

Mixed Sources
Product group from well-managed forests and other controlled sources
www.fsc.org Cert no. SA-COC-1565
© 1996 Forest Stewardship Council
FSC

Printed and bound in Great Britain by
MPG Books Group, UK

Contents

Illustrations and Maps   x

Preface and Acknowledgements   xi

Table of Quantities and Conversions   xii

Glossary   xiii

Editorial Note   xv

INTRODUCTION   xvii
    The Voyages   xvii
      1817   xvii
      1818   xx
      1820   xxi
    Scoresby's Personal and Religious Life   xxiii
    Scoresby and Arctic Exploration   xxvii
    Scientific Recognition   xxxv

THE JOURNALS OF WILLIAM SCORESBY THE YOUNGER
    Journal for 1817   3
    Journal for 1818   61
    Journal for 1820   129

APPENDIX: The Building of Arctic Whalers, by Fred M. Walker   213

WORKS CITED   237

INDEX   243

Illustrations and Maps

Illustrations

	Model of the *Baffin*.	*Frontispiece*
Figure 1.	'Dangers of the Whale Fishery'.	xlii
Figure 2.	Midship section.	224
Figure 3.	Keel scarf.	225
Figure 4.	Longitudinal structure.	225
Figure 5.	Keel.	226
Figure 6.	Frames.	226
Figure 7.	Tonnage formula.	231
Figure 8.	Scoresby's stowage plan for the *Baffin* from his notebook.	234

Maps

Map 1.	Map for the voyage of 1817.	2
Map 2.	Map for the voyage of 1818.	60
Map 3.	Map for the voyage of 1820.	128

Preface and Acknowledgements

Like the two earlier volumes, this final volume devoted to the voyages of William Scoresby the Younger, from his first command in 1811 until the publication of *An Account of the Arctic Regions* in 1820, is based on the manuscript transcripts that form part of the Scoresby Papers in the Whitby Museum of the Whitby Literary and Philosophical Society. The 1817 journal forms part of WHITM:SCO1254; that for 1818 is WHITM:SCO1255.1; and the 1819–20 journal, describing the construction of his new ship, the *Baffin*, and the 1820 voyage, is WHITM:SCO1255.2.

Throughout the decade of this editing project, the officers and staff of the Museum and the Society have provided me with great support; particular mention should be made of the Society's Registrar, Denise Gildroy. Professors Joyce Lorimer and Will Ryan have saved me from many errors through their final editing. Any that remain are my own, exemplified in the quite irrelevant caption to Figure 2 in volume II, for which I apologize.

Because the 1819–20 journal contains a detailed and perhaps unique day-by-day account of the construction of a new whaling vessel, it was an opportunity to include an appendix that could set the *Baffin*'s construction in the context of commercial shipbuilding in the heyday of wooden sailing ships. With his background as both a shipbuilder and shipping historian, Fred Walker has enhanced the value of Scoresby's account.

In Whitby's maritime pantheon, the William Scoresbys, father and son, yield only to James Cook. It seems somehow fitting, and was certainly a personal pleasure, while I have been preparing the present volume for publication, that I have also assisted Whitby's Captain Cook Memorial Museum to arrange an exhibition on 'Cook in Canada'. Both Cook, the surveyor and chart-maker of the Newfoundland coast, and the younger Scoresby, the arctic scientist, were so much more than superb navigators. It has been a privilege to be able to bring knowledge of their achievements to a wider public.

Finally, I should like to express my great personal gratitude to the Gladys Krieble Delmas Foundation of New York for its generous grant, through the American Friends of the Hakluyt Society, towards the publication of this third and final volume of Scoresby's voyages.

Montreal, Quebec   IAN JACKSON
April 2009

xi

Table of Quantities and Conversions
(approximations in most cases)

Length
1 inch = 2.5 cm   1 foot = 30 cm   1 yard (3 feet) = 91 cm
1 fathom (6 feet) = 1.8 m   1 mile = 1.6 km

Weight
1 pound (lb) = 0.45 kg   1 quarter (28 lb) = 12.7 kg
1 hundredweight (cwt, 112 lb) = 50.8 kg   1 ton (20 cwt, 2240 lb) = 1016 kg
1 chaldron (Whitby measure) = 4927 lb or 2235 kg

Temperature
A difference of 10°C is equivalent to a difference of 18°F and the Celsius and Fahrenheit scales converge at −40°, so:

0°F = −18°C   10°F = −12°C   20°F = −7°C   32°F = 0°C
40°F = 4°C   50°F = 10°C   60°F = 16°C

Atmospheric pressure
One inch of mercury is equivalent to 33.864 millibars or hectopascals. Therefore:

Inches of mercury	Millibars	Inches of mercury	Millibars
28	948	29.5	999
28.5	965	30.0	1016
29	982	30.5	1033

Cask capacities
In Scoresby's day, volumes and other dimensions were generally imprecise. The cask capacities listed below are therefore very approximate, and it is the hierarchy of cask sizes (e.g. as listed in the 'Manifest' at the end of the 1811 voyage) that is more important than the measure of capacity, especially because the casks contained blubber and not liquids.

Leaguer	=	159 imperial gallons	Butt	= 126 gallons, wine-measure
Puncheon	=	72 gallons	Barrel	= 31½ gallons

Miscellaneous
1. According to Scoresby (see note to journal entry for 26 May 1813),'Four tons of blubber by measure, generally afford three tons of oil.' and 'The ton or tun of oil is 252 gallons wine measure.' A butt cask could hold half the latter amount of oil.
2. Value of the pound sterling. Using the data in Grahame Allen's *Inflation: the Value of the Pound 1750–2002*, the equivalent purchasing power in 2002 in each of the years from 1811 to 1820 was: 1811: £49.65; 1812: £43.72; 1813: £42.64; 1814: £48.95; 1815: £54.73; 1816: £59.92; 1817 & 1818: £52.66; 1819: £53.88; 1820: £59.41.

Glossary

These entries supplement those in the glossaries of volumes I and II of these *Journals*. Most definitions are from Smyth's *Sailor's Word Book*, with others from Layton's *Dictionary of Nautical Words and Terms*.

Black-strake. 'The range of plank immediately above the wales in a ship's side; they are always covered with a mixture of tar and lamp-black ...'. (Smyth)

Breast-hooks. 'Thick pieces of timber, incurvated into the form of knees, and used to strengthen the fore-part of a ship, where they are placed at different heights, directly across the stem internally ...'. (Smyth)

Broach-to, To. 'To fly up into the wind. It generally happens when a ship is carrying a press of canvas with the wind on the quarter, and a good deal of after-sail set. The masts are endangered by the course being so altered, as to bring it more in opposition to, and thereby increasing the pressure of the wind. In extreme cases, the sails are caught flat aback, when the masts would be likely to give way, or the ship might go down stern foremost.' (Smyth)

Caboose, or *camboose.* 'The cook-room or kitchen of merchantmen on deck ... It is generally furnished with cast-iron apparatus for cooking.' (Smyth)

Cat-harpings or, *catharpin legs.* 'Ropes under the tops at the lower end of the futtock-shrouds, serving to brace in the shrouds tighter, and affording room to brace the yards more obliquely when the ship is close-hauled. They keep the shrouds taut for the better ease and safety of the mast.' (Smyth)

Clench, To. 'To secure the end of a bolt by burring the point with a hammer.' (Smyth)

Cut-water. 'The foremost part of a vessel's prow ... It cuts or divides the water before reaching the bow, which would retard progress.' (Smyth)

Deadeye. 'Hard wooden block, pierced with holes, fitted in lower end of shroud to take lanyard for setting up.' (Layton) There is also a lengthy definition in Smyth.

Dubb, To. 'To smooth and cut off with an adze the superfluous wood.' (Smyth)

Fife-rails. 'Those forming the upper fence of the bulwarks on each side of the quarter-deck and poop in men-of-war. Also the rail round the mainmast, and encircling both it and the pumps ...'. (Smyth)

Frames. 'The bends of timbers constituting the shape of the ship's body – when completed a ship is said to be *in frame.*' (Smyth)

Gammoning. 'Seven or eight turns of a rope-lashing passed alternately over the bowsprit and through a large hole in the cut-water, the better to support the stays of the foremast ...'. (Smyth)

Gut. 'A somewhat coarse term for the main part of a strait or channel.' (Smyth)

Hogged. '[I]t implies that the two ends of a ship's decks droop lower than the midship part, consequently that her keel and bottom are so strained as to curve upwards.' (Smyth)

Martingale. 'A rope extending downwards from the jib-boom end to a kind of short gaff-shaped spar, fixed perpendicularly under the cap of the bowsprit; its use is to guy the jib-boom down in the same manner as the bobstays retain the bowsprit.'

Nankin. 'A light fawn-coloured or white cotton cloth.' (Smyth)

Outward. 'A vessel is said to be entered outwards or inwards according as she is entered at the custom-house to depart for, or as having arrived from, foreign parts.' (Smyth)

Pooping, or *being pooped*. 'The breaking of a heavy sea over the stern or quarter of a boat or vessel when she scuds before the wind in a gale, which is extremely dangerous, especially if deeply laden.' (Smyth)

Spring. '[A] hawser laid out to some fixed object to slue a vessel proceeding to sea.' (Smyth)

Tender.'Said of a vessel having small righting moment; so being easily moved from her position of equilibrium, and slow in returning to it.' (Layton)

Tierce. '[A]pplied to provision casks, ... the beef-tierce contains 280 lbs., or 28 galls., whilst that of pork only contains 260 lbs., or 26 galls. Now [1867] the beef-tierce often contains 336 lbs., and the pork 300 lbs.' (Smyth)

Victualling-bill. 'A custom-house document, warranting the shipment of such bonded stores as the master of an outward-bound merchantman may require for his intended voyage.' (Smyth)

Waft. '[M]ore correctly written *wheft*. It is any flag or ensign, stopped together at the head and middle portions, slightly rolled up lengthwise, and hoisted at different positions at the after-part of a ship. Thus, at the ensign-staff, it signifies that a man has fallen overboard ... At the peak, it signifies a wish to speak; at the mast-head recals [sic] boats; or as the commander-in-chief or particular captain may direct.' (Smyth)

Wales. 'Strong planks extending all along the outward timbers on a ship's side, a little above her water-line; they are synonymous with *bends* ... The channel-wale is below the lower-deck ports ...'. (Smyth)

Editorial Note

The transcription of the manuscript text follows the original with the following exceptions:

1. Occasionally missing punctuation or letters are supplied in square brackets for greater clarity.
2. The layout of the original text in columns has been simplified for economy and ease of reading. Variations in layout are indicated in editorial notes in square brackets in the text. Marginal headings giving dates, coordinates, wind direction etc. have been placed at the head of the entry to which they refer. Dates in headings have been emboldened for ease of location, and the form of coordinates in headings has been standardized.
3. Asterisks in square brackets indicate unreadable words.
4. Words in square brackets with a question mark indicate an uncertain but probable reading.
5. Where Scoresby himself uses brackets this is normally indicated in a footnote as ('Brackets in transcript').

Introduction

In the two earlier volumes devoted to William Scoresby's whaling journals, we have seen the development of a successful whaling captain and a competent and resourceful navigator, as well as the emergence of a careful and respected arctic scientist. The journals have also provided evidence of the growing importance of religion in Scoresby's life. The pattern was one of steady progress and the maturing of Scoresby himself. The journals, mostly devoted to his months away from Whitby and his family, could not be a complete mirror of the man and his activities, but it seems reasonable to suggest that they reflect the main elements of his life between 1811 and 1816.

The journals in the present volume, though they are as detailed and eventful as the earlier ones, are much less of a self-portrait. More was happening to Scoresby between the voyages than during them. In particular, in the seventeen months between August 1817 and the end of 1818 Scoresby seriously considered giving up his sea-going career; this option was made impossible by a substantial financial loss; he became a whaling partner rather than merely a hired captain; his relationship with his father changed profoundly; he declined the opportunity to participate in the renewal of naval exploration of arctic waters; he began the move from Whitby to make his home in Liverpool; his religious convictions were powerfully strengthened; and he completed arrangements for the publication of his major work, *An Account of the Arctic Regions*. The journals show the effect of all these events, but the journals need to be read in the context of this broader background of Scoresby's life.

The Voyages

1817. After Scoresby's amazing return to Whitby in 1816 following the holing of the *Esk*'s hull at 78°N, the voyage of 1817 was a disappointing anticlimax. It began with protests on wage-cutting across the Whitby fleet, as owners took advantage of a peacetime oversupply of sailors.[1] The *Esk* was then unable to leave the port due to weather conditions until the beginning of April. The stay in Lerwick was brief and despite bad weather the *Esk* was north of 75°N by 21 April. The ship was lucky to avoid a storm in early May that caused the loss of four ships, but the first whale was not caught until 1 June. A second was caught five days later, but these two were the only successes of the entire summer. By 18 July, Scoresby was complaining in his journal that

> The fishery of the present season has been the most singular, partial, unsuccessful of any occasion witnessed of many years. Where it has been profitable it has been partial [in

---

[1] The cuts in sea pay were substantial, as can be seen from a comparison of the table of wages in 1813 (see vol. I, p. 138) and that included by Scoresby in the 1817 journal.

the?] extreme & singularly accidental. The places of resort & habits of the fish have differed so much from what is usual that it is allowed that success in the fishery has been the result of <u>chance</u> only; ... hence we can account for the fact how the experienced & judicious fishers have in general failed whilst almost every master of his <u>first year</u> has succeeded. This remark is not splenetic or for excusing our failure, ... as far as we know at least ¼ of the fishing ships which have not cargos sufficient to [answer?] their expences supposing the price of oil to be above the average.

The ostensible reason of the scarcity of whales & their pecular [*sic*] habits, is the singular state of the ice which lies at a distance from the land greater than was ever known by any fisherman now prosecuting the business ... . Hence the whales not finding their usual shelter are dispersed & prompted to the pursuit of dif*feren*t routes & the adoption of original retreats.[1]

The unusual expanse of open water where sea ice was normally to have been expected may have been a major reason for the lack of success, but the *Esk* seems also to have been particularly unlucky. Unusually for Scoresby, he spent a substantial part of the season sailing in company with his father in the *Mars* and his brother-in-law in the *John*. As he remarked later in his autobiography,

> I was indeed completely 'at fault', and for once gave up all dependence on my own judgment for near two months together, and followed my Father. Hitherto I had always made a practice of acting independently.[2]

Perhaps, though there is no evidence for this in the journal, Scoresby was dogged by memories of 1816, when the assistance of the *John* proved vital in escaping from the ice and bringing the *Esk* safely home. What is clear is that, during this period, both the *Mars* and the *John* were catching whales, but the *Esk* was not.

Scoresby's scientific experiments also had misfortune. On 28 June, after lowering his marine diver, a marine thermometer, and wood specimens to what he believed was a depth of over 7200 feet (2000 metres) without reaching the seabed, the rope broke as it was being raised, and everything was lost. 'My mortification was excessive.'[3]

One consequence of the open water was that the *Esk* sailed in longitudes west of the prime meridian from 10 June until 15 July, and again from 25 July until the ship headed homeward. Since he became a captain in 1811, Scoresby had never entered western longitudes in the whaling area until 1816, and only briefly in that year. On 9 July Scoresby estimated his longitude at 10°W which, if accurate, would, at 75°N, have put the *Esk* within about 130 nautical miles of the islands along the east coast of Greenland. Certainly there is clear evidence that the *Esk* had entered the southward-flowing East Greenland Current.

By the end of July, Scoresby gave up the search for whales. A venture in the middle of the month to the east of Spitsbergen, 'a track of the ocean which has not been

---

[1] Journal entry 18 July 1817.

[2] Scoresby's unpublished autobiography covers the years from his birth in 1789 until 1823, and is in ten parts (WHITM:SCO843.1–10). A complete transcript is available in the Whitby Museum Library. Cited hereafter as 'Autobiography'.

[3] Journal entry 28 June 1817.

visited of many years & in which we read in the Dutch authorities of much profitable fishing for whales and walruses'[1] had been blocked by ice at 12½°E, and by 29 July the *Esk*, with the *John* and the *Venerable* of Hull, was back within sight of the Greenland coast. Two days later, 'As our companions were now determined on proceeding homewards, and as we had for a long time been unable to find a single whale',[2] the three ships headed south and on 3 August arrived off the southeast coast of Jan Mayen.

Scoresby's lengthy account of the landing on Jan Mayen that he included in his journal has been omitted from this edition, because it became the basis for a revised and extended text that he included in *An Account of the Arctic Regions* (vol. I, pp. 154–69).

Sailing eastward, the *Esk* separated from the *John* and *Venerable*, probably because the other ships needed to land crew members in Shetland, and reached harbour in Whitby on 15 August. Scoresby can scarcely have been surprised that he received a very different welcome from that of a year earlier. As he wrote in his autobiography,

> I found the owners of my ship not altogether satisfied with my success & exertions. They said it was a cruel thing for me to follow my Father all the season & thus lose the chance of success which a separation of two ships, the Esk & Mars, would have afforded at least to one of them.

Scoresby's situation was not helped by the fact that his father in the *Mars* had returned with fourteen whales[3] and another Whitby ship, the *William and Ann*, brought home twenty-two.[4] The owners may also have begun to wonder whether Scoresby's scientific activities during the voyages were distracting him from their principal purpose.

If Fishburn and Brodrick intended their comments as no more than understandable grumbling about the poor returns, they may have been surprised by the reaction they provoked.

> My Father ... had had some disturbance with his crew & had been annoyed with several acts of obstinate disobedience which he was disposed to punish by withholding the wages of the offenders agreeable to law & paying them into Greenwich Hospital. The owners, however, refused their sanction to this measure, though obviously important for preserving any sort of good government on board of their ships – and declared their determination not to be troubled with any quarrels but to pay the men their wages & dismiss them. My Father felt himself so agrieved [*sic*] by this refusal of support from the owners of the ship, that he immediately gave up his command; and I, for the same reason, together with the apparent want of approbation of the owners respecting myself, and some little circumstances in their conduct that were rather unpleasant to my feelings, also gave up my Command.[5]

[1] Journal entry 16 July 1817.
[2] Journal entry 31 July 1817.
[3] 'Autobiography'.
[4] Lubbock, *Arctic Whalers*, p. 205.
[5] 'Autobiography'.

Both father and son were, by this time, impatient with the reluctance of the Whitby owners to make them partners in the whaling enterprise; had the owners done so they would have less justification for complaining about their loss, since it would have been shared with their captains. Fishburn and Brodrick were also unaware of a profound change in the son's attitude to whaling, absent from the 1817 journal, but clearly expressed in the autobiography about his return home on this voyage.

> The view of the English coast along which we were sailing produced a train of reflections on expected happiness, checked by the recollection of our scanty cargo that was productive of much manifestation to my pride & disappointment of my desire of soon gaining a comfortable independence. Methought God was working against me. My labours for three years had been increasingly unprofitable. They now hardly promised to me the supply of my necessary wants. 'I shall leave off the sea', thought I. 'The little property I have acquired will provide me 120 or 150 £ a year, and on this, with any accidental acquisition from finding out other employment, I may live in an economical manner at least, entirely on shore. I shall then be no longer exposed to the <u>freaks of fortune</u> ...'.[1]

1818. As explained later in this Introduction, Scoresby quickly learned that he could not afford to give up the sea, but it was not until the end of January 1818 that he and his father agreed that Scoresby should take command of the *Fame*, a vessel in Liverpool purchased by Scoresby, Senior two months earlier. Ownership of the vessel was agreed as one-half Scoresby, Senior, one-third his son, and one-sixth Thomas Jackson, Scoresby's brother-in-law. Strengthening and adapting the vessel for northern whaling did not begin until mid-February and when the *Fame* put to sea on 2 April Scoresby noted in his journal that 'I never experienced relief on getting to sea on any former occasion'; nevertheless, as he remarked in his autobiography, 'We were too late in starting [the conversion] & were greatly harassed in getting ready in time, and after all we were obliged to sail in a very disordered condition'.[2]

The journey through unfamiliar waters from Liverpool is described in detail in the journal. Scoresby took the *Fame* west of the Outer Hebrides, and west even of St Kilda. Instead of the usual visit to Lerwick, the ship went west and north of Shetland, pausing briefly at Baltasound on 16–17 April to complete the crew. The voyage northward was marked by adverse winds from the east, so that Scoresby was back in sight of Jan Mayen, and of volcanic activity on the island, at the end of the month, and noted in his journal on 5 May that, with the wind from the southwest, the *Fame* was making 'good speed, with the first fair wind since we passed the Isle of Man!'

By 8 May Scoresby was in familiar waters in sight of Spitsbergen; the first whale was taken on 16 May and by the end of the month the *Fame* had taken four bowheads and a narwhale. The ship was briefly beset in the ice at 79°N, and the whaleboats had dangerous encounters with whales on 1 and 22 June. By the latter date seven bowheads had been caught. Other ships had been even more successful: Thomas Jackson in the *John* had twenty-nine whales by 13 June and started homeward before the end of the month.[3]

---

[1] 'Autobiography'.
[2] 'Autobiography'.
[3] According to Lubbock, *Arctic Whalers*, p. 209, the *John* returned with 31 whales.

Much of July was spent in unsuccessful searching for whales, but by the 17th Scoresby was writing a lengthy description in the journal of the west coast of Spitsbergen and especially the glaciers that calved icebergs into the sea. On 23 July Scoresby landed on Spitsbergen, for the first time since 1809 and he and his colleagues climbed to a height of about 850m (2800 ft). Returning to sea-level, they had the good fortune to find a dead whale that had apparently escaped after being harpooned by a German whaler. Flensing the whale on shore and conveying the blubber to the *Fame* in whaleboats was a difficult task, but the 20 tons of blubber, or 12–13 tons of oil, that it provided probably made the difference between a marginal voyage and a successful one.

The *Fame* set sail for Whitby on 1 August, discharged the hired Shetlanders on the 14th, and arrived off Whitby on the 17th. On the following day, there was a near-catastrophe as the ship attempted to enter the harbour, and even after reaching the inner harbour on the 19th, the *Fame* 'grounded on a sandbank ... strained considerably, and opened several of her bilge seams'. At over 370 tons, the vessel was only marginally capable of using Whitby harbour, and Scoresby's father thereafter sailed her from Hull.

1820. After the disagreements with and separation from his father following the 1818 voyage, described later, Scoresby found new partners in Liverpool. The city became his home in 1819 when, for the first time since 1802 at the age of twelve, he did not sail to the Greenland Sea. As the 1820 journal tells, one of his tasks during 1819 was to monitor the building of the *Baffin*, from laying the keel on 25 June until her launch on 15 February 1820. The care that he put into the design and construction of the ship did not apparently extend to hiring a crew, something that he probably regretted during the voyage.[1] Scoresby also seemed unconcerned by the fact that as the ship set sail on 18 March, five members of the crew, including the cooper and a line manager, were missing.

Why Scoresby chose to replace the missing members at Loch Ryan, in southwest Scotland, rather than in Shetland is not clear. It seems likely, however, that one factor may have been that the *Baffin* would not head for Whitby on her return, but would return to Liverpool. The ship would necessarily pass close to Loch Ryan, but need not be constrained in her return route to visit Shetland. Scoresby was also following the example set by the two other Liverpool vessels engaged in the whaling trade, the *Lady Forbes* and the *James*.

Stranraer, at the head of Loch Ryan, was also the home of Captain John Ross, the leader of the Royal Navy's 1818 voyage of discovery. Scoresby's introduction to Ross was unexpected, but quickly developed into a warm acquaintance. Sailing from Loch Ryan on 26 March, Scoresby again took a northward course that was to the west of both the Hebrides and St Kilda, 'to guard against the danger and inconvenience of a westerly wind' (27 March). Scoresby described just such a storm two days later, though his belief in the influence of 'the moon in expelling

[1] In none of the journals from 1811 onwards is there any significant comment by Scoresby at the outset of the voyage about his method of crew recruitment.

dense vapours and its power in breaking through dense strata of clouds' was meteorologically unsound.

Although Scoresby was pleased by the performance of his new ship, two calamities occurred on the journey northward. On 30 March, the deck caught fire, just above 20 tons of coal, because the cooking unit was too close to the deck. 'Providentially the discovery was made in time – and only just in time'. Much more tragic was the loss of the ship's carpenter who fell overboard on 4 April and was drowned.

With a strong southwesterly wind, and a ship capable of nine or ten knots, the *Baffin* reached 75°N as early as 7 April. This brought no advantage and some hardship; on 21 April Scoresby recorded in his journal that

> The preceding five days have been a continuous series of the most disagreeable and trying weather that occurs in the arctic regions ... During this period it was continually stormy, not always blowing heavy but sometimes a hard gale. During this interval the thermometer was never above 11°, the average temperature being 6¼°.

The *Baffin* did not take her first whale until 13 May, but was very successful later in the month; seven whales, most of them small, were taken between 22 and 25 May. The success was general: 'It is probable that near 120 fish have been killed around the field .. during the last 4 or 5 days' (26 May).

The ninth bowhead was not captured until 20 June, by which date Scoresby had taken the *Baffin* westward to 8°W. This was a large whale, and its capture, like two of those described in the 1818 journal, involved the whaleboat in great danger:

> In the killing of this fish it rose beneath one of the boats, forced the keel upwards until the planks on each side burst out, gave the boatsteerer a toss in the air, threw the harponeer on his back, and cut, by means of an oar, the cheek of one of the rowers completely through into the orbit of the eye.[1]

It was during the flensing of this whale that Scoresby was faced with what amounted to a potential mutiny, described in detail in the journal entries for 20 and 22 June. Scoresby acted quickly and firmly, and although there were another 'four or five more unprincipled men' besides the ringleader, John Wright, there were no further problems until early August, when the *Baffin* was homeward bound. In the interim, Scoresby had learned something of the mutineers' background, and recorded this in the very long journal entry for 9 August.

Because of the serious nature of these events, it may seem surprising that Scoresby apparently took no action to prosecute Wright or the others after the *Baffin* returned to Liverpool.[2] In a recent paper, however, Margarette Lincoln has emphasized that the legal power of the British state, unlike many other sea-going countries, did not at

---

[1] See Fig. 1, p. xlii. There has been a tendency among later commentators to regard such illustrations as exaggerated, but it is clear that the power of a large whale made such events, though unusual, a constant possibility.

[2] It is also surprising that Scoresby-Jackson, in his *Life* of Scoresby, stated that 'Few circumstances of interest occurred during this voyage' (p. 157)! It is possible that Scoresby-Jackson was adapting a remark in Scoresby's 'Autobiography', 'Little remarkable occurred during the voyage', but that remark was made about the 1818 voyage in the *Fame*.

this time extend to merchant vessels. In describing how John Meares resisted a mutiny in the Pacific in 1788, she noted that

> The merchant captain's authority was undefined by statute, although subject to the law. Meares argued that Britain should emulate other nations by including merchant ships in the general legislation dealing with discipline at sea, which would provide a legal code that would help govern all seamen, 'a class of men who are so necessary to the commerce, the strength, and the glory of the British empire.' The integration Meares envisaged never took place: the navy's disciplinary code is part of statute law, but the legal agreement signed by merchant seamen relates only to conditions of service.[1]

Scoresby did at a later date add to the journal a separate note, adding to his knowledge of the mutineers' background (see p. 204, note 2).

Three more whales were taken in late June, and the *Baffin*'s good fortune continued in July, culminating on the 19th with the capture of the seventeenth bowhead of the season. 'This fish being calculated to fill all our casks, the boats towed it on board with flags flying, in token of a "full ship" – thanks to God for all his Mercies!'

This whale was taken within sight of the east coast of Greenland, though Scoresby's longitudes (or his estimates of the ship's distance from the coast) are unreliable. Thereafter, however, fog, gales and ice combined to prevent the *Baffin* from beginning the homeward voyage. The forefoot of the ship had been damaged earlier in the voyage (probably on 11 May), and in the journal entry for 30 July Scoresby noted that

> the keel projecting now in front without any defence, appeared liable to be struck off by a very slight blow from a tongue of ice: which danger, became very appalling, when we had the prospect of being obliged to force through a sea stream of heavy ice & in a swell, where numerous pieces appeared having tongues projecting from their corners, of 10 to 20 or 30 feet deep!

By careful navigation, however, the *Baffin* escaped into open water and by 3 August had reached the Langanes peninsula, in what was then a very remote corner of northeast Iceland. The *Baffin* continued around the northern and eastern coasts of the Faroes, landed the sailors from Loch Ryan on 20 August and reached Liverpool three days later.

Scoresby's Personal and Religious Life

As described in the Introduction to volume II of these journals, Scoresby had by 1816 come under the influence of the evangelical minister of the Anglican chapel in Baxtergate, Whitby, James Thomas Holloway. Scoresby was always ready to attribute events in his life as indications of the hand of God working directly. On the 1816 voyage, this explained the *Esk*'s remarkable escape from disaster and successful return to port; in 1817, in the same passage of his autobiography as that, already quoted, in which he contemplated giving up a seagoing life, he attributed his lack of

---

[1] Lincoln, 'Mutinous Behavior on Voyages to the South Seas and Its Impact on Eighteenth-Century Civil Society', pp. 63–4. The 1788 mutiny occurred, however, while Meares was sailing under a Portuguese flag.

success to divine influence. 'Methought God was working against me ... [M]y conscience smote me – it suggested it was not owing to the freaks of fortune that I was no longer prosperous – it was the hand of God.'

The autobiography also claims that 'the most complete surrender of heart to God, and the most perfect abandonment of reserved sin that I had ever made' took place on Sunday 13 July 1817, as a result of using one of George Burder's *Village Sermons*, though Scoresby did not mention the significance of this in his journal entry.[1]

If Scoresby was serious about his intention to give up whaling after the 1817 voyage, as he appears to have been, this was made impossible by a devastating blow to his financial situation at the end of September. His wife's brother, George Lockwood,

> to whom I had lent large sums of money, amounting in all to £1537.3s.5d,[2] for assisting him in starting business as a linen draper, had failed ... . Thus at a single & most unexpected blow, were all my hopes of competence ... blasted in a moment. This was the chief of my property – and it was probably gone.[3]

Once again, however, Scoresby chose to see this disaster as evidence of divine intervention.

> By the blessing of God, whose providence it evidently was, that brought about this event, the effect of this news was not either anguish or despair – it was resignation to the Divine will.

Having also resigned his command of the *Esk*, lost the hope of a shore-based life, and been unsuccessful in his ambition to lead a voyage of arctic exploration, Scoresby probably had little choice but to enter an agreement with his father to become commander and co-owner of the *Fame*. Even this was only possible because Scoresby, Senior, gave his son a 'gratuity' of £1000[4] towards the price of co-ownership. This placed father and son in a closer formal relationship than had existed since the son's last voyage under the command of his father in 1810. In the interval, however, the son had matured, whereas his father may only have aged; Scoresby, Senior was 58 in 1818. That year was one of only two in the thirty-three between 1791 and 1823 when the elder Scoresby did not command a whaling ship in the Greenland Sea, and he may not have welcomed the enforced idleness.

In any event, the partnership did not survive the 1818 voyage. As the end of that year's journal records, the *Fame* had a near-miraculous escape from wreckage on the

---

[1] The sermon, entitled 'Irresolution Reproved, and Decision Recommended' was published as Sermon LX in volume 5 of Burder's *Village Sermons*. It does not seem, to a modern eye, particularly well-suited to a service for a whaling crew in arctic waters, but as its title suggests, it is easy to see how it had a powerful influence on Scoresby, who was already close to making a commitment as a 'born again' Christian. In 1831 some of Scoresby's own sermons were published under the title *Discourses to Seamen*; extracts from several of these were reprinted in Scoresby-Jackson's *Life*, pp. 250–58.

[2] Equivalent to almost £81,000 in 2002, see Allen, *Inflation*, Table 2. According to Scoresby's 'Autobiography', although the details are missing, he eventually recovered 'nearly half of my debt'.

[3] This and the following quotations relating to the dissolution of the partnership between Scoresby and his father are from the 'Autobiography'.

[4] Equivalent to about £52,660 in 2002, see Allen, *Inflation*, Table 2.

Rock outside Whitby harbour, but was then damaged on a sandbank within the harbour. As Scoresby recounted in his autobiography, what followed led to his separation from the *Fame*, and indirectly to his departure from Whitby and his father.

> After the necessary repairs had been accomplished, my Father proposed and entirely against my [advice?], executed, several alterations in the vessel, which though they were very expensive, effected little more than an improvement in her appearance, but added almost nothing, in my view, to her already excellent qualifications as a whale-ship. Hence arose several instance of disagreement between us, and I was always obliged to submit to the inconvenience and expence, as well as the mortification of being subject to a constant and arbitrary control. My Father no doubt acted in his opinion for the best, and I allow made very great improvements in the ship; but he acted against our mutual interests, these improvements not being essential. But differences also occurred respecting the manufacture of the oil, which proceeded to a disagreeable length. My spirit and my pride, which were probably too great, prevented me from giving up my opinion with that frankness and that submission which it was possibly my duty to have done to a parent. Hence arose so many unpleasantnesses that I found our confidence and affection, and my duty daily injured, if not weakened. I was convinced that we should be more comfortable, & indeed more happy, were our co-partnery dissolved.

Scoresby offered his father two options. One would have transferred command and management of the *Fame* entirely to Scoresby, Senior, leaving his son as a co-owner. Alternatively, Scoresby was willing to give up command and his share of the ownership, 'thus returning to my father the gratuity of 1000£ with which he had presented me'. His father accepted this option.

From the autobiography, it is clear that Scoresby did not dissolve the partnership with his father because he had another prospect in view. 'I was now without a situation, and had not the most distant idea where to look for a new connection.' He was, however, determined that future partners would need to have religious convictions as strong as and similar to his own.

> I daily laid my case before Him ... I felt myself completely passive in the hands of God; I found myself willing to wait on shore for a year rather than join any [worldly?] persons ... . But the Lord did not put my faith to such a long trial. I had scarcely been separated from my Father a month, when I received through the hands of a gentleman of Whitby with whom I was not personally acquainted, an offer of a ship from Mess[rs] Nicholas Hurry and Gibson of Liverpool. These gentlemen being total strangers to me I made instant enquiries respecting their character, and particularly their religious views – when to my much surprise & satisfaction I was informed that both of them were men of piety: – that M[r] Hurry was a deacon of the most respectable congregation of Independents in Liverpool, under Mr (now D[r]) T Raffles[1] and that M[r] Gibson was a zealous and consistent Methodist. This proposal appears to me to be in answer to my prayer – the hand of God seemed in it.

Liverpool had other attractions for Scoresby. His experience with converting and sailing the *Fame* had given him knowledge of the port's facilities, and the city offered

[1] Thomas Raffles (1788–1863) Congregationalist minister of the Great George Street Chapel in Liverpool. See entry in *Oxford Dictionary of National Biography* (ODNB).

far more opportunity for scientific and similar interaction than Whitby. In 1818 Scoresby had already begun a friendship with Thomas Stewart Traill, a founder of both the Liverpool Literary and Philosophical Society in 1812 and the Liverpool Royal Institution in 1817.[1] Of similar significance at the time, and in Scoresby's eyes further evidence of the guiding hand of providence, was the fact that his spiritual mentor, Dr Holloway, had moved to Liverpool just as Scoresby returned from his 1818 voyage.

Hurry, Gibson and Scoresby had similar moral and religious convictions, but this did not avoid some hard bargaining over the terms of the proposed partnership. Negotiations continued up to the day before Scoresby was due to leave for Edinburgh, and he had meanwhile two other offers from potential partners in Liverpool. Hurry and Gibson eventually agreed to Scoresby's terms, 'I to take command with wages, nearly the same as I had in the Esk and Fame, and to hold one-third share of the concern'.[2]

One consequence of this new partnership that is evident in the journal of the 1820 *Baffin* voyage is the strengthened emphasis on Sabbath observance. This had of course been a feature of the earlier voyages, with the owners' knowledge and assent:

> it is but justice to those who were latterly united with me in the adventure, – Messrs. Hurry and Gibson, of Liverpool, – to mention that they ... most fully accorded ... in the practice I had adopted, – having given, indeed to another of their Captains, engaged in the same pursuit, very strict directions to sanctify the Sabbath as a day of holy rest. And not these gentlemen only, but others with whom I was previously engaged, Messrs. Fishburn and Brodrick ... most cheerfully acceded to the plan ... .[3]

Nevertheless, Scoresby wrote that 'it was not until the year 1820, that I was enabled, undeviatingly, to carry the principle into effect', and the partners' enthusiasm was not initially welcomed by the crew.

> Several of the harpooners – whose interest in the success of the voyage was such, that even a single large whale being captured yielded to them an advantage of from £6. to £8. each – were, in the early part of the voyage, very much dissatisfied with the rule ... [T]hey reasoned that our chance of a prosperous voyage was but as six to seven, when compared with that of our competitors in the fishery. The chief officer, however, was frequently known to remark, that if we, under such disadvantages, should make a successful voyage, he should then believe there indeed was something like a blessing on the observance of the Sabbath.

By mid-July, with fifteen whales already caught, he and others were apparently persuaded. 'The men were now accustomed to look for a blessing on Sabbath observances. And within the succeeding week ... the blessing was realized.'[4]

---

[1] See the entry for Traill in *ODNB*. Both Traill and Scoresby were elected Fellows of the Royal Society of Edinburgh on the same day in 1819, with Robert James as one of the proposers for both of them.

[2] 'Autobiography'.

[3] Scoresby, *Memorials of the Sea*, p. 31.

[4] This and the preceding quotations are also from *Memorials of the Sea*, pp. 35, 36, 42.

Scoresby and Arctic Exploration[1]

The voyages in this volume took place against a background of renewed British interest in arctic exploration, and especially the search for a northern passage from the Atlantic Ocean to the Pacific. With his long experience and scientific understanding of arctic waters, Scoresby had a personal interest in such discovery and an expressed desire to take a leading role. That he did not do so has frequently been attributed to antagonism and obstruction on the part of John Barrow, Second Secretary of the Admiralty for most of the years from 1804 to 1845. Scoresby's biographers, for example, claimed that

> Barrow had taken all credit for suggesting the polar expedition, wilfully suppressing Scoresby's name, and this mean act coloured all their future relationship. Barrow was a mean-spirited sycophant who had wormed his way upward by devious means and he was determined not to give way to anyone, least of all a whaling captain … .[2]

That is not the view taken in this Introduction, and that characterization of John Barrow is not consistent with the biographies of a man who occupied an important position in the British government for four decades.[3] Because many writers have tended to accept that Barrow behaved in this way towards Scoresby,[4] and because Scoresby's own ambitions and objectives in regard to arctic exploration have been relatively neglected, a reappraisal seems necessary and overdue.

Scoresby's first suggestion of such exploration was contained in a paper for the Wernerian Society of Edinburgh in 1814. He still thought it feasible when *An Account of the Arctic Regions* was published in 1820.

> I yet imagine, notwithstanding the objections which have been urged against the scheme, that it would by no means be impossible to reach the Pole by travelling across the ice from Spitzbergen … . As the journey would not exceed 1200 miles (600 miles each way), it might be performed on sledges drawn by dogs or rein-deer, or even on foot … . With favourable winds, great advantage might be derived from sails set upon the sledges; which sails, when the travellers were at rest, would serve for the erection of tents. Small vacancies in the ice would not prevent the journey, as the sledges could be adapted to answer the purpose of boats; nor would the usual unevenness of the ice, or the depth or softness of the snow, be an insurmountable difficulty, as journeys of near equal length, and under similar inconveniences, have been accomplished.[5]

He envisaged the round trip as taking about two months, or slightly less if dogs were used. It was an imaginative proposal, but the thought that Scoresby might actually attempt it in 1815 was promptly vetoed by his family, and especially by his wife. The Stamps suggested that 'Had Mrs. Scoresby concurred, her husband might well have reached the North Pole nearly a hundred years before Peary.'[6] It is far more

---

[1] Some of the material in this section was published earlier in Jackson, 'Three Puzzles from Early Nineteenth Century Arctic Exploration'.

[2] Stamp and Stamp, *William Scoresby*, p. 67.

[3] See, for example, Lloyd, *Mr. Barrow*; Fleming, *Barrow's Boys*.

[4] See, for example, Martin, 'William Scoresby (1789–1857)'.

[5] Scoresby, *Account of the Arctic Regions*, 1, pp. 54–5.

[6] Stamp & Stamp, *William Scoresby*, p. 53.

likely that such an attempt in the early nineteenth century would have been rapidly abandoned, or ended in disaster. At that time nothing was known about the south-westward drift of the arctic pack ice and, with longitude measurements difficult or unreliable, Scoresby might have found it very difficult to reach Spitzbergen on the return journey. Eight decades later, Nansen and a colleague attempted a polar journey very similar to that proposed by Scoresby, but abandoned the attempt within a couple of weeks. They did understand the probable ice circulation pattern, they were better equipped, and they had the advantage of starting at 83°N, much closer to the Pole than Spitsbergen, yet they were quickly defeated by what Scoresby envisaged as the 'usual unevenness of the ice' but what Nansen described as 'Lanes, ridges, and endless rough ice, it looks like an endless moraine of ice-blocks; and this continual lifting of the sledges over every irregularity is enough to tire out giants'.[1]

As Constance Martin and others have recognized, a crucial question in arctic exploration during this decade was whether the central arctic basin was permanently ice covered or whether, beyond the apparent ice barrier at about 80°N in the Green-land Sea, there was an 'open polar sea.' Scoresby had no belief in such open water, and said so, both in his 1814 paper and in *An Account of the Arctic Regions*, but many others, including John Barrow, were equally convinced that, if there was no land in the arctic basin, then there would also be no permanent ice.

Scoresby's 1817 journal understandably focused on the effect that the unusual absence of ice in the whaling grounds had on the catch, but he was also quick to recognize the scientific significance of the event, and he reported on it to Sir Joseph Banks, President of the Royal Society, in a letter dated 2 October 1817.[2] He also used the opportunity to make clear his own interest in exploration.

> *I do conceive there is sufficient interest attached to these remote regions to induce Government to fit out an expedition, were it properly represented. ...*
>
> I should have much satisfaction in attempting an enterprise of this kind, namely to examine and survey the islands of East Greenland or Spitzbergen, especially the eastern part, which has not been visited [for] many years past; and to ascertain, for the benefit of the whalers, whether the whales resort thither; to endeavour to reach the shore of West Greenland, determine its position, prove its insularity, and ascertain the fate of the Icelandic colony together with making researches ... relative to the north-east and north-west passages, &c. for the performance of which objects, I could point out a method by which the enterprise could be conducted with little, or possibly no expense to the nation. This would be accomplished by combining the two objects of discovery and fishing.[3]

---

[1] Nansen, *Farthest North*, II, p. 140.

[2] This was a response to a request from Banks, which is letter 132 in Chambers, *Letters of Sir Joseph Banks*, p. 329.

[3] Quoted in Scoresby-Jackson, *Life*, p. 126. Emphasis as in Scoresby-Jackson. Note that Scoresby was restricting his proposals to the latitudes where the ice had disappeared, i.e. between 74° and 80°N. By 'East Greenland', Scoresby meant Spitsbergen; similarly 'West Greenland' meant what we would now term the east coast of Greenland. Although both the Norse colonies, the 'Western Settle-ment' and the 'Eastern Settlement', had been on the west coast of Greenland, the notion that the latter was on the east coast, and its fate undetermined because of the difficulty of access, persisted into the 19th century. See Gad, *History of Greenland*, II, p. 6.

Banks's biographer[1] has suggested that not merely was Scoresby, from 1811 onwards, 'his most intelligent channel of information about the far north beyond the Arctic Circle' but also '[t]hrough this channel of scientific news the Admiralty was also nourished with ideas'. That nourishment was supplied through and welcomed by Barrow, who was not short of exploration ideas himself, though these differed significantly from those advanced by Scoresby.

The formal suggestion that the British government should resume arctic exploration was made in a letter from Banks, as President of the Royal Society, to the First Lord of the Admiralty dated 20 November 1817. The letter's opening sentences are significant:

> It will without doubt have come to your Lordship's knowledge that a considerable change of climate, inexplicable at present to us, must have taken place in the circumpolar regions by which the severity of the cold, that has for centuries past enclosed the seas in the high northern latitudes in an impenetrable barrier of ice, has been, during the last two years, greatly abated. Mr. Scoresby, a very intelligent young man, who commands a whaling-vessel from Whitby, observed last year that 2000 square leagues of ice, with which the Greenland seas between the latitudes of 74° and 80° N have been hitherto covered, has in the last two years entirely disappeared.[2]

As with most such letters, it seems reasonable to assume that Banks already knew that it would receive a favourable reception, and very probably Barrow had already begun the necessary planning and organization of the expeditions. Barrow, like Scoresby, was on close terms with Sir Joseph Banks, and when Banks acknowledged Scoresby's letter about the disappearance of the ice, his letter had been franked by Barrow.[3]

Barrow's plans for the expeditions were explained to a wider public in a lengthy essay that appeared in the October 1817 issue of the *Quarterly Review*.[4] He took as his departure point for the essay 'an extraordinary change which a few intelligent navigators remarked in the state of the arctic ice' and quoted at length (from the letter to Banks) 'the direct testimony of Mr. Scoresby the younger, a very intelligent navigator of the Greenland Seas, for the disappearance of an immense quantity of arctic ice'.

Barrow clearly accepted the evidence of Scoresby, and of other whaling captains mentioned in the essay. This is scarcely surprising in view of the confidence that

---

[1] Carter, *Sir Joseph Banks*, pp. 505–7.

[2] Chambers, *Letters of Sir Joseph Banks*, letter 132, pp. 334–5. Ross (*Polar Pioneers*, p. 29) claimed that this letter was drafted by Barrow. The First Lord (Robert Dundas, Lord Melville) replied on 12 December, with details of the proposed expeditions. That reply was presumably also drafted by Barrow.

[3] Scoresby-Jackson, *Life*, p. 125.

[4] *Quarterly Review*, 18, no. 35, 1817, pp. 200, 202. This issue was not in fact published until February 1818. Although all contributions to the *Review* were unsigned, Barrow's authorship is not in doubt; the essay was one of nearly two hundred that he contributed to that journal. The format was nominally a book review, but the book in question was dismissed unfavourably in a single paragraph and the rest of the essay was devoted to what Barrow called 'metal more attractive'. The *Quarterly Review* can be found at British Periodicals Online.

Banks had in Scoresby, but Barrow had respect gained at first hand, since he had himself sailed to the Greenland Sea in the Liverpool whaler *Peggy* as a teenager about 1780.[1]

It is also clear, from Scoresby's writings, that he believed his letter to Banks had initiated the plans for the exploring expeditions of 1818. In his autobiography he included three pages which he intended to include in the preface to *An Account of the Arctic Regions* that, with some caution, make this claim. He was persuaded to omit these pages,[2] but late in 1817 Scoresby had reason to believe that his proposal 'to combine the object of the whale fishery with that of Discovery' was receiving serious consideration in London.

That was not however the case. The main reason why the Admiralty and the British government were willing to undertake such exploration was because of the vital need to provide useful employment for the Royal Navy in the years following the final defeat of Napoleon. It is easy to forget how vast was the transformation that took place within a very few years:

> In 1812 there were 131,087 men serving in the 543 ships in commission, of which 98 were line of battle ships. By 1817 the comparable figure had fallen to 13 ships of the line and 22,944 men.[3]

Even these dramatic figures understate the problem facing the Admiralty. As Fleming has written,

> The ships were laid up 'in ordinary' and the seamen were simply thrown back onto the streets from which they had often been press-ganged in the first place. The officers, however, were a different matter. They were career men, they had political clout, and

---

[1] The Stamps, in their biography of Scoresby, dismissed this unusual qualification: 'he had made one journey to the Arctic as a lad and that had been enough for him' (Stamp & Stamp, *William Scoresby*, p. 67). This disparagement seems unjustifiable. In the otherwise rather tedious autobiography that Barrow wrote shortly before his death more than sixty years later, he devoted twelve lively pages 'entirely from memory' to that voyage, and it seems clear that during the voyage he learned a great deal about 'all the tactical parts of navigation; and the more I learned of it the more I liked it'. He observed, remembered and described the techniques of whale capture and blubber preservation, and he rowed in a whaleboat during one such capture. He did declare 'I confess that my trip to the Spitzbergen seas was a disappointment' but that was because there was no opportunity for landing; whaling was the sole focus (Barrow, *Auto-Biographical Memoir*, pp. vi, 18, 27).

[2] 'Autobiography'. The manuscript note at the foot of the first omitted page reads 'NB. The above account was printed as part of the preface of my acc^t of the Arctic Regions but was rejected & not published, from the apprehension of my friends that it would bring upon me the enmity & ill-offices of Mr Barrow who was exceedingly anxious of the honour of these expeditions.' Several possible interpretations seem possible here. Assuming the 'friends' were correct, Barrow may have wanted to be recognized as having conceived the expeditions before Scoresby's letter, or he may have wanted recognition for the fact that Scoresby's proposals were very different from the objectives set for the expeditions. A third possibility, bearing in mind that the *Account of the Arctic Regions* was not published until after the return of both expeditions, is that Barrow could have felt that the statement by Scoresby of his own objectives might be seen as a denigration of the objectives that were chosen but not achieved by the Admiralty's expeditions.

[3] Lloyd, *Mr Barrow*, p. 91.

they could not be dismissed so easily. In fact, their numbers increased until the navy, reduced to a rump of some 23,000 men from a peak of more than 130,000, had one officer for every four men … . But 90 per cent of these officers had nothing to do … . Thirty years on, the navy was still feeling the effects of the Napoleonic Wars … . In 1846, of 1,151 officers, only 172 were in full employment.[1]

It was against this background that Barrow was able to set objectives for two naval voyages of exploration that would, he was sure, prove the existence of an 'open polar sea'. These objectives were very different from those offered by Scoresby. As he wrote in the *Quarterly Review* essay,

[O]ne … is to proceed northerly into the polar basin, and to endeavour, by passing close to the pole, to make a direct course to Behring's Strait; the other is to push through Davis's Strait for the north-east coast of America; and, if successful in discovering and doubling the [north-eastern extremity of America], to proceed to the westward, with the view of passing Behring's Strait.[2]

Back in Whitby, Scoresby knew little or nothing of these plans when, in early December 1817, his father, then in London, 'was advised to send for me, with a view of my being employed in this interesting service'.[3] It was the way in which Scoresby discovered that it was not his own proposals that were being promoted that caused his biographers and others to see in Barrow a personal contempt for a mere whaling captain. As Scoresby recounted the occasion in his autobiography,

I left Whitby on the 11th of December and proceeded immediately to London, and the day or two after my arrival had an interview with Sir Joseph Banks and Mr Barrow. I found Mr Barrow was particularly anxious that my Father or I, or both of us should go in the proposed expeditions; yet to my surprise he evaded conversation on the subject, and generally avoided me in the room, until provoked by his conduct I watched an opportunity, and put the question plainly to him – Was it desired that I should have an employment in either of the expeditions; and if so, what situation it was that I might expect? He answered shortly & indirectly that if I <u>wished</u> to go on the Discovery I must call the next day at the Navy Board and give in my proposals, and then [turning?] sharply round he left the room. More than ever annoyed by this ambiguity, and general mystery that there seemed to be respecting this matter I determined to ask an explanation of Sir Joseph Banks, of whose candour and good will I had no doubt.

---

[1] Fleming, *Barrow's Boys*, pp. 1–2.

[2] *Quarterly Review*, 1817, p. 220. As he made clear in this essay, Barrow did not believe that Baffin Bay was a bay, but only a continuation of Davis Strait, with a broad channel extending into the polar basin. This was not his opinion alone; while the two expeditions were at sea in 1818, a new edition of Daines Barrington's 1775 essay appeared with a revised title, *The Possibility of Approaching the North Pole Asserted*. It contained a map that showed 'Baffin's Bay' as such, but added the words 'According to the relation of W. Baffin in 1616, but not now believed.' This has sometimes been read as casting doubt on Baffin's voyage in the tiny *Discovery* two hundred years earlier, but what was at issue in the 19th century was whether the sea he sailed was a bay or a channel.

[3] 'Autobiography'.

M. J. Ross has written, 'Barrow's curt treatment of Scoresby was inexcusable'.[1] Barrow could certainly have handled the situation better, but consider the circumstances. The occasion was one of Sir Joseph Banks' *conversazioni* at his London home, as much a social as a scientific gathering. Barrow was probably well aware that Scoresby had arrived in London hoping, and perhaps even expecting, to be offered the command of an exploring expedition on very different lines from what was going forward. Barrow was, in modern jargon, 'ambushed' by Scoresby before the latter had talked to Banks who, with Scoresby, Senior, was mainly responsible for the summons to London.

After Barrow's embarrassed departure, Scoresby then talked to Banks:

> The first interval that I perceived him to be disengaged, I stepped up to him … and put the same question to him that I had done with so little satisfaction to Mr Barrow. The substance of his answer was that they much wished, (himself & the admiralty I presumed) I should embark in one of the expeditions, but he was very sorry to say that all his endeavours to obtain me a command in one of them had failed, as the admiralty, having taken up the matter, could not employ any but their own officers as leading men. But it was hoped I might be disposed to go as a Master (namely a pilot!) having the charge of my own ship and crew; subject to the direction (namely [universal control?]) of the naval Captain. The worthy president thus in as delicate a manner as he could conveyed to me the information I wished, & repeatedly & I doubt not with perfect sincerity, expressed his dissatisfaction with the arrangements. He stated moreover that he believed the commanding officers of the four proposed ships were already appointed or at least fixed upon.
>
> I was greatly disappointed with the result of this interview from which it clearly appeared that I had undertaken a journey to London for nothing, and had been called up in such a way that I could have no claim for my expenses. Spurning the idea of embarking in a subordinate capacity, on a service that I had good reason to apprehend I was better capable of, from my experience in the icy seas, that [*sic*] any lieutenant or Captain of the Royal Navy could possibly be, I declined the proposed arrangement suggested by Mr Barrow and neither appeared at the Navy Board, nor made any further enquiries on the subject.[2]

Scoresby was understandably disappointed, but he had expected too much. Once the decision had been taken to give the task of exploration to an under-employed Royal Navy, there was no prospect of him being given a command.[3] Instead the Admiralty wished him to sail on one of the expeditions – presumably the one via the Greenland Sea – as a master. Scoresby summarily dismissed that suggestion in his

---

[1] Ross, *Polar Pioneers*, p. 30.

[2] 'Autobiography'. The Navy Board was and is concerned with the day-to-day administration of the Royal Navy. Until it was merged with the Admiralty in 1831, it was a separate institution.

[3] William Dampier in 1699 and Edmond Halley a year earlier had been given command of Royal Navy ships though not members of that service, but by the mid-18th century these precedents were resisted, so that it was not the Royal Society's nominee, Alexander Dalrymple, who commanded the *Endeavour* on her first voyage to the Pacific, but Lt. James Cook, RN. If Banks, who sailed with Cook, really had sought to obtain a naval command for Scoresby (and was not just trying to soften the blow to Scoresby's ambitions), he should have known better. I am grateful to Glyndwr Williams for drawing my attention to these precedents.

autobiography, but James Cook's biographer emphasized the responsibility of the position:

> trained by hard experience and his own ability; the chief professional on board though not the highest ranking one, the man who never ceased to retain control ... of the ship's navigation. He was subject of course to the orders from the captain, who got his orders from an admiral or the Admiralty; but it would be an unwise captain who ignored, or overrode, his subordinate's particular expertness. Apart from navigation the master was responsible, over the boatswain, for masts, yards, sails and rigging, for stores, for general management. In between navigation and management he had a special responsibility for pilotage and harbour-work ... for taking soundings and bearings and correcting or adding to charts – often enough for making new ones. He was responsible for the ship's log. His responsibilities were endless, his signature always in demand.[1]

From the Admiralty's standpoint, what was being offered to Scoresby or his father was a responsible position for an expedition to latitudes where they were recognized to have the expertise and experience. Banks' suggestion that the Admiralty would enable Scoresby to have his own ship and crew seems unrealistic; two ships could be seen as a necessary safeguard when navigating unknown ice, but three ships would surely make the task unnecessarily difficult. Probably neither John Barrow nor the Admiralty were surprised when Scoresby declined the idea – as the latter recognized, it would almost certainly involve considerable financial loss to him – but it was a genuine compliment to his ability, and in no way an attempt by Barrow to diminish him.

One could go further: even if the impossible were to happen, and Scoresby had been offered the command, his knowledge and integrity would surely have prevented him from adopting the objectives set out for the expeditions. To sail to 80°N in the Greenland Sea was for him a routine matter; to go much beyond that latitude he was convinced was impossible and to accept such a command would have guaranteed that he would fail. As he wrote to Banks from Shetland on 17 April 1818,

> [A]s to reaching the *Pole*, I confess myself sceptical. From what I have observed, I imagine probabilities are against their penetrating beyond 82° or 83°, and I readily allow I shall be *much* surprised if they should pass the eighty-fourth degree of latitude.
>
> The success of the expedition intended for the north-west is still more equivocal. Indeed, the nature of that voyage is wrapped in so much uncertainty, that, in my opinion, it cannot warrant even a conjecture. *I am persuaded a north-west passage exists – that is, as regards any obstruction from land – but how far it may or may not be blocked up with ice, so as to be always impervious, can only be determined by repeated trials.*[2]

Scoresby was to have another frustrating trip to London in 1822. This has been seen as further evidence of Scoresby being 'baulked by Barrow', but a careful examination of the events suggests quite the opposite. It has little to do with the journals in the present volume, but needs to be examined here because the incident was used to

---

[1] Beaglehole, *Life of Captain James Cook*, p. 26.
[2] Quoted in Scoresby-Jackson, *Life*, p. 129.

support the erroneous belief that Barrow was, in the Stamps' words, 'the persistent thorn in Scoresby's flesh'.[1]

As Scoresby later recounted,

> Towards the end of the year 1821, my father and I made a representation to the Board of Trade … concerning the failure of the whale-fishery, and … founded a proposal for searching and exploring the hitherto unexamined coasts on the south and east of Spitzbergen, &c., with a view of discovering some more abundant fishing station … .[2]

The Scoresbys used John Barrow as a contact in London who could forward their memorial to the Board of Trade. One obvious question is why would they have chosen this route if they had any reason to doubt Barrow's good opinion of them? From his home at Nocton[3] in Lincolnshire, the President of the Board of Trade, Frederick Robinson,[4] responded to Barrow 'I think this proposition well worthy of consideration, and I shall be very glad to see these gentlemen'. A meeting in London was suggested, and it took place in early February 1822, when Scoresby was accompanied by Barrow. If Barrow had been ambushed by Scoresby in 1817, on this occasion both of them were blindsided by a reception very different from that which they had been led to expect from the President.

> To my astonishment I found that, instead of speaking favourably of the proposal, as his correspondence implied, he now seemed altogether to waive any arrangement with me on the subject. He employed himself in endeavouring to show that our proposal was only suited to individuals, not to public boards – that though the trade showed decline, it would soon find its proper level; and intimated that the loss of private property was a matter of private, not public, consideration, and that the whole fishery had already received too much of the national support![5]

It seems evident that in the interval between Robinson's spontaneous letter from his home and the meeting in London a month later, the President of the Board of Trade had been briefed by his civil servants. As Gordon Jackson has written, this was precisely the period when long-term plans for the whaling industry 'were brought to naught by the emergence of the Free Trade spirit within the Board of Trade'.[6] Coal gas was replacing whale oil for street lighting, and reductions in the duty on imported rape seed had a similar effect on the clothing trade.

> The interests of whaler-owners clearly conflicted not only with the interests of the better end of the cloth trade, but also with the expanding seed-crushing industry, and with the benefit of hindsight one can hardly fault the Board of Trade for sacrificing the whaler-owners to what, in the circumstances, was both their natural fate and the national interest.[7]

---

[1] Stamp and Stamp, *William Scoresby*, p. 85.
[2] Quoted in Scoresby-Jackson, *Life*, p. 180.
[3] Scoresby-Jackson, *Life*, p. 181, incorrectly wrote 'Norton'. The relevant letters are quoted on that page.
[4] Later Viscount Goderich, and briefly Prime Minister in 1827–8.
[5] Quoted in Scoresby-Jackson, *Life*, p. 182.
[6] Jackson, *British Whaling Trade*, p. 120.
[7] Ibid., pp. 120–21.

The plainest proof of this new attitude was to come in 1824, when the government bounty offered to whalers ever since 1733 expired, and was not renewed. Meanwhile, in the more immediate drama of the meeting with Robinson,

> Mr. Barrow happened, in the course of the interview, to suggest that the Board of Longitude, of which he was a member, had it in their power to spend £5000 annually in valuable discoveries, and he stated he would throw out a hint at the next meeting of the Board, which was to take place on the day following, that a premium of £2000 be offered for circumnavigating Spitzbergen. On this hint Mr. Robinson immediately seized, and through it took the opportunity of disengaging himself both of me and my proposition![1]

Barrow's suggestion may have been intended more as a way to extract Scoresby and himself from a meeting that was clearly going nowhere than as a proposal likely to be successful. The Board of Longitude subsequently rejected the suggestion on the grounds that the objective was not within its remit, and it would in any case have been of no benefit to the Scoresbys, since a circumnavigation of Spitsbergen was probably beyond the capability of the sailing ships of the period, and certainly could not be anticipated in any specific year. There is, however, no evidence that Barrow was not as surprised as Scoresby by Robinson's change of attitude.

Although the evidence for an antipathy by Barrow towards Scoresby is thin to non-existent, it is still a matter of some surprise that *An Account of the Arctic Regions* was not reviewed by the *Quarterly Review* when the two volumes were published in 1820. Barrow was a prolific contributor with a special interest in the Arctic, and a review by him could have been expected.

Scientific Recognition

As noted in volume II (p. xxxi, note 3) of these journals, Scoresby's intention to write a scientific and historical study of the Arctic was already clear and explicit as early as the winter of 1814–15.[2] In addition to his own experiments recorded in the journals, it is clear from the footnotes and appendices in the *Account of the Arctic Regions* that he spent much of the next few years compiling material from a large number of sources and languages. Writing, however, was not so easy. In his autobiography, he confessed that, by late in 1818,

> I had made no great progress in the work – the whole of my M.S. scarcely exceeding 300 pages of letter press, which did not complete one-third of my plan. I found my progress however, so slow that some stimulus was requisite; and the best stimulus I could fix on

---

[1] Quoted in Scoresby-Jackson, *Life*, p. 183.

[2] Scoresby, 'On the Greenland or Polar Ice', pp. 261–338. At the end of that paper (pp. 336–8) he stated, 'In a work which I am now preparing for the press, the preceding paper, amplified and illustrated, is intended to be introduced.' He then set out eight general headings that are reflected in the *Account of the Arctic Regions*, though in a different structure. According to Bravo, it was his Edinburgh mentor, Robert Jameson, who suggested the two-volume format, with one volume devoted to arctic science and the other to whaling; see Bravo, 'Geographies of Exploration and Improvement', p. 529.

was to put the work to press which would then be a spur to my exertions & render delay inexpedient.[1]

Both Constable in Edinburgh and Longmans in London were offering to publish the *Account of the Arctic Regions*. It is Constable's name that appears on the title page, but a letter quoted by the Stamps suggests that Longmans were 'to have the offer of a share of the work from you on the usual footing'. An edition of 1000 copies was anticipated,

> to be completed in 2 Octavo volumes of about 400 pages each, and to be illustrated with various engravings, amounting all to about 20 plates ... and the retail price about 30/- in boards.[2]

It was to sign the contract and deal with other publication matters for the *Account of the Arctic Regions* that Scoresby's departure from Liverpool in December 1818 was fixed (see p. xxvi). The other major event of his stay in Edinburgh was his election as a Fellow of the Royal Society of Edinburgh on 25 January 1819. His election may have been particularly gratifying to Scoresby, because it took place before the *Account of the Arctic Regions* was published. His sponsors were Robert Jameson, John Playfair and Sir George Steuart Mackenzie of Coul. Mackenzie was one of the Society's presidents, but the fact that Jameson and Playfair, Scoresby's teachers at Edinburgh University a decade earlier, were able to unite in nominating Scoresby is significant because, as noted in the Introduction to volume I of these journals (pp. xxxi–xxxii), they were on opposite sides in the fierce debate that took place at the university on the age and character of the earth.

Scoresby and his family returned to Whitby in February 1819 because of the death of his mother, and then moved again to Liverpool in May. But the stimulus of a signed contract and a deadline was indeed a spur to his exertions, as it has been to many other authors, and by the time Scoresby sailed for the Arctic in the *Baffin* in 1820 he was able to take with him, and cite in that journal (e.g. 31 July) the completed *Account of the Arctic Regions*. Despite his assiduity, his publishers were by that time already grumbling:

> [T]he cost has greatly exceeded our original calculations. We do not think the selling price can be under £2 – at 36/- it would do little more than cover the bare cost. We would much rather it had been a cheap book.

The price was eventually set at two guineas, equivalent to about £125 in 2002, which may partly explain the lack of reviews in the quarterlies: this was not a purchase that many of their readers would be willing to contemplate. But the publishers need not have worried; by the time the *Baffin* returned in August 1820, Constable and Co. were able to tell Scoresby that

> We have every reason to be much pleased with the sale of your book – it has gone further than we could have anticipated. Upon the whole the sale has been very creditable to the

---

[1] 'Autobiography'.
[2] This and the next two quotations are also quoted in Stamp & Stamp, *William Scoresby*, pp. 74, 76 and 79.

author, at the same time, it would be wrong to flatter you with a new edition – that cannot be thought of for some time yet to come, and even then with great caution.

There was no reprint or new edition, until the facsimile reprint by David & Charles in 1969.[1]

The lack of a review of the *Account of the Arctic Regions* by the *Quarterly Review* in London has already been mentioned. Its appearance was noted by both *Blackwood's Edinburgh Magazine* and its political rival the *Edinburgh Review*,[2] but there was no review. These were primarily literary quarterlies; the main scientific periodical in the city at the time was the *Edinburgh Philosophical Journal* edited by David Brewster and Scoresby's mentor, Robert Jameson. Instead of a review, the *Journal* printed a long and detailed 'Analysis of Mr Scoresby's Account of the Arctic Regions, being a translation of the Official Report of MM. ROSSILY and ROSSEL, to Baron Portal, Minister of the French Marine'. Brewster's introductory note indicates how Scoresby was regarded by the Scottish scientific establishment:

> We have been indebted to Dr Traill for the translation of this very interesting document, which has not been published in the original; and we trust it will give much satisfaction to our readers, to see that the high merit of Captain Scoresby has been well appreciated in a foreign country. – D.B.

Scoresby himself must have been gratified by the recognition given to his work in Paris, exemplified by the following comment:

> The most remarkable character of this work is, that the reasoning in every step is supported by experiments deduced from ordinary practice, or from the most delicate and abstruse physical investigations. No general idea is discussed, of which the conclusion is not supported by some fact observed by the author, or communicated to him by persons worthy of credit.[3]

Scoresby's *Account of the Arctic Regions* did receive a formal review in another Edinburgh periodical, the *Edinburgh Monthly Review* (III, 6, June 1820, pp. 611–46). Much of its length was due to extensive quotation from the *Account*, but it was also a critical evaluation, written anonymously by someone with some scientific knowledge. Summing up, the reviewer concluded:

> Our ideas of its importance are manifested by the largeness of our notice. Though it is very creditable to the author, and undoubtedly ought to find a place in all public libraries; yet, we think, that if he had confined it to a concise narrative of the

---

[1] In terms of relative purchasing power, the £8 price of the reprint was also expensive, equivalent to almost £81 in 2002, see Allen, *Inflation*, Table 2.

[2] Listed in *Blackwood's Edinburgh Magazine*, VI, 31 October 1819, p. 103 as a 'work preparing for publication' and in the *Edinburgh Review*, LXVI, May 1820, p. 524 as recently published. Scoresby's links to Edinburgh were substantial, but it is surely an exaggeration to include him, as Hugh Montgomery's short biography did in 1982, in a series entitled 'Scottish men of science.'

[3] *Edinburgh Philosophical Journal*, IV, 8 April 1821, p. 286. According to Scoresby-Jackson, *Life*, p. 164, the French original was in fact published in *Annales maritimes et coloniales*, 7 July 1820, pp. 700–712. The quotations in the *Life* (pp. 164–7) appear to be Scoresby-Jackson's translation; they differ in style but not substance from Traill's version.

observations and remarks he had himself made during his numerous voyages to the Greenland Seas, instead of swelling it out with treatise upon treatise on every subject, animate and inanimate, connected with the polar regions … it would have been rendered still more useful, without suffering loss of interest by the abridgement. This opinion, with our objection to some unnecessary minuteness and prolixity, does not hinder us from commending it, as having furnished by far the most accurate and satisfactory account that has ever been given to the public, of the varied peculiarities of the Arctic regions.

The principal focus of the reviewer's criticism was on the fifth chapter of volume I: 'Observations on the Atmospherology of the Arctic Regions …'. With some justification the reviewer described 'atmospherology' as 'a new, barbarous, and unnecessary phrase', but the principal complaint concerned Scoresby's extrapolation of his own meteorological measurements in the Greenland Sea to conclude that the annual mean temperature at the North Pole was likely to be about 10°F (−12°C). This conclusion, 'so repugnant to what both theory and observation would lead us to expect' caused the reviewer to suggest that 'In the field of conjecture and hypothesis … into which Mr Scoresby has chosen to enter, he appears but to little advantage, and is far from displaying that intelligence and knowledge of his subject so conspicuous in other parts of the work'.[1]

Scoresby's reasoning can be criticized, but what was mainly repugnant to the reviewer was the suggestion that the mean temperature was as low as −12°. If that were the case, the reviewer argued, 'no sea could withstand the refrigerating energy' and 'the whole ocean would become a solid rock'. Since this evidently had not happened, and voyage records suggested that the annual amount of sea ice had changed little during the previous two hundred years,

> we are entitled to conclude … till we obtain more exact observation, that the mean temperature of the year, at least along the barrier of ice, will not vary much from that of the freezing point of fresh, or of sea-water; and … it [is] probable that the same degree of mean annual heat extends with little variation to the pole itself.[2]

The flaw in the reviewer's own reasoning is, of course, neglect of the insulating effect of the sea ice itself and the heat capacity of the underlying ocean. The notion that an annual mean air temperature of −12°C would freeze the 'entire ocean' is absurd, and Scoresby's estimate was in fact on the warm side. The mean annual temperature in the late twentieth century on the edge of the central polar pack at Alert (82°31′N, 62°16′W) was −18°C, and the mean for the central polar basin was very similar (−18.5°C).[3] Scoresby's reviewer is likely to have been a believer in the 'open polar sea' and this section of the review is a valuable sidelight on the flawed physical reasoning that supported this notion.

---

[1] Both quotations from p. 628 of the *Edinburgh Monthly Review*.
[2] Quotations in this paragraph from p. 629 of the *Edinburgh Monthly Review*.
[3] Alert data from Environment Canada, online. Polar basin data derived from Mark C. Serreze & Roger G. Barry, *Arctic Climate System*, Fig. 8.8, which is based on data from Russian drifting stations.

More cogent criticism of some of Scoresby's science appeared in the October 1820 issue of the *Edinburgh Philosophical Journal* (III, 6, pp. 237–43), from an unexpected source. Dr Thomas Latta had sailed with Scoresby in 1818 as the *Fame*'s surgeon, and had landed on the Spitsbergen coast on Saturday 18 July in the vicinity of the 'Seven Icebergs'.[1] His account, 'Observations on Ice-Bergs, made during a short Excursion in Spitzbergen', differs from Scoresby's journal entry, and also differs from some of Scoresby's conclusions about the character of these glaciers.[2]

As Latta described it,

> Having manned two boats, we directed our course to that part of the shore where the Seven Ice-Bergs of navigators are situated. These, however, presenting nothing novel to our Captain, after viewing the frightful precipice which terminates the seaward extremity of one of the principal masses, he returned to the ship. I, with the remaining boat, landed a little to the south of this ice-berg, and having shot a few birds, and collected some plants and minerals, the natural productions of the beach, I sent the boat round to meet me at the north side, and made preparations to cross the berg, which lies from east to west; one of the sailors accompanied me, and, armed with muskets loaded with ball, we commenced our journey.

Latta had two main sources of disagreement with Scoresby's description of these coastal glaciers. The first concerned the origin of the 'rents' (i.e. crevasses), which Scoresby attributed entirely to 'the melting of the snow'.[3] Latta advanced several reasons why this was unlikely, including the fact that

> Some of the rents had a drift of snow thrown across their mouths ... I should suppose this would have been the first to have suffered from the solvent or abrasive power of the water, had the chasms been produced through the influence of that fluid.[4]

Latta's arguments against fluid erosion are all well-founded, and indicate his excellent ability to observe and deduce. However, his own tentative explanation for crevasse formation was 'in the expansive power of water, when subjected to the freezing process'. Neither he nor Scoresby was aware that these glaciers and icefields are in motion and that crevasses are the result of tensile fractures of the ice caused by such motion.

A second significant disagreement concerned what would nowadays be termed glacier alimentation:

---

[1] 71°20′N, 11°E. The place-name is retained in Norwegian: *Dei Sju Isfjella*.

[2] Latta was at pains to emphasize 'the high respect I cherish for the distinguished talents of Captain Scoresby' (p. 237), but he drew his own conclusions based on direct experience on one of the glaciers, as the following quotation on p. 238 demonstrates.

[3] *Account of the Arctic Regions*, I, pp. 101–9, quotation from p. 105.

[4] Latta, p. 240. The surgeon fell down one such snow-filled crevasse during his crossing of the glacier: 'I imprudently stept into a narrow chasm filled with snow to the general level; and immediately plunged up to the shoulders, and might, but for the sudden extension of my arms, have been buried in the gulf. My imprudence here originated, in finding many of these coverings sufficiently strong to sustain the weight of my body; and expecting to find here the same firmness of constitution as in others, I was tempted, by way of preventing a circuitous route, to cross this, which was but a thin cake of snow laid over an unfathomable gulf, an attempt which had nearly proved fatal.' (pp. 240–41).

I do not agree in opinion with Captain Scoresby on the increase of bulk of these ice-bergs. 'Ice-bergs,' says he, 'are as permanent as the rocks on which they rest; for though large portions may be frequently separated from the *lower edge*, or *by avalanches from the mountain summit* be hurled into the sea, yet the annual growth replenishes the loss; and probably, on the whole, produces a perpetual increase. But the annual supply of ice is not only added to the upper part, but also to the *precipitous crest facing the sea*, ... In some places, indeed, where the sea is almost perpetually covered with ice, the berg or glacier makes its way to a great extent into the sea, till it reaches a depth of several hundreds of feet.'[1]

Latta suggested that there was likely to be only very minor annual accumulation at the seaward end of the glacier 'where, from the influence of the ocean, the snow-line is more elevated'. He also believed that 'all that part of the ice-berg which lies beyond a league or so from the shore, has long ago ceased to receive additions of ice, as it is now much elevated above the circle of perpetual congelation, being buried under a great body of snow'.[2] He was correct about the seaward portion, but Scoresby was closer to understanding the process of converting snow to firn and then to glacier ice when he wrote that

Snow subjected by a gentle heat to a thawing process, is first converted into large grains of ice, and these are united, and afterwards consolidated, under particular circumstances, by the water which filters through among them. If, when this imperfectly congealed mass has got cooled down below the freezing temperature by an interval of cold weather, the sun break out and operate on the upper surface so as to dissolve it, the water which results runs into the porous mass, progressively fills the cavities, and then being exposed to an internal temperature sufficiently low, freezes the whole into a solid body.[3]

Here again it was their inability to visualize the glaciers as being in motion that limited both Scoresby's and Latta's understanding of the processes at work. Scoresby concluded incorrectly that net accumulation must take place at lower altitudes near the coast, to replace what was lost to the sea; if Latta had recognized the fact that ice in the landward areas would eventually descend to lower levels, he might have been more ready to accept Scoresby's explanation for the conversion of snow to ice.

* * *

[1] Latta was quoting from the *Account of the Arctic Regions*, I, p. 108, with emphasis in italics added by Latta. Scoresby's description had been reproduced in the April 1820 issue of the *Edinburgh Philosophical Journal*, under the title 'Account of the Seven Icebergs of Spitzbergen'.
[2] Both these quotations are from Latta, p. 242.
[3] *Account of the Arctic Regions*, I, pp. 107–8. Compare this with a modern definition of 'firn'. 'Snowflakes are compressed under the weight of the overlying snowpack. ... Where the crystals touch they bond together, squeezing the air between them to the surface or into bubbles. During summer we might see the crystal metamorphosis occur more rapidly because of water percolation between the crystals. By summer's end the result is firn – a compacted snow with the appearance of wet sugar, but with a hardness that makes it resistant to all but the most dedicated snow shovelers! Several years are usually required for the snow to settle and to season into the substance we call glacier ice' (Glossary of Selected Glacier and Related Terminology, online at http://vulcan.wr.usgs.gov/Glossary/Glaciers/glacier_terminology.html).

After Scoresby's return in 1820, he made three more voyages to the Greenland Sea. His own journal of the 1821 voyage has not yet been published; the transcript is among the Scoresby Papers in Whitby Museum (WHITM:SCO1256). He was accompanied by Captain G. W. Manby, who published his own account of that voyage.[1] The 1822 voyage was that combination of whaling and exploration, along the east coast of Greenland, which Scoresby had proposed to Sir Joseph Banks in 1817; the journal was published in 1823 and reprinted in facsimile in 1980.[2] The death of his wife while Scoresby was absent on the 1822 voyage, and a largely unsuccessful voyage in 1823, led to his decision, immediately on his return in the latter year, to give up his sea-going career, and to study for the Anglican ministry.[3]

Scoresby's later life is beyond the scope of the present study but, at the conclusion of these three volumes, liberally adorned with footnotes, one final and valuable footnote to his arctic whaling career was provided by Scoresby himself. In 1824 he wrote in a letter to Francis Wrangham, the Archdeacon of Cleveland,[4] that:

> The circumstances of my having left an employment which, for the last eleven years that I pursued it, has produced me an average income of £800 per annum, whilst I have no prospect or hope of emolument in the professions which I now desire to undertake beyond that of my 'daily bread,' will at once show that I do not seek to enter the Church with secular views ... .[5]

Eight hundred pounds in 1824 had the approximate purchasing power of £54,000 in 2002. As his biographer noted, this was in marked contrast with a letter written to the newly-ordained Scoresby a year later from another Anglican priest, who expressed the hope that

> Surely some one possessed of the means (prelate or no) will confer a credit on himself, and do you common justice, by making you more than passing rich with £40 a-year in the church.[6]

---

[1] Manby, *Journal of a Voyage to Greenland in the year 1821*. Manby (1765–1854) is famous as the inventor of life-saving apparatus for use in shipwrecks, and of the modern fire extinguisher. See entry in *ODNB*.

[2] Scoresby, William, *Journal of a Voyage to the Northern Whale-Fishery*.

[3] The journal for 1823 is WHITM:SCO1258 and the Scoresby Papers in Whitby Museum also include an item entitled 'Memoranda and sketch book relating to Scoresby's Arctic voyage of 1823' (WHITM:SCO649).

[4] 1769–1842. See entry in *ODNB*.

[5] Quoted in Scoresby-Jackson, *Life*, p. 221.

[6] In Scoresby-Jackson, *Life*, p. 243. The writer, Revd Thomas Cursham of Mansfield, was not being ironic; he went on to say, 'I ride about a thousand miles a-year for rather less than this sum; but I have more than I deserve ...'.

Fig. 1. 'Dangers of the Whale Fishery'.
This engraving was the frontispiece in volume II of Scoresby's *Account of the Arctic Regions*
(1820). The whaleboat that has been tossed in the air by the whale's tail appears to have been
endeavouring to add more lances to the two already struck. Meanwhile the two boats on the right
remain fast to the whale by harpoons. Photo courtesy of Whitby Museum.

Journal for 1817

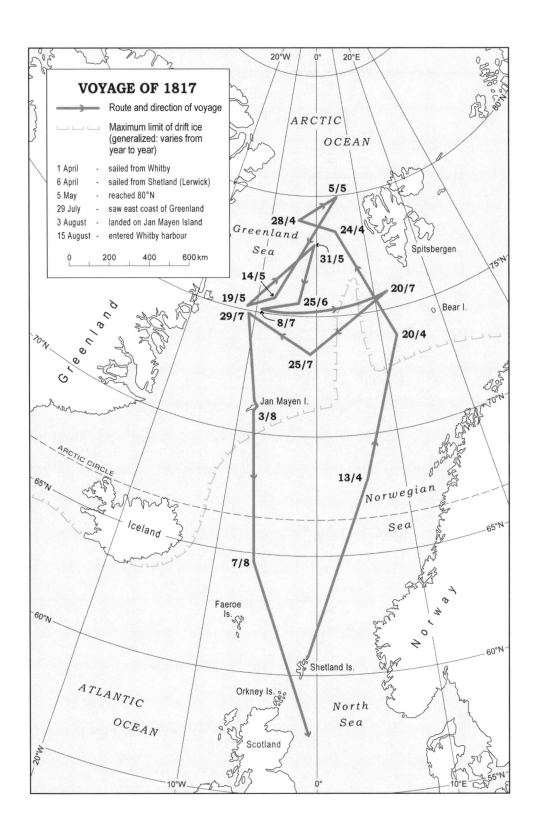

VOYAGE OF 1817

——▶ Route and direction of voyage

- - - - Maximum limit of drift ice
(generalized: varies from
year to year)

1 April	-	sailed from Whitby
6 April	-	sailed from Shetland (Lerwick)
5 May	-	reached 80°N
29 July	-	saw east coast of Greenland
3 August	-	landed on Jan Mayen Island
15 August	-	entered Whitby harbour

0   200   400   600 km

20°W   0°   20°E

ARCTIC
OCEAN

80°N

5/5

28/4   24/4

Greenland   Spitsbergen

Sea   31/5

75°N

14/5   20/7

19/5   25/6   Bear I.

29/7   8/7   20/4

25/7   70°N

70°N

Greenland   Jan Mayen I.
3/8

ARCTIC CIRCLE   13/4

65°N   *Norwegian*

Iceland   *Sea*   65°N

7/8   *N o r w a y*

Faeroe
Is.

60°N   60°N

Shetland Is.

ATLANTIC   Orkney Is.   *North*

OCEAN   *Sea*

Scotland   10°E

10°W   0°   55°N

Journal for 1817

In the beginning of February[1] the ship was hauled out of her winter moorings and removed into a convenient birth[2] for fitting out. The casks were placed in proper order in the hold, the ground tier filled with water as ballast, and the provisions, water, and other stores taken in immediately afterwards. We omitted filling the second tier of casks with water with the view of keeping the ship at as light a draught of water as possible for convenience in getting to sea – which was particularly necessary as the <u>Bar</u> ('was' *deleted*) at the mouth of the Harbour was singularly bad.[3]

About the 10ᵗʰ of March the ship was rigged, the hold completed, provisions and principal stores on board.

On the 13ᵗʰ (Thursday) it was proposed to enter into pay – the usual signal was therefore made throughout the fleet and most of the men who were provided with births repaired to their ships – but on learning that a reduction of wages was intended, notwithstanding the wages still exceeded what was paid in almost every port of Britain, the men, in general left the ships and assembled in a crowd on shore. Such as were inclined to remain on board, were forcibly taken out, those from the Volunteer in the face of the Chief Magistrate[4] who was at the time on board, and three who had signed articles on Board the Mars were dragged on shore and carried on the shoulders of others through the town, with their jackets turned inside out, as spectacles of disgust and ridicule. After they had paraded the street for some hours, they were dispersed by Henry Walker Yeoman Esqʳ who passed through the midst of them and enquired particularly into the nature of their grievances.[5]

---

[1] Like the journal for 1816, the transcript has no title-page.

[2] Possibly 'berth'.

[3] According to Young, *History of Whitby*, II, p. 539, 'the depth at neap tides is from 10 to 12 feet; at spring-tides, from 15 to 18 feet, and sometimes more'. The days on and shortly after 18 March 1817 should have been favourable for spring tides in the North Sea.

[4] 'The present magistrates, Rich. Moorsom and Christ. Richardson, Esqrs., to whom Hen. Walker Yeoman, Esq. has recently been added, have done much for the interests of the town; particularly by repressing several disorderly practices which formerly prevailed' (Young, *History of Whitby*, II, p. 604).

[5] 'Henry Walker' was listed as one of the ten current Whitby harbour and piers trustees in Young's 1817 *History of Whitby*, II, p. 540 n. Presumably the supply of sailors had increased as a result of reduced demand from the Royal Navy after 1815, but another factor in the owners' calculations may have been the decline in the price of whale oil from a peak of £50 per ton in 1813 to £28 in 1816.

The following day was a kind of armistice – the owners were determined not to give higher wages and the men though considerably cooled – yet held off; they were quiet, being threatened with a military force in case of promoting any disturbance.

On Saturday the 15th the men finding the owners determined to detain their ships a fortnight longer and then to man in Shetland as far as was allowed by law – feeling also the loss of their wages and provisions, as well as parish relief which had hitherto been afforded them but which was now, very properly suspended – they came forward and signed articles and commenced the equipment of their ships with all possible expedition.

The detention was however such that the mustering officer could not ['effect' *deleted*] complete his survey & muster of the fleet before **Tuesday Evening the 18**[th]. We were mustered in the Morning of the this [*sic*] day, and the crew paid their harbour wages and one month's advance immediately afterwards. The following is the rate of wages payable throughout the Whitby fleet.

Quality of men & officers	Hand mon. £ s	Fish mo. per size fish £ s d	Oil mo. per ton s d	Month mo. £ s d	Strik[g] Mo. £ s d
Mate & Harpooner	7 7	1 1 0	6 0	2 2 0	0 10 6
Specksioneer & harpooner	8 8	0 10 6	6 4	—	0 10 6
Harpooner	7 7	—	6 0	—	0 10 6
Second mate. skeeman, or boatswain, Extra	—	—	—	1 1 0	—
Surgeon	—	1 1 0	—	4 0 0	—
Carpenter	—	1 1 0	—	4 0 0	—
Carpenter's mate	—	—	1 6	2 10 0	—
Cooper (if boatsteerer 5/- p mo. extra)	—	—	1 6	3 10 0	—
Boatsteerer [Cook the same][1]	—	—	1 6	2 5 0	—
Linemanager	—	—	1 6	2 2 6	—
Seaman	—	—	1 6	2 0 0	—
Landman	—	—	1 0	1 10 0	—

In the afternoon of Tuesday and following morning the Lively, William & Ann, Phoenix, Volunteer, and Mars got to sea – the Valiant also made the attempt but (toutching?) on the bar she fell behind the East pier and grounded near the edge of the rock. Happily for her safety a threatening North wind kept back and she was on the following tide taken back into the harbour. A little sea and want of wind prevented any other ships from getting out. The Mars lay all day in Sandsend roads filling casks with sea water for ballast. We were all in readiness for [getting?] to sea in the morning tide; circumstances however detained us. A strong gale of wind at NNE commenced

---

[1] Square brackets, unlike the parentheses used in the previous entry.

about 2 AM. and blew tremendously accompanied with strong showers of hail. A heavy sea arose in a very short time. A sloop in attempting the harbour, at the commencement of the gale, by some mischance fell to leeward upon the rock, ['and' *deleted*] became a complete wreck in a few minutes and her crew together with a female passenger all perished. The body of the female was picked up near Saltwick at day break. The same evening prior to the gale a smuggling lugger resisted the attacks of a Brig Cutter in <u>Bay wick</u> but was after a stout action captured. Three men were killed on board the Cutter & seven wounded – the loss of the lugger in killed is unknown – the wounded were several.

The storm continued during **Thursday the 20th** and subsided in the afternoon of the following day – when the sea smoothed on Saturday the spring tides were passed and we remained along with four other fishing ships, neaped in the harbour.

Sunday the 23; the Mars, which had found shelter in Bridlington Bay appeared in the offing and took in some stores which were left on shore by mistake.

From this time to the 30th the weather was singularly fine and open – wind prevailing from NW to SW.

On Monday the 31st. the Aimwell & Valiant hauled through the Bridge and we removed into the Bridge way Birth. None sailed. Dug the Bar.

On Tuesday Morning (April 1)[1] at 1 am. we fired a signal gun and [unmoored?]. The tide was indifferent and owing to the elevation of the bar, the Aimwell only, which was of a light draught of water got to sea. The different ships during the ebb sent men to dig the sand on the bar and throw it towards the rock. The effect was trifling. At 2¾ Pm. the Valiant put to sea with a fresh gale of wind at WSW: we prepared to follow – set the sails unmoored and proceeded forward. The ship struck the Bar, as the Valiant also did, rather [***] to the southeast but never stopped. Hauled by the wind to the N^d. Reached nearly to Sandsend, tacked, and as we approached the pier discharged the pilot and [foy?] men.[2] At 4 pm. we bore up, and made sail on a NE½E course. At sun set the wind subsided and veered to the SE. During the night we had variable winds, occasionally very brisk breezes, with a continuance of charming fine weather. The Henrietta, Resolution, & Valiant, steering more E.erly, parted c°.

[Journal now assumes the normal three-column format.]

---

[1] This parenthesis inserted above the line of text.

[2] 'There are 14 pilots belonging to the port, who take charge of vessels entering or going out. They are sufficiently hardy and bold; yet such is the swell at the mouth of the harbour, that in stormy weather it is dangerous for them to venture without the outer piers' (Young, *History of Whitby*, II, pp. 539–40).

April 2ᵈ Wednesday Lat. 56°19' Lon. 1°0'W.
S. SW WSW NEerly
Light variable winds – a few gusts of wind – in the evening nearly calm. The sky was overcast the greater part of the day with dense clouds – the morning clear and bright. Steered NbE½E & NbE – in the evening by the wind close hauled NbE to NNW. Tacked in the night.

Thursday 3ᵈ April Lat. 56°53'+ Lon. 1°20'W. At 4ʰ2'30" Pm by Chronometer 1°19'45"W.
Nerly Var Calm SSW.
During the night light winds, calm all day, sky cloudless. Two or three ships were seen in the morning. Summoned all hands at 10½ AM. ['Stationed' *deleted*] apportioned them in three watches, and lotted them to the boats. Afterwards we took the Beer & provⁿ out of the afterhold, filled the second tier with water & then replaced it. During the day, caught from the ship 8 cod fish and 1 ling. In the stomach of one of the cod were two animals called by some of our crew <u>sea mice</u>. They were of a brown[1] colour on the back, beautifully fringed with iridescent hair on the sides & beset along the margin with sharp spines. The feet were [3?] on each side which with the belly were white. The largest measured 5½ inches in length & 2½ in breadth & was of an ['oval' *deleted*] oblong shape.[2]

In the evening we had a most copious fall of dew, the ['evening' *deleted*] sky was still cloudless & air calm. The therm [*sic*] suspended in its usual ['<u>Dew</u> temp. of [bodies?] on which it was deposited' *in margin*] place abaft the companion stood at 44° but another thermo*mete*r laid [flat?] on the companion on which dew was plentifully deposited fell to 30° the same instrument suspended under the drum head of the capstern where it was partially exposed to the view of the heavens rose to 40°.

Friday 4ᵗʰ April Lat 57°57'+ Lon 1°12'W By Chrono*mete*r 1 22W.
SSW
A fair wind which sprung up the preceeding evening now gradually increased to a fresh Gale, attended still with fine weather. At 5 Am. Saw Buchaness & at 9 it bore WNW Dist. 6 leagues. Made all sail & steered NNE½E – from noon until 8 Pm. our velocity was regularly 8 knots per, as we then were fast approaching Fair Isle and were likely to reach Shetland before day light we took in all the Studding sails with the mizen, &c. Continued on a NNE½E course at the rate of about 6 knots. Cloudy dark weather until the moon rose.

---

[1] Possibly 'mouse'.
[2] Smyth, *Sailor's Word Book*: 'SEA-MOUSE. The *Aphrodita aculeata*, a marine annelid, remarkable for the brilliant iridescence of the long silky hairs with which its sides are covered.' There is a modern biological description at www.marlin.ac.uk/species/Aphroditaaculeata.htm.

Saturday 5ᵗʰ April
SW WSW. W NW & NNE

A dense [haze?] universally prevailed at day break – the wind rather subsided, but a strong NW.erly swell annoyed us. Steering more westerly from 4½ to 5½ am. we saw Fair Island bearing SW Dist. [30?][1] miles – from hence we steered NE½E about 6 miles and to our astonishment saw land at NE about four miles distant. The distance between Fair Island & Shetland being upwards of 20 miles, it was a matter of doubt with us whether the land we had obscurely seen was really Fair Isle or not. The land a ['Effect of Tide' *in margin*] head certainly resembled Fitfil Head – in which case the tide must have carried us to the NW or NNW near 8 miles in about an hour! And this proved really to have been the case, for on steering <u>SE</u> about 4 miles we ['Longitude of Sumbro Head' *in margin*] rounded Sumbro Head – the Longitude of which as we passed it within 1½ miles appeared by the Chronometer to be 1°25′20″W – that is the east side or corner of the southern extremity of Shetland called Sumbro Head.[2]

['Remarks on Tide near Fair Isle' *in margin*] The strong tides which prevail in the vicinity of Fair island render the navigation here, especially in thick weather which is so frequent, most particularly troublesome, uncertain, and hazardous. Between Fair Island & Shetland on a line between the two extending also a little way to the SE of the this [*sic*] line the stream of ebb tide sets to the NW or NNW[3] with a velocity of 7 or 8 knots at spring tides & the flood in a reverse direction & only 2 or 3 knots at neap tides. A small distance further eastward the stream runs NE & SW with scarcely half the velocity of the former! Some minute observations on the tides here would be of essential service to the navigator and in the mean time the force & danger of them should be more generally known.[4]

We passed Sumbro Head to the Eastward, bearing WNW 1¼ miles at 8ʰ 46′ 50″ am. True time at ship when the time per chrono*mete*r gave the above longitude.

Steered along shore NE to E, NE, & NNE after passing Mousa Island with the wind a fresh breeze, gradually veering more to the west & NW. As we approached the entrance to Brassa Sound we perceived a packet coming out – I instantly prepared two letters & sent them on board. A pilot boarded us at 10 am.

Entered the Sound about 12½, worked through the midst of a fleet of 11 sail of ships into a good birth ['Anchor in Brassa Sound' *in margin*] in the center [*sic*] of the fleet where we anchored. The ship had not been brought up three minutes before the wind shifted in a shower of rain to the NNE!

We immediately set to work to break out the hold & fill water for ballast. We did not cease until this operation was completed & the ship deepened about one foot in the water now floating '18 inches by the stern'.

Some of the ships which sailed with us had arrived – the Valiant came in about 5 PM. and another ship, expected to be the Resolution appeared far distant to the

---

[1] Possibly '3', but the context suggests 30.

[2] Trethewey & Forand's *Lighthouse Encyclopaedia* gives the longitude as 1°16.3′W.

[3] Possibly 'WNW'.

[4] See the comments on the Sumburgh Röst tide-race in the Introduction (pp. xx, xxii) and Appendix, p. 300, to volume II of these *Journals*.

southward. The London fleet now occupies this harbour. All the ships belonging other ports having sailed to the fishery. Each of the London ['fleet' *deleted*] ships take from 15 to 20 men, one as high as 30. Men here are plentiful & to be had for very moderate wages.

At mid-night the Aurora Borealis appeared in ['Aurora Borealis & its indications' *in margin*] the North & NW – it was near the horizon, did not extend near the zenith & was without variety of colour. It appears this phenomenon has been very frequently seen in Zetland within two years – especially the last winter – much thunder & lightning also occurred. An intelligent old pilot informed me that the Northern Lights were considered as indicative of a change of weather when they had certain appearances. That when they were seen in the NW. quarter rested near the horizon & did not extend their radiation up to the zenith it indicated (in winter) frosty still weather – when they rose to the zenith [shot?] upwards & appeared red or copper coloured it indicated a storm which was usually very violent – that when they appeared in the SW quarters, a storm usually followed & in the SE. a storm with rain or sleet.

['Winter in Zetland bad!' *in margin*] The Zetlanders complain of the past as a very bad winter: The weather being almost constantly wet & stormy – wind chiefly from the west. So signs of vegetation scarcely appear at this advanced season.

In England, during last summer, especially on the east coast ['Comparison in England' *in margin*] the wind prevailed most frequently from the E & SE and scarcely a dry day occurred. The winter was open, windy constantly from the W & NW & weather generally pretty dry: in spring warm & dry weather – the dust lay as much in the roads as in general it does in summer. Vegetation highly rich, in the month of March – flowers almost out – fruit trees in blossom & gooseberry <u>set</u>. Winds still prevailed from the W^d SW – & NW but N. winds became less rare.

Sunday 6th April
N.erly to WbS.
The morning was calm – a breeze prevailed in the forenoon & seemed established in the afternoon. Most of the crew attended church, after which the wind being favourable we made signal for sailing – got under way & put to sea by the north channel. Though many of the fleet which we left (13 sail) were ready for sea none attempted to follow us. At 7 Pm. Hangcliff bore WSW distant 14 miles. Steered from the Harbour EbS to clear the Soulden rock, then E & ENE round the Skerries which we passed at 8 Pm. Blowing then very fresh & sea smooth we carried a smart sail until I believe the ship went with a velocity, scarcely less than 12 knots! 10½ knotts appeared by the log after sails were reduced. Barometer falling.

This was Mrs Scoresby's Birthday which however falling upon Sunday the occasion was celebrated on the preceding Evening when all hands had double 'mess bottles'.

Monday 7 April Lat 62°47′ Lon. 1°1′E
WbS SWbW
A strong gale prevailed the whole of this day. Our course was NEbN but indifferent steerage cast us further eastward: our velocity was regularly 8 to 9½ knotts, sometimes

greater. Between mid-night of Sunday & mid-night of this day (24 hours) our distance run was [210?][1] miles by a log of which .... feet were allowed to a [knot?] & a [glass?] of 28 seconds.

The ship though remarkably easy had nevertheless much motion from a heavy swell which accompanied the wind, but she scarcely shipped any water. Not having any ['Seasickness.' *in margin*] sea since we put to sea before many of our best seamen were effected with <u>seasickness</u>. This distressing disease producing a depression of spirit becomes more violent in proportion as the spirits sink: by hard struggling with it – eating frequently, sometimes quite against my stomach, – moving about the deck briskly at intervals – and such like means I have always been able to resist it and speedily get quite the better of it – though I scarcely ever enter upon a voyage without finding some strong symptoms of it.

Tuesday 8 April Lat. 65° Lon. 1°35′E.
WNW EbN to NbE
At 2 Am. the wind veered to WNW – abated & suddenly shifted to the ENE. In a few minutes it blew as strong as before from a quarter diametrically opposite. The sea in consequence became tumultuous and the ship rather laboursome. Snow speedily followed the change of wind & at night the therm*ometer* sank to 28° the barometer was stationary at 29.45. We reached to the northward, until the evening then wore & reduced our sails to close reefed topsails & reefed main sail and foresail.

The Aurora Borealis was very brilliant between 10 & 12 pm. It shot upwards into the Zenith with ['a' *deleted*] yellowish white streaks ['Aurora Borealis & its indications' *in margin*] which as their brilliancy subsided became of a greenish hue. This we considered as a prognostic of a further storm.

Wednesday 9ᵗʰ April Lat. 64°39′ Long. 2°6′E
NbE to [NE?]
As the wind occasionally veered from NE to N. we took advantage thereof & usally [*sic*] wore the ship for the purpose of retaining as far as possible our situation. The sea was very heavy and much increased towards night, when in the squalls it blew most tremendously which [were?] regularly accompanied by showers of thick snow. The night was dismally dark. Proceeded under two close reefed top sails & foresail. Velocity 3 knotts – leeway 3[2] to 4 points. Several persons sick.

Thursday 10 April Lat 64 29 Lon. 3°30′E
NbE to NWbN
Intermittent gales all this day, with thick showers of coarse opaque or small granular snow. Occasionally the wind blew with great fury but at intervals (during a few minutes) it was frequently nearly calm. The sea raged & the ship in consequence was laboursome & not altogether comfortable. We steered principally to the eastward or NEᵈ. Bar. rather rising.

---

[1] Possibly '220'; the second digit was altered.
[2] Originally '3½'; '½' deleted.

Friday 11 April Lat. 65°0′ Lon. 5°13′ E
NW to NE
In the morning we had greater hopes of a return of fine weather – the bar. had risen to
29.93 & the wind fell considerably – the squalls were less frequent & less powerful.
We ventured to shake a reef out of each topsail & to set the jibb, ['&' *deleted*] mizen,
& stay sails – our expectations were however baulked; the snow showers continued –
the bar*omete*r again fell – the squalls became more until at length we were obliged to
reduce sail. A tremendous head sea met us from the NNE or NE & a considerable sea
prevailed in the direction of the wind – this threatened a return of the NE wind & so
it proved for at 6 pm. in a shower of snow the wind shifted & blew with nearly its
former violence. Wore at 7 Pm. A ship in sight to the Eastward.

Saturday 12 April Lat. 65°48′ Long. 4°19′E
NE to NbE WbS to SW
We had strong squalls in the night with thick showers of snow – towards morning
the wind subsided and the snow became less abundant. The strange sail which
was seen yesterday proved to be the Aimwell of Whitby – Capt. Johnstone hoisted
his jack to us – as much as to say 'how do you' – which we returned with the
ancient.

At noon the weather cleared – called all hands, splic'd foregangers to the harpoons
and spanned them ['Spanning Harpoons' *in margin*] into the stocks. In each foreganger besides ribbons was a printed ['mark' *deleted*] parchment (usually written
leather) as well as underneath the 'serving' on the socket of the harpoon containing
the words "ESK. WHITBY SCORESBY, 1817." The use of these 'marks' is for identifying
the harpoon in case of a dispute respecting a fish which might happen to be struck by
two ships, not known to be fast when struck by the latter of the two. Disputes which
might otherwise have extended to litigation, have by this simple precaution, been
frequently prevented. The original intention of fixing pieces of ribbands in the foreganger was probable [*sic*] with the same view.[1]

Set up the backstays of the foretopmast rigging – main top mast stay, and bowsprit
shrouds – took martingale[2] & spritsail yard upon deck, &c. &c.

In the afternoon it was calm. In the evening a breeze of wind sprung up from the
westward, which soon increased (veering to the SW) to a fresh gale, accompanied
with snow, sleet, & hail in succession. Aimwell joined Company. ...

---

[1] A clearer explanation of these marks was provided by Scoresby in *Account of the Arctic
Regions*, II, p. 231: 'The foreganger is most commonly formed of white or untarred rope, which is
stronger and more flexible than tarred rope, consequently more easily extended when the harpoon
is thrown. Every harpoon is stamped with the name of the ship to which it belongs; and when
prepared for use, a private *mark*, containing the name of the ship and master, with the date of the
year, written upon leather, is concealed beneath some rope-yarns wound round the socket of the
instrument, and the same is sometimes introduced into the foreganger.'

[2] Smyth, *Sailor's Word Book*: 'MARTINGALE. A rope extending downwards from the jib-boom end
to a kind of short gaff-shaped spar, fixed perpendicularly under the cap of the bowsprit; its use is to
guy the jib-boom down in the same manner as the bobstays retain the bowsprit.'

Sunday 13 April Lat. 68.3 Lon 6°3′E
SW to WNW

A strong gale in the night with snow, sleet, and rain – in the forenoon it abated and suddenly veered to WNW: set top gall*ant* sails. Our course was NEbN all the day; velocity from 4 to 9 knots. The low state of the bar. (29.07) threatened a storm & indeed it was evident that a storm prevailed on every side of ['Three swells at the same time!' *in margin*] us; in proof of which, we had a heavy swell from the west, a considerable sea from the NW and a very heavy swell from the SSE all three of which were clearly apparent, if not at the same time, at least they were alternately observable within every five minutes; two out of these three swells were always distinguishable – the combined effect of these three swells operating at once was very curious, they produced a perfect jumble in the sea. Hence a gale of wind most certainly prevailed at a short distance from at least two very different quarters, but with us the wind continued moderate all the day, though squally in the showers. Towards mid-night much rain fell & immediately afterwards ['**Monday 14 April** Lat 69. 25 Lon 6°32′E NE to E & SEbE to E.' *in margin*] the wind shifted at once to the NE and instantly blew a hard gale. Steered to the ESE five hours, then wore and steered to the NW–NNW–N. & latterly NE½N – close hauled by the wind in general, under a brisk sail. The wind speedily subsided after day light (4 am.) and we had moderate weather, cloudy, with snow showers all day until evening when a NE swell which had prevailed ['all day' *deleted*] for many hours became excessively heavy & in a shower of snow a heavy gale commenced in a moment. All hands ['Sudden Storm' *in margin*] sprung up to reef sails & in an hour we proceeded under two treble reefed top sails & reef'd foresail. Aimwell in C°.

Tuesday 15 April Lat. 70°27′+ Lon 4°42′E
East to NE

Blowing a very hard gale, throughout this day with exceeding heavy sea & rain & snow. At noon the sea being on the beam, the ship became very 'laboursome' & some seas broke on deck – wore and reached to the SE^d under two close reef'd topsails & [treble?] reef'd fore sail. Bar. from 29.10 to 29.35 rising. Therm. 28°.

Wednesday 16 April Lat. 70°0′ Lon 6°2′E
NEbE to NbW

Showers of snow with heavy squalls – wind somewhat more moderate and sea less heavy – blowing still however a strong gale. Reached two hours NW and then wore again; & stood constantly to the E^d. Bar. rose to 29.62 at noon.

I have frequently remarked that the amendment of weather after a storm does not keep pace with the rise of the ['Barometer.' *in margin*] barometer. Whenever the bar. falls very low, it frequently rises ¼ inch or even more as soon as the predicted storm commenced; It in fact seems to sink beneath its natural level & rises for sometime [*sic*] without indication a cessation of the storm.

Thursday 17 April At 9ʰ[58'?] AM Long by Chronometer 9°28'30"E By account Lat.
70°12 Lon.[8?]°¹40'E
NbE to NNW

After mid-night the wind began to abate, the squalls became less frequent & less
heavy. At 9 am. we made sail, sent top gallant yards up, &c.

It is worthy of observation that the heavy storms which ['On Storms' *in margin*]
occur in Greenland in April frequently continue about three days – when they arise at
E or SE they generally veer progressively to the N & subside at WNW or NW. SE or
S storms on the contrary frequently take a contrary course. The storms which have so
commonly prevailed since we left Shetland have been rather remarkable on account
of their frequency & duration.

The cables having been aired on a former occasion they were now put into the
cable stage – the ice ropes [placed?] in the Cable tier – the crow's nest fixed in its place
– two provision casks placed on the <u>quarter deck</u> – and sundry other useful alterations accomplished.

Steering by the wind to the ENE- NEbN. Aimwell in C°.

Friday 18 April Lat 71.56 Lon. 10°16'E
SSW. S. to SEbS. WbN.

Calm at Mid-night. At 2 am. a southerly wind arose, which progressively increased
until it had attained the pitch of a most tremendous storm at 2 pm. accompanied
meanwhile with thick snow incessantly. Steered NbE, NNE & NE as the gale
increased, fearful of falling in with ice. At 3 Pm. we were reduced to two close reef'd
top sails & close reef'd foresail under which the ship scudded with a velocity of 10
knotts or upwards. The sea was now prodigiously heavy; after reefing ['Heavy Storm'
in margin] the top sails with all hands, we sent down top Gallant yards, & made all
snug for the storm, secured the boats by extra lashings, &c. The ship was every
moment ['Left the Aimwell out of sight astern' *in margin*] in danger of being pooped²
or of broaching too³ – the weather being truly dismal, we [carefully?] hauled to the
wind to the Eᵈ at 3 Pm.& furled the fore top sail. The ship laboured heavy; the lee
rail was frequently under water as well as the cabin windows (the dark lights were all
in but one) some of the lee bulwark washed away – the snow at the same time was so
thick that we could not see three ships lengths.

The Barometer had rapidly subsided from 29.87 to ['29' *deleted*] 28.75 (1.12
inches) in the space of 20 hours, which warned us of the storm & expected a <u>long</u>

---

¹ '8' appears to be written over '7' or '9'.

² Smyth, *Sailor's Word Book*: 'POOPING, OR BEING POOPED. The breaking of a heavy sea over the
stern or quarter of a boat or vessel when she scuds before the wind in a gale, which is extremely
dangerous, especially if deeply laden.'

³ Smyth, *Sailor's Word Book*: 'BROACH-TO, To. To fly up into the wind. It generally happens
when a ship is carrying a press of canvas with the wind on the quarter, and a good deal of after-
sail set. The masts are endangered by the course being so altered, as to bring it more in
opposition to, and thereby increasing the pressure of the wind. In extreme cases, the sails are
caught flat aback, when the masts would be likely to give way, or the ship might go down stern
foremost.'

<u>gale</u> – but at 11 Pm. we were surprised with sudden shift of wind to the W^d. The sea then became astonishingly tumultuous it rose in perfect columns – what is termed mountains high and appeared all in a foam. We directed the ship's head towards the south until mid-night & then wore & found the ship on the whole, easier but she ['**Saturday 19th April** Lat. 73°13′ Lon. 11°46′E W.– Variable. Calm. Var.' *in margin*] dipped the stern[1] nearly underwater sometimes.

From 4 am. the wind began to subside and at 8. it was nearly calm. Afterwards we had a breeze from various quarters and heavy swells from the W. & particularly SW. The ship laboured much & frequently dipped the cabin windows in the water. It was therefore evident, as the SW. sea continued without abatement that a few leagues to the S^d the gale still continued with undiminished violence – whilst the calmness of the air here was owing to the struggles of different opposite ['<u>diverse</u>' *inserted above the line of text*] winds.

Our advance in the day was trifling; the direction of it was principally towards the ENE. The evening was fine & serene. The sun set late: say 9 or 9½ pm. & at mid-night a strong twilight remained in the sky. A ['**Sunday 20 April** Lat. 73°25′ Lon. 11°30′[2] NEbN to N. to W to SW. & WNW' *in margin*] strong NE. swell commenced early in the morning and a light breeze blew from the same quarter. It brought forward a heavy black cloud, which as it approached our zenith divided & part proceeded to the S^d & part to the W^d. Tacked at 2 am. & stood to the NW^d until 9 am. when we again tacked & the wind progressively veered to the NNW, NW, W. & settled in the SW. in the afternoon. The sky became presently obscured – frequent showers of prismatic snow fell & the wind increased to a gale. Steered NNE & NbE – velocity at noon 3½ knots at 6 pm. 10! A strange sail seen in the morning.

Monday 21 April at noon Lat. 76°5½+ Long. 13°22½E+
NWbN Variable
Steered by the wind (a fresh gale with showery weather) generally at the rate of 6 or 7 knots. Saw a stream of ice at 10 am. and at noon entered among a quantity of heavy drift ice in the same streams. At Pm. [*sic*] having penetrated 10 miles or ['Made the ice in Lat. 76° Long 13½E' *in margin*] upward saw land (suppose Horn Mount or [Hedgehog?] Mount) bearing NEbE dist*ant* 30 – Whence its Long. (from Chron*ome*ter 10 am.) is estimated at 15°0′E. A heavy sea falling in upon the ice amidst which we navigated obliged us to go the same way back for some distance. After we reached the sea a strong gale commenced which blew exceedingly hard in the squalls towards mid-night with a heavy sea. Stood [but?][3] to the W^d until 8 pm. tacked & wore again near the ice at mid-night. [Close?] reef'd topsails & set close reefd foresail. Therm. 26–20. Three ships seen. All hands in Greenland Costume.

---

[1] Possibly 'stem'.
[2] The normal 'E' longitude indication is absent.
[3] Possibly 'out'.

Tuesday 22ᵈ April Lat 75°50′ Lon. 12°50′E
NW. NbW Var. Calm. E.

The wind abated towards noon & the squalls & showers were less considerable. We wore at 8 am. & at 3 Pm. approaching the edge of a pack tacked – made sail (the wind having fallen) and stood to the westward. Fine weather in the evening. At 4 Pm. Horn Mount NE dist*ant* 40 miles. Set the topmast rigging up, which was slack. The sea from the NNW being very heavy we expect much [water?] in that direction probably an open country. Calm at 10 pm. & a little afterwards a breeze from the Eᵈ sprung up,['**Wednesday 23 April** Lat. 77°24 Lon. 7°0′E. E to SE to ENE' *in margin*] increasing rapidly to a strong gale and accompanied with snow. Steered Nb[W?] supposing that course would carry us clear of ice which proved correct. Saw the land at 3 am. and a pack of ice constantly to windward (but no ice elsewhere to be seen) from 7 am to noon – during a run of 35 or 40 miles. Treble reef'd the top sails. At 2 Pm. the wind abated & veered to the ENE made all sail we could safely carry on a North to NbW course. Saw no ice after <u>noon</u> and the weather being heavy the land was rarely visible. Saw in the evening, several cetaceous animals which we imagined were Razor backs but could not exactly determine.

Thursday 24ᵗʰ April Lat. 78°21 Lon.2°23′E
E to ENE. NbE

Moderate weather in the morning – but cloudy and very dark in the north and SE. Being however in a fishing latitude, we called all hands at 6 am. took the two boats out of the twin decks & suspended them at the quarters of the ship & began to coyl the lines. We had made but small progress when the heavy cloud seen in the north advanced, a prodigious northerly swell assailed us, showers of snow commenced & shortly a strong gale of wind from the threatened quarter. Reefed topsails & stowed all the other sails. Finished the lines of the two boats in the twin deck, but were obliged to suspend the rest until better weather.

All the harpooners dined with me, when I took advantage ['Advice to Harpooners' *in margin*] of giving them some directions for the regulation of their conduct in the fishery which amounted to this. In all cases to make use of the most powerful exertions of activity & perseverance – to <u>rise in time</u> when approaching a fish and always to get up at a ship's length distance at least when meeting ['General Rules for the regulation of their conduct in the fishery' *in margin*] a running fish – to form a circle with the boats round a fast boat when is at risk and always distribute the boats at a considerable distance from each other – one boat with lines to always stay near the fast boat when her velocity is not great – & when at rest some boats lay to leeward – &c. &c. When approaching a lone[1] fish in still weather [on her eye?], if sufficiently far off not to be seen may take [a sweep?] but must never increase their distance from the fish, but let them be always approaching her – if the fish be in fast motion always steer for her tail

---

[1] Previous two words possibly 'above'.

which will without trouble bring the boat behind her – assist all ships whatever which need it, when it can be done without disparagement to the prosperity or success of our own ship, &c. and in all cases to exercise their own judgment guiding it by these [few?] general maxims – taking care to keep their harpoons clean & sharp & to have always their harpoon & foreganger clear as soon as they enter the boat – if they chase a lone fish a long way from the ship always return as soon as ever they lose sight of her, or give up the chase.

At 5 Pm. fell in with loose ice – wore stood off till 10 pm. & then wore again. Saw two ships.

Friday 25th April Lat. 78°0' Lon. 1°35'W[1]
N. Var. NNW

Strong gales during the night with some snow & much frost rime. We had no frost rime with a temp. ['Frost rime' *in margin*] of 16 but when it fell to 14 it immediately commenced. Moderate breezes towards noon – therm. 10°. Coyled 2 boats lines at the quarters complete & fitted them for the fishery. Reached to the westward among very detached pieces of drift ice at noon – passed some streams at 1 pm. proceeded through open ice & streams & perceiving nothing inviting we tacked & reached to the NEbE among streams of ice.

Expecting that cold diminished the magnetic energy, as ['Cold does not diminish the power of magnetism' *in margin*] it evidently prevents compasses from traversing[2] – I took a magnetic which will usually with difficulty sustain 7 [lb?] & had some trouble in getting it support such a weight at temp. 50° on deck temp. 8° it supported the 7 [lb?] & after a while 1 [lb?] more but would not carry 9 [lb?] & when the 8 [lb?] was removed, it would then only carry 7[lb?]. I therefore conclude that cold does not diminish the magnetic energy, but if anything increases it – the effect however produced by it is by no means considerable.[3]

When the therm. attatched [*sic*] to the companion indicated a cold ['Temp. of deck & mast Head' *in margin*] of 8°[,] at the mast head $\frac{(85)}{90}$^{ft4} high it marked a temp of 3½° – the temp. at the companion being 8 on the windward rail it was 7°. Hence the radiation of heat from the ship has some effect in raising the temp.. & shewing the average heat as somewhat more than what is strictly correct.[5]

[1] On this and for the next several days up to and including 1 May (except 28 April) the 'W' designation of longitude appears to have been overwritten on 'E', as a later correction.

[2] *OED*, s.v. 'traverse': '... to turn about on a pivot (as the needle of the compass)'. The actual cause may have been contraction of the needle on the pivot as the temperature fell.

[3] Scoresby was correct in concluding that the temperature variations in his experiment had little or no effect on the magnet. Only if a magnetic material is heated to its 'Curie temperature' – 1043°K or 770°C in the case of iron – will it lose its magnetism.

[4] Though clearly written as a fraction in the transcript, this presumably means '85 to 90 feet'.

[5] Scoresby was correct in his conclusion, although a small part of the difference in temperature was probably due to the normal atmospheric decline in temperature (typically about 4°F per 1000 feet of altitude).

Saturday 26ᵗʰ April Lat. 78°23′+ Lon. 0°55′W
NNW. NEbN
Continued our reach under a moderate or light breeze of wind to the NE all night and until the evening of this day. Saw little ice, that consisting of a few detached lumps. At 3 Pm. a fish was seen, sent two boats in pursuit. In the course of the evening saw 3 or 4 more, but all were running ['Saw whales' *in margin*] with great velocity in differ*ent* directions. The frost rime cleared away when the temp. rose to 14° & commenced in the evening when it sunk to 11°. Spoke the Guilder with 500 seals & the Mars without success. Above 50 sail of ships in sight.

Sunday 27 April Lat. 78°20′ Lon. 1°40′W
NE to NEbE
Lay too from Mid-nᵗ to 10 am. the wind then blowing a fresh breeze, made sail & worked to windward by the edge of a body of open heavy ice. Snow showers in the afternoon. ['on Frost rime' *in margin*] Therm*ome*ter rose to 20°. Frost rime was seen last night when there was no curl or breaking in the lipper.

In the afternoon we had a fresh gale of wind accompanied in the evening with showers of snow & strong squalls. Tacked at the edge of the ice at 6 pm. & continued our reach to sea or eastward all night & soon lost sight of both ice & ships. The therm. at 8 pm had fallen to 12° when it stood at 14° there was the first appearance of frost rime.

Monday 28 April Lat 78.5 Lon. 3°50′E [*sic*]
NE to N
We had a fresh or strong gale with frequent snow showers and strong squalls all the day. Tacked at 2 Pm & returned to the westward. Though the therm*ome*ter was never above 14° we had very little appearance of frost rime. Having seen frost rime at a temp. of 22° & in great & thickening profusion at temp. 16° especially with strong winds I imagine that this phenomena [*sic*] depends on the ['Frost rime: its dependence on dampness & dryness' *in margin*] dryness & dampness of the air as well as its temp. but in very damp states of the atmosphere at this time it is not abundant at a temp. of 12°.[1] This idea is confirmed by the circumstance of little snow fall*ing* when it is very abundant and the contrary when it is not seen with very low temp*eratures*.

This day in spite of a constant excellent fire the temp. ['Cabin disagreeable from Cold & smoke' *in margin*]of the cabin 4 feet from the fire was constantly below the freezing point – the therm. marked 29°. Ink froze in the pen repeatedly when in the act of writing. The smoke of the cabin was intollerable at times.

Tuesday 29 April Lat 77.54 Lon. 2°40′W.
N. Var.
Fresh gales of wind, strong squalls, snow showers, & constant frost rime. Temp. air 4° to 8°. Plying to windward near the ice among straggling pieces. Much swell. Several ships. ['Temp Cabin 20° = 32°' *in margin*]

---

[1] Scoresby's comments about ice crystal formation at 22° and 12°F (5.5° and 11°C) are reflected in the diffusion chamber photograph that appears as Fig. 1 in volume II, of these *Journals*.

Wednesday 30 April Lat. 77.48 Lon. 3°20' W.
N. Var.
Strong gales & fresh breezes of wind, some snow & constant thick frost rime. Much swell. Plying all day off the edge of the ice – in the evening joined C° with the John ['Spoke the John' *in margin*] reached into the W^d in smooth water among streams & open heavy ice. Many ships occasionally seen. No fish.

Thursday 1 May Lat. 77. 55 Lon. 2.10 W
N to NE Very var*iabl*e E.erly
Suspended the garland with the usual ceremonies. The day was "calmish" – employed all hands some hours in cutting the ice away from the ships sides, bows & head which had accumulated to the amount of some tons. Worked under all sail to windward – but on account of light & variable winds made very little progress. In the evening had a fresh breeze from the E^d sailed into a bight of the ice & saw a fish. Remained in the bight during the night. About 40 ships in sight. John & [Phoenix?][1] in C°.

Friday 2^d May Lat. 78°5 Lon. 2°50'W
E to N. very var.
Moderate or fresh breezes with strong squalls, very variable showers of snow. Under the influence of which we plyed to the NE^d along the [uneven?] edge of a heavy pack of ice. Saw 3 or 4 fish. The Lively of WBy captured one near us. Proceeded under a brisk sail. Several ships in sight.

Saturday 3 May Lat. 78°28' Lon. 1°20'W
NE to N. & variable SSE
Working off the edge of the pack to the NE^d all night under a brisk sail with a fresh gale of wind & frequent snow of the crystallized kind, in great abundance.

In tacking at 7 am. the word "main sail haul" was given before the top sail brace was let go, the ['Carried away the Main Top Sail Yard' *in margin*] consequence was, the yard broke in the centre. All hands were employed 3 Hours in clearing away the [wreck?], sending up the sprit-sail yard (which by the bye was 4 feet too short) and bending a spare [spritsail?] theron as the yard would not spread the main one. The John spoke us at 10 am. & offered a spar for a main topsail yard which we cheerfully & thankfully accepted.

Lay too under shelter of some ice & took the spar on board. It was [9?]7.4 inch in length, two feet shorter than the original yard, but is expected to be sufficient to stretch the sail.

['Change of wind, phenomenon attendant on.' *in margin*] Calm weather succeeded at noon, with a heavy SSE swell, & much snow on rise of temperature of 6 degrees. A SE gale from the state of the Bar. was confidently expected, which at 9 Pm. actually commenced but not with great violence. [Dogged?][2] near the same place during the night. Saw 2 fish & had boats out.

---

[1] The name is very badly written, at the foot of a page, but see journal entry for 7 May.
[2] Transcription error for 'dogged'?

Sunday 4 May Lat. 78°55′ Lon. 0°0′¹
SEbs to E & SE. ESE to SSE
Fresh gales to light breezes & afterwards in the afternoon an increase again, attended with much snow & strong [S?]erly swell. At 8 am. made sail to the [NEᵈ?] & at 9 saw a fish. Upwards of 30 sail of ships in sight.

In the evening clear weather slight wind with a heavy SSE swell. At 5pm. tacked near a pack lying in a zigzag direction E & W to the south of us & NNE & SSW to the Nᵈ. The Mars killed a fish. Reached to the SSWᵈ–SWᵈ from 5 pm till midnight with a considerable increase of wind & then tacked.

Monday 5 May Lon. Chronometer 4°41′31″E at 9ʰ16²47″ Am. Lat 79°40 46+ Lon. 5.35′E³
SSE–East.
Steered by the wind ENE–NE under a brisk sail, with strong SEerly swell. At 2 Pm. saw land bearing ESE – 40–50′ distant 38 sail in sight. At noon fine clear weather. Long. per Chronometer 5°35′E Leslie's Hydrometer⁴ (not corrected) sheltered from the sun 33 temp. air 30°. Tremendous swell.

The whole forenoon & morning the wind blew a brisk gale but far from hard, so that we set top gallant sails at ['Situation of the ice near the Headland – w. Ice lay 40′ from it' *in margin*] noon, but the sea from the SSE was prodigiously heavy. Hence though the Bar. was not very low (29.80) we were certain a heavy storm must prevail to the southward at a very short distance. At 4 Pm. being in lat. 80.05 or 80.10N. we came to a core of ice from whence it trended E & W & seemed to run in with the land. The ice was a ragged pack to the Nᵈ to the Wᵈ was the ice 5 or 6 miles off, but to the NW was a deep bay. Saw a small fish & was near to getting fast to it. 20 sail of ships in sight at this time or [***]⁵!

In the evening bore down to the W. ice & the reached to the SWᵈ under a light or mod. breeze of wind. When near the ['Greenland Currents or Tide.' *in margin*] ice the ship drifted NW by the current near 2 miles in an hour. A strong rippling, as of a tide was observed on the surface of the water.

Tuesday 6ᵗʰ May Lat. 79°18′ Lon. 3°45′E
SE to SbE
Continued our reach to the SW or SSW – all the day under all sails, (top gallant sails, &c.) against a prodigious S.erly swell. At 10 am. passed closely to windward of a point of the pack ice & afterwards saw no ice but a few small pieces. The weather from Morn till night was thick with snow & the wind usually a fresh breeze. The

---

¹ 'E' deleted, confirming that the vessel appeared to be precisely on the prime meridian.
² Possibly '10'.
³ These latter coordinates are presumably the noon position.
⁴ Leslie was professor of mathematics at Edinburgh University. See Scoresby's journal entry for 21 May 1816, vol. II of this work, p. 230. There are illustrations and a description of Leslie's hygrometer, taken from the 1893 edition of *Encyclopædia Britannica*, at http://etc.usf.edu/clipart/27100/27187/leslies_hygr_27187.htm.
⁵ Possibly 'afterward'.

snow was ['Beautiful crystallizations of snow' *in margin*] beautifully & most variously crystallized. It fell 3 inches deep on the deck every particle of which was probably most exquisitely formed. It was partly lamellar & partly had collateral crystallizations attatched to the principal plane in the usual angle of 60°. The greater part was transparent & beautifully marked with fine white lines, but some crystals were spotted & opaque. The variety was immense. The bar. stood at 29.85 thermometer 26 to 28° wind SE to SSE.

Wednesday 7 May Lat 78.55 Lon. 1°E
S–SE to ENE
Light or moderate winds with heavy weather all the day. Steered westward several hours & at 9 am fell in with the Henrietta & Phoenix. The masters both came on board & were afterwards joined by my Father. I was concerned to learn that a fish which had been struck & killed by the Mars people ['Mars: lost a fish after being killed & parted with 2 boats crews in a gale of wind.' *in margin*] on Sunday, broke adrift during a hard SE gale which followed & was picked up today by the Triad of Banf [*sic*] not above a mile from the Mars which was then in search of her. ['Inequitability of the Greenland laws' *in margin*] This was a mortifying circumstance to lose a fish so narrowly; but so is the Greenland law, which though not in all cases equitable as in this for instance, is nevertheless simple & prevents frequent litigation. The Mars had 2 boats crews employed in getting the lines in who were separated from the ship by the storm, but they had the happiness of perceiving their boats on board a ship which approached them, & consequently could not doubt of the safety ['Storm of wind, remarkably partial!' *in margin*] of the men. It is curious that on Monday & Tuesday (yesterday) when we carried top gall*ant* sails with ease; the Mars & other ships in the place we now are had most <u>tremendous storm</u>!

   In the evening fine clear weather with a light breeze of wind. Stretched to the pack edge & ran into a northwestern bight where we saw 2 or 3 fish – but had no success.

Thursday 8 May Lat.78.50 Lon. 1.10W
EbN to SEbS
Beat about in the bight all night, laying too occasionally with several ships in the neighbourhood among which a fish was now and then seen. Made a stretch to the SSE from 11 am. found the ice all the way under our lee, at intervals; finding the breeze increase & threaten a gale with thick weather, I conceived it a favourable opportunity for exploring the southern parts of the fishing ground accordingly, we made all sail to the southward steering usually by the wind from S. to SW. with a velocity of 3 to 6 knots. Blowing strong at mid-night with thick disagreeable w*eathe*r & considerable swell – reefed topsails & courses & took in the waist boats.

Friday 9 May Lat. 77.20 Lon. 2°W
SE to ESE to S
Fresh breezes prevailed from about 4 am. with frequent snow or sleety showers – made all speed towards the SSW by the wind. Saw 4 fish during the day, one of which we pursued. The John in Cº. Scarcely any ice seen.

In the evening we had a real thick fog for some hours with occasional attenuation.

At 7 Pm. we observed a ship 4 or 5 miles to leeward with ['Receive the Mars' men who were separated from the ship by the late Storm.' *in margin*] her ancient hoisted: supposing she had got the Mars' men we bore down & were happy to find our conjecture correct & all the men 13 in number safe and well. The sea was extremely high at the time they were picked up by the Ellen, Capt*a*in Spence (the ship)[1] above alluded to) – the 6 Oared boat was twice filled with water – they had got the lines in some time before & every ship was out of sight but two. Their escape was highly Providential. It is supposed they would have foundered, had they remained much longer in the boats & had they not been able to reach the Ellen it is almost certain they must have perished. Capt*a*ins Spence & Jackson (of the John) supped with me. Capt. S. would not accept of any provision for ['the' *deleted*] what had been consumed by the Mars' people. They now came on board of us with their 2 boats. At 11 Pm. we made sail to the N^d in search of the Mars, blowing a fresh gale of wind.

Saturday 10 May Lat. 77.52 Lon. 2°10W
SE to SSW
Blowing strong with considerable sea & thick weather with snow sleet or fog – lay too at 2 am. At 8 made sail NW with a signal flying at the F.T.M. Head as agreed with the Mars. Approach the ice (a heavy close pack) at 11 am. tacked & steered East, in search of the Mars or <u>fish</u>. We were ['Distresses produced by the late Gale.' *in margin*] informed by Capt. Spence that 7 sail (Mr Craig says 11) were driven into the pack near us in the late gale, in which from the tremendous storm, sea, & heavy ice they have suffered great distress & that one or more of them was in a sinking state, if not already wrecked. At this time[2] we had fine weather: so partial are the winds in high latitudes. My Father tells me he was once plying to the N^d under a low sail opposed ['Remarks on the partial winds of high Latitudes' *in margin*] by a North ['wind' *deleted*] storm with thick weather. Presently of a sudden, the wind fell the weather cleared, & some ships passed into a <u>south</u> wind under top gall*a*nt sail, & asked my Father what he was about under such a low sail. They expressed the greatest astonishment when he told them he had just had a heavy storm; they said they had experienced a heavy north sea, & had seen a black cloud to the north of them but had had no other wind but that from the south. The meeting of two winds readily accounts for the black cloud seen by the other captains & the heavy fall of snow experienced by my Father.

In the evening; weather fine but a little foggy, fixed a new wheel for steering by the Rudder Head, which we had prepared before, the [barrel?] being made of a part of the broken top-sail yard.

Sunday 11 May Lat. 78°2'11" Lon. 3°0'30"+W
SSW to WbS
Stood to seaward till Mid n*igh*t seeing no fish, nor the Mars among a fleet of about 30 sail – stretched to the NW & at the edge of the ice fell in with the Volunteer with a

---

[1] *Sic.* Closure of the parenthesis at this point was presumably a transcription error.
[2] I.e., at the time others were experiencing the gale.

signal hoisted to us. The master told us the Mars was to the southward that he passed them on Friday. we now began to work back again along the edge of the pack.

In the day we had fine weather – clear – & a fresh breeze of wind: made good progress.

['Delivered Mars' Crew' *in margin*] In the afternoon saw the Mars, bearing towards us; joined her at 4 Pm & put her men on board. In the evening reached to the S or SSE by the wind. Mod. weather: Prismatic snow. Several ships. Saw 3 fish.

Monday 12 May Lat. 77.50 Lon. 2.40W
SW. NEbE
Light winds, calm, or fresh breezes, with frequent showers of prismatic snow & occasional fog. The carpenter made a new main topsail yard which was sent up & bent to it the main topsail at 4 Pm. Several ships around us. Fish very scarce. In the evening steered along the edge of the pack to the southward. Spoke the Dexterity, Geary, who informed us that the Dauntless ['of London' *deleted*] and Fortitude of London, ['Loss of 4 Ships.' *in margin*] Leviathan of Shields, & Lion of Liverpool were wrecked in attempting to get out of the ice in the gale of the 5 & 6th which we avoided by going to the northward; that the Superior & some other ships which were forced into the pack at the same time were severely stove. This will be a severe loss to the poor fellows belonging the wrecked ships who must now [proceed?] the voyage probably for nothing, as well as to the underwriters. The number of British Greenland ships are 90, the losses already are amounting to $4\frac{4}{9}$ per cent, whilst premiums of insurance against total loss is only 2 guineas per Cent!

Prismatic snow has fallen repeatedly for some days; it ['Prismatic Snow described.' *in margin*] comes in showers like fog, hangs heavy in clouds like fog, which obscure the vision from the mast head whilst on deck you see more beneath it & consequently to a greater distance. It consists of fine spiculæ ⅛ to ¼ inch in length of rough prisms about the thickness of horse hair. But some finer particles are crystallized more perfectly & transparent. [Many?] particles seem to be formed or 4 or more put together as in a bundle.

Tuesday 13 May Lat. 76.50 Lon. 2.50W
NEbE to E. – NE
Steered SWbS, SbE [for?] ice, then SW, W, WNW, NW, & latterly N. After 4 am. when we had hauled out to the eastward for a point of ice we saw no more ['until ... pm' *deleted*] during the day. In the morning many ships were in C° but a thick fog commencing at 11 am. & continuing most of the day, in the evening when pretty clear only 4 sail were to be seen. Saw a fish at 6 Pm. The wind which blew fresh in the morning, subsided in the afternoon. Prismatic snow occurred along with the fog.

Wednesday 14 May Lat 76.15 Lon. 7.40W
NE variable to NNE
Steered by the wind the NW^d–NNW under a brisk breeze of wind all night. At 6 am. fell in with ice; being thick with fog & snow alternately lay too. Clear weather at 2 Pm. made sail to the NW & soon made a close pack of very heavy ice along which we

steered W. per compass but only SW½S per True Course, until 6 pm. when we tacked. At this time our long. by chronometer was 8°25′30″W – variation of the compass mean of two sets <u>with the ship's head west</u> = 49°40′20″W & variation with the <u>ship's Head East</u> 30°50′40″W. – Hence the mean of the two is the true variation = 40°15½W.[1] The sky was perfectly clear at this time & though we were ..... <u>leagues upon the</u> west Land by the Dutch Charts yet no land or appearance thereof was to be seen; hence we may safely conclude that the W. land or Old Greenland must lay at least 3½[2] degrees farther west or beyond longitude 12°W.

['Lat. at mid nᵗ 75°59′53‴ *in margin*] Finding only a rare fish here & there we stood now to the eastward & worked NEerly during the night, blowing a strong Gale of wind with cloudy weather.

Thursday 15 May Lat 75°53′+ Lon. 7°W
NE

Under a hard gale of wind & [dry?] weather plyed to the NEᵈ amongst [loose?] brash ice or streams. Split the mizen top sail – unbent it, repaired it, & replaced it in a few hours. Temp. 15°. In the afternoon, kept our reach to the ESE under close reef'd topsails & reef'd courses: met a high sea & passed some dangerous pieces of ice in violent agitation. Mars & John in Cᵒ.

Friday 16 May Lat. 75.12 Lon. 6°20′W
NE–NNE

Blowing tremendously hard with thick snow a little past mid-night – but subsiding a little as the day advanced. Stood to the ESE under three topsails only, having a heavy swell until 8 am. when we wore. In the afternoon fell in with much heavy ice violently [commoded?] by the swell: tacked & stood off until 8 pm. when we again tacked & stood to the NWᵈ. The sea now [rolled?] heavily from the East to ESE.

Saturday 17 May Lat. 75.16 Lon.[3?]°50′W
NE

During the preceding storm the bar. was for the most part so high as 30.00–30.10 inches – but the air was then dry & evaporation went briskly on under a temp. of 15° to 18°. After however the bar. [sunk?] ['Barometer & weather' *in margin*] to 29.70 thick snow commenced.

Entered the ice in the forenoon, having a moderate wind but still dull heavy weather: reached four hours NNW amongst heavy loose ice, streams, or patches:

---

[1] I am grateful to George Huxtable for pointing out that Scoresby was attempting to correct for what would nowadays be termed the compass *deviation*, i.e. the effect on the needle of iron in the ship. The influence of this deviation would have increased as the ship sailed to ever higher latitudes, because the horizontal component of the earth's magnetic field rapidly diminishes. Scoresby's attempt to determine the variation by averaging total compass error from two opposite headings was inadequate; it was, however, one of his earliest experiments in what was to become a lifelong interest in magnetism and the difficulty of obtaining accurate compass determinations in high latitudes.

[2] '3' written over '4'. At 76°15′N, the east coast of Greenland is in fact at 18°30′W.

falling into navigable water we then worked under all sails towards the NE. At 7 Pm. a fog which had some time prevailed became so thick that falling in with much ice we were confounded & obliged to lay. At 11 pm. we reached ['**Sunday 18 May** Lat.75°28′ Lon. 4°40′W NE' *in margin*] a little eastward & then found rather opener ice, among which we plyed towards the ENE all night. Clearing at 6 am. we saw the Mars scarcely two miles from us. A swell from the South appeared about 8 am, & very shortly increased and became very considerable. Much ice appeared to the E^d & apparently a close body to the NNE near which a foreign ship was seen flinching a whale. Made all possible dispatch to windward, though we had a light wind & consequently could not make very rapid progress. Fog showers during the day, the dampness of which adhering to the rigging became a coat of transparent ice.

Spoke the Noord stern,[1] flinching; had seen 2 or 3 other whales. A thick fog prevailed at this time stretched to the N^d towards an ice blink before seen where we fell in with a close pack then tacked & proceeded amongst crowded heavy[2] & strong S. swell towards the SE. The sky clearing when I was at the mast head I happened to hit upon an object with the spy glass which excited my ['A wreck seen' *in margin, with small sketch*] attention: on being viewed by a good telescope[3] it proved to be a wrecked ship, the main mast of which stood complete, but the lower mast of the foremast was only standing. Afterwards I saw the bowsprit likewise level with the ice. As this vessel was 5 or 6 miles off within a heavy pack I could not ascertain whether it was a brig or a ship with the mizen mast cut away. Anxious to be of service to the crew in case they should remain by her we hoisted an ancient – but seeing no signal returned when we had approached as near the ice would permit we ['**Monday 19 May** Lat. 75.23 Lon. 11°W ENE to EbS' *in margin*] concluded the crew had deserted her. Lest however this should not be the case we lay too all night.

Fog & snow showers (of the prismatic kind in large flakes) ['Prismatic snow accompanied & alternated with fog.' *in margin*] alternated so that the weather was almost constantly thick. Wind in a light breeze.

At 9 am. made sail with the view if possible of extricating ourselves from among this dangerous ice, wherin a swell still prevailed & in which we had seen but one fish. Steered by the wind to the S–SSE fell in with much heavy ice which lay very awkwardly & afforded but a difficult & occasionally dangerous navigation. At noon got a respite in a slack place of the ice in which we plyed towards the SE the ice being very close to the S^d of us & very heavy. Wind a light to moderate breeze: The Mars in C°.

Having worked to the SE^d under a very [smart?] sail for several hours, we found the ice which[4] to the SW^d of us proved to be a sea stream gradually narrower until at length we were able to put thro' it & escaped to sea, much to our satisfaction for the wind now blew strong gale & the sea was high.

---

[1] *Sic.* If a German vessel, presumably *Nord Stern*, 'North Star'.

[2] Transcription error: 'ice' omitted?

[3] The distinction that Scoresby here drew between a 'spy glass' and a 'good telescope' is not evident in *OED*, which defines 'spyglass' as 'A telescope; a field-glass' and cites Marryat in 1847: 'A telescope, or spy-glass, as sailors generally call them.'

[4] Transcription error: 'lay' omitted?

Tuesday 20 May Lat. 75.30 Lon. 10°10′W
E
Under a strong gale of wind, high sea, & hazy w*eathe*r we plyed under a smart sail all day to windw*ar*d but scarcely held our ground: we regularly stood 4 hours off the ice. The Mars nearly out of sight to windward.

Wednesday 21 May Lat. 75°30′ Lon. 10°W
E to ENE
The fore part of this day the wind blew a strong gale and was as usual accompanied with a high sea. Continued ['plying' *deleted*] beating to windw*ar*d under as much sail as we could carry along the edge of the pack, standing regularly 4 hours. In the evening cloudy weather with an abatement of the wind. Made sail. The Mars out of sight to windward.

Thursday 22ᵈ May Lat. 75°34′ Lon. 10°W
EbN
Continued plying to windw*ar*d along the edge of the pack, with a fresh breeze of wind diminishing to a calm. Saw a fish ab*ou*t 4 pm. among brash ice, but like all the fish we have almost yet seen[1] it escaped us without again appearing. A heavy swell has constantly prevailed ['Intermittent swells' *in margin*] for several days from the SE, which on this occasion was near drifting us into the pack. It is curious, this swell which evidently arises from a distant wind comes in gusts as it were – that is every now & then come severe heavy waves & then for a little it disappears: the same phenomenon was still more evident when we were in the ice, Sunday last.

   Took on board a stock of fresh water ice. The whole surface of every lump was covered with conchoidal indentation.

Friday 23 May Lat 75°45′ Lon. 9°30′W
NE to NNW to NE.
Slight breeze commenced at 2 am. & prevailed with a small increase throughout the day; during the whole of which we towed a boat but never saw a fish. Several unicorns however played[2] about us. The weather was a little showery (small pris-m*ati*c snow) but very fine & the sea smooth. Saw 4 ships like ourselves working under all sails towards the NE. Perceived floes a little distance within the ice.

Saturday 24 May Lat. 75.58 Lon. 9°10′W
NE to N. Var.
Moderate breeze of wind dark weather with a little snow. Beating to windw*ar*d under every sail we could set. No fish to be seen. The ice a close pack to the Wᵈ and NWᵈ of us. Saw three ships to the SWᵈ of us & 2 to windw*ar*d. The pack here trends generally NEbE & SWbW but the edge is filled with deep sinuosities.

---

   [1] *Sic*: 'like almost all the fish we have yet seen' intended?
   [2] '<u>spouted</u>' inserted above the line of text.

Sunday 25 May Lat. 76.15+ Lon. 7.52.45+W
NE. Var SSE
Moderate winds with cloudy weather: in the afternoon calm. Continued beating to windward with pretty good effect so long as we had any wind. With a light air of wind in the evening steered ENE.

Monday 26 May Lat. 76.37.7+ Lon. 5°55′15″W
[SbEast?]
With a progress of about 2 knots per hour we advanced to the E^d early in the morning saw ice to the E–SE & SSE hauled by the wind, passed thro' some open ice at 8 am. & at 2 pm. tacked at a close stream of prodigious heavy ice. At 6 pm. again approached the same stream which was here about a mile in breadth consisting of large masses of field ice with fragments of ice bergs – perceiving no means of circumnavigating it we pushed into it and after 4 hours arduous labour warping, &c. we happily succeeded in passing it into an open sea on the E. side. Some of this ice was 20–30 *feet* in height above the water and pieces were observed upwards of that deep, some of them must ['Curious alteration in the ice.' *in margin*] have been at least 100 *feet* thick. This great accumulation of ice joining the W. pack & extending far into the sea must have ['come' *deleted*] drifted in the late gales from Point Look out, or between it & Cherry Island of which idea the number of <u>icebergs</u> is a strong proof. One ship pursued the same course as ourselves & likewise escaped – five other ships returned to attempt to double the windward ice – in the light wind prevailing at the time this must require a considerable interval for its performance.

Tuesday 27 May Lat. 77°7′ Lon 3°40′W
S to SE
Steered from hence NE along the edge of the pack – at [3?] am. saw a ship beset in the pack – seeing ice again to the E^d & S^d hauled by the wind at 5 am. (lay EbS) passed thro' much slack ice from 12 to 2 Pm. and then proceeded among loose heavy ice to the ENE. 5 ships in sight all pursuing a similar course. In the evening the weather was calm & fine. Saw one fish.
   A man of the name of [Robson?] came on board of us ['Loss of the Leviathan, Dauntless, Fortitude and Lyon[1] May 4th [Vide 16th of June.]' *in margin*] from the London, requesting a passage to Whitby: he belonged to the Leviathan of Shields which was wrecked with three more on the 5th [*sic*] of May. At the time we enjoyed fine weather in lat. 80° the Superior, Enterprize, [Norfolk?],[2] Dauntless, Lyon, Leviathan, & Fortitude were contending with a most tremendous storm of wind, sleet, and swell, which caught them within a sea stream of the pack in lat. 78°.

---

[1] *Sic.* Lubbock, *Arctic Whalers*, p. 204, clearly stated that this was the *Lion* of Liverpool.

[2] This and the similar name later in this day's entry are only tentative identifications. However, Lubbock, *Arctic Whalers*, mentioned the *Norfolk* of Berwick in whaling seasons both before and after 1817. There is a blank space, followed by another comma, after this name, indicating another unnamed vessel.

Baffled in every attempt to escape by the force of the wind, swell, & obscurity of the atmosphere they at length after contending in vain for some time & receiving some heavy blows from the ice, resigned all the ships to the pack – here they received a dreadful beating – the Dauntless was wrecked in an hour, afterwards the Lion [*sic*]; the Leviathan after carrying away her bowsprit & rudder against the ice was kept up, 2 hours by means of the assistance of the Dauntless' crew & then the water gaining on them, they had scarcely time to save their provisions & clothes before the ship went down head foremost & sank to the bottom! A quantity of iron ballast was the reason of this rare circumstance in a fishing ship. The Fortitude soon after shared the same fate. The crews of the 4 wrecked ships 196 in number lodged themselves on the ice 6 or 7 days in tents. They slept in casks, two together with one end out: by that means though terribly cramped they were defended considerably from the inclemency of the cold. They cooked provisions in a kind of hearth constructed of iron hoops, burning the mizen mast of the ['Leviathan' *deleted*] Dauntless for fuel. After this the ice slacked some ships approached & they with their boats got on board of them. The Lion broke in two pieces, & the Fortitude fell over on one side: the ['Leviathan' *deleted*] Dauntless continued upright. This ship it appears it must have been that we saw in Lat. 75½ which had drifted above 150'[1] in the space of 14 days, as she was boarded by another ship at ['Disasters by SE gale of 4th May.' *in margin*] sea near that place.

It appears the Superior & Enterprize were much stove & Robson says the [Norfolk?] had a large piece of ['[32 ships in sight This day]' *in margin*] ice sticking in her bilge when she escaped, which they endeavour to secure fast to prevent the ship from sinking. This piece of ice was afterwards removed & no leak ensued: it was supposed not to penetrate.[2]

Wednesday 28 May Lat. 77.25 Lon. 3.10W
E.rly Calm NE.rly
Had a light air of wind in the morning but calm all the day with a heavy SE.rly swell – clear to the N[d] but dark & heavy clouds to the E[d]. The swell drove us very near a projection of the pack formed of a lately broken floe – [towed?] occasionally. Several ships around us, but no fish. Slight breeze from the NE[d] sprang up towards midnight.

Thursday 29 May Lat. 77.34 Lon. 2[o]3W
ENE to N. Var.
Light to fresh breezes, cloudy fine weather. Worked to windward all the day but owing to variable winds made little progress. At night attained the head of a bay of heavy ice where we lay too. A brig killed a fish. Several ships seen running toward the south, suppose 20 sail. Capt. Bennet of the Venerable supped with me – he had not yet got fish, understands that the fishery has hitherto but little advanced.

---

[1] I.e. 150 nautical miles.
[2] This sentence appears to be a later insertion.
[3] The minutes are illegible.

Friday 30 May Lat. 77°39′+ Lon. 2°W
N to NWbW

The wind veering to the NW about 6 am. passed thro' a sea stream to the eastward into the Sea & then reached toward the North. The Capt. of the Amsterdam ship Greenland (the only Dutch ship out while there are . 3 ..¹ from the Elbe) Jacob Broerties dined with me as well as Capt. Jackson. Broerties gives a good account of Spitzbergen which he has circumnavigated² wanting only 10 Dutch miles on the NE side. Has seen fish in all the bays occasionally, once saw the west land, &c. He seems to possess an enlightened knowledge of the Country. His son a fine youth of about 15 years of age accompanied him in his visit. Saw 2 fish in the evening & one ship in the act of flinching. Some ships ran off to the southward about a dozen sail remain in sight.

['Various coloured water: the way in which they are [united?]: distinct' *in margin*] Entered an olive green coloured sea at [noon?] in lat. 77°39′, the first we have this year noticed – it being hitherto always an "ultramarine coloured transparent blue". The edges of the two different coloured waters were perfectly distinct even as disunited as fresh water from a river & the sea when they unite. A strong rippling as of a current was between them. Its breadth was small (olive green water) for in an hour sail we would sometimes get into greenish blue water then olive green & then transparent blue ['Currents & examination of minute molluscæ & "filiformes".' *in margin*] all within 10 miles. In the olive green water I examined to the little [***] substances which give it its colour & found them consisting of globular molluscæ (I suppose*³) about the size of a common pin's head. Each contained of about 12 distinct patches of double dots [*small sketch inserted*] of a brownish colour & each patch contained 16 pairs or 4 pairs of ['double' *deleted*] these dots. The moluscous [*sic*] part was not visible but it evidently existed from the effects produced on the patches of dots when the thing happened to turn over or aside: the "filiformes" was also very evident in this water resembling the [horn?] of some flies [*small sketch inserted*] thus:⁴ The mollusca were very numerous.

Strong currents appear to exist amongst the ice here & near it – ships sometimes drift to the Sᵈ when they expect they have gained 10 or 15 miles towards the north in the space of one day's sailing.

Saturday 31ˢᵗ May Lat. 78.2 Lon. 0°50′W
W to WNW, NNW & N.

In the evening saw 3 or 4 fish: sent boats in pursuit without effect. Lay near the place all night where a fish was occasionally seen. The John succeeded in capturing one.

---

¹ *Sic*: possibly the '3' was a later insertion, anticipated by the ellipsis points.

² In commenting on the 1818 season Lubbock, *Arctic Whalers*, p. 205, noted that '... many Arctic voyagers still held that land joined the north-east corner of Greenland to the north-west corner of Spitzbergen, which was still called by many seamen Old Greenland.' Scoresby clearly was not one of these, and the Phipps expedition of 1773 and later whaling voyages had virtually disproved the existence of such a land connection.

³ Note in margin: '*Class Radiaises of Lamarck nearly allied to the Beroë globuleux. The family is Molluscous, class Radiaises, order Mollesses. Lamarck vol. II 470.'

⁴ A transcription error? The sketch precedes 'thus:'.

In the forenoon stretched to the N[d] & in company with several ships penetrated the ice for 6 hours, in a most critical navigation occasionally; the ice being very crowded & many of the pieces very heavy. At mid-night gained the edge of an impervious pack where we lay too. Wind a mod. breeze.

Sunday 1st June Lat. 78.29′.11+ Lon. 1°50′W[1]
In the morning we had a mod. breeze of wind with thick showers of hoar frost or frost rime on which was impressed a bow resembling the rain bow but more dull & broader. ['Hoar frost bow!' *in margin*] At noon this bow formed the segment of a circle the alt. of which was about 9° & the chord (along the horizon) 50°.[2]

Seeing no prospect of getting into the ice & no fish, steered out of the ice to the E[d] from 9 am until 1 pm. when having gained the sea steered SE & SSE, in search of the olive green coloured water where we had seen the fish, with a view also of attempting the ice in about lat. 78°–78°10′. The wind being[3] light our progress was but slow: at 7½ Pm. however we fell into a narrow stream of olive green water, then a narrow stream of blue & in five minutes or less, a still more opaque water. At 10 pm. saw a fish which we pursued [' **Monday 2[d] June** Lat 78°15′ Lon. 0°5′W. Var. WSW to SW' *in margin*] unsuccessfully during 3 hours. The wind veering to theW[d] we stretched a little to the SSW & again met with fish. At 5 [A?]m, we had the happiness of being aroused by the alarum of a "fall". The fish struck descended 3 lines & returned to the surface in about 15′ after running with great celerity to the S[d] shortly it again

John Greenwood **M.** No. 1 = 13[ft] 7in bone!

descended appeared in about 15′ more & three more harpoons were struck – it was killed in about an hour, generally avoiding the lances by repeatedly shifting its course & diving a few fathoms under water. At 7½ Am. it was taken alongside & a flinch gut prepared for its reception. The men having gotten their breakfasts, the flinching was commenced at 9 am: but owing to a fresh breeze of wind & considerable lipper which appeared we did not finish until 2 Pm. This whale was of the longest ['Dimensions of the above fish' *in margin*] whalebone I ever saw killed – it measured along the curve 13.7 and on a straight line 13 [ft] 6 in. The fish was very bulky in circumf*erence* but not remarkably large in other respects. Its tail was 20.10 broad – its fin (from the extremity of the knuckle to the tip) 10f[t]: the lip 6 [ft] 2 by 19 [ft] 6; the length of the body 46 feet, of the rump & tail 6 [ft] making the total length 52 [ft]. The length of the cant on the stretch was 31 [ft] 6 in. but as the external side or skin was slack I esteem that the real circumference in this part must have been 36 [ft] allowing

---

[1] There is no indication of wind direction.

[2] Presumably Scoresby meant that the bases of the bow on the horizon subtended an angle of 50°. He was observing what would now be described as a fogbow. See also the journal entries for 6 and 11 July 1817.There is a photograph of a fogbow over the Arctic Ocean at 81°N at www.sundog.clara.co.uk/droplets/arctic1.htm.

[3] This word is repeated in the transcript, and the repetition was deleted.

an increase of 18 inches diam*eter* for the contraction of the skin on blubber 12 inches thick. The jaw bones were fᵗ ... in length & adjoining to the knuckle ... fᵗ ... in. in circumference.

In the water when this fish was killed, a vast quantity ['Shrimps in the sea' *in margin*] of shrimps were seen. Several ships in sight.

The tail of the above fish around the edges was varied by ['Remarks on the tail & whale bone' *in margin*] numerous white scratches evidently arising from wounds, which had the appearance of scratches from the teeth of some animal: the scratches were 2 or 3 inches asunder. The thin edge of the tail was very uneven apparently owing to the same cause. The whale bone was marked at intervals of 6–8 inches with a hollow on the concave side as if cankered: this I have before imagined may give some idea of the age of the animal.[1]

The flinching finished & wind blowing a strong breeze we reached NW until ['made' *deleted*] came to the ice about mid nᵗ. Several foreign ships.

Tuesday 3ᵈ of June Lat. 77°56′21″+ Lon. 0°10′W
SW to SSW
About 4 am. the wind ['abated &' *deleted*] subsided into a moderate breeze we therefore (seeing no fish) reached to the SSE – fell in with fish about 8 am. & were in frequent pursuit during the whole day afterwards. We saw about a dozen fish & were very <u>nearly successful</u>. Several ships around us, none of which succeeded. In the evening we had snow showers.

Wednesday 4ᵗʰ of June Lat 78° Lon. 0°10′W
S to SE
With a fresh breeze of wind accompanied by showers of snow we worked most of the day towards the SE, saw 3 or 4 fish, but made no capture. In the evening we passed a detatched stream of ice ['forming' *deleted*] being one of many forming a kind of chain from the main ice 20 or 30′ to the SE. Here we spoke the Mars with 2 fish.

[1] Scoresby returned to this topic in *Account of the Arctic Regions*, II, p. 457: 'In some whales, a curious hollow on one side, and ridge on the other, occurs in many of the central blades of whalebone, at regular intervals of 6 or inches. May not this irregularity, like the rings in the horns of an ox, afford an intimation of the age of the whale? If so, twice the number of running feet in the longest lamina of whalebone in the head of a whale not full grown, would represent its age in years.' In their chapter in Burns, *Bowhead Whale*, Schell and Saupe referred to Scoresby's suggestion, and showed from isotope data that the variations were indeed mainly a reflection of the whales' annual migrations between feeding grounds, although wear from the distal end of the baleen plate was a complicating factor. From empirical data, Schell and Saupe ('Feeding and Growth', p. 502) found that 'Field Measurement of one of the longest baleen plates appears to provide a reasonable means of age determination in harvested subadult bowhead whales where

$$(\text{age in years}) = 2.14 \ (\text{baleen length in meters})^{2.271}.\text{'}$$

Fig. 12.9 in their chapter, and the result of the above calculation (53.90) suggests that the age of the whale caught on 2 June 1817 could have been fifty years or more.

Thursday 5th of June Lat. 77°54′ Lon. 0°20′W
ESE to SbE & SE.
Seeing no fish we steered a considerable distance to the N^d until we got to leeward of most of the accompanying ships: here we fell in with fish & pursued several. At length we were favoured with entangling one, which in the space of two hours we killed. It remained underwater 15′ during which time it

John Allen F.   No. 2 = 9..9

ran out 7 lines very obliquely downwards: it shewed itself 5′ & was then down again 5′ & on its next appearance was with difficulty secured by a second harpoon. The flinching was commenced about 10½ Pm. & did not conclude until after midnight.

In one of the snow showers during the day, we had a most brilliant & perfect rain bow or rather 'snow bow'.

Wind all day fresh to a light breeze, snow showers. Several ships.

Friday 6th June Lat. 77°56′ Lon. 0°15′+ W
SE to SSW. to SSE
Fresh to light winds accompanied by showers of snow: in the afternoon beautiful clear weather.

Plyed some distance to the SW^d saw no fish: penetrated a few scattered streams but still saw no fish. Conceiving therefore the opportunity favourable we commenced clearing the after hold at 8 pm. & after close reefing the topsails & making all snug we began to make off about mid-night. 20 ships in sight.

Variation of the Compass at 6½ pm. ships head East 20°¾W; ship's head west 45½°W & ship's head north 33¼°W! Long. by Chron. 0°15′W.

Saturday 7 June Lat. 78.2+ Long. 10′W.
SE–E, S, W. Var.
Mild, fine, calm weather. Ship laying too. About 2 Pm. finished making off, having filled 65 casks = 95 butts in 14 hours being 7 butts per ['Made off: 65 Casks = 95 B' *in margin*] hour, nearly. The first fish filled 62 butts of blubber, the last 33.

In the evening continuing calm. I sent down the marine diver to the depth of 761 fathoms & along with it various kinds of wood, metals, &c. to ascertain the degree of impregnation which would be produced by pressure: the result was curious. The particulars are related in the book of meteorological registers [at large?].[1] The temp. passed thro' by the inst*rumen*t was 32 to 38; the surface being 32°: by means of a wire gauze stretched across the upper valve, 3 curious animals were caught; a squalus or shrimp,[2] a round rough [conglomerate?] [mass?] like [spawn?] & a smaller animal.

---

[1] This sounding was described, with a table of the results, in *Account of the Arctic Regions*, I, pp. 193–5.
[2] In *Account of the Arctic Regions*, I, pp. 538–40, Scoresby used the Latin name *Squalus borealis* for the Greenland shark (now *Somnisosus microcephalus*). It is not easy to imagine how this relatively large creature could be confused with a shrimp.

Sunday 8ᵗʰ June Lat. 78°10 Lon. 20′W.
Variable NE.rly.
Light variable winds, with fog or snow showers. Having seen no fish of 2 or 3 days we penetrated the ice pursuing a NW.rly course for 10 hours, in a most intricate navigation occasionally – when at length we were stopped by a solid pack: floes appeared to the N & W. but were inaccessible, some we ['**Monday 9 June** Lat. 78°12′ Long. 2°W. NE.rly Var.' *in margin*] approached within 2 or 3 miles but saw no fish by them. Made the ship fast to a piece of ice in the morning, lay until 6 Pm. & then cast off and steered back to the SEᵈ with a light variable breeze, taking advantage of an interval of the fog which prevailed from 6 or 8 am. until this period. Several ships to the Eᵈ & Sᵈ but none to the W or N. The bilge water gass evolved from the ['Colours produced on metals by bilgewater gass.' *in margin*] casks when making off on Saturday discoloured metals as follows. Copper became of an iron grey, brass of a fine gold lacquer colour with a shade of rich crimson, silver assumed to the colour of lead & gold was likewise tarnished: the gilt frame of a looking glass resisted it as well as varnished metals. Litharge[1] became black & adhesive plaster the metallic colour & luster of lead.

Tuesday 10 June Lat. 78°20′ 0°00′W.[2]
W.rly. N.rly; var.
At 6 am. issued into the sea: steered NNE–NE under a mod. breeze of wind 15 or 20 miles & then began to ply in the ice again. A foreign ship killed a fish near us: upwards of 30 ships in sight about one half of them "Elbers."[3]

Wednesday 11 June Lat. 78. 26 Long. 1°W
N. NW.rly to N.
A fresh breeze of wind with fine cloudy or clear weather. Having beat to windward several hours occasionally in a troublesome navigation, but generally in an open bight of the ice, we saw several ships running towards us from the N & NW. Lay too & sent for Captain Souter of the Resolution[4] of Peterhead: [she has 3 fish 30 tons of oil] who informed us he had penetrated the ice as far as it was possible to navigate without seeing an[5] floes or open ice beyond him: here he got a little fish & is now pursuing his way towards the NE with the view of doubling the pack of ice which lays hereabout. Several of the Peterhead fleet are still <u>clean</u>. Notwithstanding this information, on the wind increasing to a strong breeze from a quarter favourable for opening the ice we made all sail & plyed in a roomy navigation towards the NNW. John, Mars, Aimwell, &c. in Cᵒ.

---

[1] Litharge is lead monoxide, PbO. Scoresby may have been referring to lead-glazed items.

[2] The usual 'Long.' is omitted, and the 'W' indication is incorrect if, as indicated, the vessel was exactly on the prime meridian. The '00' minutes were however overwritten on an illegible value.

[3] Presumably whaling ships from Hamburg and other ports on the River Elbe.

[4] The Whitby *Resolution* commanded by Scoresby in 1811 and 1812 was sold to Peterhead, but not until 1829; this was an earlier vessel of 400 tons that began whaling from Peterhead in 1813 and was one of the nineteen British ships lost in Davis Strait and Baffin Bay in 1830 (Lubbock, *Arctic Whalers*, pp. 278–9 and Appendix G).

[5] Transcript error: 'any' intended?

Thursday 12 June Lat. 78.34 Lon. 2°10′W
N. or NbW
Found ample room in the ice until 8 am. when we began to fall into crowded ice & at
noon found ourselves at the extremity of the navigation; floes in sight, wind blowing
a strong gale. The ice being all in motion had frequently to shift our ground to obtain
a convenient navigation. Towards mid-night had a hard gale of wind with snow
showers. 5 ships near us.

Friday 13 June Lat. 78°28′+ Lon. 2°0′W
NW to NNE to NWbN
The wind abating a little about noon made more sail (having plyed during the night
under close reef'd top sails) and worked into the windward ice which opened out &
[exposed?] floes – the Mars killed a small whale as we advanced. In the afternoon had
a very critical navigation among heavy drift ice & small floes in motion – pushed
thro' a narrow neck of ice into an opening by the lee of a firm considerable floe where
we looked in vain for fish. Perceiving a 'sea of water' to the Wd of us into which a
narrow channel opening about 8 pm. we entered it & steered 15 miles WSW to W. &
then began to ply into a narrow deep bay formed by floes & loose ice. ['**Saturday 14
June** Lat. 78°17′+ Lon. 2°40′W NNW to NNE. EbS to NE' *in margin*] & leading in a
NW direction into the body of the main western ice. Finding however the ice rapidly
closing & the weather being very thick with small snow we ran out steered a little to
the NEd & began to ply to windward. The John only in sight.

About 7 am the Mars joined us: the wind veered to the Ed and blew a very hard
gale accompanied with thick snow showers. Dodged under the three reef'd topsail.
Clearer weather in the afternoon made fast ['along with the Mars' *deleted*] to a small
floe. In this operation the wind blew so hard that the bit head was cut 2 inches into
the solid wood by a new 6¼ inch towline, before the ship could be brought up. The
Mars killed a size fish though we saw none. 4 ships in sight.

Sunday 15 June Lat. 78.4 Lon. 3°25′W
NEbN to N.
Blowing a hard gale of wind most of the day. We were obliged to cast loose from the
ice by the interference of other floes joined the Mars & again moored to a small floe
to which she had been some time fast.

Monday 16 June Lat. 77°54′ Long. 3°50′W
N.
The gale was renewed & continued with increased violence the whole of this day.
Much snow fell. The Aurora of Hull with 3 fish = 50 tons of oil worked up to us &
moored to the same floe. Gives account of the Neptune (Munro) with 5 to 7 fish;
Enterprize (Sanderson) 5 large fish; ['&' *deleted*] some others well fished; & a number
of ships still clean. Capt. Jackson sent me a bird, apparently of the Duck kind (Order
[Ameres?], Genus Anas) of which the following is a description. Bill straight,
depressed, ['Black duck described.' *in margin*] & serrated; 1½ inches in length & 6/8
in breadth at the base; nostrils oval or oblong. Feet with four toes, 3 of them fully

webbed. The bill & legs black; the back, tail wings, ['head' *deleted*] brownish black, the neck & head raven black; the coverts of the tail & [vent?][1] feathers white; the belly <u>brownish</u> grey. The edges or ends of the feathers of the belly & back are of a lighter shade.*[2] The wings spread 3 feet & the body measures in length 1 f^t 10 in.: and weighs 4¼ lbs. This bird was shot near us on the 12th inst*ant* whilst it with several others of the species were resting on ['the ice' *deleted*] a piece of ice. They appeared much fatigued so that when disturbed by being fired at they alighted at a short distance & allowed the boat to approach again within shot.

Capt. Souter of the Resolution last week gave us some ['Further particulars respecting the loss of the Dauntless, &c. & the damage caused by the storm of the 5th of May: Vide May 4, 7, 9, 10 18 & 27.' *in margin*] further particulars relative to the loss of the four ships in the storm of the ... of last month. 10 sail were plying within a sea stream on the Sunday preceding (4th May) a swell arose & a fresh gale of wind from the SE succeeded. Two ships which first made the attempt escaped; the other [*sic*] on trying later were unable to penetrate the seastream which had then collapsed. After an ineffectual trial & reaching sometime [*illegible deletion*] too & froe, finding the sea & wind increase & their situation every moment more hazardous they began to attempt to seek shelter in the main ice which however from the delay to their misfortune had closed to a solid mass. The Alert[3] steered by the wind towards the NE fell happily into shelter of a projecting point of ice & fixed in safety – the others less happy (some of them indeed were unable to follow the course of the Alert which was to windw*ard* of them) alternately took to the main ice but were unable to penetrate it in the least so close ['[had?]' *deleted*] was it already forced by the swell. One was wrecked in a few minutes & two others speedily shared the same fate, the last of the four survived for some time. The Enterprize Norfolk & Superior[4] were preserved by fothering them with snow shovelled off the pieces of ice against which they lay. On effecting their release about 8 or "10"[5] days afterwards a piece of ice was found beneath the bilge of the Norfolk but the ship on examination being found "unstove" it was got out & beneath the Enterprize a piece of vast size was lodged beneath her keel with which 3 ships made several trials, two with their sterns to the Enterprize's stern with hawsers fast to the piece of ice & the third fastened to the bow of the Enterprize all making sail together to draw it away, before they succeeded. This mass of ice must have weighed "80 or 100 tons" or upwards. The Superior was stove & leaked considerably, as well as the Enterprize & Norfolk in some measure. In the same gale, (whilst we carried top gall*ant* sails & sent boats in pursuit of a whale though at sea) the Walker had a boat washed away, the Aurora's boats were all

---

[1] Possibly 'vest'.

[2] Note in margin: "*It has two lengthened white spots on its neck, one on either side a small whitish spot under the eye. The other animals of the same flock appeared much larger than the one described. It seems to be the 'Anas Bernicla' or Brent Goose.' From the description, it appears to have been a subspecies of the Brent or Brant Goose, *Branta bernicla hrota*: the 'light-bellied Brent Goose', also known as the 'Atlantic Brant'.

[3] Lubbock, *Arctic Whalers*, mentions the *Alert* of Peterhead, but not before 1823.

[4] 'Norfolk' inserted above the line, where it was preceded by a deletion, possibly 'North Briton'.

[5] Possibly '16'.

[scuttled?] & one nearly torn to pieces, &c. so tremendous was the storm. The wreck of the Dauntless was seen in lat. 73½° in the month of May.

Tuesday 17 June Lat. 77°20′ Lon. 2°0′W
N to ENE
The gale continued until the morning & then subsided into a strong breeze. The ice encompassed us in such a way before I was informed of it that we had all hands to [rouse?] & the utmost exertion to use in warping the ship to windward to prevent her from getting beset. We were free by 8 am. Made sail & steered to the eastward, finding a roomy situation towards the NE we worked up by the edge of the floes. ['At' *deleted*] In the evening we were at the extremity of the opening: the situation of the ice appeared uncommonly favourable for the fishing but not ['At mid-nᵗ Lat observed 77°17′+' *in margin*] a single whale was to be seen. About 11 Pm. we ['undertook' *deleted*] ventured on a very intricate & difficult navigation leading in a southerly direction towards slack ice to the eastward.

Wednesday 18 June Lat. 77. 27′+ Lon. 2. 51+W[1]
NE to NbW
At 1 Am. we were in navigable ice where we saw a fish; which having escaped us we worked to the NEᵈ or Eᵈ until the afternoon. The wind then veered to the NbW. An extensive sheet of water appearing in that direction we plyed up it the rest of the day. The Mars & John in Cº 3 other ships in sight. Variation of the Compass ....
At mid-night wind a gentle breeze: fine clear weather.

Thursday 19 June Lat. 77. 36+ Lon. 1°55′W
NW.rly to NE.rly
Light airs or calm: charming clear, warm weather. Seeing some ships running out of the ice into which we were plying we steered to the Eᵈ with the view of gaining the sea & attempting the ice further towards the north. In the evening met an interruption from a heavy compact body of ice lying NW & SE through which in passing a slackish part we experienced great inconvenience & difficulty, having to tow 4 hours ['A strong SSE swell' *in margin*] with four boats. Passed it about mid-night Mars & John in Cº.

Friday 20 June Lat. 77. 41+ Lon. 0°20′E
NEbE
From hence we experienced little inconvenience from the ice, but reached the sea about 6 Am. the wind then springing up a fine breeze we steered to the ESEᵈ until 2 Pm. & then tacked. In returning we saw a razorback to which we gave chase mistaking it for a whale. ['[sea deep olive green]' *in margin*] The sky was cloudless until noon. A heavy bank of cloud then arose in the SE & soon enveloped the whole atmosphere.

---

[1] '6 pm' added beneath the longitude.

In the evening as we approached the ice saw a whale which was ['Velocity, stay down, & blowing of a whale' *in margin*] pursued some distance towards the SW. Its velocity was 5–5½ miles per hour: it blew 8 times during 2 minutes which it stopped at the surface & then dived during 19 or 18 minutes: it was considered to stop long down!

Saturday 21 June Lat. 77.58 Lon. 0°20'W
NEbE to NNE
Fresh to strong gales of wind with frequent showers of prismatic snow in flakes. Plying all day to windward under a press of sail. About 8 pm. passed through with difficulty an extensive stream of ice lying many miles NE & SW. We ['[Sea Green]' *in margin*] then entered the sea again to the NW^d of it & met another similar ['A strong S.rly swell' *in margin*] but impervious stream 4 or 6 miles to the NW. Plyed to windward between the two streams. John in C^o.

Sunday 22^d June Lat. 78. 20 Lon. 2°0'W
NEbN. to N.
Blowing a strong gale of wind, with snow showers. Beat to windward during the greater part of the day. At noon passed with some difficulty, by the help of all hands, the western stream of ice & found an open sea beyond it. In the evening we were in lat. about 78.30 near the edge of a floe, but not a fish to be seen. Steered to the eastward 10–15 miles & found a body of ice which had ['**Monday 23 June** Lat 77°30' Lon. 3°W NNW or N' *in margin*] drifted from the land & joined the main western ice. Steered SW and SSE and gained the open sea about 6 am. From hence, the wind becoming more moderate & weather clear, we made sail to the SW or WSW along the edge of the ice. In the afternoon spoke the Walker of Hull with 2 fish: the Capt.[1] gave us intelligence of several ships having made a good fishing in the open sea in a Southern latitude during the preceding weeks. Mars & John in Co. Continued our course to the SW^d.[2]

Tuesday 24 June Lat. 76.30+ Lon. 4°30'W
N. NW.rly Var.
Fine clear weather: wind a light breeze. Hauled up by the wind to the W^d reached to the edge of the pack, saw no fish, ran to the SE^d & in the evening had the pleasure of chasing a whale, tho' the chase ended in disappointment. At night nearly calm. 17 ships in sight.

Wednesday 25 June Lat. 76.17+ Lon. 3°50'W
WSW to SW
A fresh breeze of wind sprang up in the morning & soon increased to a fresh gale, attended with hazy or showery W*eathe*r. Joined the Phoenix with 5 fish: the master gives account of some ships having made a successful fishery in a high northern lat.

---

[1] Richard Walker, according to Credland, *Hull Whaling Trade*, Appendix 3.
[2] Possibly 'NW^d'.

from whence on the disappearance of the whales, he has but just ['Situation of the land ice' *in margin*] returned. The land pack Capt. Dawson says stretched from Point Look Out NNW.rly to the lat. 78½ where it joins to the main western body. It is impervious to the southw*ar*d of 78°.

Lay too part of the day: saw several seals but no whales.

Thursday 26 June Lat. 76.26 Lon. 5°20'W
SW to SSW
Blowing a strong gale with hazy or thick foggy weather. About 5 am. entered the ice for shelter. Steered a NW.rly course a distance of 20–30 miles & after much difficult sailing & making several tacks, guided by the blink we gained the edge of a field. The John, Mars, [Rookewood?],[1] & Alert in the same situation. Loose ice joins the field on the SE, S, W, & NW leaving only E, NE, & N. parts clear. To the northern part of the field we moored at 6 Pm, and spent ['the night' *deleted*] comfortably a very boisterous and gloomy night – the fog being intensely thick.

Friday 27 June Lat. 76.26 Lon. 5.40W
SSW
The weather continued without amendment; wind a hard gale & fog so thick that we could rarely see 100 yards. The revolving of the field brought us in contact with a quantity of heavy ice & obliged us to unmoored [*sic*]. Beat along the eastern edge to a point of ice containing a deep bay adjoining where we again moored. Saw a razorback, a white whale, some narwhales, an arctic gull, &c. 2 or 3 whales were also seen by the ships around us but we saw none.

Saturday 28 June Lat. 76°30'+ Lon.5.45.37+[2]
SW to NW. WSW. SSE. var.
After mid night the wind moderated & the atmosphere cleared. Cast off at 6 am. steered along the edge of the field several miles (about 10) to the SW in which course we saw a fish: attempted to beat through an opening formed by floes & [***] in a W.rly direction but the ice closing in we were prevented. Returned back along the edge of the field & made fast to a point of the ice.

The weather being fine & nearly calm I thought it a favourable ['Preparation for an experiment on the pressure of the sea, temp. & spec. grav. at a great depth' *in margin*] opportunity for completing my experiments on the pressure, temp. & spec. gravity of the sea at great depths. I had previously prepared 20 articles for submersion, consisting of fir wood of various sizes & shapes, hickory, lignum vitæ, ash, elm, beech, oak & cork: bone, jet, and various metals. A counterpart of each of the specimens of wood I had likewise prepared from the same piece, similar in shape, size, & exactly of the same weight. These counterparts I proposed to immerse in a bucket of sea water during the time the other pieces were underwater, & hence the difference of weight of

[1] Lubbock, *Arctic Whalers*, mentions the *Rookwood* of London, but not before 1825.
[2] Below these coordinates is a marginal note: '[Long. by means of 2 sets of Obs*ervati*ons by Chron. PM. corrected 4°48'W.]'.

the two sets of pieces would show the degree of impregnation produced by pressure. All things being in readiness about [3?][1] Pm. the marine diver containing a six's thermometer[2] (a present from Sir J. Banks) & a wire gauze frame stretched beneath the upper valve for catching any little animals which might happen to pass ['through' *deleted*] into it in its descent: & connected with the line near the diver were the specimens of wood &c. together with two tin vessels for ['Apparatus sent down 1200 fathoms or 7200 feet!' *in margin*] ascertaining the depth – were sunk to the depth of upwards of 1200 fathoms (or ['upwards' *deleted*] more than 1¼ miles). The field drifting towards the north the line passed obliquely underwater & trended strongly towards the south (per compass). For the purpose therefore of allowing it to descend perpendicular the end of the line was fastened to a boat & the boat ['taken' *deleted*] removed towards the south until the line became perpendicular. The boat still moved through the water towards the south: so that though we immediately cast the ship off & began to beat to windward we could not fetch it in the space of 1½ hours. A whale line being now taken to the boat it was drawn to the ship; the sails reduced & the line begun to be ['drawn' *deleted*] hauled in. The instrument weighed [***] 20 lb. ['but' *deleted*] yet the strain was about a hundred weight or upward. About 120 fathoms was taken on board when lo! to my great grief & mortification the line broke within a yard of one of the men's hands, but so ['The line breaks & the apparatus is all lost !!' *in margin*] sudden was its retration[3] that it flew through the blocks & disappeared in a moment! Thus was defeated & baulked expectations the most sanguine of some highly interesting result & thus was sacrificed my original apparatus value (with 1100 fathoms of line) upwards of £20. The marine diver was of brass well finished & illuminated with plate glass & was the only instrument of the kind in "existence" that I know ['History of the marine diver' *in margin*] of. The original of it was ['invented by' *deleted*] made by Mr Cary under the direction of Messrs <u>Cavendish</u> & ..... both of whom, died before it was completed, & presented to me by Sir Jos. Banks together with a Six's thermometer. This instrument however being of deal swelled so with the pressure of the water by impregnation that it became leaky & the illuminators were broken on the first trial. I therefore made a model & got a cast ['of' *deleted*] in brass, on a similar plan. It was finished by an excellent workman & the valves of the original instrument applyed to it. It was a handsome instrument & answered every intention in the most exquisite manner. The two valves opening upwards permitted the water to flow freely through it whilst it was descending & the moment it stopped closed & brought the water up, received at its lowest descent. My mortification was excessive. Though the value of the [*illegible deletion*] apparatus was considerable I felt more for the failure of an experiment which I had never heard performed or suggested by any other. It was not idle curiosity by which I was influenced but a desire to further the ['Objects of the Experiment' *in margin*] objects of science. In this experiment I had expected to ascertain the temp, specific gravity, &

---

[1] Possibly '9'.

[2] Named for its British inventor, James Six, FRS (1731–93). Invented in 1782, it is still the device normally used to record both maximum and minimum temperatures over a period of time.

[3] *Sic*: 'retraction' intended?

constituents of the sea at the depth of 1200 fa*thom*s to add perhaps some little animal or other to our collections of nat. hist. & above all the prove [*sic*] the degree of impregnation by sea water which would take place in wood of various forms, sizes & descriptions. Thus having sent down fir in a cube, oblong, prismoid, & wedge shape, dif*feren*t in bulk as well as in shape I should have ascertained whether the pressure of the sea would impregnate each form & size in the same degree & if so I anticipated I should be able to give some facts for the adoption of a new method of ascertaining great depths simply by the specific gravity of wood sent down. That this would probably answer I conceived from observing a higher spec. gra*vity* was procured by greater immersion in three former experiments & I had no reason to doubt but the rule might hold most generally; neither could I be ['assured' *deleted*] certain but metals might be likewise increased in weight by being subjected to such enormous pressure.

['Pressure of the sea enormous' *in margin*] A column of sea water $33\frac{3}{4}$ feet in height presses with a force of near 15 lb (about 14.7) on every square inch of surface, consequently with a pressure equal to that of the atmosphere. Now the perpendicular depth of the apparatus was 1200 fa*thom*s or 7200 feet. Hence 7200 ÷ by $33\frac{3}{4}$ = $213\frac{1}{3}$ atmospheres. ['Pressure of the sea at the depth of 7200 feet = $1\frac{1}{3}$ tons per square inch!!' *in margin*] But a column of sea water 1 foot in height & 1 inch square weighs 0.444¹ lb avoirdupois: hence 7200 feet of depth x by 0.444 gives 3088.88 lb² pressure on every square inch or 1$^\text{ton}$ 7$^\text{cwt}$ 65$^\text{lb}$. If to this we add the usual atmospheric pressure of 15 lb the amount of pressure per inch will be 1 ton 7 cwt 80 lb. The fir & oak cubes were 2 inches each way, consequently contained 24 square inches of surface. Then 1 ton 7 cwt 80 lb x by 24 = 33 tons 5 cwt. 16 lb pressure upon a cube of 2 inches each side. The effect of which can scarcely be conjectured.

The occasion of the loss of the apparatus proved to be a ['Colour of sea trans*paren*t Blue' *in margin*] <u>bad place</u> in the thickest line which was out. Some of the lines which looked suspicious were tried by the strength of 2 or 3 men before they were applied but the one which broke appeared calculated to sustain at least treble the weight which was upon ['the line' *deleted*] it at the moment when it broke. The rotten part of the line (produced by some accidental wet when reeled up) was not above 2 or 3 inches in extent.³

The field of ice by which we lay & indeed much of the ['Ice dirty: fields & other large ice: hence it may have been formed near land.' *in margin*] ice in the neighbourhood abounds with dirty or earthy places proving it to have been adjoining to some land at some recent period. At mid-night made sail & plyed to the SSE$^\text{d}$ in company with the John. The Neptune of Aberdeen near us, clean. Shot a bear but it escaped.

---

¹ The last digit, here and twice in the following line, has a backslash, presumably to indicate the recurring decimal.

² Scoresby's arithmetic is inaccurate.

³ Understandably, Scoresby devoted only a paragraph to this failed experiment in *Account of the Arctic Regions*, I, p. 188, with none of the details included in this journal entry.

Sunday 29 June Lat. 76.24+ Lon. 6°0W
Var. W.rly SW.rly.
Light var. winds or calm with occasional snow showers. Stretched & plyed about 15 miles towards the SW in the course of the day among open drift ice & floes. Towed most of the day with one boat.

Monday 30 June Lat. 76. 4+ Long. 7°20W
SW.rly SSW S
Clear weather in the morning saw a fish which escaped us. After doubling a point of ice we stretched 8 or 10 hours (by the wind) to the WSW, during a continuance of thick fog. Mars & John in C°.

Tuesday 1 July Lat. 75°55′ Lon. 7°20′W.
SW.rly to S.
Wind a moderate or fresh breeze with almost uninterrupted thick fog. Lay too about 2 pm. having entered a more convenient situation for spending the night in, than the very crowded drift ice thro' which we had passed. During half an hour of rather clearer weather some fish were seen. One of them had a narrow escape from the John's boats & another was struck killed by the Mar's boats in the space of probably 20 or 30 minutes which proved a most admirable prize of 25 tons of oil, &c. In the course of the day stretched 20 miles to the NW saw but one fish & falling into transparent blue water, returned 12 miles & then lay too. Fog intensely thick.

Wednesday 2ᵈ July Lat.75.30 Lon. 9.10W
SW to W. SW
Impenetrable fog all day: wind a fresh breeze. Being among much heavy drift ice; moored to the largest piece we could find and took a quantity of water from its surface[.] Heard the blowing of a fish. The John in C°.

Thursday 3ᵈ July Lon: 8°20′[1]
SW
The fog continued without a moments attenuation. Lay moored all day. Saw several narwhales.

Friday 4 July Lat. 75.40 Lon. 8.20
SSW to W. SWbW
Light wind; fog a little less dense at intervals, but never clear. 'Made a loose fall' after a fish in the forenoon, but without success. Killed a narwhale with a 5 feet horn (externally).[2] It was a male. Its stomach was filled with the remains of cuttle fish,

---

[1] In this extremely brief daily entry there is no indication of latitude, and the usual 'W' longitude indication is also missing.

[2] The 'dimensions and particulars' of this narwhal were listed by Scoresby in *Account of the Arctic Regions*, I, p. 495. The four tusks exhibited in the Cook & Scoresby wing of the Whitby Museum are all longer than the '60½ inches' noted there; the shortest is approximately 62 inches.

innumerable <u>eyes</u> and beaks like those of a small bird. It likewise contained some arcarides or worms. Cast off from the ice in the afternoon, plyed a few miles to windward & saw 3 or 4 fish. [A second?] time we summoned all hands & sent 6 boats in pursuit, but altho'. they approached [amazingly?] near[,] this expedition like all our former (2 excepted) terminated without success. The Venerable (with 4 fish, all of which have been taken hereabout since the 22ᵈ ult.) struck a fish but lost it. The Mars again with more success ['**Saturday 5 July** Lat. 75.50 Lon. 8°0'W. SSW to W' *in margin*] struck another large fish & presently captured it! This makes 4 fish about 55 tons of oil which the Mars has procured close by us without our being able to obtain any! In the course of the night though the weather kept constantly foggy, sometimes however so clear that we could see a mile, we plyed some distance to the SWᵈ amongst heavy ice & small floes. Saw one fish about 11 am. Lay too & dodged the rest of the day.

Sunday 6 July Lat. 75.48 Lon. 8.10
W.rly: NErly E.rly: var.
Drifted to the SWᵈ or Sᵈ most of the night during a fog most obscure below but above us apparently scarcely 100 feet high quite clear through which the sun shone with brilliancy. We saw a fine fog bow.

Heard a fish <u>blowing</u> but could not find it. In the morning on a small attenuation of the fog, being nearly calm, we found ourselves surrounded by ice of almost massy[1] description & so nearly embayed that we were obliged to tow with a boat all the day when we had a very light air of variable wind. Most of the pieces of ice about us sustained hummocks 10 to 30 fᵗ in height and abounded in black dirty patches both above & on their sides, indicative of their having been resting against some land or perhaps having their formation there. In the evening we gained a more roomy situation & were joined by the John.

Monday 7 July Lat 75°53' Lon. 8°20'E[2]
S.rly: SW to W.
Wind a light or moderate breeze, mostly thick fog. Finding a body of ice lying to the Sᵈ & Eᵈ of us through which there scarcely seemed to be any passage we persevered towards the west, searching for fish but found none. The Venerable joined us in the afternoon. At 10 am the fog being intensely thick made fast to a piece of ice.

Tuesday 8 July Lat. 75°50' Lon. 9 20W
WSW. W. SW: Var.
A Gentle breeze of wind all day. Whilst we lay moored to the ice we pumped water on board & filled 15 or 16 casks for trimming the ship & better ballasting her. The Mars joined us at 4 am. The weather being then a little more clear we cast off & steered to the NW or NNW among ['[open?]' *deleted*] drift ice, more open as we proceeded for a distance of 15 or 16 miles – the fog then had recommenced & meeting much ice tacked. Beat to windward during the rest of the day. Fog very thick. Perceived a piece

---

[1] Probably a transcription error for 'a most massy'.
[2] *Sic*: evidently an error; should be 'W'.

of ice in motion as with a swell. At midnight moored to a small floe; the John &
Venerable followed our example.

Wednesday 9 July Lat 75°10′ Lon. 10°W
WSW, SW
About 10 am. there were intervals in the fog in which we could see for 2 miles. Cast
off & plyed a little distance to windward, when meeting much ice, the fog recom-
mencing, & finding our latitude more southerly than we expected, lay too. Saw the
Mars 2 or 3 miles to the NE of us, we lost her in the fog.

Our drift towards the south with Serly & SW.rly winds is surprising. During
several days past we have done little better than lay too & yet we appear to have
advanced 20 or 30′ southerly. This proves the prevalence of a strong S.rly current
which I imagine cannot ['Strong SW.rly current proved' *in margin*] run less than 12 or
18′ S. per day though against a wind which has now prevailed incessantly for ....
days. In 4 days included between the 13 & 17 June we drifted along with heavy floes
60 miles or 15′ per day, wind at SW to ENE & the last day of the 4 we appear to have
drifted above 25′. Here when we could expect the ice to drive at ['Sea transparent
Green' *in margin*] least 10′ per day towards the north it evidently advances against
the wind nearly that distance per day towards the S or SW.[1]

Thursday 10 July Lat. 75°18′ Lon. 8°W
SW to W.
We lay too all night during a thick fog & fresh breeze of wind. At 10 am. made sail &
ran towards the E, ENE, ESE, SE, N, NW, NE & S. in all which courses we had occasion to proceed to avoid the numerous floes, & patches of heavy ice which opposed
our navigation towards the E^d. We found more room after 2 Pm. & continued our
stretch to the S. during 4 hours. The water (sea) then became of a ['clear' *deleted*]
transparent blue, such as we have not seen whales in during the whole season. Steered
8 miles NE & then moored to a large floe; the John & Venerable in C°. The weather
was hazy during 5 or 6 hours of the day when we could see around occasionally 2 or
3 miles: this was the clearest interval we have experienced of 10 days.

Friday 11 July Lat. by artificial horizon 75°12′+[2]
Killed a bear. It measured in length of body & head 6..8′; circumference round the middle
of the body 5..8, of the neck 2..9; breadth across the belly between the hind legs 1..6, ditto
forelegs 1..4; ['Dimensions of a bear' *in margin*] stands 3..6 high on the forelegs & 3..7
or 3..8 behind; length of the foreleg 2..8, circumf. at the shoulder 2..2 & near the paw
1..5; length of hind leg 2..6 (about), circum. at shoulder 2..8 & near the paw 1..7. In its

---

[1] It seems evident that the *Esk*, at Scoresby's estimated longitude of 10°W, had entered the
East Greenland Current (EGC). 'As the only major southward flowing current in the Greenland Sea,
the EGC transports recirculating Atlantic Water, Arctic Ocean water masses, and >90% of the ice
exported from the Arctic Ocean ... [I]n the upper 500 m of the EGC at 79°N, the one-year mean speeds
of the current were as high as 9.5 cms°-1' (Gyory, Mariano & Ryan, 'The East Greenland Current'). 9.5
metres per second is equivalent to 21.2 mph or over 18 knots, consistent with Scoresby's account.

[2] No wind directions are indicated in the margin, and there is no longitude estimate.

stomach was nothing, but in the intestines 2 claws of seals were found. A stake [*sic*] cut from the ham on being cooked could not be distinguished from beef.[1]

Thick fog & fresh breeze of wind prevailed during the night; we had occasional intervals in which we could see objects at the distance of a mile. Found the latitude by artificial horizon 75..12..16 & by a quadrant used in a boat scarcely 3 feet above the surface of the water[2] ['Utility of a low elevation for finding the latitude in foggy weather or in the immediate vicinity of land' *in margin*] 75..12 but used on deck 75..3. Hence we have a mode of finding the latitude whenever the sun is seen through a fog or even in the neighbourhood of land provided the surface of the sea can be seen at the distance of ['a' *deleted*] 1½ or 2 mile, which at the elevation of 3 feet will be nearly the true or visible horizon: whilst on the deck of a ship at the height of 15 feet the horizon is at the distance of 4½ miles. At all events the error of observation will be much diminished by making the observation in about as near as possible to the surface of the sea. Besides should the fog or land form an app*aren*t horizon at the distance of a mile instead of 2 which is the distance it is visible in clear w*eathe*r at the height of 3 feet the error of observation will only be ½ a minute to a minute of alt: but on the deck say at 15 f^t elevation the error of observation were the hor*izo*n one mile distant would amount to 5.3 minutes; also suppose the visible hor*izo*n at the distance of ½ a mile, the error at 3 feet would be only 3' but at 15 = 13' thus rapidly increasing as the distance of visible hor*izo*n decreases. Hence by observing at a low elevation (near the surface of the water when the weather will permit) and applying the dip of the sea at the estimated distance of the visible horizon from the observer, as found in the tables ['Degree of accuracy to be expected from observations made in a fog at diff*eren*t degrees of elevation' *in margin*] the lat. may generally be found whenever the sun is visible even in the thickest fog to within 3 or 4 ['miles' *deleted*] or at most half a dozen or 8 miles whilst in the usual situation at 15 feet elevation an error of a degree or more may easily be committed. For instance if we suppose the hor*izo*n to be distant 2/10 of a mile & it should happen to be only 1/10, which on account of the great decption [*sic*] of distance in a fog would probably be the case in general, it would make an error of only about 8¼' at the height of 3 feet, but of 43' at the height of 15 feet!'

This suggestion might be of great service occasionally when the sea is smooth & ships are expecting to make land in foggy weather, & the sun happens to shine through the fog which is frequently the case.[3]

---

[1] 'I once treated my surgeon with a dinner of bear's-ham, who knew not, for above a month after-wards, but that it was beef-steak' (*Account of the Arctic Regions*, I, p. 520). It seems surprising that, when including all this data in his journal, Scoresby did not indicate the sex of the bear.

[2] Scoresby was presumably unwilling to risk losing his sextant if the boat capsized, so used a quadrant instead.

[3] This paragraph suggests that either Scoresby was the first navigator to use this technique of taking an artificial horizon close to the sea surface in fog, or that it was a relatively unknown method at the time. He described the method again, saying it was 'a very simple contrivance, which I adopted some years ago' in *Account of the Arctic Regions*, I, pp. 442–5. Much later in the century it was similarly explained and recommended in Lecky's popular manual of navigation:

Every seaman knows that by going aloft in clear weather his range of view is extended … In like manner, by descending towards the surface of the water his range of view is lessened, and the horizon approaches him. Advantage of this can be taken to get observations in foggy weather. By sitting

After we had found our latitude which again proved farther south than we expected, we cast off & steered to the N, or NE followed by the John & Venerable, in search of fish or [dark?] coloured water in which we had alone seen fish. For some time we found the ice open & navigable, but about 6 Pm. we ran ourselves into a bight among heavy floes & drift-ice out of which we were glad to make our escape by making a tack to windward. Steering SE.rly we found a body of floes extending 10 or 16 miles on our larboard hand – at length we doubled a point where the sea being a little greener than usual, we steered under the ['Fog-bow seen' *in margin*] lee of a floe and moored. Several narwhales were seen sporting about the edge of it but no whales. Observed a complete circular ['Rain cleared the sky of fog' *in margin*] fog bow from the mast head with a halo in the center [*sic*]. A strong shower of rain fell in the night after which we saw 3 or 4 miles.

Saturday 12 July Lat. 75.20 Lon. 5°W.
WSW to W.
When the rain had cleared the density of the fog we found ourselves on the windward side of a body of floes in close aggregation & our situation consequently critical should any loose or lighter ice drift from the south, which might readily beset us. We therefore immediately unmoored and steered 40 miles to the SSE. We then found ourselves in open drift ice with some floes. The wind freshening about noon we ran under the lee of a small floe & made fast as also did the John & Venerable. At the floes in the morning we got two bears a ['she' *deleted*] female with two cubs one of which was taken alive by the John's people. The other which was nearly as large as the mother was taken alive by our men but being wounded with a lance it died in the course of the day. It exhibited many marks of affection for its parent which lay slain before it.

I took the opportunity of leisure time when the ship was moored to ascertain ['Specific gravity of diff*eren*t kinds of ice' *in margin*] the specific gravity of diff*eren*t specimens of ice. For this purpose I took a piece of lead which weighed in fresh water $2^{oz.} 6.6^{dr}$ & in salt water $2^{oz} 6.5^{dr}$ avoirdupois & fastening it to various limbs of ice examined their weight in salt & fresh water temp. 34° to 36°. The following results were obtained. viz.[1]

---

in the bottom of a small boat, or on the lowest step of the accommodation ladder, the eye will be about two feet above the sea level, at which height the horizon is little more than a mile and a quarter distant, so that unless the fog is very dense, serviceable observations are quite possible.

The writer, on three different occasions, when at anchor off the River Plate, during fog, has been enabled to ascertain the ship's position in the way described, and after verifying it by the lead, has proceeded up to Monte Video without seeing land' (Lecky, *Wrinkles*, pp. 59–60).

[1] Some of the 'ounce' and 'dram' superscripts in the transcript have been omitted in these tables as unnecessary; their inclusion in the transcript was also inconsistent. These results were summarized in Appendix VIII, 'Experiments for Determining the Specific Gravity of Ice', in *Account of the Arctic Regions*, vol. I. In that appendix, Scoresby gave the results from two sets of data, but gave no date for either. It is clear from the journals in the present volume that the measurements on which he placed greater reliance were made on 15 May 1818; 'These experiments', he wrote in the appendix, 'with similar kinds of ice, and under similar circumstances, were repeated on another voyage, in which the coincidence of the results are remarkable.' He then went on to cite some of the results from this other voyage; they are those indicated in this 1817 journal, showing that these results did not *repeat* but *preceded* those in 1818.

Nᵒ		Weight in air	Weight in fresh water when attached to the piece of lead	Ditto in <u>salt</u> water	Wᵗ of an equal bulk of water	Spec grav^y
1	Thin opaque ice apparently salt water & porous	5ᵒᶻ 10.4ᵈʳ	1ᵒᶻ 14.9ᵈʳ	[1. 14.9 – 2. 6.6 + 5. 10.4]	6ᵒᶻ 2.1ᵈʳ	0.9215
2	Solid fresh water ice without any bubbles	8. 10.3	1. 10.0	[2. 6.6 – 1. 10 + 8. 10.3]	9. 6.9	0.9165
3	Salt water ice from a <u>tongue</u>; semi-transpᵗ	7. 14.6	1. 11.6	[2. 6.6 – 1. 11.6 + 7. 14.6]	8. 9.6	0.9200

Compared with salt water

		Wᵗ in salt water with lead attatch*ed*	Weight in air			The Spec. gravity compared to salt water 35°, as 1.0000.
Same as No. 2	Solid fresh water ice¹	1. 9.0	7. 2.1	[2. 6.5 – 1. 9.0 = 13. 5 + 7. 2.1 =]		0.8942
Same as No. 3	Porous ice from a tongue of saltwater ice	1. 9.6	6. 13.2	2. 6.5 – 1. 9.6 = 12. 9 + 6. 13.2 =	7. 10.1	0.8943

This mode of finding specific gravities of a <u>wasting</u> substance such as ice seems only capable of an accuracy to the 2ᵈ or at most the 3ᵈ place of decimals. Solid fresh water ice perfectly diaphanous may I think be considered of the spec. gravity of 0.92.

In the night we had thick fog as usual.

Sunday 13 July Lat. observed in a boat at water's edge = 75. 16 Lon. 5°10′W WbN

At noon, the wind blowing fresh & fog occasionally a little attenuated cast off steered to the Eᵈ some hours but falling in with much ice & the fog again becoming dense hauled up south & lay too all night drifting towards the ['South or' *deleted*] SE.²

¹ This replaces 'in salt water at temp 34°' deleted.
² Although this daily entry is very brief, Scoresby later wrote in his autobiography that the day was of great importance in shaping his religious life. 'On my passage home, the most complete surrender of heart to God, and the most perfect abandonment of reserved sin that I had ever made occurred. It was on Sunday, the 13ᵗʰ of July, and was the effect, I believe, of reading to the sailors, with more than ordinary attention, from the text, – 'And Elijah came unto all the people and said, *How long halt ye between two opinions? If the* LORD *be God, follow him; but if Baal, then follow him*' (1 Kings xviii. 21).' Quoted, with additional text from the autobiography, in Scoresby-Jackson, *Life*, p. 112; emphasis in original. The statement that on this date Scoresby was 'On my passage home' is clearly incorrect. See Introduction, p. xxiv.

Monday 14 July Lat 74°59′+ Lon. 3°40′W
WNW NWbW
Made sail at 9 am. & steered to the E^d & NE all the day. At night found ourselves at sea. About 10 pm. the fog cleared and the first time of 16 days the atmosphere was clear. Spoke the Spencer of Montrose clean & Valiant with 10 fish.

Tuesday 15 July Lat. 75. 58 Lon. 0.
NNW to NE^d
Stretched 9 hours to the eastward in the open water, tacked at noon & in the evening approached some scattered streams of ice, which with the sea around ['were' *deleted*] swarmed with seals. Sent two boats to hunt them but they fled to the water so precipitately that we got only 5. The John & Venerable in C°. Towards mid-night thick fog & weather calm.

Wednesday 16 July Lat 76.20+ Lon. 1°33′+W
NNW to NE.
A breeze springing up about 4 am. we stretched to the North until 10 am. the fog then began to clear away & we saw a body of ice close ['to the' *deleted*] ahead of us extending from the NW to the South. A large floe lying at the outer edge we lay too on its weather side about 2 hours but saw no fish neither signs of any. The sea was very blue & perfectly transparent. Feeling hopeless of succeeding in the ice & seeing no prospect of finding fish in this advanced state of the season in these latitudes, I determined (Deo volente) to make a stretch to the eastward of Point Look Out provided the situation of the ice & state of the winds & weather should admit, and explore a track of the ocean which has not been visited of many ['Motives for visiting new region with the hopes of finding whales' *in margin*] years & in which we read in the Dutch authorities of much profitable fishing for whales & walruses being obtained. At 1Pm. made sail, stretched to the south until we doubled the point of ice, which was not until ['Long. by Obs*ervati*on of Chron. 6 pm 1°33′30″' *in margin*] 7½ Pm. and then shaped our course SEbE for the intended destination. The John & Venerable accompanied us. Saw 2 ['Var*iati*on of compass ship's head South mean of [many?] observation = 28° W.' *in margin*] ships, one of them the Manchester,[1] Adair, still a <u>clean</u> ship bore up & followed us, as did the other also (the British Queen) ['**Thursday 17 July** Lat 75.56 Lon 2°49′E WSW, NW. NE.rly' *in margin*] during the night but in the forenoon she hauled by the wind & parted C°.

A thick fog prevailed during 3 or 4 hours in the forenoon: it cleared away at noon. In the evening was fine clear weather but rather calm. Two strange sail in sight. I paid a visit to Cap*tai*n Adair who is ill & has been for some time indisposed.

Friday 18 July Lat 75°45′ Lon. 5°30′E
E.rly: NW. to NNE
The fishery of the present season has been the most singular, partial, unsuccessful of any occasion witnessed of many years. Where it has been profitable it has been

---

[1] The 'Old' *Manchester*, or *Manchester I*, of Hull, captained by James Adair from 1812 to 1817.

partial [in the?] extreme & singularly accidental. The places of ['Cause of the failure of the present year's fishing: remarks on.' *in margin*] resort & habits of the fish have differed so much from what is usual that it is allowed that success in the fishery has been the result of <u>chance</u> only; because throughout the season 'inference & deduction the most sagacious in appearance' have had no 'tendency but to mislead the navigator' from the very objects of his search; hence we can account for the fact how the experienced & judicious fishers have in general failed whilst almost every master of his <u>first year</u> has succeeded. This remark is not splenetic or for excusing our failure, for it is fully satisfied by the circumstance of there being yet known to be .... clean ships and as far as we know at least ¼ of the fishing ships which have not cargos sufficient to [answer?] their expences supposing the price of oil to be above the average.

The ostensible reason of the scarcity of whales & their pecular [*sic*] habits, is the singular state of the ice which lies at a distance from the land greater than was ever known by any fisherman now prosecuting the business. I calculate that at this time & indeed throughout the season, there has been .... square leagues[1] of water bare of ice which is generally totally covered with it. Hence the whales not finding their usual shelter are dispersed & prompted to the pursuit of dif*fere*nt routes & the adoption of original retreats. So thin is the ice dispersed through the country, that it is creditably asserted that a brig from the Elbe has penetrated without hindrance to the West land and coasted along the shore to a vast distance & returned again to the eastward without difficulty, but without finding any whales!

The weather was calm in the morning, a gentle breeze prevailed during the day with which we advanced some distance towards the east. A strange sail making towards us in the NW quarter.

Saturday 19 July Lat. 76°20′ Lon. 9°30′E
NWrly, W to SW, W.
Made considerable progress towards the EbS, having a brisk W. wind, which though fair was not such a wind as we could have wished on account of it not permitting us to return in case of meeting with ice. The weather however continuing favourable (free from fog) we pushed boldly on. At 4 Pm. saw land extending from NE to E distant 40 to 50 miles: our longitude by chron*ome*ter at this time (reckoned from an observation 22 hours previous) was .... E and the long. by the situation of the land 12½°E. Hence the chron*ome*ter seems to have performed well. At 5 saw ice extending to the SE – hauled up SE, SSE. S, & at 7 pm. close hauled by the wind, the ice in the form of an open pack extending from SWbW or WSW to S, E, & N or even by ['Saw a number of Razor Backs' *in margin*] the blink to NW. This interruption was mortifying especially as it had the appearance of altogether preventing our projected cruize.

---

[1] Though left blank in the journal, Scoresby later quoted from a letter written to Sir Joseph Banks on 2 October 1817: 'I found, on my last voyage, about 2000 square leagues of the surface of the Greenland Sea, included between the parallels of 74° and 80° north, perfectly void of ice, which is usually covered with it' (Scoresby-Jackson, *Life*, p. 123). See Introduction, p. xxviii.

Sunday 20 July Lat. 76.4 Lon. 12°10'E
WNW to W: WNW.
Stood off & on by the southern ice all night & at 2 am. doubled the point of ice. Continued our reach by the wind, with ice under our lee until 10 am. when we passed beyond a point, the last we saw. Strong currents were all day observably forming eddies same as a tide in shallow water. These eddies seemed ['Visible Currents' *in margin*] principally to extend in a line NbW & SbE, one only seemed to lay NE & SW. Sounded in 150 Fa*thom*s but found no bottom. The Phoenix of Whitby joined us. The Manchester, John, & Venerable also in company.

Monday 21ˢᵗ July Lat. 75.15 Lon.11.42E
W.rly Var.
Light winds or calm. Fine cloudy weather. Saw several finners with a tall dorsal fin (some call them herring catchers) sent 2 boats in pursuit of them. They took the alarm on seeing one of the boats & fled. The little distance we sailed this day was towards the SW.

Tuesday 22ᵈ July Lat. 75.5 Lon. 10°38'E
Var. SE.rly to SSW
A breeze sprang up at 3 am. Stood to the Eᵈ two hours but the ship lying a course not calculated to double the ice we passed on Sunday evening provided even it should there recede towards the E. we tacked & made all sail on a West or WbN course accompanied by the ships before named. In the evening the weather was still cloudy; wind a moderate breeze.

Wednesday 23 July Lat. 74.20 Lon. 5°58E
SEbE to SSE & SW.
Steered all this day WbN by the compass with the view of making the ice between the parallels of 73 & 74°of lat. Our progress was usually 3 to 4 knots per hour. A thick fog commenced about noon & continued throughout the day. Ships as before in Company.

Thursday 24 July Lat. 73°49' Lon. 0°58'E[1]
SSW to WSW to NNW.
All this day the fog was intensely thick. I have some reason to suppose that fogs are much more frequent & lasting in westerly longitudes than towards Spitzbergen. In our recent cruize after ['Fog less prevalent near Spitzbergen than to the westward.' *in margin*] passing to the eastward of the meridian of 3° or 4°E we had never a thick day during 6 days – but immediately that we passed to the Wᵈ the meridian of 6°E it recommenced; whether the weather was regularly clear during this interval to the westward remains to be ascertained.[2]

---

[1] These coordinates are preceded by the words 'at noon.'

[2] Scoresby's suggestion is a reasonable one. The relatively warm northward-moving Spitsbergen current in the eastern part of the Greenland Sea could be expected to evaporate moisture in the overlying air, whereas the cold East Greenland Current in the west would cool the air towards its dewpoint and cause shallow fog formation.

I observed with much interest at 1½ Pm. that the decks which were ['Observation on a remarkable <u>drying fog</u>:' *in margin*] 3 hours previous <u>splashy</u> wet, were[1] become perfectly dry nearly fore & aft; though in the interval the fog had been so constantly intense that we could never perceive the accompanying ships or any other object beyond the distance of 100 or 150 yards frequently much less. The hygrometer (uncorrected) stood at 12°, which is I believe 6° above absolute humidity.[2] Perceiving every object about the decks quite dry but moisture dripping from aloft I ascending [*sic*] the rigging & made the following observations. The standing lower rigging was quite dry the rattlings[3] & rough running ropes wet; on reaching the main cat-<u>harpings</u>[4] I perceived the standing rigging & top mast back bays become moist on the weather side & every object above the top was moist; the topmast rigging, top, [& running?] ropes, &c. absolutely dripping wet. The temp. of the air was at this time 45° the sun had been occasionally visible but was now quite obscure. It was curious to observe evaporation going on so rapidly during a fog so dense. The mist seemed equally dense from the deck as it appeared from the top mast rigging. At 5 Pm. a wetting mist commenced which speedily [***] the whole exterior of the ship & its appendages.

From the longitude of 12°E. to the meridian of 0°30′E the colour of the ['Observations on the colour of the Sea' *in margin*] sea was transparent blue. The tinge was ultramarine with a tinge of black (the sky being always dull & heavy). After we had passed the above meridian it suddenly became green & less transparent. The shade was nearest <u>grass green</u> with a tinge of black. In this water we saw much grease floating, which covered acres of surface & appearances of the substance ejected from the blowholes of the whale.

A strong SW.rly swell. Course WbN, NW, NbE. Tacked at mid-night.

---

[1] A repeated 'were' was deleted.

[2] Though using the same physical principle, the techniques and calibration of modern humidity measurements differ from those of Leslie's hygrometer, used by Scoresby. Nowadays, two thermometers are used – dry-bulb and wet-bulb - and values are expressed as 'relative humidity', i.e. the proportion, expressed as a percentage, of water vapour in the air compared to the amount of water that the air is capable of holding in vapour form (saturation vapour pressure) at that dry-bulb temperature. Leslie's hygrometer was a single instrument, with the dry bulb and wet bulbs at opposite ends of a U-shaped tube with a liquid such as sulphuric acid separating the volumes of air beneath each bulb. In saturated air, the volumes would be identical, but normally the cooling effect of evaporation displaced the liquid towards the cooler and therefore denser volume beneath the wet bulb. The amount of displacement is a measure of the relative dryness of the air. As Scoresby's friend Dr Traill wrote in the *Library of Useful Knowledge*, 'When this hygrometer stands at 15°, the air feels damp; from 30° to 40° we reckon it dry; from 50° to 60° very dry; and from 70° upwards, we should call it intensely dry ... In thick fogs it keeps almost at the beginning of the scale' (Traill, p. 42). Leslie's scale is hence the inverse of relative humidity.

[3] *Sic*. The normal spelling is 'ratlines' or 'ratlings'.

[4] Smyth, *Sailor's Word Book*: CAT-HARPINGS, OR CATHARPIN LEGS. Ropes under the tops at the lower end of the futtock-shrouds, serving to brace in the shrouds tighter, and affording room to brace the yards more obliquely when the ship is close-hauled. They keep the shrouds taut for the better ease and safety of the mast.'

Friday 25 July Lat. 73°55′ Lon. 1°5′W
WNW NW, var
Tacked at 4 am. to the NbW. The wind blew fresh & the fog was thick. Parted Company
with the Manchester. At 8 am. the Phoenix hoisted an ancient indicating the intention
of proceeding homeward. We tacked and having prepared [***][1] letters I sent them on
board along with Wᵐ Robson the shipwrecked mariner whom we ['took' *deleted*][2] came
to us from the London in the month of May. He had been constantly since in ill health,
but was of late much recovered. Our seamen made a subscription in his behalf which
with a trifle from myself – amounted to 22/- part he got in sugar, coffee, &c. the
remainder 7/- I gave him in cash. About 11 am. the Phoenix parted Co steering to the
SSW, we reached to the Wᵈ. A heavy SW.rly sea rolled towards us, but the gale by which
it was raised never reached us. Towards mid-night nearly calm.

Saturday 26 July Lat. 73°35′ Lon. 1°40′W
Variable. Calm.
Lay Becalmed all day. A thick fog generally prevailed, but in a break in the obscurity
about 4 Pm. showed us two ships to the NWᵈ of us. The fog was <u>dry</u> from 9 am to 2
Pm. in which interval the sun was frequently visible. The hygro*mete*r (uncorrected) in
a shade ['indicated' *deleted*] where the sun had not shone during the day stood at 14
at 11 am. & 12 at 2 Pm. indicating a degree of dryness of about 6 & 5°. The decks
dried rapidly though there was not a breath of wind. I was informed that the inhabitants of Newfoundland, frequently dry their fish in foggy weather when the sun by
shining through the fog has heated the rocks. The SW.rly swell was still considerable,
but in the "<u>act of falling</u>".

Sunday 27ᵗʰ July Lat. 73.27 Lon. 1°45W
NE.rly
The calm, accompanied by fog, continued until about mid-day. A breeze of wind then
sprang up, but the fog did not disperse. Steered to the NW.

Monday 28 July Lat. 73. 56 Long. by a/c from the land ... 5°59′W
ESE, ENE East.
The wind increased as the <u>barometer fell,</u> and soon fulfilled this instrument's indication of a gale. Fog showers prevailed along with it. Our course was NW until 10 am.
when we steered NNW along the weather side of an extensive range of drift ice. The
ice was under our lee lying SSE & NNW during a run of 40 miles. At 4 Pm. we came
to <u>open drift ice</u>, & close streams, among which we were on the point of entering
when a thick fog shower rendered every object invisible & induced us to tack. Stood
off and on all night under easy sail, the wind blowing a strong gale. At 6 Pm., long. by
Chron*omete*r 7°2′W. The time by chron*omete*r was 6ʰ21′9″ – its rate 2′22″ = 6ʰ18′47
time at ['At 6 pm Long. by Chron*omete*r 7°2′W. Ditto by reckoning from the land ..
7°23′W' *in margin*] Greenwich. Sun's true alt. 19°30′. Lat. 74°5½′N. At 4ʰ4′10″ Pm.

---

[1] Apparently a numeral, but not recognizable.
[2] Grammatically, the phrase should evidently read 'who came to us'.

by chronometer – 2′22″ + 4^h ....; observed alt. sun centre (true) 28°33′ lat. 74°9′N. Venerable & John in Company.

Tuesday 29 July[1]
ENE to NE & NE.
Having tollerably clear weather in the morning, made sail at 10 am. steered NNW, entered a sea stream at noon & afterwards pursued a course towards the NW. viz. 29′ NWbW & 17′NW. when we tacked at 8 pm. Passed several large floes in ['our passage' *deleted*] much drift ice though in general we found ample room. At 6 pm. the Venerable made fast to water but perceiving a land blink & appearance of land in the NW. quarter we stood on until 8 pm. The sun seemed to shine on several hills on the first sight – I saw the blink again at 7½ Pm. And at 10 pm. the land was to be seen with a glass in a satisfactory manner. The blink was yellow, or orange yellow & continued stationary from 6 Pm. until 1 am. when the weather became very heavy. The nearest or highest blink, that in which land was first seen bore by compass NNW to NWbN (variation about 4 Points) a lower blink was visible at WNW in which we also saw land and a very low blink joined the two but no land was to be seen in it. After tacking at 8 pm we returned back to the SE to a floe to which we made fast & took on board a large stock of water from one of the numerous pools which were upon its surface. At this time when the land was most distinct, our lat. was 74°5′N & from an observation of the[2] chronometer at 5^{h}43′30″ rate –2′23″ = 5^{h}41.7 Greenwich time was 10°46¼′W. Saw[3] the land appeared to me to be distant near 50 miles or say 3° of longitude; this makes the nearest point of land bearing NWbW in lat 74.15 & long. 13°46′W. The land in the Dutch charts ([4]the only authorities who ['accept' *deleted*] pretend to have seen it above the lat. of 70° excepting Hudson, is in their parallel of 74° laid down in long. 6° to 7°W. whereas its true situation must be ['above' *deleted*] at least 7° farther west![5] Between us & the land at 10pm there seemed to be much less ice than we had passed through. This as far as could be seen consisted of drift ice without floes & very open. To the southward of us appeared to be a vast body of ice, extending from WSW to SEbS. Much ice seemed likewise to lie in diff*erent* directions[6] to the northward of us.

Wednesday 30 July Lat. 73.46 Lon. 10°W.
NE.rly.
The wind had now fallen to a moderate breeze but the fog became very dense at 2 am. Having finished watering and seeing no symptoms of whales, & scarcely any

[1] The usual noon coordinates are absent, but see the other notations of position in the margin and text for this day.
[2] At this point there is the following marginal note: 'At 5 pm: lat. 74.5 Long. 10°46′W. At 9 pm. 74.6 11°50′W. being our greatest W. long.
Error of Chronometer by [***] observ*ation* fast 4′51″ in time or 1°12′45″ in long . Hence the long. at 9pm corrected True is = 10°37′15″W.'
[3] Possibly 'Now'.
[4] There is no closing parenthesis.
[5] Probably the nearest land in that general direction from the supposed position of the *Esk* is the island of Shannon, the southeast coast of which is at 75°00′N 17°21′W.
[6] 'positions' inserted above this word.

living creature except a few seals, a narwhale, & a very few birds, we thought it prudent to remove to the eastward as we were at the time 40' from the sea the way we came in & as this was a deep bight at least 80' from the sea in a SSE direction. Steered therefore towards the SE, found crowded ice having missed the roomy track on which we entered. At 10 am. we perceived a swell, the first & most certain indication of our approach to the ice edge.

Some days ago we examined in the state of our provision, &c. and finding it more reduced than we expected the seamens allowance was somewhat diminished. Our coals were found more nearly expended; 16 bushels only remained out of 7 chaldron: we were therefore obliged to parcel out a certain quantity for each day which was not sufficient to serve ⅓ ['half' *deleted*] the 24 hours. Two or three bags from the Venerable & a quantity from the John did us great service, which Captains J. & B.[1] were kind enough to send us.

During the afternoon & evening we were entangled amongst a great quantity of heavy drift ice in motion with the swell. The wind being very light we continually fell foul of the pieces, though we towed with 2 boats & sometimes 3. Our situation was extremely embarrassing – the fog was so dense that we could not ascertain our best course. An impenetrable sea stream lay [***][2] us. We plyed within side[3] of it though terribly annoyed with ice until near mid-night when the fog dispersed ['**Thursday 31st July** Lat. 73°46'20"+ Lon. 9°25'W E.rly: W.rly to NE'.[4] *in margin*] & we perceived a channel of communication with the sea at a few furlongs distance, but owing to the lightness of the wind & its direction (E.rly) we did not get clear of this ice until about noon of the 31st.

A commanding breeze of wind sprang up in the afternoon under which we steered to the S, & SSE along the edge of a great quantity of ice lying to the Sd of us, we hauled up SE & E in the evening and after all could not find our way round ['some' *deleted*] a narrow but lengthened stream without passing through it. We escaped ['At 5h pm by chronometer Lon. 8°49'30"W. Variation Compass 37°33W [ship's head SbW.]' *in margin*] into what was evidently the sea at mid-night. The John & Venerable in Company. As our companions were now determined on proceeding homewards, and as we had for a long time been unable to find a single whale we pursued a S.rly course, with the wish however of keeping near the ice to a low latitude provided the weather allowed us. Saw a ship to the Nd of us.

Friday 1st August Lat. 73.46 Lon. 7°9'W Bar. 29.76 Ther. 33, 35, 33
NbW N.
Fresh to light breezes. Foggy occasionally, in the intervals cloudy. Steered S, SW, S, & SbE as we found the ice trending. Passed an extreme point of ice at 7 pm. after which we steered SW. About 9 pm. saw Jan Mayne Island ['which bearing [WSW?]' *deleted*] which at mid-night bore West per compass, suppose 80 miles

---

[1] Jackson of the *John* and Bennett of the *Venerable*.
[2] Possibly 'without'.
[3] *Sic*: 'sight' intended?
[4] Originally 'NNE' but the first 'N' struck through.

distant. Steered ['**Saturday 2ᵈ August** Lat. 71.35.8+ Long. 7.50W. NbW Erly Bar 29.72 Ther. 34, 38, 35' *in margin*] towards it. Fell into dark olive green water in the forenoon, in which we saw razor backs in abundance & some <u>finners</u>. The land was concealed from us by <u>heavy</u> clouds & the wind falling to nearly calm our ['[Operation of Footing skins]' *in margin*] approach was extremely slow. Employed the crew for some days in <u>footing</u>[1] bear's & seal skins. In the afternoon saw Beerenberg[2] bearing W¼N; which though at the distance of .... miles & its top [encapped?] in clouds subtended an angle of 1°15'. It did not clear during the day.

[*At this point in the journal is inserted a lengthy description of the landing on Jan Mayen. It represents a first draft, heavily amended throughout, of 'Narrative of an Excursion on the Island of Jan Mayen', published in the* Memoirs of the Wernerian Society *in 1818, and then as 'Account of Jan Mayen Island' in* Account of the Arctic Regions, I, pp. 154–69. *Also included in the journal at this point are (a) a list of 13 items entitled 'References to Lavas &c. from the island of Jan Mayen'; (b) 5 items forming a 'List of some of the plants found on Jan Mayen'; (c) most unusually, a page of entries from the ship's log (as distinct from Scoresby's journal), in nautical day format, covering the period from 2 p.m. on 29 July to noon on 4 August.*]

Sunday 3ᵈ August Bar. 29.72 Therm. 38, 42, 40'[3]
ENE to NNE. E.rly
Clouds constantly hung over the land so that the lower part of it only was visible. Steered towards it & in the evening went into "<u>Great Wood Bay</u>".[4] Took angle of the coast as far as we could see, which latterly was the whole extent of the SE'rn coast from which I proposed to draw a plan.

The top of Beerenberg cleared for a minute about 9 & 10 Pm. on which ['intervals' *deleted*] occasions I took angles of its elevation from whence to determine its distance & perpendicular height. The upper part was an entire iceberg a few hundred feet from the summit black rocks were seen in a few places

---

[1] There is nothing in *OED* in such a context. However, both Smyth and *OED* define a nautical use of the verb 'to foot' from which Scoresby's use may have been derived, e.g. 'To push or shove with the feet. Chiefly *Naut.*' Another possibility is that Scoresby adapted a whaling term to the task of stripping bear and seal skins of extraneous matter. In *Account of the Arctic Regions*, II, p. 402, in describing the process of boiling the whale blubber after returning to port, he noted that 'the blubber of the whale ... affords a considerable quantity of watery liquor ... on the surface of which, some of the fenks, and all the greasy animal matter called *footje* or *footing*. float.' *OED* cited this reference, and also the following, from Simmonds, *Dictionary of Trade Products* (1858): '*Footing*, the finer detached fragments of the fenks, or refuse whale blubber, not wholly deprived of oil.'

[2] The active volcano at the northern end of Jan Mayen (71.1°N 8.2°W). Its present elevation is 7468 ft (2277 m).

[3] No coordinates are given for this date.

[4] See the very detailed map that Scoresby included as Plate VI in vol. II of *Account of the Arctic Regions*.

peeping through the snow & ice. This remarkable hill never cleared whilst we were on the N. or E. side, but when we got under the <u>lee of</u> it, it was distinctly seen for some hours whilst a thick fog was seen ['**Monday 4 August** Lat. 70.34+ Lon. 9°11'W Bar. 29.98. Therm. 38, 40' *in margin*][1] hanging over the opposite verge of it & the neighbouring mountains.

The ship being becalmed 3 miles from the shore & the weather fine accompanied by Captains Bennet[2] & Jackson, with our respective surgeons, &c. I went on shore. We landed at 2½ am. & returned to the ship at 6½ am. after a most interesting exploration.

['Long. at 6ʰ52' am: chr. 8°51'7W
        Error   −1. 14.45
                <u>7. 36.22W</u>' *in margin*]

A fresh gale of wind sprang up at 8 am. Made sail & steered to the SW & W. At noon observed in lat. 70°33'. At 1 Pm. (having sailed West 5' from noon) the SW.ern hook of Jan Mayne bore 9°E & the SE hook N56½°E.

For a number of days past, ever since indeed we came from the eastward, a considerable difference has appeared between our lat. by a/c & observation, the latter being invariably <u>less</u>[3] than the former, the usual amount has been 6 to 10' per day. This proves the constant [action?] of a current setting to the Sᵈ. It indeed influenced my angles taken on Jan Mayne so much that I was obliged to make a regular allowance of a drift towards the South before I could accomplish my satisfactory intersections where I had taken more than two bearings. The ship when becalmed near "Wood Bay" set directly out to the Sᵈ. As I shall reserve my remarks on Jan Mayne for a paper by itself, it is needless to repeat them here.

We looked in vain (though the weather was very clear) for a rock laid down by the Dutch[4] to the Sᵈ of Jan Mayne. We were probably too much to the Eastward for seeing it.

Our researches for whales having been so long in vain [&?] the wind being favourable bore up for <u>dolce dominum</u>. Rigged royal masts & set all sails.

Tuesday 5ᵗʰ August Lat. 68.30 Lon. 9°47'W Bar. 29.80 Ther. 40, 45, 42
NNE. NE Variable: ESE
Wind fair, blowing a fresh or light breeze, and charming fine weather. Employed all hands cleaning ship inside & outside, washed the whalelines, the footing of bear's skins going on, as well as variety of other useful and ornamental work.

Steered SW by the way of keeping well to the westward that we might yet have visited the ice should a contrary or S.rly wind have occurred whilst we were yet north of Iceland. Finding however our Southing rapidly increasing we steered SWbS & afterwards SSW. John & Venerable in Cᵒ.

---

[1] No wind directions are provided for this date.

[2] 'Bennett' according to Credland, *Hull Whaling Trade*, Appendix 3.

[3] 'Less' in the sense that the observation yielded a lower (more southerly) latitude than dead reckoning.

[4] I.e. shown on the Dutch charts.

Wednesday 6 August Lat. 67.10+ Lon. 9°33 W. Bar. 29.73 Ther. 42, 46, 43
SE ESE, E
Still fine weather, some showers of rain & fair brisk wind. Course SSW, velocity 3 to 8 knotts per hour, Considerable S.rly, & NE.rly swells. The John & the Venerable still in Company. Long. by Chronometer 6ʰ21′58″ pm = 8°58′15″W.

Thursday 7 August Lat. 64.20 Lon. 7°7′W. Bar. 29.60 Ther. 45, 46, 44
E, ENE
Strong gales with rain. Steered SSW until 9 am. when the John made a signal to speak with us & then she & the Venerable parted company; they steering about SWbS, we SbW & S. Our velocity was regularly 7 to 9½ knotts per hour. Our distance run in the 24 hours ending at noon was 184′ by the log. Stars which were seen for the first time these 3 months, ['last' *deleted*] in the preceding evening, were deemed such a curiosity as to draw all the idlers [upon?] out to gaze at them.

Friday 8 July[1] Lat 61.50 Long a/c:[2] Bar. 29.57 Therm. 50, 52
ENE, NE
Fresh gales with rain or hazy weather. Steering South until 8 am. Our run in the 24 hours ending at noon was again 180 miles. Strong SW.rly swell, which abated & indeed was imperceptible for some hours in the morning: this we imagined was owing the proximity of Farro which intercepted the swell, as towards noon it was again very evident. Saw a strange sail in the afternoon steering to the SSWᵈ. Long. by the chronometer at 3ʰ5′ pm. was 5°10′30″ Pm;[3] by a/c 3°15′W (from observation of Chronometer on the 6th inst.[)] The evening came on with strong squalls, thick dark weather & boisterous sea. Tried for soundings at 8 & 10 pm.: but found no ground with 130 fat. perpendicular. This confirmed us in the western situation of the ship. Our latitude at 10 pm. was 60°50′. I considered the hazard of proceeding so great on account of the Skerries & Havre degrind;[4] each of which rocks (the latter blind rocks) lay 4 or 5 miles from land; our proximity to which was evident but the distance very uncertain, as our lat. had not been corrected ['Saw some birds called 'Mother Carey's Chickens',[5] fulmars, kittywakes, & ['solon geese' *deleted*] & some land birds during the day.' *in margin*] by solar observation in a run of near 400 miles & our longitude equally uncertain from my ignorance of the rate of the chronometer no means of determining which to any degree of accuracy[6] had occurred in the course of the voyage. We therefore reduced sail & lay too.

---

[1] In this and the following day's entry, 'July' has been struck through, but was not replaced by 'August'.

[2] No value was indicated, but see text of this day.

[3] *Sic*: 'W' presumably intended.

[4] *Sic*. See entry for 29 July 1815, in volume I of these *Journals*.

[5] The stormy petrel, *Procellaria pelagica*.

[6] Originally 'accurracy', but the second 'r' struck out.

Saturday 9 ['July' *deleted*] At 10 am: Lat. 60°7 Long. 2°24′W. Bar. 29.26 Ther. 53, 54, 54.

NE to ESE. NNE Var.

The night for summer season was dismal and the gloom only was dispelled by day light for the rain & mist was so thick we seldom could see above half a mile. Finding no soundings however, though the wind blew a strong gale & the sea was ['Saw several solon geese & fulmars' *in margin*] much increased from different quarters, we made sail & proceeded under double reefed topsails & jib on a SE course wishing to make Shetland for fear of slipping behind Orkney to ['Made Fula' *in margin*] the westward. No soundings at 6 am. At 8 am. I corrected our night's run & made the lat. 60°11′ & long. from the last observation of chronometer 2°42′. At 10ʰ10′ am. saw land (the weather having cleared in that quarter) which proved to be Fula, bearing SE½S, per compass distant about 10 miles. By our reckoning reduced from 8 am. I made the lat. of Fula 60°1½′ and its long. 2°8′W. The coincidence is singular. ['Bar. 29.26 Ther. 53, 54, 54.' *in margin*] My reckoning to my own astonishment, for I could only attribute its singular accuracy to chance, corresponded with the position in which Fula island is laid down in the best tables to half a minute of a latitude & one minute of long.![1] From however a sight of the sun which I got at 8ʰ39′30″Am. my long. was 3°41′15″W which differed 1° from my reckoning conducted only through a single night! Whether this error was in the reckoning or in the observations (which indeed were not very excellent) I could not determine: probably it was in both. From the last observation Fula's long. was 3°7′W. which differs a degree from what I take to be the truth. If the observation was correct & the position of Fula be likewise accurately determined the chronometer must have gained 4′ of time or 1° of longitude W. in the course of the voyage: or say from the 7ᵗʰ of March, when its supposed rate of was [*sic*] only 1″ per day fast.

The wind subsided towards noon: made sail on a course S½E. Passed Fair Island at 7 Pm. bearing East dist 5′. At 10 pm. the "Start Light" of Sanda (Orkney) bore WSW distant about 10 miles.[2]

Sunday 10 August Lat. 58.32+ Lon. 1°24′W. Bar. 29.80 Ther. 54, 55, 53
NbW NWbW

In the morning we had a moderate breeze of wind, fine weather in the evening blowing strong: velocity of the ship from 3 to 9½ knots: course steered SbW & SSW. Several strange vessels seen. At 7 Pm. saw the coast of Scotland & at 8 "Moor Mount" near Buchaness bore NW½W distant 15 or 20 miles. About mid-night the wind abated, & rain commenced.[3]

---

[1] Foula is at 60°8′N 2°5′W; Scoresby's determination was even more accurate than he thought.

[2] The Start Point lighthouse, on the east coast of Sanday (59°16′N 2°23W), constructed in 1806 as the first revolving light in Scotland, and still operational (Trethewey and Forand, *Lighthouse Encyclopaedia*).

[3] There follows, at the foot of the page, a two-line insertion in pencil that is barely legible. It appears to note that the voyage from Jan Mayen to Buchaness had taken only six days; it also was intended to note the distance travelled, but the value in miles was left blank.

Monday 11ᵗʰ August Lat 56.30+ Lon. 1°34′W. Bar. 29.50 Ther 53, 55, 54
WbS. Var. SSW to SEbS
Light variable winds the fore part, the latter part of the day blowing strong with a heavy fall of rain. Made land about 2 Pm. Stretched by the wind to the SWᵈ & fetched in a little windward of Dunbar. Tacked close in shore at 9 Pm.

Tuesday 12 August Lat 56°4′+ Lon. [*blank space*] Bar. 29.23 Ther. 54, 58.
SSE Calm. Var. W.rly:
Fresh gales with heavy rain in the night. Tacked at 2 am. stood in shore, fetched only about the place where we left in the evening; tacked off at 7 am. Towards noon inclinable to calm.

When near the land in shallow water, the colour of the sea was apple green, varying according to the nature of the ['Observations of the <u>Colour of the sea</u> in various situations.' *in margin*] ground: white sand producing pale green, dark yellow deep green, rocks brownish, &c. In all ['remote' *deleted*] deep seas, remote from land which I have yet visited I have invariably found the colour of the sea ultramarine blue (deep shade) or [azure blue?] or a slight tinge of greenish blue, the Greenland seas only excepted. Hence in deep ['S.erly' *in margin*] seas the colour is nearly that of the azure of the atmosphere ['['above us?']' *deleted*] and probably arising from the same cause.[1] Near the mouths of large rivers the sea is coloured with the mud & fresh water from the rivers with the various substances washed from its supplying mountains which is held in suspension in the water – in strong tides & shallow water we see sometimes grey [***] [motley?] coloured sea or of other shades according to the nature of substances removed from the bottom & the colour of the ground itself – near shore in still water or in all still shallow seas the native colour of the sea commixed with that of the bottom of the sea ['forms all' *deleted*] constitutes all the varieties of colour & intensity which we observe.

In the evening a fresh breeze of wind prevailed but not ['very' *deleted*] fair; reached to the SEᵈ. Many coasters & 2 Greenlandmen in sight.

Wednesday 13 August Lat. 55°40′ Lon. 1°27′W. Bar 29.22 Ther 56, 58, 54.
S.erly: Var. Calm: W.
Heavy rain in the morning, calm in the forenoon. Having as yet had no opportunity of drying our whale lines we suspended them in the forenoon, being previously washed – but a fresh gale of wind commencing & the ship pitching heavy against a strong SSErly [swell?] we were obliged to take them down, after a very short time.

At 10 pm. Tinmouth light at WbS dist*ant* 20 miles.

---

[1] Scoresby was not quite correct. The blue of the sky is the result of the scattering of much of the blue end of the visible spectrum by air molecules as solar radiation passes through the atmosphere. The blue of the sea is caused by reflection of the blue sky from the sea surface to the eye of the observer. Scoresby expanded considerably on these comments about sea and sky colour in *Account of the Arctic Regions*, I, pp. 173–5.

Thursday 14 August Lat.54°48′ Lon. 1°0′W Bar. 29.50 Ther 57, 59
SW.rly Var. SWbS.
Tacked at 3 Am. having steered far off the land, stood in shore until 10½ Am. when
we tacked a little to the S^d of Sunderland in 7 fat. water. In a squall of wind & rain at
1 am. carried the foretop gall*ant* mast away: cleared the wreck & set about making a
new top gall*ant* mast of a topsail yard we picked up at sea. About 6 pm. passed Huntcliff but the wind scanting had to make a tack which the tide of flood was expended.
Hoisted our flag in sight of Whitby at dusk. Blowing a hard gale of wind no boat
appeared.[1]

Friday 15 August Lat. 54.30 Lon. 0°26′W Bar 29.65 Ther. [*blank space*]
SW to W
Stretched to the S^d ['all' *deleted*] until mid-night, still blowing hard, & then tacked;
fetched no higher than Huntcliff: carried a pressure of sail, passed Whitby in the
offing at 9 am. & it was not till near noon in returning that a boat boarded us when I
was rejoiced to hear of the health of all my dearest connections – thank God. Brought
up in [Louden?] Ness at [1?] Pm. weighed anchor at 4 pm. at 5½ pm. sailed by Pier
end clewed sails up and [shot?] into the harbour. Passed through bridge & mustered
the crew. Were informed a hard gale of wind had blown at Whitby during three days
past which account for the low state of [the Bar?].

---

[1] Scoresby needed a pilot to enter the harbour. see entry for 1 April 1817.

Journal for 1818

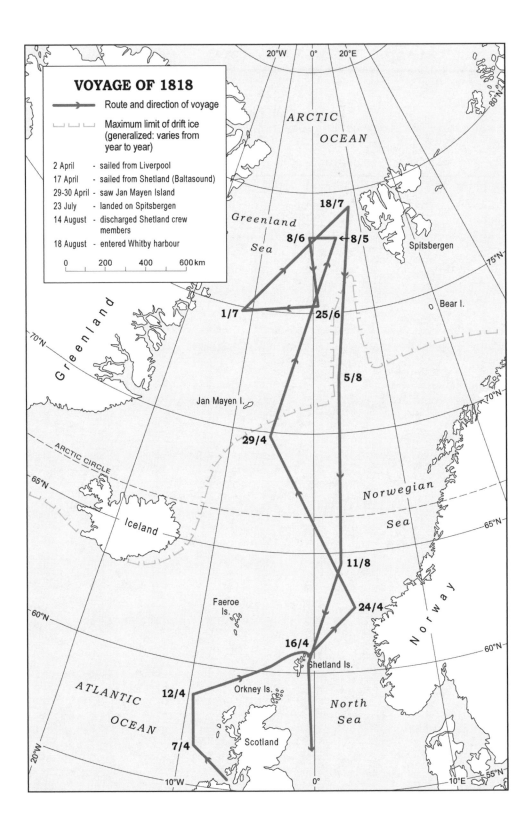

VOYAGE OF 1818

→ Route and direction of voyage

⊔ ⊔ ⊔ Maximum limit of drift ice
(generalized: varies from
year to year)

2 April	- sailed from Liverpool
17 April	- sailed from Shetland (Baltasound)
29-30 April	- saw Jan Mayen Island
23 July	- landed on Spitsbergen
14 August	- discharged Shetland crew members
18 August	- entered Whitby harbour

0   200   400   600 km

Journal of a Whale fishing voyage Under Divine Providence In the ship Fame from Liverpool to Greenland and Whitby By William Scoresby, Junior, Commander. 1818.

Introduction

The Fame, a teak built vessel, taken from the Portuguese by the French Privateer Marseilles and retaken by his Majesty's Frigate Blanche, was "sold pursuant to an order of the Court of Vice Admiralty held at Roseau Dominica[1] the 18th day of June 1794 and his Majesty's duty for the said vessel was[2] paid at Liverpool the 9th Fleby 1795 as appears by a certificate of Registry granted at Liverpool the 28 Jany 1814" – and after passing through different hands was purchased by my Father in the month of November 1817, with a view of fitting her for the whale fishery.

As, however, I was at the same time engaged in a treaty for another vessel belonging to Whitby no arrangements were made for her equipment until an advanced season.[3]

The general openness of the Greenland seas in the year 1817 owing to vast[4] quantity of floating ice having drifted to the southward, was observed by all the whale fishers, and as this openness presented me with an opportunity of getting sight of the E. coast of <u>lost</u> Greenland[5] the uncommon circumstance was circulated abroad through the medium of the public [prints?]; these facts in connection with various evidence of extraordinary bodies of ice having been met with in the vicinity of Newfoundland – led the valued President & some of the members of the Royal Society to investigate into the peculiarities of these facts. In reply to a letter from Sir Joseph Banks, with whom I had for some time had the honor [sic] and advantage of corresponding,

---

[1] Roseau is the capital of Dominica, in the Windward Islands of the Caribbean.

[2] This word, at the end of a line, was repeated at the beginning of the next line, but the latter was deleted.

[3] This is the only mention of an intended voyage from Whitby in 1818; there is no suggestion of it in Scoresby's 'Autobiography'.

[4] Possibly 'past', but in a letter to Sir Joseph Banks dated 2 October 1817, and quoted in Scoresby-Jackson, *Life*, p. 23, Scoresby noted that in 1817 'I found ... about 2000 square leagues of the Greenland Sea ... perfectly void of ice, which is usually covered with it. Now all this ice has disappeared within the last two years, and there is little doubt but that it has been drifted to the southward into warmer climates, and there dissolved.' See also the remark later in this paragraph.

[5] As indicated later in this paragraph ('ancient Icelandic Colony') Scoresby was referring to the widely-held belief that one of the two main mediaeval Norse settlements had been on the east coast of Greenland, and that descendants of them might still be living there. In fact, both the Norse 'Western Settlement' and the 'Eastern Settlement' had been on the west coast of Greenland; the later notion that the latter was on the east coast was mainly due to fanciful mapmaking in the seventeenth century. Gad (*History of Greenland*, I, p. 237) has commented that, even then, 'The idea that there were still Norse people living in Greenland must have been due to a kind of stubbornness or mental inertia', but it was an idea that persisted into the 19th century.

making some enquiries on these subjects, I stated that I had seen the Coast of Greenland, had landed on Jan Mayne Island, that 2000[1] square leagues of ice, or upwards,
had quitted the Greenland seas in the course of three years, and that if I had been
engaging in discovery in place of fishing, I could have no doubt but not only might I
have landed on Greenland, probably ascertained the Fate of ancient Icelandic Colony
established there, but might also have resolved the problem as to the existence of a
NW passage.[2] ['Whether' *deleted*] I also mentioned my willingness to undertake such
a voyage in the ensuing season, and suggested a plan of combining the objects of fishing & discovery so as to cover in a great measure the expence, which an expedition of
this kind might be to the nation. Whether these hints were informed on[3] or the same
ideas had occurred to others I cannot say, but a short time afterwards, it appeared
application had been made by the Royal Society to the Admiralty requesting that an
expedition in the Polarseas [*sic*] might be fitted out. Shortly afterwards it was intimated to me through Sir J. Banks that government had determined on fitting out two
expeditions, one for discovery towards the Pole and the other towards the NW.
through Baffin's Bay, so called. On the same occasion he expressed his desire that I
might be placed at the Head of one of these expeditions, and subsequently, through
my Father who was then in London, requested that I might be sent for. I accordingly
proceeded to London, but found that the plans of the Admiralty were already laid, as
to the command of the expeditions, and their plans resembling the "Laws of the
Medes & Persians which altereth not",[4] I presently ascertained that I indeed might
proceed in one of the expeditions & as such was requested to send in my proposals to
the Navy Board, but that it must be in a subsidiary capacity.[5] My determination was
already made. I never presented my self at the Navy Board; but after spending two or
three weeks in research after information on the Ancient History of Greenland & the
whale fisheries, in which I was kindly ['aided[?]' *deleted*] assisted by the influence of
Sir J. Banks in procuring me access to the MSS. preserved in the British Museum as
well as in lending me some scarce books which were in ['[***] among' *deleted*] his
own library; I returned to Whitby. It was not until the **end of January** that we decided
on fitting the Fame for the fishery, at which time I joined my Father by agreeing for ⅓
share of the ship, and engaging to take the Command for the fishery in the ensuing
season.

Some urgent engagements prevented me from quitting Whitby to proceed to
Liverpool where the Fame lay for two or three weeks. My father left home on the 3ᵈ
of February reached Liverpool on the Saturday[6] following. Agreeable to prior
arrangements the Fame was <u>docked</u> on the 10ᵗʰ **February**. The copper was

---

[1] The value was added later in pencil, over ellipsis points, as also was 'three' later in the same
sentence.

[2] In terms of modern geography, this seems a strange remark, but in the early 19th century there
was still debate as to whether Greenland was a single land mass or an archipelago.

[3] Possibly 'improved on'.

[4] Daniel 6:12, though 'law' is there singular.

[5] See Introduction, p. xxxii.

[6] Another pencil insertion over ellipsis points. The elder Scoresby therefore arrived in Liverpool
on 8 February.

immediately ['taken off' *deleted and replaced in pencil by* 'stripped'] as well as the sheating (*sic*) or doubling which descended from the wales downward 5 or 6 feet. The bottom was found sound & strong, and altogether the ship <u>opened out</u> well. The stern timbers were stripped, & the [***] which originally terminated in the gun-room, opened through the cabin and poop decks. The masts, rigging, & stores were all removed and the greater part of the ['two last[?]' *deleted*] remaining rigging & stores condemned.

On the 17th myself & Mrs Scoresby, left Whitby for Liverpool where we arrived at **mid-night of the 19**th and repaired the following day to a lodging previously provided by my father. The carpenters were engaged all the week in <u>dubbing</u>[1] the bottom & sides of the ship, and did not commence the operation of doubling before the 25th. From the six feet mark upward to the 16th on the bows and adjoining the stern were put logs of timber 12 or 14 inches thick diminishing to three or 2½ Inch plank at the forechains, and likewise diminishing upward so as to terminate evenly with the wales excepting at the stern where it suddenly diminished. The doubling was proposed to extend ['to the' *deleted*] from the wales fore & aft to the 6 feet mark forward & the 8 feet mark abaft. Plank of 1½, ['Inch' *deleted*] 2, & 2½ inches thick, being provided, the doubling was commenced as proposed; a coat of plaster consisting of lime, sand, water, and linseed oil being laid upon the plank beneath, so as to make the doubling lay solid and keep out the water where the iron was decayed or any other openings should be produced in the plank.

Finding our progress slow notwithstanding above 40 carpenters were employed, and ['being un' *deleted*][2] finding we should not be able to leave the dock before the last springs ['which occur' *deleted*] of March, we removed, on the **12 March**, from the high end to the gates of the dry dock that we might be at liberty, on account of the greater depth of water at this end of the dock, to ballast the ship and take on board our stores without any risk of <u>not</u> floating.

On the same day commenced rigging; and stowed the first cask in the hold on the 14th having previously taken 36 tons of shingle ballast on board. From this time we were engaged in the most laborious service in rigging, stowing hold, filling water, taking in stores, doubling, fortifying, fitting davits, skeeds, new windlass, new rudder, in fitting cabin, galley, and lodgings for the crew, and a great variety of other operations.

On the 20th took 2 tons of bread on board, and **on the 21**st <u>bent</u> courses and top-sails, took bread, coal, oatmeal, pease, whale-lines, ice ropes, cables, and other stores and apparatus on board.

On the 23, 24, & 25 in the morning, we were employing taking stores on board, finishing rigging and hold, and the blacksmiths in <u>plating</u> the stern with strong sheet iron. The doubling, cabin, twin decks, galley, &c. were finished, the windlass, stern,

---

[1] Smyth, *Sailor's Word Book*: 'DUBB, To. To smooth and cut off with an adze the superfluous wood.'

[2] Originally 'unable', with the first two letters deleted.

fortifications, skeeds, &c. well advanced but still incomplete. **On the latter day (25ᵗʰ)** we left the <u>Graving Dock</u>, and hauled into the <u>King's</u> Dock, where we advanced in our various operations. Filled an additional quantity of water in the hold, ['&c' *deleted*], built blacksmith's shop & erected a forge, &c.

Friday the 27, at 4 Pm. the proper officer of Customs came on board and mustered the Crew 42 in number, including myself, & on Saturday we '<u>entered the ship outwards</u>'¹ (a victualling bill² having been taken out some time before) and by the extraordinary exertions of the Collector of the Customs, we were enabled to Clear out the same day. I cannot refrain from mentioning the great urbanity and uncommon attention we received from this Gentleman. Had it not been for those excellenies (*sic*) in his Character we could not have cleared before Monday, and of course, suffered detention thereby. Gave the men a promissory note each, for two months advance payable 14 days after the sailing of the ship.

In the afternoon we hauled out of dock and got safely into the River where we brought up with Chain Cable opposite the ['Kings D' *deleted*] ..... **On Monday** hired a large boat & a sloop which took the remainder of our stores on board consisting of coals, casks, ['wines &' *deleted*] and sundry small materials. Took boats onboard. Paid harbour pay to the crew until Friday 27 Inclusive.

On Tuesday 31ˢᵗ the wind being unfavourable we lay still at anchor and employed ourselves in putting our stores into order and the ship into a convenient state for going to sea.

April the 1st. the wind blew favourable; made signal for sailing. Seeking after two officers who were absent, prevented us from getting to sea – we however dropped down to the [Rock?]³ to be in readiness for the next opportunity: the afternoon tide was too late for clearing the sands before dark. Two men Charles Evans, and Peter Swinny left the ship against orders. The latter we pursued overtook and brought on board, and took strict measures for securing him. His conduct was daring and highly insubordinate.

At day light of the 2ᵈ prepared for sea. The wind was light but still favourable. Weighed anchor at 7 am. and cleared the Sands at 10 am. when a Pilot Boat approached us and took on board our pilot. Steered NNW at a brisk rate for the Isle of Man which we descryed at 4 pm. Passed the Calf of Man at 7. pm. blowing strong from the ENE, reefed top sails & courses and hauled by the wind. At

---

¹ Smyth, *Sailor's Word Book*, s.v. OUTWARD. 'A vessel is said to be entered outwards or inwards according as she is entered at the custom-house to depart for, or as having arrived from, foreign parts.'

² Smyth, *Sailor's Word Book*: 'VICTUALLING-BILL. A custom-house document, warranting the shipment of such bonded stores as the master of an outward-bound merchantman may require for his intended voyage.'

³ Probably Perch Rock, off New Brighton at the entrance to the Mersey. A lighthouse was erected there in 1830.

mid-night saw the new Light of the N&S. Rock[1] on the Coast of Ireland. A strong swell drifted us towards the shore and induced us to set more sail. **At 4 am. of the 3ᵈ** saw the Light of Copeland Island.[2] At day Light the coasts of Scotland & Ireland were both in sight. Several ships near. The day was beautifully fine and mild & the Sun brilliant & hot. At noon passed the maiden rocks[3] on the NE. coast of Ireland, near which the tide exhibited violent eddies and the sea was in a foam.

In the evening, the tide swept us during a calm, towards the Island of <u>Arran</u>; The Pladdin light[4] was in sight which at first we mistook for the light on the Mull of Cantire.[5] A breeze springing up from the SW we steered Nerly and at mid-night saw the <u>Cantire</u> Light and passed it at **1 am. of the 4**.

At day Light we were within sight of Cantire, the Mull of Kino, Rachlin[6] Island & the N. coast of Ireland; and most of the day we lay becalmed between Mull of Kino[7] & <u>Rachlin</u> Island. The day was beautiful and <u>hot</u>. Stowed the boats in sea order and secured them. Carpenter & his crew with the [***], preparing apparatus for the fishery. Latitude at Noon 55.30.

I never experienced relief on getting to sea on any former occasion. On the present however, notwithstanding the difficulties of the navigation in the Channel, and the careful watching it required I experienced ease of body & mind compared with the unremitting exertion & harass which I had endured during my stay in Liverpool. The Fame had been fitted, her stores made, casks manufactured, the ship doubled, fortifyed, repaired, ['and' *deleted*] altered, and adapted for the whale fishery, in a space of time less ['than' *deleted*] by one half than was requisite to have performed these <u>multitudinous</u> operations with ease and comfort to ourselves. The attention requisite in ordering the stores, all of which required to accurate[8] described & drawn, as the mechanics were totally unacquainted with their formation, was incalculable. The carpenters, who performed their work idly and frequently very ill, required constant superintendance. Hence I experienced a relief when we finished, which I was before quite a stranger to. Thus are ['evils' *deleted*] inconveniences lessened by comparison & frequently altogether lost ['by' *deleted*] when contrasted with greater evils.

---

[1] The North and South Rocks are off the Ards peninsula, County Down. The lighthouse known as South Rock or Kilwarlin (54°24′N 5°22′W) was erected in 1797. There is a detailed history of its problems in the early 19th century at the website of the Commissioners of Irish Lights, but this does not mention a 'new light' about 1818.

[2] There was a lighthouse on Copeland Island at the entrance to Belfast Lough (54°42′N 5°31′W) from 1700, but Scoresby was referring to the one erected in 1815.

[3] The Hulin or Maiden Rocks off the coast of Co. Antrim, 54°56′N 5°44′W.

[4] Presumably the Pladda lighthouse (55°26′N 5°7′W), erected in 1790 on an island off the south coast of Arran in the Firth of Clyde.

[5] The lighthouse on the Mull of Kintyre (55°19′N 5°48′W) was erected in 1788.

[6] This is still an alternative spelling for what is now normally mapped as Rathlin Island, off the coast of Co. Antrim.

[7] The 'Mull of Kino' is now known as the Mull of Oa, on the south coast of Islay. See note to journal entry for 20 August 1820.

[8] Presumably a transcription error for 'to be accurately'.

At 8 pm. the light of Inisterhol[1] (Ireland) bore W½N p Compass. Strong eddies of tide around us: wind a moderate breeze at ENE. Steered NbW to avoid the dangerous rocks which extend from the Islands of Mull & Tiri, the former stretching SW.rly 10 miles & the latter 15 miles into the Sea! Calm during the night. Barom. 30.44 – falling.

The <u>Fame</u> is thus described in the <u>Register</u>[2] – "Foreign built – has one deck and half deck, and three masts." "Length from the fore part of the main stem to the after part of the stern post 103^{ft} 3 in.: breadth at the Broadest part above the main wales 29 feet; height between decks 5^{ft} 4 in. and admeasurement 370^{58}⁄₉₄ tons." "Square sterned, with a raised quarter deck, no Gallery, woman's Head" (female Figure of Fame with a wreath of laurel in the left hand and trumpet in the right).[3] Willm Scoresby, Wm Scoresby Junr & Thomas Jackson, the sole owners, in proportions as follows. W.S. ½; W.S. Junr ⅓; & T.J. ⅙ part.

Specific Gravity of the Sea between the Mull of Cantire & Rachlin Island [by Hyd. N° 4 = [*blank space*] temp. 58°][4] = [*blank space*].

Sunday 5 April. Calm most of the morning: [hazy?] weather. No land in sight. Steered ['by wind' *deleted*] to the N^d on a breeze springing up at Noon from the SE, E, and veering to ENE. The Bar. fell to 29.60 and the wind increased to a strong gale. A heavy head sea caused the ship to plunge very violently and obliged us to take all sail in but 2 close reef'd topsails & double reef'd main sail. 3 ships in sight. Lat. at noon 55.53 Long. 7°7'W.

Monday 6th. Blowing strong all day with showers of hail & considerable swell. Steered NW.rly by the wind (wind NE) until noon; wore and made more sail. At 6 pm. blowing hard in the showers tacked & reduced sails, supposing ourselves astream of Barra Head Dist. 20 miles. Lat at noon 56.30+[5] Long. 8°33'W. Bar 29.60. <u>Many Fulmars</u>.

Tuesday 7th. Fine weather during the day: set all sails and stood off and on. Lat. at noon 56.32+ Long 8°49'W. Heavy swell from the northward. The Bar kept low and rather subsided: agreeable to its indications, the wind freshened in the evening & towards mid-night blew a gale.[6]

[1] Inishtrahull lighthouse (55°26'N,7°15'W), on an island off the coast of Co. Donegal, had been constructed earlier in the decade.

[2] There were at this time two competing Registers of British shipping: the 'Green Book' published by Lloyd's Register Society, and the 'Red Book' New Register Book of Shipping, also known as the Shipowners' Register.

[3] The name and trumpet identify her as the Greek goddess Pheme (Roman 'Fama'), reputedly a tremendous gossip about the affairs of gods and mortals.

[4] These brackets '[by Hyd.... . 58°]' are in the transcript; they are not editorial inserts.

[5] Possibly '38+', but 30 is more consistent with the noon latitude on the following day.

[6] This Introduction ends close to the foot of a page. Beneath it, there is a pencil note indicating latitudes and longitudes as follows:
'Tues   56.32+   8.49W
Wed   57.27−   9.40W'
Note however that the longitude entry for Wednesday on the following page is an inked entry of 10°40'W, the '10' clearly overwritten over '9'. If nothing else, this implies that the pencil insertions, here and earlier, were broadly contemporaneous with the preparation of the transcript, and not added much later.

[Journal now assumes the usual three-column format.]

Wednesday 8ᵗʰ April Lat. 57.27+ Lon. 10°40′W. Bar. 29.40
E: EbN
All day we had a strong gale with heavy squalls in showers of snow or hail, and tremendous cross sea. The ship was very laboursome. Steered Northward until noon, under two close reef'd topsails & courses, when we wore and furled the courses. The ship rolled so heavily that we were in duced [*sic*] to wear again at 6 pm. to the Nᵈ. The smoke was so intollerable that we were obliged to put the cabin fire out. Our situation was uncomfortable.

Thursday 9ᵗʰ Ap. Lat. 57.36 Lon. 11°47′W. Bar. 29.40.
EbN ENE.
Blowing excessively hard with showers of hail, sleet, & snow. Ship laboursome but tollerably tight. Reached principally to the southward, under two close reefed topsails. T.G. yards on deck.

Friday 10ᵗʰ Ap. Lat. 56.58+ Lon. 10°54′W Bar. 29.60
NE, ENE[,] E,
The wind rather subsided towards noon & in the evening we had moderate weather, squally however with showers of hail or sleet. Made sail in the evening and stood to the Nᵈ. Bar. 29.60.

Saturday 11 April Lat. 57.40+ Lon.11.30′W[1] Bar 29.70
E to NE & NNW to NE
Fine weather in the morning, showery, turbulent sea considering the ['wind' *deleted*] little wind we had. Reached northward until 6 am. then tacked & stood to the Eᵈ. At 10 am. wind shifted suddenly in a shower and blew fresh. It increased so rapidly that by 2 Pm. we were under treble reef'd top sails. At noon, by estimation Stromness Orkney bore ENE (due course) 210′ Barra & Rona Islands[2] ENE¼N = 186′ and Butt of the Lewises ENE[¼?]N 120′. Spec. gravity of the sea at noon by Hydr. Nº 4 = 4°7 below, temp. 60. Temp of the surface 48°. The sea was considerable; but the wind abated towards night and fell nearly to calm.

Sunday 12 April Lat 57.40+ Lon. 9.40 Bar. 29.90 at 10 pm. 29.70
NEbE, Var. E, SE SSE, S.
Light variable winds in the morning with beautifully clear weather. Aired the beds of some of the men which had been wet with the sea having poured down the hatchways

---

[1] Longitude entry a substitution for '9.30 W.' deleted.

[2] By 'Rona' Scoresby was clearly referring to the island now normally known as North Rona (59°7′N 5°49′W). More remote even than St Kilda, it was still inhabited at that time. 'Barra' means the small rocky island of Sula Sgeir, about 10 miles west of North Rona. An alternative spelling was 'Sulisker', and on Blachford's 1846 'chart of the coast of Scotland including Orkney and Shetland Islands', the island is shown as 'Sulisker or Barra'.

during the late Gales. A fresh breeze sprang up at noon – steered E¼N and in the evening East. At 4 pm. saw Sᵗ Kilda bearing ESE and at 8 pm. the same island bore South dist. 20 miles. The weather now became cloudy and again boisterous which reduced us to double reefed top sails & courses: velocity of the ship was 5 to 8 Knots.

Monday 13 April Lat 59.15+ Lon. 6.20 Bar. 29.60 – 50.
SbE. to SSE. S
Strong Gales all day, hazy weather, cross tumultuous sea. Having occasion to call at Orkney or Shetland for the purpose of procuring 6 or 8 men, our present crew being only 44 in number we hauled as close to the wind as the ship could conveniently lay, making a due course little better than NE¼E or NEbE. ['Temp. Sea at surface 46¼.' *in margin*] In the evening the sea was heavy from the westward & considerable from the southward. Passed to the Nᵈ (out of sight) of Barra & Rona, and all land of the British Dominions.[1]

Tuesday 14 April Lat 60.15+ Lon. 3.16W. Bar. 29.55
SbE or S.
Still blowing hard with heavy sea: the motion of the ship, owing to various swells prevailing at the same time, was extremely curious and violent. Carried a brisk sail but fell to leeward of the Orkneys. The wind declined towards mid-night.

Wednesday 15 April Lat 60.50 Lon. 30'W. Bar 29. 70
South.
At 2 am. saw land, viz. the northern extremity of Shetland – which at 6 we passed to leeward of at the distance of 6 miles. Worked briskly to windward and at 8 [pm.?] reached the northern entrance of Balta Sound, but could not in the wind not being suitable & before we could reach the southern entrance, having to work round Balta Island the ebb tide commenced & kept us back. Stood off until midnight, blowing a fresh gale of wind.

Thursday 16 April Bar. 29.70
South SSW
At day break steered in for the land, descried Balta Island and bore away for the harbour. At 6 am. entered the Sound ['Sun rose p Chron. 4.40 am.' *in margin in pencil*] and brought up in the inner harbour. A pilot boat boarded us just as we reached the anchorage.[2]

['Balta Sound.' *in margin*] I immediately sent for an agent to procure me some men but before his arrival several had come on board. I found most of them raw lads; such as had been before to Greenland expected high wages. In the course of the forenoon I engaged 12 young men with the proviso that they should be in readiness early on the ensuing morning as the wind was fair & the season fast advancing. This was a notice

---

[1] Clearly incorrect, since Orkney and Shetland were part of the 'British Dominions'.

[2] Baltasound, on the island of Yell, was a logical alternative to Lerwick for Scoresby, because of his past visits there in 1807 and 1812. See the entries for 12–19 April 1812 in volume I of these journals.

not half so long as they were accustomed to nevertheless seeing I was determined on sailing without them should any of them not be[1] in readiness, they made great exertions to equip themselves with the very scanty ['Baltasound' *in margin*] supplies which the island afforded. Though it boasted different <u>merchants</u> neither sugar, coffee, boots, jackets, or other similar articles could be obtained & even mitts & stockings (of a common kind) though the principal manufacture of the Island were[2] to be had.

All hands now set to work to secure the masts by setting up the rigging, &c. an extra security was adapted for the main stay: the boats skeeds were fitted, the casks in the hold better secured; those in the twin-decks shaked & put up in packs that they might occupy less room; and a variety of other highly useful work which could scarcely be done at sea. The day was particularly favourable for our purpose.

I landed after dinner. The beach was strewed ['150 ['Belugæ' *deleted*] Delphinus [melas? *in pencil*] stranded in 1814. Some remarks on them.' *in margin*] with the skulls of the ['Beluga or' *deleted*] Bottlenose whale, 150 of which animals were driven onshore here four years ago.[3] These skulls bear a very close analogy to those of narwhales both in size & form, neither is the snout so different as might be expected. The principal difference, as far as cursory observation served, consisted in the small teeth of the Beluga[4] and in the want of the sheaths or sockets for the prominent tusks of the narwhales. The practice formerly so inequitable with regard to the division of these animals when driven on shore, has been subjected to some modification, since M[r] Neill visited those Islands.[5] These ['Mode of distribution.' *in margin*] whales when stranded, formerly, were divided into three equal shares – the one belonging to the person who ['had' *deleted*] was endued with the Admiraltyship of the islands, another to the proprietors of the land on which they were taken; and the third to the [salvers?]. The portion usually paid to the deputy ['Usage of distribution modified.' *in margin*] of the Admiral, who always claimed it as for ['his' *deleted*] the Admiral, was first with-held a few years ago. The deputy summoned the[6] fishers to the Sheriff court at Lerwick from whence the cause was transferred to the court at Edinburgh. But Lord Dundass who is possessed of the prerogative of the Admiralty of the Zetland Islands, is said to have declared his disapprobation of the exaction of this tribute and that he would not appear against them. As such the action was suspended and the prizes in question divided into two share – one moiety to the salvers & the other to the land holders on whose property the fish were cast.

[1] Originally 'being'; 'ing' deleted.

[2] 'were not' presumably intended.

[3] Scoresby mentioned this stranding again in *Account of the Arctic Regions*, I, p. 499, and referred (p. 498) to the illustration in II, Plate XIII, Fig. 1. From that engraving, and the description of behaviour, it seems probable that these were not bottlenose dolphins (*Tursiops truncatus*) but pilot whales (*Globicephala melaena*).

[4] It appears that Scoresby neglected to correct this repeated reference to Belugas. In *Account of the Arctic Regions*, I, pp. 496–501, he clearly distinguished between the black 'Ca'ing or Leading Whales' and the white Belugas, and identified those stranded on Shetland as the former.

[5] Neill, *A Tour*, Edinburgh, 1806, p. 221, and so cited in *Account of the Arctic Regions*, I, p. 496.

[6] Originally 'them'; last letter deleted.

Towards to [*sic*] top of the Sound I observed the bones ['Razor back stranded, some account of' *in margin*] of a large whale, of Physalis kind or the Razor Back of the fishers. It was embayed & killed during the winter. It measured 82 feet in length. The jaw bones were 21 feet long and the largest whalebone about 3 feet. It [*sic*] belly & sides about the thorax were <u>ruffled</u> in the way of rugæ[1] running longitudinally in parallel lines. It provided about 5 tons of oil of an inferior quality some of it very viscid and bad. It was valued clear of all expences at 60£ sterling. The whalebone was much stiffer & harder than that of the common whale & the fringe consisted of bristly fibres of whale bone rather than hair. A third of the fish it seems was claimed by the Depute-Admiral.

Friday 17 April[2] Bar. 29.72
S.rly calm. var. E.rly
Light airs or calm; in the evening a moderate breeze; beautiful weather. We were in readiness for sea by 9 am but a calm kept us at rest. In the afternoon we weighed; towed, sailed, & <u>kedged</u>[3] to an anchorage in the ['Balta Sound.' *in margin*] outer Sound where we brought up: but a few minutes afterwards a commanding breeze of wind at EbS sprang up: we immediately weighed, worked out of the south entry and got to sea at 9 pm. We had variable light winds all night and some swell which prevented us making any way: in fact we lost considerable ground. In the ['**Saturday 18 April** Lat. 60.35 Lon. 0.5′W NErly. variable Bar. 29.72′' *in margin*] morning we were opposite to Fetlar Head. 55 hands on board. A sick man William Mc[Kenzie?] mustered at Liverpool, being in a dangerous state was landed at Balta Sound and supplied with money suffi*cie*nt to take him home: furnished partly by myself & partly by subscription from the crew. We supplied his place with John McBride, a seaman from Liverpool. Made little progress during the day.

Having no medical practitioner in the Island of Unst, our surgeon ['Mode of Bleeding in Unst!' *in margin*] had repeated applications from the sick and solicitations to visit other sick persons at a short distance from Balta Sound. ['Having' *deleted*] The inhabitants having recently adopted some improved method of ventilating their cottages attribute an imaginary increase of complaints to the deficiency of their usual quantity of smoke! Two persons only in the Island, it seems have ventured on the operation of Bleeding; the one a midwife cuts the <u>vein across with a razor</u> and the other a school-master uses an old ['ill' *deleted*] abused lancet, which when at all out of order he <u>sharps upon the first stone he</u> ['meets' *deleted*] <u>comes to upon the road.</u>

[The journal is here interrupted by a page devoted to the following table.]

---

[1] OED: 'Ruga ... *Bot. Zool.*, etc. ... A wrinkle, fold, or ridge.'
[2] Scoresby's letter to Sir Joseph Banks concerning the Royal Navy's voyages of arctic exploration bears this date. See Introduction, p. xxxiii.
[3] Smyth, *Sailor's Word Book*: 'To kedge. To warp a ship a-head, though the tide be contrary, by means of the kedge-anchor and hawser.'

Names of the Fames Crew & their distribution into 3 watches and six Boat's Crews.

Mate's Watch	Specksioneer's Watch	Captain's Watch
Wm Clark; Ch^{f} Mate 1st off^{r}	John Dawson Specksion^{r}	George Welborn: 2^{d} Mate.
Thos Townsend. Boatst^{r}	Edw Clark. Boatsteerer	Peter Swinny. B.
Robt Boyd, Linecoyler.	Wm Wilson. Lineman	Robt Meldrum. L.
John Hughes. Seaman	James Young Seam^{n}	Robt Howland. Sea.
Robt Goodile	John Lace	Joseph Blacker
Arthur Harrison	And^{w} Matthewson	Joseph Park
Magnus Walterson }[1]	Wm Jones }	Owen Owens }
James Russel }	Charles Spence }	And^{w} Sinclair }
Thos Lashley: Harpooner	[Law?]:[2] Harp^{r}	John Anderson. H.
John Skinner: B.	John [Tiboad?]. B	Wm Shepherd. B.
John O'Neal L.	Henry Richards L.	Charles Evans L.
John Clark. Seaman	John McBride Seam^{n}	W^{m} [Clucus?] Seam.
John Brown	R^{d} Oldcroft	James Manson
Thos. Turner	Fred^{k} Stickl.	Matt^{w} Johnson
Wm Nesbit }	Wm Harrison }	W^{m} [Barniele?] }
Hugh Hughes }	John Peters }	– Matthews }
Geo. Smith }	Wm Skelton }	John Pearson }

Also ...

Self:

Thomas Latta: Surgeon.

Thos Robson; Steward.

Matt^{w} Robinson. Armourer

In all 55 men & Boys

Sunday 19 April Lat. 60.41+ Lon. 0°20'W Bar. 29.72
NE.rly ENE Var.
Light variable winds, squally with Showers of snow, hail, or sleet. With difficulty weathered the Island of Balta, but still could not double the northern promontory.

Monday 20 April Lat 61.10 Lon. 39'W. Bar. 29.73
Still light winds and variable: fine weather. Doubled the N end of Shetland and proceeded by the wind to the North. All hands employed in fitting various fishing apparatus; the carpenters caulking decks, drying cable and warps, painting new work &c. &c. &c.

[1] All the men whose names are linked by the braces are categorized as 'Extra'.

[2] The name 'Thos Lashley' is repeated from the first column, but deleted, and 'Law' [?] inserted above the deletion. However, from the entry for 17 May 1817, it appears that this harpooner was named 'Ladley' or, if he was related to the harpooner in the Mate's watch, 'Lashley'. 'Law' may be an abbreviation for 'Lawrence'.

Snow showers occasionally. At 9ʰ41′25″ Appᵗ time, an alt. of the Sun (supposing the N end of Shetland to lie in long. 38′W.[1]) gave the Chronometer slow of Greenwich 3′39″ and its daily rate gaining 10″.

Tuesday 21 April Lat. 61°30′ Lon. 1°W. Bar. 29.74–80
NE.rly Var. ENE NbE, E
A heavy NE.rly swell arose about noon and the rising cloud and increasing gloom of the atmosphere in the northern horizon, threatened a storm: the barometer however did not fall, and its indication proved correct for though the sky continued threatening and the swell increased no storm commenced. Rain,[2] Sleet, snow, &c. in the evening. Close hauled by the wind sometimes one tack & sometimes the other.

Wednesday 22 April Lat 62°o Lon. 1°20′W Bar.29.72
N. NW NE.rly. E.rly.
Blowing a fresh breeze, squally with a few showers of snow. Very heavy NE.rly swell. All hands employed preparing the fishing apparatus. Carpenter caulking waterways armourers, [blockmakers?], joiner, & riggers, employed in various needful ['occupations' *deleted*] work. Close hauled by the wind; ['Aur. Borealis; seen' *in margin*] standing principally to the Eastward.

Thursday 23 April Lat. 62°30′ Lon. 1°34′E Bar. 29.70.
NbE
A strong breeze with squalls and showers of snow or hail throughout the day. Very heavy swell from the N. or NE. Stood all day to the Eastward.
    Saw a great number of the ['<u>Beluga</u>' *deleted, replaced by* 'Bottlenose' *in pencil*] Whale, running southward. ['Aurora Borealis, seen' *in margin*]

Friday 24 April Lat. 62.46 Lon. 3°50′E
N. Var. NNW
Blowing strong with showers of snow, and high northeasterly swell the former part of the day. Less wind in the afternoon near calm. All day reaching to the eastward. Thermometer 32–34°.

Saturday 25 April Lat. Lon.[3] Bar. 29.72
Var. Calm. E. EbN. to NE
An easterly wind sprung up in the morning – made all sail upon a NNE to N. course. Employed all hands again in fitting apparatus for the fishery. <u>Sea Green</u>. The coast of <u>Norway</u> was seen at 7 am. bearing SbE, distant 30 or 40 miles. The sea was yet very rough.

---

    [1] Muckle Flugga lighthouse is at 54′W; the north coast extends some distance east of this, but not as far as 38′W.
    [2] This word is either crossed through or underlined.
    [3] The abbreviations are written, but no values inserted.

Sunday 26 April Lat 64.0 Lon.[1] Bar. 29.76 – 30.05.
ENE to E. & NEbE
Moderate of [2] fresh breezes of wind – fine clear weather but most tumultuous sea. The swell rolled from the NE. with amazing violence, indication a heavy tempest at the distance ['Heavy swells from the N. & NE. during 7 days without wind' *in margin*] of a very few leagues. It is worthy of remark that this is the 7th day in succession on which a considerable swell from the N. or NE. has prevailed, and doubtless a little to the northward of our situation a storm has prevailed during the week whilst we have never, except in an occasional squall, had more than a top-gall*an*t breeze. It is therefore probable we are not much in the rear of the large fleet which had some days the start of us from Shetland. In the evening the swell rather subsided; wind fresh breeze.

Monday 27 April Lat. Lon. Bar. 29.04. Ther. 34.
NEbE ENE
Fine cloudy weather with a moderate or brisk breeze of wind. Proceeded under all sails towards the N & NbW, close hauled by the wind. The sea being smooth for the first time since we left Shetland, though the wind was not fair yet we made considerable progress towards the north & west. Cloudy W[r].

Tuesday 28 April Lat. Lon. Bar. 30.20 Ther. 32°.
ENE to E. Var.
Light variable winds, towards evening a fresh breeze, with dense cloudy atmosphere. At 5 am. saw a fishing ship ahead 10 or 15′ distant & at 9½ pm. passed under her lee about half a mile off! Erected an insulated conductor of electricity ['Electricity of the Atmosphere tried.' *in margin*] 8 feet above the main top Gall*an*t mast head & formed a <u>wire</u> communication with the deck; but no signs of electricity were exhibited with Bennet's gold leaf electrometer.[3] NB. The electrometer each time it was in the air could not be excited with glass or wax until warmed.

Wednesday 29 April Lat. 69.40 Lon. 6°W Bar. ['29' *deleted*] 30.05 Ther. 30
E. EbN. to EbS.
Moderate winds, fine cloudy weather. Sea particularly smooth. At 3 am left the ship seen yesterday out of sight on the weather quarter. Course NbE, generally 7 knots p hour, close hauled by the wind. At noon, saw a blink of ice or land, ahead of the ship and at 1 Pm. from the masthead saw Beerenberg, Jan Mayen, distinctly from the masthead. ['Jan Mayen seen' *in margin*] bearing p compass NbE – NbE¼N; at 1½ Pm. it was visible from the deck.

---

[1] No longitude value is inserted, and no values for either latitude or longitude for the next two days.

[2] *Sic*: 'or' presumably intended.

[3] Nowadays termed an 'electroscope', and invented in 1786 by Revd Abraham Bennet (1749–99). There are illustration of Bennet's and other electroscopes at http://physics.kenyon.edu/EarlyApparatus/Static_Electricity/Electroscope/Electroscope.html, and Bennet's description of his instrument, as published in The Royal Society's *Philosophical Transactions*, 77, 1787, pp. 26–34, is reproduced at http://www.wirksworth.org.uk/BEN-PT-1.htm.

It is observable that we have not seen the sun during three ['The effect of land or ice to clear the air, with N, W, or E winds' *in margin*] days, and yet over the land the air is perfectly free from clouds. Land or ice when compact has usually this effect.[1]

At 8 Pm. saw a piece of ice. The ship's velocity at this time 'close hauled' & 'sails lifting' was 8 knots and about a point off the wind it was 9 miles per hour. Again tried the electricity ['Elect. of Atm' *in margin*] of the atmosphere, when the air was full of low clouds and threatened showers, but no electricity was apparent.[2]

Falling in with much brash ice, interspersed with some heavy pieces , and the wind veering directly on the ice, at ['Beerenberg seen $\frac{100'}{95}$ off from the deck.' *in margin*] 9½ Pm. tacked Beerenberg then bearing N¼E, dist*a*nt 30 miles. Since Beerenberg was seen from the deck we had advanced directly towards it per log 50 miles and it was yet at least 45 dist*a*nt if not 50, making the distance visible at 16 feet elevation 95 or 100 miles. as appears by subsequent observ*a*tion[.]*[3] Snow showers.

Thursday 30 April Lat.70.34 Lon. 6°54'+W. Bar. 30.25 Ther. 29–30.
EbS, E, Var.
Light winds or fresh breezes. Fine clear weather. Stood off and on of the ice during the night. At 10 am. p chron*o*meter Beerenberg bore N. p compass 47' Dis. At 10ʰ 2'45" Am p chron*o*meter ☉'s true alt. (mean of 3 obs.) 30°21', whence the long. of the ship = 6°54'W. And by mer*idi*an alt of Sun lat. = 70°31'21" run between 10 am. Due Course NbW dist. 14'; whence long. at noon = 7°2W. At noon Beerenberg bore NWbN (due course) Dist. = 33 and <u>SW</u> Cape WNW¾W dist*a*nt ... miles. Tried Atmosp. Elect. but found no signs of excitement.

['Killed 10 Seals. Volcano in action' *in margin*] Reached a few miles into loose ice, brash streams, where we saw a few seals & killed 10 young ones. About 2 Pm. we observed thick volumes of smoke occasionally rising from (apparently) Egg Island, which ascended at intervals. As this is quite a volcanic country we took it be some volcano which has begun to act. I conceived it possible a shipwrecked crew might have taken refuge here, but saw no signal though I minutely examined from mast-head all the adjoining hills.[4] Stood out to Sea.

---

[1] Cold air passing over a relatively warmer ocean is warmed and evaporates moisture from the sea surface. But as this air rises and cools, its saturation vapour pressure decreases and the moisture is condensed out as clouds or fog.

[2] The clouds were unlikely to have the large vertical development characteristic of thunderstorms, so no electrical activity was to be expected.

[3] Note in margin: '*NB. The cliffs where the icebergs are situated were <u>visible: they are 1284 fᵗ high</u> hence the distance = 46.' It is possible that 'visible' could be read as 'invisible', but this is unlikely, because the marginal note implies a trigonometrical estimate of the distance from the ship that would depend on the cliffs being visible.

[4] Scoresby elaborated on this in *Account of the Arctic Regions*, I, pp. 166–7: 'From about the north side of Egg Island, near Esk Mount, we were surprised with the sight of considerable jets of smoke discharged from the earth, at intervals of every three or four minutes. At first, we imagined the smoke was raised by some sailors, having suffered the calamity of shipwreck; but after person-ally examining the phenomenon from the mast-head, for upwards of an hour, I was convinced that it could be nothing else than the feeble action of a volcano. The smoke was projected with great velocity, and seemed to rise to twice the height of the land, or about 4000 feet.'

Friday 1 May Lat. 70.50 Lon. 6.50W

E. ESE, SEbE

The wind still prevailed from the eastward, and blew a fresh breeze. Stretched in among the ice, which principally consisted of pancake (bay) ice, intermixed with massy lumps, formed into streams and extensive patches, until 6 pm, when we reached the borders of continuous and unvarying pack, extending towards the land & ['State of the ice' *in margin*] the edge lying NEbE & SWbW. This pack was bay & heavy ice intermixed. Saw no seals in it, returned to the S^d by the wind and came up with a foreign brig which I went on board off [*sic*]. She had procured 2000 seals to the westward of Jan Mayen & was now on her way to the whale fishery stations of Spitzbergen, together with a brig & ship to lee-ward of us; all of which were to windward in the morning. From a list furnished to me by the captain of the Harmonie (the name of the brig) it appears that 53 sail of whale & seal fishers have been fitted ['Hamburgh measures' *in margin*] from the Elbe & the Weser for the fishing of the present season. The Harmonie's seals, filled 60 [quardeclen?] of blubber equal to 200 tons (Hamburgh) of oil. 224 Hamburgh [lb?] ['Expence of a foreign fisher' *in margin*] are a ton. This vessel which seemed to be about 250 tons burthen, new, doubled with about 6 inch oak nearly fore and aft and trebled with about 2 inch plank, fitted and victualled for sea cost (this year) only 74,000 marks =16^d English each or £4933..6..8 sterling: the same kind of vessel in England, with 7 boats & 50 men, as this has, would not have cost less than 6500 to 7000£.

In the evening reached out to sea.

Saturday 2 May Lat. 71.10 Lon. 6°20'W

ESE EbS

Plying all day to the eastward under a brisk sail, generally with a fresh ['gale' *deleted*] breeze of wind; weather cloudy. In the evening clear; an appearance resembling aurora borealis during the ['Appearance like Aur. Borealis in the day. No signs of electricity!' *in margin*] day light. The ships in company yesterday: nearly out of sight leeward – five sail came within sight of, to windward, and gained rapidly upon them. Beerenberg in sight at 10 pm. distant 40–45 miles bearing W. per Compass.

Sunday 3^d May Lat. 71°34'+ Lon. 5°28'+

EbS

Moderate or fresh breezes, fine weather: in the night a fresh gale. Came up with & passed three of the five vessels which only appeared in sight yesterday and approached very near the other two. Hence we conceive the Fame sails amazingly fast by the wind. Hitherto we have seen no vessel, she has not decidedly beat, and that in a distinguished manner. Several foreign seal fishers hove in sight about 4 Pm. some of which were steering to the SWbW. One was a small schooner, the rest were principally brigs. Sent a boat onboard of a brig, which had come from lat. 73° & only got[1] 100 seals. Many of these sealers have no apparatus for the whalefishing.

---

[1] Originally 'gotten'; 'ten' deleted.

Monday 4 May Lat. 72°1' Lon. 4°20'W.

EbS to SEbE SSE, SbE

Our longitude on the 30ᵗʰ April at 10 am. was 6°54'W. by chron*ome*ter. From thence steered (due course) NbW 14' to [noon?] & observed in lat. 70.31: hence our long at noon 7°2'W (Diff. long. being 8') Beerenberg at this time bore NWbN¼N (due course); N. p compass, 10' as ascertained by its diff. lat. and bearing 2¾; whence ['Longitude of Jan Mayen, proved.' *in margin*] the departure 20'.6 and diff. long = 12'W+ long ship 7°2 = 8°4'W long. of Beerenberg. By former observation last year the long was found to be 7°35½' difference 28½' of long. or 9½ geogr. miles or 1'54" of time. But as our distance on the present occasion was considerable and as the rate of chron*ome*ter was only determined from the long of the N. end of Shetland at some distance, which might be inaccurate, the former observation is of course more satisfactory. It was pleasing however to find, that the difference was not greater.[1]

Made great efforts all day to get to windward and succeeded well. We were amongst much loose & bay ice, in the morning: at 11 Am reached to seaward until 3 pm & then tacked. Thick snow then commenced together with a gale of wind. Stretched to the ENE until 11 pm. when meeting much heavy ice in violent & dangerous agitation with the sea, we wore and under reduced sail stood to the SWᵈ.

The shaking of the mast & force of the wind broke the ['my' *deleted*] insulating glass rod of my electrical apparatus & the rod, & appendages were lost. Several ships near us. The top Gall*ant* yard (main) being sprung sent it down.

Tuesday 5 May Lat. 72°30' Lon. 3°0'E[2]

SbE to SSW, SW

Blowing strong with impenetrable snow or mist during the morning; which induced us to stand off the ice or rather obliquely off until 3 Am then wore. Steered SEbE until 8 am. & then perceiving less ice we bore up E. and made all sail possible.

The Carpenters having finished a new main top Gall*ant* yard, it was sent up at 4 Pm.

The weather cleared at noon: saw 2 or 3 ships: steered ENE at 4 Pm. and afterwards, made good speed, with the first fair wind since we passed the Isle of Man!!

Wednesday 6ᵗʰ May Lat. 74.40 Lon 1°44E

W, NW NNW, &c. var.

Steered NE principally, after passing some loose ice and patches which obliged us to haul for a short time to the eastward. Saw no ice during the day, after about 10 am. The weather being mild and fine, we commenced coyling whale lines and had all the boats completely fitted for the fishery before night.

['Coyled lines' *in margin*] As each of the boat's lines were finished, three cheers from the crew announced ['the effec' *deleted*] event, and it seems was heartily urged as a usual <u>invokative</u>[3] [*sic*] of "good luck". Passed 6 sail of ships and came up with two others, one of which, however outsailed us in her turn, in the evening when the breeze abated. Nearly calm in the night.

---

[1] In fact, it was the 1818 determination that was more accurate; the *Times Atlas* gives the longitude of Beerenberg as 8°5'W.

[2] Corrected from 'W' deleted.

[3] Not in *OED*, where 'invokative' is included only as an adjective.

Thursday 7 May Lat. 75.39 Lon. 2°40′E.

Var. EbS, SE to SW

An easterly wind commenced in the morning accompanied by much snow: it veered gradually to the SE, S, & SW, freshening as it veered & the snow ceasing was followed by fog. At 10 Pm. a strong gale had arisen & the weather was somewhat clearer. Courses steered NNE, NEbE, NE, NEbN, and as soon as the fog disappeared, North. No ice was seen throughout the day. All the harpooners dined with me, when I took occasion to give them various directions for their conduct in the fishery, exhorting them to harmony, activity, & perseverance.

Friday 8 May Lat. 78°10′ Lon. 5°10′E

SW to W. WNW

Strong gales; dark cloudy weather. About 3 am. fell in with loose ice & streams, steered E half an hour & then NEbN. At 9 am. ice again interrupted us; bore away ESE, E, ENE to NE and then hauled up to North at noon. Spitzbergen appeared at 11 am. bearing ['Saw Spitzbergen' *in margin*] NEbE distant 40 miles. Saw a <u>whale</u> at 7 am. but the sea being transparent blue indicated it to be a whale ['Saw a Whale' *in margin*] of passage only. We therefore proceeded forward as we could not lower a boat on account of the sea & wind. Continued by the wind to the North, until 9 pm. when we tacked for shelter, having proceeded 2 hours from beneath the lee of some heavy streams and met a strong swell from the NNW. We also found our distance from the land less than we could have wished, though it was still probably 15 miles distant, whereas in the snow, it seemed not more than 3 or 4. Plyed to windward all night amongst loose ice and heavy streams with smooth sea.

Saturday 9 May Lat 78.30 Lon. 6.20

NWbW [W, NbE?]

In the morning we had light winds and fine clear w^r occasionally calm. Exercised the Shetland men and others in ['to' *deleted*] the manner of rowing the whaleboats. The sea having frozen over in the morning and we being in danger of being arrested by it, made all efforts to reach the northern water. Succeeded in passing the sea stream at 2 pm. 3 ships in sight. Stood to the NW.

At 1½ Pm. I took the following angles and bearings on Charles' Island or the Foreland. ['Observations at 1½ pm. for determining the height of the mountains of Charles Island' *in margin*]

| | | Bearing of Middle Hook | |
		At 2½ pm	At 3½pm
(Southern ['Hill' *deleted*] Mountain)	E.12°N =	E 3°N. =	E 3°S
North End of Foreland ...	E 50 N =	E 45 N =	E 43°N
South end . ——	E 45 S =	E 50½ S.	——

Ship's course between   1½ pm & 2½ pm = NbW distance 3½ miles.

     2½ —— 3½   = NbW —— 3 ——

Altitudes: Middle Hook Southern Mount = $1°36'$
   at 2^d ———————————————   1.31
$1\frac{1}{2}$ pm.   3 ———————————————   1.30½
          4 ———————————————   1.29
          5 (northern mountain of the five) 1.32

Made the following experiments with seal & sperma-ceti oils. The seal oil was extracted 4th of May & the sperma-ceti oil, purchased at Liverpool and declared to be genuine.

Two thirds the fill of a wine glass of each was taken on deck, in two wine glasses and exposed to a temperature of 22°. The following ['Experiments on the quality & freezing of oils' *in margin*][1] alterations took place; viz.

Seal oil.	Temperature	Sperma-ceti oil.
[NB. Poured off clear at the temp. of 40°]		
No apparent change	32½	First crystals about the edge of the glass observed.
A little less limpid but no change in colour	28	Generally obscure & much thickened. of the consistence of starch or thick cream.
Ditto	25	In colour and consistence resembling honey – still however semi fluid like.
Semi-transparent: little alteration indeed except a small thickening, which yet was not greater than the sperm oil was at first!	23	So thick that it would not run out of the glass though turned over and laid for several minutes on its side.
No change	39	First vestige of cloudiness.
	38	Generally obscure, semi transp*aren*t
	40	Perfectly transparent

Second Experiment 12 May

Seal oil perfectly Transparent		Spermaceti oil as before
Unaltered	33	Quite cloudy; congealed on the edges.
First exhibited signs of a streaky cloudiness, very faint & subsequently did not alter	32	Ditto
So clear that the smallest print (diamond type) was easily read through a body of it in a wine glass, about ¼ an inch thick & still so limpid that it readily left the bulb of the thermometer in drops!	14	Thick as soft soap.

[1] Across the middle of the table is a sentence in pencil, the latter half of which is illegible: 'NB repeat this experiment with [linseed?] oil; ...'

Sunday 10 May Lat. Lon.[1]

N.erly

Fine weather: wind light or moderate breeze. At 3 am. fell in with ice: the first we saw after leaving the land ice. Plyed to windward, by and in it – occasionally passing close streams. Saw 10 ships, but communicated with none of them. In the evening, being near much ice, ships around us seeing fish, and the colour of the water (olive green & very turbid) being excellent for fishing we lay too and soon after a whale pursued by the boats of the Juno passed us. Lay too all night.

Monday 11 May Lat. Lon.

NEbE to NbW

The wind increased to a fresh gale, and snow showers prevailed. Made sail at 8 am. and stretched into crowded ice in various winding and obscure channels during 7 or 8 hours. At 3 pm. saw a whale: three boats went in pursuit & on its next appearance, the indiscretion of a harpooner in rowing up towards it when ill situated whilst an adjoining boat was in the [back?][2] position, alarmed it and it escaped, after allowing the boats to approach it with 8 or 9 yards. Soon afterwards we saw another, ['and it' *deleted*] which was also alarmed by the approach of a boat; nevertheless it allowed its advance to within a boat's length, when the inertness[3] of harpooner, permitted it to escape without hurt. A third whale was seen about 9 pm. & was long pursued by <u>five</u> boats but without success. Dodged in an opening during the night. Keen frost thermom*eter* 14°. This day I spent 11 hours at the mast head, where the temperature was from 16 to 10°.

Tuesday 12 May Lat. 78.6+ Lon.

NNW, NW. &c.

Blowing strong in the morning, with clear atmosphere & keen frost. It was remarkable that with a temperature of 14° under such circumstances there was no appearance of <u>frost rime</u>. ['<u>Frost rime</u>: not seen at a low temper.' *in margin*] Leslie's hyg.[4] pointed out only 2° of dryness, though the sun was so powerful that the sides of the ship were heated to 70 or 80°.

   Saw a whale at 6 am. which gave us a fruitless chase of 4 or 5 hours. A heavy S.rly swell penetrating the ice, no other whales appearing, & there being some risk of our getting frozen up or otherwise beset we spent the day in our progress towards the sea; the margin of which we did not reach before 10 pm. In our progress (4 Pm.) a whale rose close by the ship, but dived under the ship's keel before a boat could reach it. Afterwards, it was slightly entangled by one of our harpooners, and ran out 1½ lines: the harpoon then came out. Thus again [stronger?] hopes of success were excited and as speedily blasted. These circumstances though very mortifying to human nature,

---

   [1] Although these abbreviations are inserted in the margin, there are no entries for latitude until 12 May, or for longitude until 13 May.

   [2] Possibly 'best'.

   [3] Presumably a transcription error for 'ineptness'.

   [4] See journal entries for 21 May 1816 and 5 May 1817.

are¹ doubtless ['their' *deleted*] designed for some beneficial end by the author of our being and Salvation.

In the evening 25 ships were in sight.

Our navigation out of the ice was hazardous and difficult. ['Ice roaring² in a swell' *in margin*] The ice was in such violent motion, and the drift of the pieces so dissimilar that it was impossible to avoid the whole. We only struck one piece of any magnitude. The roaring of the sea upon the sides of the ice was like the raging of a storm upon a sloping beach.

The sea beginning to freeze we steered to the south-eastward during the night and soon obtained a situation [froze?]³ of every description of ice.

Wednesday 13 May Lat. 78. 0 Lon. 4°20′E
SSW, W. to NW & NNE

Light or moderate winds; seeing no whales in the sea we approached the ice; ran to the northward within the sea streams and in the evening hauled in to the ice to the NNWᵈ. At 10 pm. lay too. Upwards of 30 ships seen.

Thursday 14 May Lat. 78°27′+ Lon. 3°55′
NE to E & SE

Light variable winds. Early in the morning steered to the NW or NNW among much loose ice: at 10 am. were surrounded with bay ice & at 2 pm. were nearly as far west as we could get. The wind veering to the SE we steered to the Sᵈ and saw a whale which we pursued but without effect. Began to ply to the ENE amidst much ice. Saw a <u>running</u> fish at 11 pm. it afforded us a chase of some hours and then took alarm on the near approach of one of the boats.

Friday 15 May Lat. 78.35 Lon. 4.20E
SE.rly. SEbS

Inclinable to Calm. Lay too great part of the day. Made the following Experiments on the specific gravity of ice.⁴

Took three masses of ice of different qualities; allowed the salt water to run from them and washed them in clean fresh water; the most porous was allowed to drain a [*sic*] warm place. This done each of the pieces were alternately weighed immersed in fresh water at the freezing temperature, upon deck where the temp. of the air was 30°, having a copper ball attatched to them to sink them, and then being dried with a <u>cold</u>

---

¹ Originally 'have' and then amended, presumably to conform with the subsequent deletion of 'their'.

² Could also be read as 'rearing', which might be more expected; however 'roaring' is consistent with the main text.

³ A transcription error: 'free' intended?

⁴ See footnote to journal entry for 12 July 1817: it was these results in 1818 that Scoresby emphasized in Appendix VIII to volume I of *Account of the Arctic Regions*. The numerical values in that appendix are identical to those here, but the text headings were made more easily understandable, and the positive and negative signs in the last column of rows 1 and 2 (but not 3) are absent.

towel were weighed in air without ['any' *deleted*] the copper ball, and the following results were obtained; viz.[1] ['Specific Gravity of *Ice* accurately determined' *in margin*]

	Weight (grams)					
	In air.	In fresh w^r with Ball	W^t of ball in water	The ice less heavy than its bulk of water	W^t of an equal bulk W^r	Specific gravity to W^r at 32°
Transparent fresh water ice without a visible pore	3333	1922	2233	311	3644	0.9146+
Semitransp*arent* ice from a <u>tongue</u> of saltwater ice; tasted fresh	3661	1898	2233	335	3996	0.9162−
Bay ice, porous, and opaque when drained tasted nearly quite fresh	4892	1838	2233	395	5287	0.925 +
Copper ball (bolt copper[2])	2515		2233		282	8.918

It is curious that the most ['dense' *deleted*] solid ice appears to have the least specific gravity, and the most porous the greatest. The latter (Bay ice) obtained its spec. grav. by containing much water in its pores which I could not properly drain out. It now appears that all solid ice is of the same specific gravity within an unit or two in the third place of decimals. The above experiments were performed to a gram or two at the most, and as the temp. of the air was so favourable that no melting could occur during the experiments.

In the evening a breeze of wind springing up at SEbS made a stretch to the SW and in the middle of an open patch found a whale. It was pursued by 2 boats and the mate succeeded in shooting it with a harpoon from the harpoon gun & the next instant had the opportunity of fastening or striking his hand harpoon also. This was about mid-night.

Saturday 16 May Lat. 78°26′ Lon. [*blank space*]
Variable all round the compass. SSE to ESE
In about 35 minutes the fish appeared blowing furiously a mixture of blood and air and dying the sea around with a stream of blood issuing from an immense

[Wm Clark F 20 T N°. 1 = 10.6 *in margin*]

---

[1] At the beginning of the following table there are several deletions, clearly due to the transcriber's errors in the initial layout of the table. It is unnecessary to repeat them here. The word 'grams' has also been transferred to the title; in the transcript it appears above the first numerical entry '3333'.

[2] The phrase is clearly written, but is not in *OED*. However, 'bolt copper' appears to have been a fairly common term in the 19th century, perhaps especially in the United States. See for example a description of a copper mill in New Jersey: 'At one time the plant was turning out 350 tons of sheet and bolt copper per year' (http://www.firstbaptistbloomfield.org/belleville.htm).

gash in her body produced by the gun harpoon. The boats were all at a distance expecting her appearance elsewhere. During their advance, the fish after blowing a few times fell over on its side & erected its fin, with every appearance of ['Actions of the struck whale & effect of harpoon Gun.' *in margin*] being dead. After laying thus a few minutes, it roused, on inhaling a quantity of water, which was evident from

['Wm Clark A narwhale' *in margin*][1]

the bubbling it made at the surface, and commenced a circular motion. It however never disappeared longer than a few seconds until it was secured by three more harpoons and ['Profusion of blood from the fish' *in margin*] mortally wounded with lances. It died about 1½ AM. It proved a fine prize. The flinching operation was not concluded of near 12 hours owing to the extreme awkwardness of some ['Fulmars, character of' *in margin*] of our officers. We were surrounded by an immense number of burgomasters, kittywakes, and fulmars. The latter however was prominent as to its boldness greediness, and the voracity of its appetite, which it continued to gorge until it could scarcely get to a piece of ice on which to rest during the process of ['Shark: gorge [***]' *in margin*] digestion. A very large shark, apparently 10 or 12 feet long and at least 7 or 8 in circumference, appeared near the fish and was killed. In its stomach or rather its belly we found I suppose 150 to 200 lb weight of blubber which it had scarfed from the whale and its liver filled a cask of 60 gallons capacity or above 400 lb. weight!

During the capture of the whale the lancers as well as their ['Size of male narwhale' *in margin*] boats were literally covered with blood discharged from the blowholes[2] of the fish. The mate also killed a narwhale: a male, with a tusk about 4 feet long externally. The length of the body including the tail but excluding the tusk was 12½ fᵗ and its greatest circumference; two feet <u>behind</u> the fins 8 feet. The blubber filled a cask of about 120 gallons. In the cavity adjoining the ear were thousands of living ascarides[3] the size of common sewing needles. large worms in the stomach.*[4]

Sunday 17 May Lat. 78.36 Lon. 1°30′E
East
The wind had increased about midnight and soon afterwards blew a strong gale. Previously, however, having stood

['Law. Ladley[5] M 15T Nº 2 = 9.6' in margin]

---

[1] This marginal entry has the whale tail at approximately one-third the size of the normal size, as used for 'No. 1' in the same column.

[2] The bowhead has four blowholes, arranged in pairs (Haldiman & Tarpley, 'Anatomy and Physiology', in Burns, *Bowhead Whale*, p. 90 & Fig. 4.2A). Scoresby believed that there were two blowholes (*Account of the Arctic Regions*, I, p. 456).

[3] *Ascarides* are intestinal worms, but the meaning is clear.

[4] The following marginal note may have been placed there only in order to complete the day's entry without needing a new page. '*The stomach full of sepiae & shrimps.'

[5] *Sic.* See note on crew list, 18 April 1817.

to the NNE a distance of 10 or 12 miles in open ice, we fell in with 3 or 4 whales and had the happiness of entangling one of them. It died after two or three hours. The lines of the first harpooner were slipped by the harpooner for want of assistance, but were recovered as soon as the fish was killed. The ice about us being rather heavy, the fragments of some field or floe recently broken, I conceived it desirable to moor the ship; this we effected after much trouble to two of the largest pieces we could meet with, hanging the ship by the stern as the ice was not sufficiently heavy to keep her clear of pieces to leeward. We had much trouble in getting the fish alongside, so that it was 11 am. before we began to flinch, and late in the afternoon before we finished.

In the evening we had much heavy ice about us; the wind blowing hard and the weather thick with snow.

Monday 18 May
East ENE
Strong gales with thick snow most generally. I felt thankful[1] in being comfortably situated during this gale. No sea amongst us and the ice from to leeward but seldom troubled us. Saw a whale about noon & two others in the evening: prepared to make off.

<u>On oil</u>. Some narwhale oil extracted by boiling on Saturday ['Experiments on Narwhale oil to ascertain the nature and properties thereof' *in margin*] last was put to the test of some experiments as to its congelation &c. A quantity poured off clear at temp. 34° remained transparent for several degrees below, but at the bottom of the vessel I found a white substance [concreted?] in the way of honey, from which I filtered the oil at temp. 38°and by pressure procured a substance which to use the words of the ['Doctor' *deleted*] Surgeon resembled "<u>a good stiff turnip poultice</u>". It was firmer than [***] and nearly as ['perfectly' *deleted*] white, but granular in its texture. A quantity of it was melted and filtered at 75° temp. & reserved for future experiment. It dissolved at about 60 to 70°. Query, Is it any thing allied to sperma-ceti? This substance separated prevents fish oil from freezing.

Tuesday 19 May Lat. 78.10 Lon. 0°50W
ENE
Tempestuous gloomy weather. Had some difficulty in holding the ship with two occa-sionally three ropes & as many pieces of ice, our ice-anchors sometimes flying out. Commenced making off about 2 am. in the fore hold.

Observed a close pack within two or three miles of us to the ['west' *deleted*] North-ward along the edge of which we regularly drifted, passing through various streams & patches: loosing from one piece of ice and fastening to another larger, as it was passed by the ship. A ship seen to the eastward under ['way' *deleted*] sail.

The frost very keen therm. 18° ropes ends having[2] overboard ['Ice-<u>pears</u> on ropes' *in margin*] have a pear-shaped mass of ice formed on them which in some instances becoming too ponderous for the strength of the rope break it and carry it away.

---

[1] This word appears to have been deleted, but the sentence is meaningless without it.
[2] 'hanging' intended?

Hitherto we had had the cabin at all times warm, seldom ['Temp of cabin freezing' *in margin*] indeed was the temp. below 50° or 60° whereas since this storm commenced it has usually been at or below the freezing point.

Wednesday 20 May Lat. 77.55 Lon. 0.55W
NE
Hard gales: clear weather. Finished making off, after having filled 45 with whale's blubber and one butt with unicorn blubber making in capacity 100 butts. Having drifted to the very edge of a heavy pack and being nearly surrounded with ice we prepared to 'get on the way'. But whilst we set the sails the ['Made off 46 casks 100 butts' *in margin*] last anchor broke out of the ice and was lost – the ship however happily escaped without hitting any of the ice. Proceeded to the eastward a few miles into a large opening towards the head of which we plied and then lay too. 3 ships in sight. ['Lat. mid-n^t 77°55″ *in margin*]

Thursday 21 May Lat. 77.57 Lon. 0°40′W
NNE to NNW or NW
About mid-night the gale having abated to a strong breeze we made sail and by a very difficult & somewhat hazardous navigation worked through a body of loose drift ice, into an extensive opening lying to the North. Here under a pressure of sail we beat up towards the North and at the extremity of the opening saw a number of fish, in ['pur' *deleted*] chace [*sic*] of which we sent all our boats, one that was stove with the ice excepted. In the course of the forenoon the mate struck a whale at a distance from the ship & all the boats but one. It ran out 13 lines (1560 fa*thom*s) in the direction of a heavy pack of floe and drift ice recently broken from floes

['Wm Clark **M 15 T** N°3 = 10.9' *in margin*][1]

the edge of which it reached as two boats came up with it, struck 2 more harpoons and presently dispatched it. Made the ship fast to a large piece of ice and took the fish alongside: we had scarcely commenced flinching before the windward ice poured down upon us, urged by a large floe, and surrounded us in the space of a few minutes. We escaped <u>stern first</u>, after considerable exertion and completed the flinching in an adjoining hole of water. The wind was very light towards evening and the atmosphere beautifully clear. The sun was so bright at <u>midnight</u> that the darkest skreen[2] ever required for observations was requisite in taking an altitude below the pole, in the mid-night of the preceding day & of the present. 20 ships in sight to the eastward.

Friday 22 May Lat 78.0 Lon. 1°W
NW. W.rly, Var.
Light winds, inclinable to calm: ['beautifully' *deleted*] fine weather cloudy. Saw a number of whales in the course of the 24 hours, but the formation of bay ice, always

---

[1] Beneath this entry is the additional note 'Taken with a single barbed harpoon, which held admirably & scarcely drew at all from its original situation.'
[2] Originally 'sckreen'; 'c' deleted.

hindered the approach of our boats sufficiently near before the fish took the alarm. 20 or 30 ships in sight. Lay too most of the day.

Saturday 23 May Lat. 77.58 Lon 1.2W[1]
NE.rly Var. calm SEbE
Light variable winds, occasionally calm. Clear w^r in the morning, at night cloudy. Were in pursuit of whales almost the whole day with 2 to 4 boats but without success. The only chance we had, which indeed was an excellent one, our boat was disappointed by the interference of that of another ship which alarmed the fish by rowing towards its eye, without any possibility of its success! 30 ships in sight. Stretched into ['Whale oil: the products of blubbers &c.' *in margin*] an adjoining opening less encumbered with ice than the place where we lay, and lay too during the night. Whale oil froze at temp of about 30° in the manner of sperm-oil & at 24° would not pour out of a quart bottle. It was of a salmon colour, the blubber from which it was extracted being the same. The thick crystalline part was not deposited at temp. [60?] or thereabout same as in the narwhale oil. A quantity of glue was formed at the bottom of the [pail?] in which the oil cooled.

Sunday 24 May
ESE to E.
Wind a moderate or fresh breeze: some snow; fine cloudy weather. Saw different whales in the place where we lay too. In the morning one of them was struck. It sought refuge in a patch of ice, formed of heavy pieces, cemented by large sheets of bay ice of

['Wm Clark'  *in margin*][2]

considerable consistence. The boats being unable to make much progress in it we ran the ship in and towed a boat to the neighbourhood of the fish. The crew were singularly inactive, notwithstanding they reached here[3] within the distance of 3 or 4 yards, before she disappeared and afforded an excellent opportunity for heaving the harpoon into her; but the harpooner being astonishingly deficient in this art actually missed the fish! The consequence was she furiously set off towards the lee-pack, ['Reflections on the singular inability of our officers & crew' *in margin*] drew the harpoon and escaped. The singular inability of our officers and crew in general is so striking, that certainly if we succeed even tollerably in the fishery, their exertions must be supported & directed by a power higher and wiser than themselves. Or in other words, we must have the blessing of the Almighty upon us if we succeed: for certainly our instruments are most deficient. In flinching they are worse than in fishing. Each of the three fish we have taken have cost them 8 or 9 hours each, whereas the usual time is but 3½ to 4'.

---

[1] Possibly '1.0W'.
[2] Note beneath the tail: 'Lost by the inability of our harpooner.'
[3] *Sic*: 'her' intended?

After the striker had got his lines on board his boat (11½ of which were out) we made sail and worked up to the eastward ['Tendency of whales to get to windward by the ice drifting over the place affording them food.' *in margin*] supposing the whales might have taken in that direction; or rather that the ice might have drifted to leeward of them, supposing their situation in the water to have been stationary. In strong winds, where the whales are at ease in a situation affording plenty of food, this effect of ice drifting over them is constantly displayed; hence when the ice hangs so compactly together to windward that though fish may breathe but the ships cannot sail, the former find a secure retreat and soon disappear from the sight of the fishers. One of our officers hit the ship a terrible blow against the ice in stays.

Monday 25 May
ENE to NE
Blowing a fresh gale all day with thick snow in the forenoon and occasional showers afterwards. Thermometer 19° to 18°. During the snow, made a stretch into the ice towards the N. though it occurred in large compact patches and altogether very crowded. At the borders[1] of a <u>bay floe</u> ['Vast number of whales' *in margin*] saw a number of whales, after which we ['lay' *deleted*] sent 5 boats. Worked round the west side of the floe in a narrow channel incommoded with drift ice, and reached the edge of a large heavy floe apparently forming the margin of the main ['Difficult navigations' *in margin*] western ice, as it was impossible in this place or indeed within sight to get a mile farther to the west. Saw no fish here, the water being transparent blue & where we left the boats opaque green. Worked round the bay floe until we gained the weather side where a considerable opening was produced by the rapid drift of the floe. Here a great number of whales were seen and one struck. It was killed ['Difficulties and dangers of the fishery.' *in margin*] after about 2 hours by the side of another bay floe within a few pieces of heavy ice closely compacted together, which pieces were accumulated by the accession of others so rapidly that in about an hour the fish & boats were beset within ¼ of mile of ice or more. The ice around closing with great rapidity there was great danger of getting the other ship beset; I therefore made a signal (a <u>wheft</u>[2]) for the boats to come on board and leave the fish. On this after getting one boat much crushed and upset they proceeded to launch the others over the ice, which with much labour was effected in the course of three or four hours. Meanwhile the ice round the floe suddenly slacked to where the fish was, and the prize, which I had deemed altogether ['**Tuesday 26 May** NE – NNE' *in margin*] lost was mercifully restored to us; for by a few minutes of prompt exertion they got the fish realeased [*sic*] & the stove boat with her lines and implements to the ship. The first fast ['[One ship only in sight]' *in margin*] boat & a companion, with 6 or 7 lines

---

[1] Originally 'boarders'; 'a' deleted.

[2] *OED* Gives 'wheft' as a 19th-century and nautical variant spelling of 'waft': '*Naut.* A flag (or some substitute) hoisted as a signal'. See also Smyth, *Sailor's Word Book*: 'WAFT ... more correctly written *wheft*. It is any flag or ensign, stopped together at the head and middle portions, slightly rolled up lengthwise, and hoisted at different positions at the after-part of a ship. Thus, at the ensign-staff, it signifies that a man has fallen overboard ... At the peak, it signifies a wish to speak; at the mast-head recals [*sic*] boats; or as the commander-in-chief or particular captain may direct.'

out yet remained beset. Took the fish in tow and dragged her 2 or 3 miles to the SE into a place of greater safety, where we moored the ship; but the ice falling rapidly down upon the bay floe, we were

['Thos. Lashley F.   T. 11 N° 4 = 9.3' *in margin*]

obliged after securing the fish to cast off and drift to the S.[1] I was under great anxiety for the safety of the two boats & crews left beset, no assistance to whom we could have yet afforded them without ['risking' *deleted*] sacrificing the liberty of the ship by getting beset, as the only ['point' *deleted*] channel of egress closed up a few minutes after we cast off and drifted out of the opening. Having cleaned a good telescope, I proceeded for the 3^d or 4th time to the mast head to endeavour to discover the boats & by a painful exercise of attention I at length discovered them ['Two boats and crews exposed to inclement weather and considerable danger' *in margin*] at the distance of about 4 miles, with a flag flying, and the boats apparently on the ice. Whilst I reflected on the best move of affording them assistance I perceived one of the boats had moved and disappeared & soon afterwards I was rejoiced to ['perceive' *deleted*] find they moved rapidly along. I attentively watched them until both boats had cleared every danger and surmounted all the difficulties, excepting the point which had closed after the ship was unmoored, and then retired with comfort and gratitude for the mercies of the day, to my bed.

['The fish being flinched' *deleted*] The two boats arrived about an hour afterwards, but the crews were miserably starved and fatigued: they could scarcely walk. [Long?] exposure to A[2] temp. of 16° which it latterly was, without extra clothing or food, to keep them in heat, and some of them wet, must indeed have been severe. They did not fail to give a dismal account of their sufferings.

The fish being flinched, I arose, we made sail, finding the whales which during the night had appeared in considerable numbers together had disappeared, and the colour of the water had changed to a clear blue – and proceeded to the eastward into a convenient navigation and then with all ['Sudden changes of colour in the sea' *in margin*] dispatch to windward in search of the fish.

The water changed colour, sometimes from transparent blue to deep green in one minutes sail; but I could never observe the contact.

Wednesday 27 May Lat. 77.27+ Lon. 0.40W.
NW to SWbW
The weather was fine and a number of fish astir about mid-night. Four boats went out in pursuit & one boat was ['Fish lost by incapacity' *in margin*] upon the back of a fine whale and the harpooner made two strikes at it, but instead of piercing the fish bent his harpoon! Thus was another fish sacrificed by the incapacity of an harpooner. Being unsuccessful, we made sail after the fish disappeared an [*sic*] cruized about among the ice during most of the day without meeting with any. About 4 Pm. we

---

[1] Originally 'S.E.'; 'E.' deleted.
[2] The first three words of the sentence were an insertion, and this article remained capitalized.

unexpectedly found ourselves at sea. Steered to the NE along the exterior of the ice, saw one whale at 8 pm. and at 9 lay too in a bay of the ice. Some ships seen.

Thursday 28 May Lat 78°0′ Lon. 0°50′W
SW to SbE & SW or W.
A strong gale of wind arose in the night attended with thick snow. It moderated in the morning, and whilst a thick fog prevailed, the ship being at sea, we prepared to embrace the opportunity to make off. Cleared the after hold and whilst the ship reached to the SE^d under two treble reef'd topsail we commenced operations at 4 Pm.

Hitherto our labours had been conducted in the most careless and idle way imaginable; Our crew having proved the worst I ever saw. By the way of stimulating them to some ['Addressed the Crew' *in margin*] degree of exertion I made an address to them before they commenced making off, threatening the punishment of withholding wages (for the benefit of Greenwich Hospital[1]) from such as should here after conduct themselves so idly, as also to those who remained below in their watches; and also all men who were sick or pretended to be sick, who should not previously to their absenting themselves from duty, make a regular application to the surgeon, &c. This I was gratified to find seem [*sic*] to produce a good effect as they made a most vigorous start and for a long while continued their unremitted exertions.

Friday 29 May
W to NW
At mid-night being nearly calm, slightly foggy, ['and' *deleted*] little or no ice in sight, and all hands in vigorous employment, I retired to ['rest' *deleted*] seek a few hours rest: that I might be prepared to superintend the <u>winding up of the concern</u>, the purifying, cleaning, and straightening operations, as well as to get the ship in the way of a cruize for searching for fish. Little did I imagine a possibility of danger; but in this adventurous voyage we are certainly in continual jeopardy and require the unremitting guidance and support of a Gracious Providence, ['Danger of the ice in a calm; inexpert danger of the ship' *in margin*] even when we feel ourselves the most secure. I had not long slept when I was awoke by a noise upon deck & a shout of "lower away the boats" – I leaped out of bed slipped on a coat which always hangs by me and was on deck before I was clearly awake – the sight however was sufficient to rouse me. The ship lay nearly becalmed, the fog was intensely thick[,] a heavy swell rolled against her, and a tremendous island of ice, sufficient ['to' *deleted*] for a mooring in any other circumstances of still water, was within a few yards of her side – and approaching it with a velocity of 2 or 3 miles per hour – the sea beating and roaring upon it like as on a lee shore, and agitating the mass with tremendous violence. Its approach was terrific, it threatened the destruction of the ship. Before the boats could be efficient the mass was along side. The first shock was happily moderated by a favourable <u>roll</u> of the ship and by the ice passing beneath the ship's bottom. It struck

---

[1] In 1818 Greenwich was still a hospital for the Royal Navy, and continued so until 1869. The Seamen's Hospital Society, serving current or former members of the merchant navy or fishing fleet, was not created until 1821.

her 3 or 4 times and then passed astern of her, and we flattered ourselves she had sustained no injury. Of this however we could have no assurance, excepting the test of leak.¹ The pump was therefore set to work & we were relieved by finding all still sound or if not sound at least water proof. Our escape considered providential.

A fresh gale at NW, arose before we finished making off and the weather cleared. We concluded about noon having filled 42 casks of 84 butts with blubber and two casks with Krang (or blubber & flesh mixed).

After this made sail and steered by the wind towards the North.

About 9 Pm. we came into a bight of the ice where was much scattered ice, up which we plyed until we found [' **Saturday 30 May** Lat 78.30 Lon. 0. 10'E+ NW, W, SW, S, Calm'² *in margin*] shelter from the sea. At mid night having reached the extremity we passed through much dangerous ice towards the NE & entered an opening which lead towards the NW to the edge of some floes: in this we worked all night and about noon were at the extremity saw no fish, steered a few miles NE & then lay too. At night calm. Several ships in sight two of which were seen to capture a whale each.

Sunday 31 May Lat 78.28 Lon. 0.30E
Calm NE to NNE
Calm to a Strong Gale with snow showers. Dodged in a roomy opening of the ice all day. I was much concerned to find on the preceding evening that the blow the ship received on the 24 inst*ant* against a piece of ice when tacking had broken the cut-water³ and turned it along with the ice plates to one side from the 8 to 12 feet water mark. The loss of this security against a front ['Ship's cutwater injured' *in margin*] blow is a serious concern & particularly so, as it is quite out of our power to repair it.

Monday 1 June Lat 78.25 Lon. 0°30E
NNE
The ice began to close about us early in the morning, in consequence of which we made a vigorous effort to pass a windward stream which on the second attempt we accomplished in safety, without touching any ice. Proceeded ['Fish lifted a boat out of the water & stove it' *in margin*] to windward under a brisk sail & whilst searching for fish in every patch & stream of ice about us we spyed one about 3 Pm. which was presently struck at about ¾ of a mile distance from a western pack. On its descent, it struck the boat beneath the keel with such violence as to lift it and the crew out of the water &

['Thoˢ Lashley F.  16T Nº5 = 11.7 Length 50 fᵗ tail 17 fᵗ broad' *in margin*]

---

¹ Originally 'leakage'; 'age' deleted.

² Before these entries of wind direction, those for the following day, 31 May, had been entered and then deleted, suggesting that the transcriber had briefly erred when copying.

³ Smyth, *Sailor's Word Book*: 'CUT-WATER. The foremost part of a vessel's prow … It cuts or divides the water before reaching the bow, which would retard progress.'

projected the harpooner some feet into the air. The violence of the blow broke the keel and two thwarts of the boat & occasioned it to sink in the course of a few minutes; but not until assistance arrived. On the 3ᵈ appearance of the fish it received 4 more harpoons and was killed about 5 Pm. Clewed the sails up and flinched it ['John's fish 57 fᵗ kent 31 fᵗ bone 12 fᵗ' *in margin*] whilst drifting to leeward amongst streams of loose ice. Saw several more whales whilst flinching and sent two boats in chace of them. 15 ships in sight.

Tuesday 2ᵈ June Lat. 78.20 Lon. 0°10′W
N. NNW
A fresh gale of wind prevailed most of the day with cloudy weather. Seeing no whales, in the forenoon we stretched to the Wᵈ as far as we could get, being prevented from going further by a firm stream of heavy ice. Beyond it was much open water, floes, and 22 sail of ships, several of which seemed to be fishing. Returned towards the NE amongst crowded heavy ice. Saw but one whale, which narrowly escaped us. Upwards of 40 sail insight. Light winds at mid-night.

Wednesday 3ᵈ June Lat. 78.28 Lon. 1°10′E
NWbW NNW.
Light variable winds, fine weather. Plying towards the North, among much heavy drift ice with floes in sight. Saw 2 or 3 fish; but were unsuccessful in the chase[1] of them.

Thursday 4 June Lat 78.35+ Lon. 0°55′E.
N, NNW
Mostly light winds, fog, haze, rain, or snow. Small[2] rain occurred when the temp. was 26° and covered the rigging with transparent ice. This indicated a warmer stratum of air in the middle regions of the clouds.[3] Beating to windward under all sails. Passed a heavy large floe, but it afforded no fish. Many ships in sight.

Friday 5 June Lat. 78°50′ Lon. 0°20′W.
NW
Moderate or fresh breezes of wind, with snow or fog showers. Made rapid progress to windward. Spoke the James of Liverpool with 6 fish; gives account of Cherub, Jackson 26 & Perseverance (Peterhead) 29 fish! 150–160 tons of oil each; taken near the place we now navigate. Found immense spaces of water free of ice 10 or 15 square leagues of surface and large sheets of ice, many of which on the <u>eastern</u> hand[4] could not be seen across from the mast head; but towards the N, NW, W, & SW, scarcely any ice was to be seen. About noon perceiving no fish or any signs of them; but on the contrary having fallen in with clear sea water of ultramarine blue, in place

---

[1] Spelled here in normal form, but the 's' appears to be a correction over 'c'.
[2] *OED*: 'Composed or fine or minute particles, drops, etc. In later use chiefly of rain.'
[3] Scoresby was accurately explaining what would now be termed 'freezing rain'.
[4] Possibly 'land'.

of the olive green coloured sea in which their choicest food seems to occur, we bore up and steered along the edge of the fields and floes the way we came in. At 6 Pm. fell into green coloured water & where a ship near us saw a fish. Lay too until 8 pm. & then made sail again towards the SW, S, and SE. 22 ships in sight.

Saturday 6 June Lat. 78.22+ Lon. 0.40E
W. WSW
At the edge of a field lay too and saw 2 or 3 whales and an immense number of narwhales. Two of the latter we got. One a male with a 5 feet tusk,*[1] 13 f^t in length from snout to tail; the other a female, no external tusk 13 f^t 4 in in length. A foetus 4 inches in

['Narwhales  M. tusk: <u>Mate</u>

Narwhale N° 3: female: <u>Specksioneer</u>' *in margin*]

length quite perfect was found in its uterus. The former the mate shot with the harpoon gun, which passed quite through the middle of the body at the distance of near 15 yards. The stomachs of each as usual were filled with the remains of sepiæ; which the green water around us seems to afford in vast profusion.

Blowing fresh with foggy weather in the afternoon, moored to the field & placed 3 boats on watch for whales. Upwards of ['Size of narwhales, &c.' *in margin*] 20 ships in sight. The blubber of the <u>two</u> narwhales amounted to about 200 gallons.

Sunday 7 June Lat 78.28 Lon. 0°30′E
SW to S
In the morning it blew a hard gale of wind accompanied by thick snow, sleet, fog, rain, and hail. When the rain fell the fog cleared. The hail was apparently round like very small shot, but from the very acute cutting sensation it produced on ['Hail & Rain' *in margin*] the face it was doubtless angular: some larger grains indeed were evidently so. They consisted of hard, ['compact' *deleted*] transparent ice. The rain fell in heavy showers, when the wind was less. In the height of the storm the boats of the Anne Marie, Capt. [Bruher?] of Hamburgh, having a stout fish in tow sought refuge on board of us; their ship was about 2 miles to windward & perfectly inaccessible to them. I gave the men a dram of some refreshment, whilst our officers treated the harpooners with Coffee. A floe setting up towards us at the time obliged us to cast off about noon, and we[2] were under the necessity of parting with them; not however without furnishing them with a large bag of biscuits in case they should remain long

---

[1] Footnote in transcript: '*This tusk had about 3 or 4 inches broken from the end & was worn smooth at the edge of the fracture: hence it seems to indicate that the tusk is used ['by' *deleted*] for some particular purpose: but whether broken in [using?] or by accidentally foul of a piece of ice or other hard substance is not clear.'

[2] Originally 'were'; 're' deleted.

seperated from their ship. – We drifted to leeward into a considerable opening and in the evening moored to a ['detatched' *deleted*] floe attached to the same field. 15 ships in sight occasionally. Weather more moderate.

Monday 8 June Lat 78.35 Lon. 0.30W.
S.rly: SE to EbN
Soon after mid-night we cleared the after hold and commenced making off our 5th fish; which we had ['Made off 23 casks of whale's & 1 of narwh*ale*'s blubber equiva-*len*t to 48 butts' *in margin*] scarcely completed before the approach of floes from the N. obliged us to cast off. The ship laying against the ice, we had to exert every art to Cast her off having a warp as a spring [***]¹ of the stern, which after some time we accomplished. A ship to leeward <u>careening</u> appears to be stove. The field seems to have moved rapidly to the W^d as a vast clear opening was formed on the E. side. Made a brisk sail & stood by the wind (after 2 or 3 tacked to the SSE along the weather side of the field.[)] At 10 pm. fell in with a sea stream.

Tuesday 9 June Lat 78.20 Lon. 0°5′E
NE, NNE
Fresh gales of wind with snow or fog showers. The fog deposited on the rigging freezes into transparent ice, whereby the ropes were ['Ropes like Glass' *in margin*] this morning so completely glazed, that they resembled the cordage of a ship imitated in glass.

The Greenland seas where the water is blue is probably more ['Amazing trans-parency of Green*land* Seas' *in margin*] transparent than in any part of the world. Capt. Wood in his voyage of Discovery of a NE passage, saw the bottom clearly near Nova Zembla, where the depth was 80 fathoms. See his voyage p. 165 in "<u>An acc^t of several late voyages of Disc. towards the S. & N.</u>"²

Finding our provision rapidly on the decrease, we this ['Estimate of provision used by 49 men; very surprising!!' *in margin*] morning took an estimate of what was expended & what was left whereby we found that in 70 days an average of 50 men had consumed 6820 lb of beef & pork, 4700 lb of bread 1200 lb of flour; 400 lb of oatmeal, a large quantity of pease & barley, and about 50 bushels of potatoes; at which rate our remaining provision could only be sufficient for to serve from 8 to 10 weeks; as such a reduction in the daily consumption became absolutely necessary. The quantity of each kind of provision consumed a day of late by 49 men & boys; the cabin consumption being omitted; is as follows.

---

¹ Possibly a badly-written 'out'. In Smyth, *Sailor's Word Book* , a spring is 'a hawser laid out to some fixed object to slue a vessel proceeding to sea'; this appears to be the intent here.

² Scoresby was citing the 'Journal, In His Majesties Ship the Speedwell, Captain John Wood Commander, Bound for the Discovery of a Passage to the East-Indies, by the North-East: Sailing about Nova Zembla, and Tartary, and so to Japan. 1676', which is included in Sir John Nar-borough's *Account of several late Voyages*, 1694. The journal entry for Tuesday 27 June 1676 (pp. 164-5) includes the statement 'We Sounded and had 80 Fathom Water green Oar, at which time we saw the Ground plain, being very smooth Water.'

		quantity p man
Beef (salt)	110 lb	$2\,^{12}/_{49}$
Bread*[1]	80 to 120 lb	$1\,^{29}/_{49}$
Potatoes	60 lb	$1\,^{11}/_{49}$
4 lb of Barley for broth	40 quarts	$^{4}/_{5}$ quart.
12 lb Oatmeal: Porridge or Burgoo[2]	30 quarts	$^{3}/_{5}$ ——
Beer	25 gallons	2 quarts

Or:	Beef	95
	Flour	30
	Broth or Soup	40 quarts
	Porridge	30 —
	Beer	100.

And on some occasions with the above allowance the crew complained of not having sufficient. I now reduced them to 75 to 90 lb of beef; 50 lb of Bread, soup & potatoes as before; or, 64 lb of pork & other things as usual: when puddings are prepared 30 lb of flour to be considered as 15 lb of beef or pork. When fishing or hunting after fish 16 lb of beef extra (say 90 lb) or 8 lb of pork.

Beat up by the edge of the sea stream, without finding an opening to admit our escape. Came to the NE.rn extremity of the opening about 8 am. where two ships of 35 sail, captured fish; we saw but one. Searched all the windward ice as far as navigable, when meeting with nothing & the sea being generally blue, at noon, we steered to the S^d found an opening in the sea stream & passed out to Sea. Stood under a brisk sail to the E^d. Three ships followed us out; the rest of the fleet as long as we could see them remained. Several ships met with at sea. A strong Easterly swell.

Wednesday 10 June Lat. 78.30 Lon. 2°0E
NE. ENE
Beat to windward all night & this day, under all sails. The former part of the day we had much wind but the latter was moderate. Above 20 sail in sight. No fish seen.

Thursday 11 June Lat. 78°34′+ Lon. 1°40′E
NE, var. Calm. SW.
Light variable winds. Thick showers of snow. Continued pressing to the northward along the edge of a pack. In the evening came into the extremity of a bight where a fish or two were seen by the ships in company. Searched the crowded ice of the bight but found nothing excepting an immense number of unicorns all of which escaped us. Towards mid-night reached along the lee ice (wind SW.rly) towards the SE which we found ['**Friday 12 June** Lat. 78.50 Lon. 2°20′E SWbS. SSW. Srly SErly.' *in margin*]

---

[1] Note in margin: '*11 men used for many successive days 28–30 lb of bread!! p day'.

[2] Smyth, *Sailor's Word Book*: 'BURGOO. A seafaring dish made of boiled oat-meal seasoned with salt, butter, and sugar.'

trended 15 or 20 miles in that direction and terminated in a point. Lay too towards morning & at 8 am. pursued our course, the wind however falling & veering to the S or SE^d prevented us weathering the point. Observed a ship boring out of the lee ice into a lateral opening which proved to be the Resolution of Whitby with 17 fish about the same quantity of blubber as ourselves. Mr Kearsley came on board & gave intelligence of the John nearly full & some other ships. Ajax stove; North Briton stove & foremast carried away by the London running foul of her, &c. &c. The light winds which occurred prevented us weathering the SE point of the ice during the day.

Saturday 13 June Lat. 78.47 Lon. 3.0E
S. SSE.
Light or moderate breeze of wind – some fog, cloudy w*eather* generally and fine. Passed to windward of the most S.rn point of ice at 9 am. steered ENE to the next point & then towards the north. Saw a small fish at 2 pm.: Lay too. 25 sail in sight many of them in pursuit of fish. The John of Greenock joined us with 29 fish 200 tons of oil! principally captured within the last two weeks about the adjoining ice.
   Lay too all night.

Sunday 14 June Lat 79.10 Lon. 3.20E
S to WSW.
Moderate or fresh breezes of wind: hazy weather: Drifted all day towards the NE along the edge of a pack. Saw several fish, but being Sabbath day, endeavoured to keep it Holy.

Monday 15 June Lat 79.18 Lon. 3.10E
West &^1 var.
Having come towards the extremity of a deep bight of the ice,

['John Dawson F 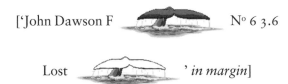 N° 6 3.6

Lost ' *in margin*]

where we saw fish [.] Sent our boats in chace, one they struck but the harpoon drew, a second a harpooner missed by a blunder ['and' *deleted*] but a third was more effectually entangled. We killed it after some trouble – it having taken refuge amidst some thick ice. Towards midnight sent all our boats to the edge of an adjoining [**'Tuesday 16 June** Lat. 79.26 Lon. 2.40E var. Calm' *in margin*] field from whence the loose ice was beginning to clear. They saw several fish & struck one, but it escaped them. Several ships around us. Saw a multitude of narwhales.

['Lost  ' *in margin*]

---

¹ These words replacing 'Calm or' deleted.

A slight swell arose in the afternoon though not at all perceptible except by the move-
ments of the ice, yet broke several large masses from the sides of the field, where the
ice was from 10 to 30 feet thick, ['the ice' *deleted*] blue coloured, and ['quite' *deleted*]
altogether fine fresh water ice. 25 sail in sight. Ice seen to the E^d & SE of us.

Wednesday 17 June
Calm. var. NE.rly
Being clear weather in the morning we found that ['notwith' *deleted*] though there
was not a flake of ice to the sea ward of us ['on' *deleted*] ([SSW?][1] to ENE or NE) on
Sunday last, nor any in sight on ['Strange manner in which the ice has imperceptibly
entrapped us' *in margin*] Monday as we drifted down towards the NE. yet today ['we
found' *deleted*] there lay a bar of ice extending quite round us & completely enclosing
us, which, on approaching it with a view to endeavour to escape ['from' *deleted*]
beyond it we found it at the narrowest part 6 or 8 miles in breadth & so compact that
['we' *deleted*] I considered it in vain to attempt to pass through it with the wind as it
now was. Searched all round the enclosure but found no opening! Such is the strange
manner in which the ice occasionally moves. The ice which encloses us seems to be
that point ['of ice' *deleted*] which we passed on Saturday morning last, which has
drifted round to the eastward of us & retained its continuity by the beat of the swell
until it formed a junction with a NE point (near 20 miles distant on Saturday).
Light winds, variable occasionally calm.

Thursday 18 June
Calm: var. NW.rly. W.rly. SW
We had calm or extremely light winds during the night & in the morning until 11
Am. when a small breeze of wind sprang up from the westward. This permitting us to
sail ['readily' *deleted*] easily to the SE, E, or NE, the course which we must principally
make to get out, we took the ice about noon, though with little hopes of getting away
altogether ['Difficult navigation in escaping from the ice.' *in margin*] on this occasion
for a complete solid stream seemed to bar our passage: By means of a boat towing
however and another clearing the way of small pieces, we succeeded to admiration.
We left 15 or 16 sail in the opening to the westward five of which speedily attempted
to follow us, but the ice closing as we went they all stuck fast before they had penetrated a mile, excepting one ship. We found the large ice & the small approaching
each other though near calm, without any apparent cause with a velocity of 1¼ or 2
miles per hour, so that a hundred yards behind the ship her track was completely
"eradicated". About 5 Pm. the meeting of the ice caught us, but steering to the W^d we
gained a slack, sailed round a few large pieces of ice & then turned to the S^d again. We
now approached the sea, but the navigation to it was the most difficult & hazardous.
We employed 3 boats to ['tow the' *deleted*] assist the ship in making evolutions occasionally where the turns were difficult & in towing when we had occasion to sail
considerably against the wind. In accomplishing the last mile we steered in every

[1] Originally 'WSW', but this was deleted and 'SS' inserted immediately adjacent to the deleted
text.

possible course from SW to E, & NE, ['& N, NW' *deleted*] making a distance of near 4 miles. The ice was amazingly large & heavy & having recently broken from heavy floes abounded with hard acute angles, which rendered our progress particularly dangerous: we however were highly favoured never having touched one large piece of ice during our lengthened navigation. At 10 pm. we found ourselves at sea. All the ships we left except one were yet in <u>statu quo</u>[1] as at 10 pm. those which attempted to follow us however showed some signs of moving – steered by the wind to the SSE.

Friday 19 June
SW to WbS
Moderate to fresh breezes of wind; with snow showers. Reached to the SE & S. all night and until 2 Pm. We then saw Razor backs, but no whales, which induced us to tack & stand to the NW. Passed a number of ships.

<u>Experiments on whale oil & references to bottles of oil</u>.

['Experiments on the nature & properties of whale oil' *in margin*] N° 1. "Oil of Red blubber". This bottle contains the grosser parts of two bottles of oil which [subsided?] by standing whilst the clearer part was poured off into – N° 2.

N° 2. "Oil of Red blubber", the clear part poured off the former at temp. about 50°.

N° 3. "Whale oil filtered at temp. 32°–34°." This is the oil of the last young whale, which is extremely beautiful. When exposed to a cool air, it became [candied?][2] and by filtration ['the' *deleted*] in the open air (temp. 30–32°) the pure oil was obtained which remains perfectly transparent at a very low temperature. Two bottles of this.

N° 4 "Refuse of whale oil". This contains the crystalline or candied part of the oil, separated by filtration & compression but not of course freed entirely from the oil: It however remains of the consistence of an ointment at the temp. of 60 and seems to require near 80 or 90° to reduce it to the fluid state. This substance it seems is what [freezes?] in the oil. When combined in the proportion in which it naturally exists, it seems not to be separated until it become of the temp. of about 40°, but in proportion as the oil is filtered it requires a higher temp. to dissolve it. Perhaps it is a substance which is soluble in oil in a small quantity at about 32°, not at all soluble below that temp. & increasing in solubility at a higher temp. until the oil dissolves any quantity of it approaching the point of its natural concretion; say 90 or 100°. This substance has much the appearance of <u>sperma ceti</u> . It occurs in oil in concretions or crystals of the size & appearance of sea sand. Query. If all the oil can be separated, will the remaining substance be inflammible [*sic*]? Or is this substance a mixture of gelatine & oil? Fish oil has been examined and analysed by M. Berard & his analysis is given in the "<u>Bulletin des Sciences</u>" for July or Aug*ust* 1817. [<u>vide</u>][3]

---

[1] Scoresby's use of the Latin term is correct, although 'in' should also have been underlined.

[2] If this reading is correct, the verb appears to be used in the sense of 'To form into crystals, congeal in a crystalline form' (*OED*).

[3] Brackets are in transcript. This citation has not been traced. However, Jacques Etienne Bérard (1789–1869) was the author of 'Essai sur l'analyse des substances animales', *Annales de chimie et de physique*, 1817. See Holmes, 'Elementary Analysis', *Isis*, 1, 1963, pp. 50–81.

Blowing fresh in the evening. Made the ice near the place where we left: a ship lying beset. Above 20 ships in sight. Thick snow showers.

Saturday 20 June Lat. 78°31′+ Lon. 4°E
W to SW. & WbN
Fresh or moderate winds, fine weather. Beating to windward under all sails. Towards mid-night, ['reached' *deleted*] stood into the same deep NW bight where we lay on the 11ᵗʰ inst*ant*. Left most of the ships out of sight.

Sunday 21 June Lat 78°10′ Lon. 1°E
W to SW. ['& W' *deleted*] var.
Thick fog early in the morning: charming weather[.] Beating to windward; near the main ice which now appears streamed & open. Saw several unicorns but no whales. From noon until 10 Pm. stood to the Southward. 3 or 4 ships.

Monday 22 June
Var. Calm. NE.rly
A Calm commenced this day. Saw a number of narwhales which we unsuccessfully pursued. Made off the young ['[Made off small fish]' *in margin*] fish which filled 4 casks = [*blank space*] butts of blubber. I omitted in my remarks on Saturday to notice having ['Razor backs : some remarks on' *in margin*] seen a number of Razor backs. Some of these animals only remained underwater about 2 minutes together, but then they generally blew but twice. Others which remained longer down blew 5 or more times. The interval between their blowing was 10 to 12 seconds.

A breeze springing up about 4 am. stretched by the wind towards the NW made some streams at 8 am. and ['Chaced a fish 5 or 6 hours' *in margin*] soon after saw a fish. We gave chace to it with the ship & at first 3 boats but subsequently with 6 boats until 2 Pm. but it at length escaped us. Having seen another fish during the chace far to leeward we spent the afternoon in searching for it, running about 10 miles to leeward & then plying back on the contrary side of a stream. About 10 pm. we got sight of a fish, whether it was the same or not we could not tell. Pursued it to leeward with 2 boats &

['James Anderson. F.  18 T Nᵒ 7 = 11.6 bone

Length 56 fᵗ Tail 20 fᵗ 3 broad' *in margin*]

the ship & at 11 Pm. we were favoured to get fast to it. It descended but a few fathoms before it returned to the surface & beat the water with its fins & tail in a tremendous manner. Soon however a second harpoon was fastened. It then descended about 250 fathoms & on returning to breathe was active & [wicked?] as before. The mate fired ['Fish blows blood from one blowhole' *in margin*] the gun harpoon into it, which penetrated out of sight, being buried in its body. This had an admirable effect. It presently blew blood from one side ['of the' *deleted*] or blowhole in powerful jets, drenching the men & boats therewith; whilst the other blowhole discharged only its usual matters of air & mucus. The boats crowding together about it, ['**Tuesday 23 June** Lat. 77.40 Lon 1°45′E NE' *in margin*] were repeatedly hoisted out of the water, ['with' *deleted*] together with their crews & lines with the same facility as a man would lift his hat! At length one of them upset & the ['A boat upset & many others lifted by the fish' *in margin*] crew were thrown out. A Shetland boy was a considerable time underwater & narrowly escaped death. He, with his comrades, was conveyed to the ship & after discharging a quantity of water from his stomach found himself relieved. The sunk boat's lines were saved, not by the harpoon which stuck in the fish, for <u>it broke</u>, but by their getting entangled with the other lines & wound about the fish's <u>rump</u>. Including the gun harpoon, seven harpoons were struck. The fish died about 1 Am. However ['three' *deleted*] four hours or more were expended in clearing the lines away: so that it was 5 am. before, the fish was gotten alongside[.] A compact body of ice lying under our lee (apparently a floe or broken floe) we had to carry all sails until 6½ Am. before we could conveniently lay bye to flinch.

A remarkable circumstance occurred in firing[1] at the whale. The <u>wad</u>, consisting of a well fitted piece of cork, cut by means of a tool: though it lay between the powder & the harpoon was found lodged in the gun, 2 or 3 inches from the muzzle!! This extraordinary circumstance equalls [*sic*] almost those recorded by the famous traveller <u>Munchausen</u>. In his style we might assert that the wad struck the fish, & from the great elasticity of both substance (the fish & the cork) it rebounded and returned into the muzzle of the gun![2] The only possible explanation which occurs to me, is that[3] some of the men had found it in the water & replaced it in the gun.

The whale being a female we examined its uterus with the hope of finding a foetus but were disappointed.

Made sail to return to the place we drifted from about 2 Pm.

The wind lipper ['being' *deleted*] was considerable in the afternoon. All our researches for whales being in vain, we steered to the eastward of all the ice in sight and towards mid night bore away to the SW^d with a view to examine the state of the

---

[1] At this point the following marginal note was written, but then deleted: 'Remarkable case of a wad found in the harpoon gun after the harpoon was discharged!!'

[2] Raspe's *Baron Munchausen's Narrative* was published in 1785. Scoresby was clearly indicating that the incident with the whale gun seemed as improbable as the events in the *Travels*, not that it replicated an incident in the book. It is worth noting, however, that in chapter 13 of the *Travels*, Munchausen claims that 'We all remember Captain Phipps's (now Lord Mulgrave) last voyage of discovery to the north. I accompanied the captain, not as an officer, but a private friend.' The chapter goes on to recount how Munchausen single-handedly slaughtered thousands of polar bears and loaded their hams and skins on to Phipps's ship, the furs later being given to the Empress of Russia. 'Some people have very illiberally reported that Captain Phipps did not proceed as far as he might have done upon that expedition. Here it becomes my duty to acquit him; our ship was in a very proper trim till I loaded it with such an immense quantity of bear-skins and ham, after which it would have been madness to have attempted to proceed further, as we were now scarcely able to combat a brisk gale, much less those mountains of ice which lay in the higher latitudes.'

[3] At this point in the text, the following words were written, but then deleted in favour of what appears above as the remainder of the sentence: 'it had not left the gun any considerable distance before the [reaching?] in of the air into the vacuum formed by the explosion …' (The remaining 4–5 words of the deletion are illegible.)

fishery ['Whales proceed from P^t Look Out to the W. ice in lat. 76: usually at a certain season' *in margin*] in a more southern latitude; the whales being frequently observed to run across from Point Look-Out to the ice in lat. 76° about the middle of June, and have occasionally afforded a plentiful harvest to those ships which succeeded in discovering them.

Wednesday 24 June Lat. 77.1 Long. 1°30E
NNE to E
Fine cloudy weather with a moderate breeze of wind; towards night hazy with increase of wind & threatening appearances of a storm: the bar. having subsided to 29.60 and in a falling state. We overtook the John, on her way homeward, joined company & visited Capt. J. They have seen but one fish since we parted with them & got none. The [*sic*] encountered great difficulty & many severe blows in getting out of the ice where we left them.

Our course was SSW, SW, W, S, SE, &c. accordingly as the points of ice trended.

Thursday 25 June Lat. 75.40 Lon. 0°30′E
E to ESE
The indication of the barometer proved perfectly correct, as a storm gradually commenced about midnight & presently put us under close reefed topsails. Conceiving ourselves sufficiently far to the south, lay too at 4 am. until 8. The John meanwhile we presumed embraced the opportunity of a favourable wind and parted company on her way homeward.

The sea <u>made heavy</u> and the wind veered more upon the ice, so that we found it prudent to make sail & steer to the southward. Such has been the smoothness of the sea, since ever we came into the country, that some of our people were now sea sick, even some of the seamen, were affected with the nausea. Wore at 8 Pm.

Friday 26 June Lat 75.44+ Lon 2°W.
ESE. SE & var.
The weather cleared and the wind abated in the morning. Steered WNW. The John unexpected rejoined us having steered 15–20 miles to the south*war*d & returned. 6[1] ships in sight. In the evening being little wind & the sea much fallen began to make off in the main hold. Finished after only an ['**Saturday 27 June** Lat 76°10′ Lon. [*blank space*] SE.rly ESE' *in margin*] 8 or 10 hours spell: filled 21 casks = 57 butts of blubber, by gauge. The wind increased in the forenoon, and the weather became hazy. Steered NW & N. Saw a fish running towards the N. after which we chaced about 5 hours from NbE to WNW course & velocity 3½ to 5 knotts. ['Extreme velocity & usual velocity on passage of the whale' *in margin*] It appeared to be a fish of passage. Its regular velocity was about 4 knotts, which appeared to be as great a speed as the fish could accomplish for any great distance. When the ship went 5½ knotts per log we came fast up with it – but a boat could not keep pace with it. I procured a harpoon from one of the boats & waited on the ship's forecastle hoping to strike it from the

---

[1] Corrected from '5'.

bow – but when the ship was only 10 or 15 yards from it, it took the alarm & dashed forward with vast increase in velocity. I suppose it might go 8 or 10 miles per hour for about a mile – but its velocity then ceased again to its former rate & after a while we began again to come up with it. I now got upon the spritsail yard with the harpoon – but when within an [ace?] of reaching it – it again saw or heard the ship & set forward as before about ¼ mile ahead of the ship. We now fixed the harpoon gun to the anchor stock, with the hope of getting within shot, but the wind now falling & a thick fog commencing, we lost sight of it – hove too in falling in with ice & the fog cleared soon afterwards found ourselves near a pack edge.

Our provision having suffered an uncommon reduction for the period, Mʳ Jackson of the John furnished us with a supply of 2 tierces[1] of beef & 2 barrels of pork which enabled me to make a small increase in the allowance of provision. About mid-night the John ['steered away' *deleted*] after taking in a stock of fresh ice, steered homeward.

Sunday 28 June Lat. Lon.
SE to S.
Accompanied the John to the Sᵈ until 6 Am. & then tacked & steered NNW. Lay too during a fog. In the evening steered the WNW. Spoke the Phoenix with 5 fish. Gave intelligence of a great number of fish having been seen here during the last week one of which she got.

Approached the ice about 8 Pm. and observed it to be slack within, but could find no place wherin we could conveniently make an entry through the sea stream, which was compact & in great motion with a strong S.rly swell. Lay too during the night. Hazy.

Monday 29 June Lat. Lon.
Var. ENE, NE, NNE.
The weather being somewhat clear in the morning I observed sufficient room to the NW within the ice; supposing fish to be there, we beat up to the NE along the edge of the sea stream towards a place which appeared to be rather slack. Though a thick fog commenced with a fresh gale of wind, & the ice was very heavy, we yet ventured in and partly groped our way into the midst of crowded ice. Occasionally we had to push small pieces out of the way, but generally we found a clear though most intricate passage, & had sometimes to tack & return the way we had come. The atmosphere clearing a little about noon I perceived navigable ice farther towards the NW and pushed forward until we could get no farther. The ice being now exceedingly <u>cross</u>, heavy, & Dangerous owing to a great increase of wind; that I was anxious to make the ship fast to the largest piece within reach. After making several short tacks, a piece of ice was found & the ship moored on the second attempt. The rope broke the first time. Here we saw two whales & a multitude of narwhales. ['**Tuesday 30 June** Lat.

---

[1] Smyth, *Sailor's Word Book*: 'TIERCE. Is specially applied to provision casks, ... the beef-tierce contains 280 lbs., or 28 galls., whilst that of pork only contains 260 lbs., or 26 galls. Now [1867] the beef-tierce often contains 336 lbs., and the pork 300 lbs.'

Lon. NNE' *in margin*] Sent out 3 boats in pursuit. The storm continued all night – the fog was intensely thick & ice more & more crowded. At length it accumulated so thick about us that when I arose from my bed I found the ship closely beset, amidst heavy ice.

The fog cleared about noon & the ['wind' *deleted*] storm rather subsided. I perceived we were in the midst of a close pack, with scarcely room to tack a ship within sight. To leeward, however (SSW) the sea was in sight at the distance of 5 or 6 miles. I was grievously disappointed that the ice had so closed & we had not opportunity of penetrating further into the interior, the cause of which closing of the ice was evidently owing to the opposite action of a heavy SE swell & a strong NNE wind. As the ice was heavier towards the Sea than towards the N. there was little hope of its speedy opening. I therefore deemed it a matter of prudence to attempt to get out again. In the shattered state of the cutwater, which in ['Dangerous enterprise in getting out of the ice' *in margin*] forcing through the ice, ['ought' *deleted*] must receive some heavy blows, we were obliged to adopt a method of caution which rendered our progress amazingly slow. This consisted in fastening a small but heavy piece of ice to the stern of the ship whereby she was prevented from going above a velocity of half a mile to a mile per hour more than surrounding ice. By this means we proceeded very safely from noon until about 6 Pm. at which time we had passed through some very heavy ice, & the southerly swell which had made its appearance before we commenced, now finding less interruption made a fearful commotion among the ice. And what further increase [*sic*] the danger was that we were forcing directly ['into' *deleted*] towards a very heavy body of ice to clear which it was necessary to proceed a little more westerly – therefore we were obliged to cast loose our piece of ice and to advance without any protection. In this enterprize we drifted & forced the ship in the most favourable channels, avoiding as much as possible striking the ice with the [stem?] or drifting against any sharp angles of the ice, & succeeded well until about 9 Pm. when we were about to drift through a still heavier stream of ice than we had yet encountered & in such violent agitation that one piece 15–20 feet thick broke into three as we approached it & others were divided into two. Selecting a flat even sided piece to lay against we escaped this danger without any material blows – but a fog commencing thicker than we had yet experienced & a swell more formidable than before making way among the ice reduced us to a state of great hazard & perplexity. ['Dangers of the ice & swell' *in margin*] Happily I had observed the direction we had to proceed with great minuteness – but as there was only one track & that of a very zigzag ['directio' *deleted*] character I felt seriously alarmed with the danger of our situation. Commending myself however to Him who seeeth[1] in all circumstances for His guidance we continued to advance, for indeed we could not lay too or moor, the swell being too heavy & the ice too crowded & in a violent commotion, using the precaution of easy sail & occasionally sending a boat under sail to seek out a passage for us by the motion of which we had more distance & time to perform our evolutions. By these means we providentially made a safe egress and reached a roomy situation bordering on the sea about midnight. The fog immediately afterwards cleared away & we had a fine clear night. We

---

[1] Originally 'seeketh'; 'k' deleted.

saw 3 or 4 whales in the course of our navigation out. One of which we chased & got within shot of – but the powder having lain too long in the gun the harpoon fell short. The fish was beyond the reach of a heave.

Wednesday 1st July Lat.74°53′43″+ Lon.11°32′+W
NNW. Calm. W.
Approached the pack edge in the morning, after a calm, having a moderate breeze of wind & the weather beautifully clear. Saw 3 whales in the course of the day. A fog commencing about 6 PM. we made sail and plied towards the West between the pack & a body of ice lying to the eastward.

Thursday 2d July Lat. 74°20′ Lon. 10°W.
WSW to NW
We had thick fog & a fresh of wind [*sic*] all night, under which we plied to the W. & SW. until we found crowded ice, and a very difficult navigation. Our search after fish being without success[.] The fog did not clear as we expected we therefore steered back to the NE & reached a free navigation as the fog cleared away.

Stretched all night with light winds, towards the NNE & NE. The John of Hull passed us apparently homeward bound, her success we did not ascertain.

Friday 3 July
NW. N. Var. Calm SW.
Light variable winds, occasionally calm. Made some little progress towards the NE by the edge of the W. pack, having a body of ice to the SE of us which had beat round us within 2 or 3 days, & now forms a bight of 30 miles deep extending to the West, and towards the seaward side not above 2 or 3 miles in breadth. Passed into the sea about 10 pm.

We found several pieces of drift wood here. Two pieces were trees of 10–15 feet long 5 or 6 in. diameter & ['Drift wood' *in margin*] had the roots attached. One of them yet retained the sap & some of the <u>bark</u>, consequently it cannot have been long in the sea. None of the pieces were worm-eaten. On the ['Drift wood of Spitzbergen' *in margin*] coast of Spitzbergen my father found a large log of timber, [unhewn?] nearly sufficient for a bowsprit; and on the shore near the Head Land, vast quantities were found, of smaller wood.

Saturday 4 July Lat. 75.50 Lon. 8°0W.
SW.
Steered to the NE or E. occasionally SE along the edge of the ice which was very irregular and had numerous large sinuosities. At noon passed under the lee of a small stream of ice, the wind blowing a strong breeze, where we saw a fish. Called all hands and sent 7 boats after it. About 2 Pm. one of them came up with it and fixed his harpoon in its back. The wind lipper

['James Anderson  Fish Lost']

was considerable, having in this place no shelter but from a small broken stream at the distance of 8 or 10 miles to windward. The fish remained down about half an hour and advanced a little to windward. We were too far distant with the ship to urge the boats to pull that way & they did not go beyond 300 yards whereas they ought to have rowed at least a mile. I urged them forward as soon as we reached the place with the ship, but it was then too late for the fish immediately appeared near ¼ of a mile to windward of all the boats, and was in considerable advance in the same direction. Their efforts then to reach it were unavailing. The Valiant of Whitby had recently passed, before the fish appeared & made no stay & the Lively was to windward about 200 yards ['Proceedings in pursuit of a fast fish' *in margin*] when the fish appeared, & excellently situated to afford us assistance. But she neither backed a yard, nor lowered a boat, though no other fish was to be seen! Our boats now gave general chase to windward but the fish fast out-stripped them and they were all glad to [***][1] the fast boat, which with 4 or 5 boats & 9 or 10 lines, was drawn away to windward about twice as fast as the ship could work, though we had a fresh gale of wind, every sail set, & some shelter from the sea stream. The Valiant now returned as if meaning to assist us, but the intention was too late – she could not fetch the fish. The fish continued to advance until about 5 Pm. with unabated velocity. It then rather lessened its speed, & 3 boats pushed off, rather gained on it, but as it passed the sea stream about 6 or 7 PM. they then had to contend against a very high sea, and the fish was continually increasing its distance. The fast boat ['passed' *deleted*] was dragged through the sea stream & soon afterwards the harpoon drew. By this time the ship was got up with the windward boats – the fish having been then long out of sight & the sea so much that a boat could but barely swim, we took two boats up and ran down to the fast boat, and found the fish was off. The ['weat' *deleted*] sky now became obscure & a thick fog commenced. Lay too under shelter of the sea-stream [**Sunday 5 July** Lat. 76.0 Lon. 7.30W SW to W. Var.' *in margin*] & got all the boats on board about 1 am. The wind had already abated.

We had foggy weather throughout the day. The wind fell to calm in the afternoon. Lay too within the sea stream.

Monday 6 July Lat. 76.10 Lon. 7°W.
SErly. E ENE
Moderate to fresh breezes of wind. Thick haze, fog, snow, sleet or small sharp hail, throughout the day. Beating to windward under all sails, by the edge of what appeared to be a heavy close pack, into which we could gain no admission. Sea Blue. No fish.

Tuesday 7 July Lat. 75°56′ Lon.6°30′W
NE. NEbE
Thick fog all day except for an interval of a few minutes when we could occasionally see a distance of a mile or upward. The wind was a fresh breeze, under which we beat towards the ESE along the edge of a large extensive and compact stream of ice,

---

[1] The sense of the text seems to be that the supporting boats linked themselves to the fast boat, so that all were towed by the whale. If the word 'be' were added to the transcript, the latter could be read as 'all glad to be towed by the fast boat'.

extending nearly in a straight line, as we progressively [gained?] 20 or 30 miles. In the evening fell into green water, but saw no whales.

Wednesday 8 July Lat. 75°50′ Lon. 5°50′W.
NE.rly. Var. Calm.
Calm, the greater part of the day, generally foggy. Saw several narwhales in the evening in a <u>blue</u> sea, in which we perceived a number of <u>shrimps</u>. At 8 pm. I began to prepare for sounding by fixing to a 20 lb lead, various specimens of wood of different kinds, shapes & weights to ascertain the effect of the pressure of the sea thereon.[1] At every 80 or 90 fat*hom*s I also ['placed' *deleted*] fixed a cube of ['Sounded in 1058 fat*hom*s or 1⅕ miles; no bottom! Effects of pressure on wood.' *in margin*] ash, of ['containing' *deleted*] one cubic inch solid contents, each cube of the same shape & of the same weight to the tenth of a gram; & all cut from the same piece of wood, and well dried before ['weighing' *deleted*] adjusted. At 8¾ Pm. put the lead over and at 9ʰ 50′ the whole was overboard, amounting to 1058 fat*hom*s or 6348 feet or 1⅕ English mile, without striking bottom. It was a dead calm & the line hung nearly perpendicular, a slight inclination of the line however was observed towards the SE (p Compass) indication [*sic*] a trifling upper current towards the NW or lower current in a contrary direction.[2] ['As' *deleted*] The cavity in the base of the lead was filled with hog's lard & not the least impression was observed upon: I was confident therefore that it had not been to the bottom. It remained at rest, an hour, before we began to haul which was at 10ʰ 50′pm & at 11ʰ 50′ the lead was brought up. Finding the Spec. Grav. of the pieces of wood occupied me until near 3 am.

Thursday 9 July Lat. 75°58′+ Lon. 6°W.
Calm. SSW
The results of the experiments on the pressure of the sea at great depth was [*sic*] differ*en*t from what I anticipated: but as I have not yet completed the calculations I

---

[1] In *Account of the Arctic Regions,* I, pp. 196–203, Scoresby described this day's experiment at much greater length and detail, although he stated there that it took place 'on the 18th July 1818', not the 8th. In particular, he mentioned (pp. 196–7) the underlying reason for this work. 'Finding, on former trials, that pieces of fir wood sent down 4000 feet, were more impregnated with sea-water than others immersed only half that depth, I was in hopes that the degree of impregnation of similar pieces of the same kind of wood, might be applicable as a measure of depth. If this were the case, it would serve a very valuable purpose, since all the plans hitherto contrived for measuring depths from a vessel, when sailing slowly, or drifting through the water, cease to be useful beyond 200 or 300 fathoms.' From that standpoint the experiment was unsuccessful (p. 202: '... it is clear that no use can be made of this effect of pressure, for determining the depth, unless it be within 2000 feet of the surface; and even in this limit, the results may be uncertain.') It is also worth noting that, because of the depths and calculations involved, Scoresby must have had in mind that the 'very valuable purpose' related to the advance of scientific knowledge, not to any practical use in ordinary navigation.

[2] The 2008 version of the International Bathymetric Chart of the Arctic Ocean (IBCAO), online at http://www.ngdc.noaa.gov/mgg/bathymetry/arctic/arctic.html, indicates that in a wide area around Scoresby's presumed position for this date, the ocean depth is greater than 2500 m (8200 feet). See Jakobsson et al., 'An improved bathymetric', *Geophysical Research Letters,* 35, 2008, L07602, doi:10.1029/2008GL033520.

must defer my remarks to a future day. I may however just observe that it is probable that at ['Result of Experiments on the impregnation of wood with Sea Water' *in margin*] a certain depth (perhaps 300 or 400 fa*thom*s) the greatest impregnation is produced on open grained wood such as ash, elm, &c. ['but' *deleted*] or at least if sent to greater depths & any greater impregnation takes place, the air confined in the pores of the wood, by its elasticity, forces out part of the water before it reaches the surface. This was visibly the case with the fir, teak, elm, & some others; but after a certain quantity was expelled, so long as the wood was kept underwater no further loss of moisture took place.

This morning was clear. Doubled a promontory of the ice the extremity of the stream along which we had been beating during 2 or 3 days & then steered NW, N, & NE by the exterior of patches & extensive streams of ice. Finding by communication with a Scotch Brig, that fish had been seen hereabout during the week I conceived they might be still lurking about the ice or a little in the interior. The blink of the ice having shown signs of slack ice in the WNW we steered that way, though a thick fog immediately commenced, following the course of some heavy streams until we found ourselves quite sheltered from the sea & the ice growing rather crowded we lay too & dodged ['**Friday 10 July** Lat. 76°30′ Lon. 5°W. SSE. SE' *in margin*] during the night. The fog rather cleared about 7 am. & though the wind was now directly upon the ice (SSE to SE) on observing the ice slack towards the N[1] & NE we steered that way about 20 miles & rested in a considerable opening on the fog recommencing about noon. The water here was of a deep olive green colour and very cloudy. Many narwhales were seen & some seals (one of which we killed) but no whales. Wishing to ascertain the state of the NW.rn ice we moored to a large piece meaning to wait a favourable opportunity for exploring the western & northern quarters of the ice. Wind a fresh breeze.

Saturday 11 July Lat. 76°30′ Lon. 5°20′W
SE to S & E.
The weather was exceedingly gloomy all day & several appearances threatened a storm, ['but the' *deleted*] which in the quarter the wind was would have been exceedingly dangerous to us & would probably have beset us, but the barometer indicated no such circumstance. But though a heavy SE swell arose the wind abated. In the night saw a whale, which the mate hove his harpoon at, but did not entangle. In the morning though still foggy, we cast off & plyed towards the E. amongst much ice & had a heavy swell & roaring of the ice which showed our proximity to the sea, between us & which, however was a heavy stream of ice.

It was nearly calm in the evening: again moored.

Sunday 12 July Lat. 76°30′ Lon. 5°30′W
NE to NNE
Light winds: foggy most generally. The ice crowding about us obliged us to cast off about 4 am. steered to the NW & plyed to windward in an obscure & difficult

[1] Original 'NE'; 'E' deleted.

navigation amongst the heaviest ice which Greenland affords. The fog clearing somewhat about 3 Pm. we steered NW as far as we could get within a furlong or two & finding the ice still larger & more crowded, being nothing less than an open or slackish pack & perceiving no appearance of whales or probability of finding any, we embraced the clear interval & with some trouble we made our way to sea without damage, in one only navigation ['**Monday 13 July** Lat. 76.25+ Lon. 4°W. W.rly. var.' *in margin*] which was within sight & that narrow & crooked. Found a heavy swell on the outside. Steered an E or ESE course towards a the [*sic*] farthest point of ice in sight & then along the edge of the pack towards the E, SE, S, & latterly SSW. The fog having returned with increased obscurity we navigated in great uncertainty & although we kept the starboard hand clear of ice yet some how or other we got involved & during the whole day could discover no means of extricating ourselves either to the NE, N, NW, SW, S, SE or E. We therefore plyed under light variable winds towards the W.

Tuesday 14 July Lat. 76°20′ Lon. 3°10′W
W.rly. SW.
About 1 am. we had beat to the NW & W. to the extremity of a bight where was no egress though we felt assured this must have been the way we entered. The fog now happily thinning we ranged the ice to the S^d of us [along?] towards the ['Ship strangely involved in the ice during a fog.' *in margin*] E & SE & at length discovered a narrow opening between two extensive heavy patches leading in a SW.rly direction apparently to sea as indicated by the increase of swell. Here the wind failing us we towed in crowded ice & narrow navigation, with considerable swell with 3 boats for some hours & when we fancied ourselves safe the closing of the ice again alarmed us & induced us to tow with all boats. At 8 am. we gained the sea. Steered SE along the ice and finding it trending (by the blink) more northerly at 4 Pm. bore away ENE. We had an interval of clear weather in the forenoon, but about 5 Pm. an intense thick fog overspread the atmosphere & again involved us in obscurity. Carpenters employed fixing steering wheel adjoining the rudder: the rest of the crew scraping & suspending three pairs of jaw bones from the main mast.
    Fell in with ice at 9 PM. hauled out SE.

Wednesday 15 July Lat.77.10 Lon. 0°15′W
WSW
A considerable fall of rain having somewhat cleared the fog about 6 am. bore away to the NE, NNE, & N. Fell in with ice at 6 pm. lay too a short time & then steered to the E &ENE with a brisk gale of wind & rain or fog. Saw 4 ships.

Thursday 16 July Lat. 77.55 Lon. 0°50′E
WSW to SbE to SW
Fell into a bight of the ice at 6 Am. which took until noon to beat out. The wind being then in a direction which prevented the ice from affording any shelter & the sea being turbulent, we steered towards the land on an EbS course, velocity 5 to 8 knots. We had much rain all the day. Saw 2 ships.

Friday 17 July Lat. 78.40 Lon. 7°E
SW – SbE Var. Calm

At 6 am. we got sight of the land & lay too, the atmosphere being very hazy. Somewhat clearer at noon, stretched inshore until we could see the beakers [*sic*] upon some rocks from the deck, when we had 35 fathoms water; tacked & lay too. Considerable sea. The land nearest to us proved to be the middle hook of the Foreland. Steered NNE 6 miles & were then becalmed. Soundings 35 fathoms rocks. Thick fog. A breeze at NNW took us off shore a few miles when we tacked ['**Saturday 18 July** Lat. 79°00° [*sic*] Lon. 8°10′E NNW' *in margin*] & stood to the NNE. Passed the N. end of the Foreland at 8 am. at the distance of 6 or 7 miles. Kept our stretch NE & NEbE taking a few angles of the coast when the intervals of the fog would permit & at 2 Pm. approached the ['north' *deleted*] shore of the main land at the place where the southernmost of the 7 icebergs rests. Here we had no soundings 4¼ miles from the shore. At about 3¼ miles distant we had 50 fathoms, half a furlong nearer 30 fathoms next cast 23 & next 17, rocks & shells. Tacked. ['Products of Spitzbergen' *in margin*] Sent a boat on shore to seek for seahorses, several of which we saw in the water & to bring off specimens of the natural productions of the country. They brought off a few birds, minerals, & vegetables. The minerals were principally quartzose, calcareous, and micaceous with some pieces of talc. They observed a hut on the shore & the graves or rather coffins of two or three men, ['one' *deleted*] which were laid in the ground [barely?] covered with a few stones. ['The lapse of time does not produce that decay in animal & vegetable substances which it does in warmer climates' *in margin*] One of the coffins ['which' *deleted*] appeared by an inscription on a piece of wood set up by it, to contain the body of a native of Britain, who had died in the year 1788 & though the coffin had lain exposed during a period of 30 years, the wood was undecayed & appeared quite fresh. It was painted red, & the colour was but little injured. On the beach was much small & principally old drift wood, with the fragments of a boat which in some places had been joined by cord instead of nails – the ribs & jaw bones of some species of whale, &c.

['Description of the land & coast' *in margin*] The coast in this place, as well as in almost every other part of this remarkable country is replete with novelty & grandeur. The hills between which occur the icebergs described by Marten's [*sic*] & Phipps[1] were

---

[1] An English translation (from the original German) of Frederick Martens's 'Voyage into Spitzbergen and Greenland' in 1671 was included in Narborough's *Account of several late voyages* in 1694. It was reprinted in the Hakluyt Society's *Collection of Documents on Spitzbergen* (1855), edited by Adam White, and the latter volume was itself republished in facsimile by the University Press of the Pacific in 2003. The account of the 1773 Phipps's expedition in HMS *Racehorse* and *Carcass*, entitled *Voyage towards the North Pole ...*, was published in 1774. Martens' reference to these glaciers ('icebergs') is at pp. 18–19 in the Hakluyt Society edition: 'Below, at the feet of the mountains, stand the hills of ice very high, and reach to the tops of the mountains; the cliffs are filled up with snow, wherefore the snow mountains show very strange to those that never saw them before; they appear like dry trees with branches and twigs, and when the snow falleth upon them they get leaves, as it were, which soon after melt, and others come in the room of them.
There are seven large Ice-mountains in a line in these countries, that lye between the high rocks, which look a glorious blew colour, as also is the ice, with a great many cracks and holes in them; they are hollowed out, melted away, and cut in grooves by the rain and snow water that runs down;

here narrow precipices proudly erecting their crests over the edge of the ocean to an elevation I suppose 1500 to 2000 feet. They consist of a rock the external colour of which is brownish black, and scarcely bear any snow upon them. They exhibit a number of acute angular points forming a surface the most rugged as possible.

Between each hill, which merely forms the termination on the side of the ocean of an immense chain of mountains, is a deep ['Icebergs in the Valleys' *in margin*] valley about a mile across, filled to the height of 150 to 200 feet or there about ['with' *deleted*] on the front, with solid ice & proceeding many miles backward ['inland' *deleted*] from the sea. The mountains on Charles' ['Mountains described' *in margin*] Island a few leagues to the SW of this place are even more beautiful than these. They commence with a base at the water's edge & by a continued ['& regular' *deleted*] ascent of an angle of first about 30° & increasing to about 45 degrees or more they come to a point with the elevation of upwards of a "mile". The termination of several of them are form[1] so fine a point that the imagination cannot descry a plain on which an adventurer attempting the hazardous exploit of climbing to the Summit, might rest. Were such an undertaking practicable [it?] is evident it could only be effected by the utmost powers of exertion, aided by extraordinary strength, perseverance, & courage. Some of the mountains of Spitzbergen form well-proportioned foursided pyramids, having each the base of 1½ miles square & an elevation of a mile; others form angular chains receding from the shore in parallel ridges, ['into the distant perspective,' *deleted*] until they dwindle into obscurity in the distant perspective. ['The Three Crowns' *in margin*] Some exhibit the effects of art, but in a style of grandeur even exceeding the famed pyramids of the east or even the more famed Tower of Babel, the presumptive design and continuation of which was checked by the miraculous confession[2] of tongues. Such regular & magnificent works of nature occur about King's bay, ['& are' *deleted*] known by the name of "The Three Crowns". They rest on the top of the ordinary mountains commencing with a square table or horizontal stratum of rock forming a complete square, on the top of which is

---

they are encreased greatly by the snow, as the other ice that swimmeth in the sea is also: they are augmented likewise by the melted snow from the rocks, and from the rain that falls on them.

These seven mountains of ice are esteemed to be the highest in the country; indeed they shewed very high as we sailed by them underneath: the snow look'd dark from the shades of the skies, which shewed very neat and curious, with the blew cracks where the ice was broken off.' See also Introduction, pp. xxix–xl.

Phipps's comment described a glacier further north, in the vicinity of Fair Haven:

'Icebergs are large bodies of ice filling the vallies between the high mountains; the face towards the sea is nearly perpendicular, and of a very lively light green colour. That represented in the engraving [in Phipps's account], from a sketch taken by Mr D'Auvergne upon the spot, was about three hundred feet high, with a cascade of water issuing out of it. The black mountains, white snow, and beautiful colour of the ice, make a very romantick and uncommon picture. Large pieces frequently break off from the Icebergs, and fall with a great noise into the water: we observed one piece which had floated out into the bay, and grounded in twenty-four fathom; it was fifty feet above the surface of the water, and of the same beautiful colour as the Iceberg.' (p. 70).

[1] 'form' inserted above the line, but 'are' not deleted.

[2] *Sic.* Evidently a transcription error for 'confusion'. Scoresby was referring to the account in *Genesis*, xi, 1–9.

another of similar form & height but ['narrower' *deleted*] a smaller square, this is continued by a third & a fourth, and so on each succeeding one being less than the last below it until it forms a complete pyramid of steps on every side, to appearance as regular as if worked by art.[1] I don't know if ever they have been visited. The appearance I have attempted to describe is that which they exhibit at the distance of 15 or 20 miles.

The sea ['being' *deleted*] was considerably turbulent when the boat landed, which circumstance with occasional fogs, rain & snow, with the rocky quality of the shore, prevented me from landing. I however took advantage of a favourable interval of fine weather to visit one of the icebergs. By the edge ['sides' *deleted*] of which we arrived at 10½ PM.

['Icebergs described' *in margin*] It is not easy to form an adequate conception of these truly wonderful productions of nature. They have their name from the Dutch, isberg, signifying ice mountain. They are met with in various parts of the coast of Spitzbergen. Their upper surfaces ['have' *deleted*] are generally concave in the line of the coast, ['gently' *deleted*] sloping towards the sea, where they terminate in abrupt precipices. The front of each usually lies parallel with the shore & though it rests upon the strand is washed by the sea, & undermined to such an extent, that when it becomes cracked by action of frost & the running of streams of water over its surface & through its chasms, immense masses break asunder and fall into the sea, but as the water is mostly shallow beside them the fragments are much reduced before they can float, which [serves?] to account for the purity of ice islands in the Spitzbergen seas. The surface of the iceberg I visited was rent in all directions near its front edge, but these rents extended ['were' *deleted*] mostly perpendicularly downwards dividing the iceberg into numerous columns. Some of our people walked across it & found the surface very <u>rough</u> & full of furrows & fissures, the former apparently occasioned by the running of water, streams of which could be heard bubbling beneath, & the latter probably by the expansion of these streams when frozen. The chasms were in some places some yards wide in others a few inches & occasionally filled with snow; into which they imprudently stepped & were nearly buried. An iceberg I observed near Horn Sound, was .... feet perpendicular in the front, but the one I now visited did not seem to be more than 100 to 150 feet high. The front surface is glistening and uneven. Wherever a mass has recently broken off the colour is a beautiful greenish blue, approaching to emerald green, but such parts as have been long exposed are of a greenish grey. The glistening green of these icebergs, ['adjoining' *deleted*] the glowing shades of ['blackish' *deleted*] brown, ['blackish' *deleted*] green, & ['blackish' *deleted*] purple ['Grandeur of the Spitzbergen scenery' *in margin*] of the naked rocks, & soil adjoining, contrasted with pure white of the snow which conceals the higher rocks & the greater part of the earth, aided by the occasional [etherial?][2] brilliancy of the atmosphere & calm serenity of the sea – present a picture novel and magnificent.

---

[1] This description is illustrated in Scoresby's sketch of 'The Three Crowns' (*Account of the Arctic Regions*, II, Plate III, no. 2.)

[2] *OED* accepts this as an alternative to 'ethereal', noting that 'The uncertainty of the spelling began in Latin ...'.

There is a kind of majesty not to be conveyed in words in these prodigious productions of ice and accumulations of cliff above rock, and snow & ice above cliff, reaching beyond the ordinary elevation of the clouds, particularly ['heightened by the strong contrast of light & shade – and bursting on the senses like magic' *deleted*] when ['by this after being' *deleted*]¹ it is concealed as you approach it by the impenetrable gloom a² summer fog and the fog rapidly disperses like the drawing of curtain & leaving a cloudless atmosphere & a powerful sun, heightens the strong contrast of light & shade and bursts on the senses like the production of magic.

I was particularly fortunate in witnessing one of the ['Falling of an iceberg' *in margin*] effects of the sea on the iceberg. A strong NW swell having for some hours beat upon the shore had loosened a number of the ['detatched' *deleted*] fragments on the iceberg, and various heaps of broken ice denoted recent shoots of the seaward edge. ['Whilst' *deleted*] As³ we rowed towards it with a view of proceeding close to its base I observed a few small fragments fall into the sea, and whilst my eye was upon the place an immense column, probably 50 feet square & 150 fᵗ high began to ['move' *deleted*] leave the iceberg at the summit & with an accelerated velocity [majestically?] leaned forward ['until' *deleted*] and ['at length' *deleted*] fell into the sea with a most awful crash. The water ['converting the waves' *deleted*] into which it fell was converted into an appearance of vapour and smoke⁴ like that from a ['[***]' *deleted*]⁵ [cannonading?]. The noise was equal to that of thunder, ['a' *deleted*] which it nearly resembled. The column which fell was square & seemed like the falling of a church. It broke into thousands of pieces. This circumstance was a happy caution to me for I might inadvertently have gone to the very base of the icy cliff, from whence masses I perceived were continually breaking.⁶

A moderate temperature acting upon ice seems to produce an ['Effect of warmth in resolving ice into columns or pillars.' *in margin*] effect different from that of a high temperature. At least the resolution of fresh water ice into perpendicular columns or pillars is an effect which a high temp. seems not to produce. Whether it is produced by the action of the sun's rays upon the water collected in little cavities & from its

---

¹ A replacement for this phrase, 'it is concealed as you', was also deleted, with 'it is' being the words finally chosen to replace those between 'When' and 'concealed' in the original text.

² *Sic*; 'of a' intended?

³ Unlike the preceding alterations, this replacement ('As') and those in the remainder of this day's journal entry are in pencil.

⁴ 'and smoke' was deleted, but there is a 'stet' balloon in the margin.

⁵ The word inserted as a replacement is also illegible.

⁶ Scoresby used much of this description of the glaciers in *Account of the Arctic Regions*, I, pp. 101–9. Although he continued to use the term 'iceberg', he noted (p. 102) that 'They are exactly of the nature and appearance of glaciers' and (p. 107) 'Icebergs are probably formed of more solid ice than glaciers; but in every other respect they are very similar.' Perhaps it was also the sheer size of the feature that encouraged him to maintain this distinction, similar to that nowadays between 'glacier' and 'icefield'.

Scoresby's description in the *Account of the Arctic Regions* was reprinted in the April 1820 issue of the *Edinburgh Philosophical Journal*. It was followed, in the October issue, by an article 'Observations on Ice-Bergs, made during a short Excursion in Spitzbergen' written by Thomas Latta, who was the surgeon on the 1818 voyage. Though it contradicts some of Scoresby's conclusions, neither Scoresby nor Latta seem to have realized that these bodies of ice were in motion. See Introduction, p. xxxix.

greater density than ice forming a kind of lens I cannot say – though were that the case it might account for the perpendicularity of the fissure observed in the icebergs.

The animals seen were seahorses (none on the shore) <u>traces</u> of foxes, the burgomasters, kittywakes, fulmars, puffins, Greenl*an*d swallows (....) roches, looms, dovecas, icebirds ([emberiza?] nivalis)[1] a very small red crested bird,[2] ducks, geese, divers.[3]

Sunday 19 July Lat. 79.15 Lon. 5°30′E mid n^t 79.14+
NNW.[4] Var. W. Calm.
When the boat returned from the shore we made sail & steered to the NW until noon: tacked & at 4 Pm. were becalmed. Open ice in sight to the NW & N. In the course of the day I saw a vast number of Razor backs [physalis] & a kind of finner resembling a bottlenose or Shetland whale, but much larger: it appeared to be 30 feet in length & had a hooked fin[5][...] about 18 In. high in the back. Sent some boats in pursuit of ['**Monday 20 July** Lat. 79.22+ Lon. 5°55′E WSW Calm' *in margin*] these animals having a buoy attached to the line at the distance of 120 fa*thom*s from the harpoon. They chased several and at length

['Razorback Mate  Line broke' *In margin*]

[2½ am.] the mate struck one of the Razorbacks, which I suppose would be 100[6] feet in length. The sudden jerk of the line when the buoy was drawn under water, (the fish having immense velocity) broke the line. We lost a gun harpoon & about 30 fa*thom*s of line value 50/-.

These animals are the swiftest of the whale tribe. They are not at all shy. They seem to take no other notice of a boat than to ['Razorbacks described their habits' *in margin*] avoid coming up underneath it & when disturbed by one, if not wounded it merely takes a little sheer & then proceeds in its usual way & course. Even some of them which the mate fired at & missed gave him subsequent opportunities of getting again within shot. They do not remain under water so long as a whale nor blow so often. Their speed is probably one half faster than that of a whale or even twice as fast; and their practice of running to an immense distance along the surface with a greater speed than any boat can go, prevents their being usually attacked.

The finners above mentioned were equally careless of the boats & ['A kind of finner described' *in margin*] would allow them to come near them many times successively, but if they attempted to pass before them, they either <u>shot</u> beyond the boats or changed their course.

---

[1] Identified in *Account of the Arctic Regions*, I, p. 537, as the snow-bunting (now *Plectrophenax nivalis*).

[2] Identified in *Account of the Arctic Regions*, I, p. 537, as the Lesser Redpole (*Fringilla linaria*). Presumably what is now termed the Hoary Redpoll (*Carduelis hornemanni*).

[3] This lengthy entry for 18 July ends at this point with a comma rather than a full stop, and with the remaining third of the page left blank.

[4] Possibly 'SSW.'

[5] Here follows a bracket enclosing a sketch of the fin.

[6] Possibly '160'.

The weather was ['a' *deleted*] clear until [3?] am. when a thick fog, commenced. Hazy during the day. reached into loose ice until it became troublesome & having taken several tons of fresh ice on board, tacked. Calm in the evening.

Tuesday 21 July Lat. 79°19′+ Lon. 6°0E
E.rly SErly Var. Calm
Chiefly calm. Beautifully clear weather. Sun hot. Thermometer in the shade 45° & hung against the ship's side on which the sun had for some time shone on black paint it rose to 92°. Spitzbergen from the Head Land to the Foreland in sight: the former bearing ENE, the latter SSE; the nearest land 25 miles dist*ant* (supposed.].¹ A ship in sight.

['Razor back Specksioneer Foreganger broke' *in margin*]

A number of Razor backs appeared in the afternoon: sent 4 boats in pursuit & struck one of them but ere 2 lines were run out & before ever the buoy went overboard or the line became tight, the foreganger broke. The fish seems to have broken it by getting it entangled with its tail, or more probably cut it by means of the horny hump or dorsal fin.

At 4ʰ4′0″ PM. by Chron*ometer* ☉'s true alt. .... = 24°26′⎱ Lat 79 17 Nearest pᵗ of
At 4ʰ11′9″ PM ———————————— = 24 8 ⎰ coast EbS 25′.

Spoke the Ipswitch's boat in the evening. She had been in Magdalena Bay caulking. Her success is about 60 tons.

Wednesday 22ᵈ July Lat. 79. 11+ Lon. 6°0′E
Var. calm.
Lay becalmed most of the day. The weather was generally clear, mild, and exhilerating [*sic*]. Some rain & fog however occurred towards night. What progress we made was towards the land.

Thursday 23ᵈ July Lat 79°18′+ Lon. 7°30′E
Var. Calm. SW.rly: NErly E.rly.
The greater part of the day calm, weather beautifully clear & pleasant. The thermometer 44° to 42. A breeze of wind from the ENE enabled us to approach the shore towards evening; we had a fine breeze in the top gall*ant* sails & topsails, whilst on the water was not a breath of wind. This was owing to our proximity to high land over which the wind blew. At 6¼ PM. we were about 4 miles from shore a little to the southward of the southern iceberg & only 2 or 3 miles from where our boat was on the shore before. I took two boats and ['landed' *deleted*] went on shore on a flat of land near the SW point of Cross bay, where the ground was ['Landed on Spitzbergen.' *in margin*] rocky at a considerable distance from the shore.² It was table land, extending about 6 miles N & S, & 2 or 3 miles E & W. from whence on the east the mountainous

---

¹ *Sic*: opens with a parenthesis and closes with a bracket.
² Scoresby described the events of 23–9 July 1818 again in *Account of the Arctic Regions*, I, pp. 118–35.

country ['Beech (sic) described.' in margin] takes its sudden rise. Calcareous rocks bordered the sea; in some places, a shingly or sandy beech, embanking by the action of the sea the whole flat of land above named, which appears at no remote period to have been occasionally covered by the sea. A micaceous shistus occurs a small distance from the shore[1] and then an immense bed of calcareous stone in small angular fragments; here & there pools or lakes of fresh water, beds of snow, and lastly towards the foot of the mountains extensive swamps, in which we sunk nearly to the knees. Some unhealthy looking mosses grow on the bogs in places, but the most boggy parts were ['free' deleted] void of vegetation. It was a marly peat kind of soil to look at, and the surface was curiously marked with polygonal figures formed by small ridges a few yards in circumference,[2] joining each other on all sides and giving the ground the appearance which is exhibited by a section of honey comb.[3] An ascent from the marsh, of a few yards, brought us to the foot of the mountains, one of which apparently 3000 f[t] in elevation we commenced to ascend.[4] The slope was by measurement an angle of 45° with the horizon. The side of the hill consisted of ['Steep hills' in margin] small angular fragments of calcareous & quartzoze stones; few pieces of which ['weighed' deleted] would[5] weigh more than 2 or 3 lb. Some masses of a stone resembling whinstone also occurred. Granite was seen on the beech but none on the hills. The ascent was amazingly difficult. The stones on the side being all loose gave way [under?] the feet & rolled down in showers at every footstep. Some rocks showed themselves through the hill side*[6] The side near the summit of the first range ['of' deleted] or lower hills was covered with [***] snow and ice[7] which in a direct ascent we tried in vain to surmount. We had to go along the side of the cliff about 200 yards before we could gain the summit. Here we rested whilst I took a few angles of the prominent parts of the Coast & their bearings, collected, a few plants & specimens of the minerals. We then passed along the ridge of a calcareous mountain, all broken into angular pieces smaller than what is [used?] by the high roads, which ridge was so narrow that I sat across it as on horseback! One side was an ∠ of 45° to 50° with the horizon the other of 40 to 45. Even the very ridge afforded no specimen of stone above the weight of 1½ or 2 lb., and no appearance of earth. This was a yellowish or reddish yellow stone: a kind of marble. The fracture seemed tollerably fresh & no earth or soil was to be seen. After passing this ridge, which extending about ¼ to ½ a mile, we descended a short

---

[1] In the Account of the Arctic Regions (p. 119) 'about half a furlong from the sea, we met with mica-slate, in nearly perpendicular strata'.

[2] In the Account of the Arctic Regions (p. 120) 'from one to three yards in diameter'.

[3] Polygonal soils, created by repeated freeze-thaw action in the active layer of the permafrost, have long been the subject of research, e.g. Elton, 'The Nature and Origin', Quarterly Journal of the Geological Society, 83, 1927, pp. 163–94.

[4] The Account of the Arctic Regions (p. 120) mentions several plant species at the base of and on the initial slope of the hill.

[5] Possibly 'could'.

[6] Note in margin: '*but they were cracked in every direction so that it was with difficulty a specimen of 7 pounds w[t] was got in a solid mass.'

[7] In the Account of the Arctic Regions (p. 121) Scoresby wrote 'Along the side of the first range of hills near the summit, was extended a band of ice and snow, which, in the direct ascent, we tried in vain to surmount.'

distance & reached the side of the principal mountain. No solid rock here occurred any more than those we had hitherto passed; but such as showed themselves by the side of the mountain were rent in every direction & [easily?] broken. ['Rocks all cracked & broken' *in margin*] Probably this state of the rocks is produced by the action of frost. The calcareous rocks especially seemed capable of absorbing some moisture which may be the means of ['cracking' *deleted*] rending them, when the moisture becomes frozen, in the state in which they were observed. The ascent of the higher ridge was even more difficult than the former at least far more fatiguing. We were glad to rest every 50 or 100 paces so that it took a long time performing the rise. ['**Friday 24 July** Var. Calm.' *in margin*] At length we completed the arduous task just as the sun had reached the meridian below the pole & shed his reviving rays upon a small flat covered with snow & ice which occurred on the top of the mountains. The thermometer placed in the shade near the summit of the mountain among some ['Summit of a mountain about 3000 f^t high' *in margin*] stones stood at 37°, on the 1st hill at 42 below it was 44 or 46°. The masses of stone at the summit were larger than any we had yet met with & the fracture less fresh. They were all overgrown & incorporated with moss, [or?] lichens.[1] The moss was the lichen islandicus, a <u>blackish</u> green moss, the common yellowish moss of Britain & a whitish <u>mineral</u> moss. The incrustasions on the stone were yellow, black, & red. Some pieces were beautifully embossed with the latter. Besides the quartz &c. occurred a fibrous slaty kind of stone, some pieces resembling serpentine & traces of iron on some stones. Down the side of the steep in which we ascended, the men with me frequently by accident ['& d' *deleted*] as well as design detached[2] lumps of stone which rolled down, whatever might be their[3] shape & size with great & accelerated velocity ['[driving?]' *deleted*] raising a cloud of smoke from the blows they struck the stones as they fell & rebounded ['[downward?]' *deleted*] forward, driving numerous other pieces along with or before them, until they ['were stopped' *deleted*] gained a most surprising speed & were stopped at length in a bed of snow at the foot 2000 feet below the place where they were set in motion. Most of the larger stones which were set in motion broke into a number of pieces, but some of a flattish form, rolled invariable on their edges & resisted the shock better than the others, making most prodigious bounds.[4]

The prospect from this mountain was extensive & grand. A fine bay was seen on the ['west' *deleted*] east;[5] mountain beyond mountain on the north, ['&'

---

[1] There are several corrections here, mostly illegible, but 'lichens' is clearly written, and in the *Account of the Arctic Regions* the stones are simply described as 'more generally covered with lichens'.

[2] Originally detatched'; 't' deleted.

[3] At the head of the margin on the next page of the manuscript, and the one following, is the following: 'Description of Spitzbergen & its products'.

[4] In the manuscript there is no following paragraph break; however one appears to have been indicated in pencil. In the *Account of the Arctic Regions*, this sentence forms the beginning of a lengthy paragraph describing the panorama around them. In the manuscript a marginal note (also in pencil and with only a few words legible) was added at the end of this new paragraph.

[5] From modern maps, it seems probable that Scoresby had reached the summit of a mountain at about 2810 feet (856 m) a.s.l., 79°17′N 11°25′E, and was looking eastward down into Lilliehöök-fjorden.

deleted] east, & SE: numerous ice bergs in various directions & beds of ice & snow extending between ranges of hills towards the NE as far as the eye could discern.

After a short rest in which we were really refreshed by the breeze which here prevailed & after surveying the surrounding scenery as long as it afforded anything ['new' *deleted*] striking we commenced the descent. We found this task much more hazardous than we had anticipated. The stones were so sharp ['and loose &' *deleted*][1] that they cut our boots & so loose that they gave way beneath our steps & frequently threw us ['against' *deleted*] backward against the hill. We marched abreast as it was very unsafe going before each other on account of the stones which were every now & then displaced. To save the labour of climbing along the side of the sharp ridge before mentioned we descended one of the steepest parts[2] where the stones were small by sliding down it in a sitting posture. We found this a most expeditious mode, especially where there was snow; but in places where ice occurred we narrowly escaped without an accident such was the vast velocity we obtained. All the party however reach'd the foot in safety.

[3]On the flat of land next the sea we met with the horns of reindeer, and many skulls & bones of sea horses, narwhales, whales, foxes and seals. The coffins containing human bones were laid naked on the shingle. Two Russian lodges & the ruins of a third formed of logs of pine appeared to have been recently occupied by Russian hunters (chips of wood & other matters being seen which appeared not to have been hewed 2 or 3 weeks). One of the hutts was a tollerable lodging, but smelt most offensively of smoke. Many domestic utensils were within it and about it. A new hurdle lay by the door and traps for foxes & birds were scattered all along the beach. The hutts were built upon the ridge of shingle adjoining the sea [beach?]. A hut which I formerly visited on the [Forland?] was much more comfortable than those I saw here [Describe].[4]

Among the shingle of the beech[5] were found many nests in which were eggs of duck, sea swallows,[6] and burgomasters, and several young birds; with the burgomasters & swallows belonging to them hovering & crying over them, repelling the artic [sic] gull, which seemed to have an eye upon the eggs or birds, and other

---

[1] The deletion, and the equivalent insertion ('& so loose that they') later in the sentence are in pencil. It seems evident that these alterations represent a draft of the version that appears in the *Account of the Arctic Regions*.

[2] In the *Account of the Arctic Regions* (p. 129), 'the inclination of which was little less than fifty degrees'.

[3] Throughout this paragraph, the original text has been heavily altered in pencil, with deletions, insertions, and marginal additions, some of which have themselves been amended and in other cases are barely legible. The present text is my interpretation of the result of these alterations, but I have not individually identified the latter here, as they normally are elsewhere, and other interpretations are possible.

[4] The brackets are in the original. The preceding sentence is not included in *Account of the Arctic Regions*.

[5] This spelling seems consistent in the repeated mention of the beach in the following paragraphs.

[6] 'terns', not sea swallows, in *Account of the Arctic Regions*, p. 130.

depradators, which they attacked with great fury. Even some of our men who took up the young of a swallow & a burgomaster were frequently nearly assailed by the old birds. At least they darted upon them within two or three feet repeatedly. So near indeed that one of the swallows was killed with a stone. They took the two young birds on board together with a swallow egg. The former they fed & the latter they hatched in warm saw dust, but the bird died soon after it broke the shell.[1]

On the beech I observed an innumerable quantity of very small green insects (of the <u>midge</u> or fly kind?) & the sea along the coast teemed with the clio borealis,[2] sea spiders, shrimps of a small kind, of the latter many millions.

I paid particular attention to the drift wood and ['Worm eaten drift wood' *in margin*] observed two pieces, one a large log, decidely [*sic*] worm eaten. They were perforated with holes of dif*fere*nt sides,[3] evidently the work of worms. I was wishful to ascertain this point as it excited some surprise among some philosophers, when I mentioned having seen worm eaten wood in Jan Mayen Isl*a*nd.

The beech was covered with great beds of sea weed, chifly [*sic*] [***], and a broad largeleafed sea weed, together with some of the smaller kinds of arborescent appearance.[4] But though this shore [& the hills?] adjacent disappointed us as to the want of interest in many of the productions the beech at length afforded to our research a prize of vast value; namely, a large <u>dead whale</u>.*[5] This at once fixed our attention & took it from objects of mere curiosity. It was much swoln, embedded in the shingle and fixed so fast that there was little hope of getting it off. We therefore determined on flinching it as it lay upon the shore and carrying the blubber it afforded to the ship in boats. To this end we brought the ship, with the first

['G. Welborn found it Dead fish: no bone. N° 8' *in margin*]

breeze of wind as near shore, as its rocky & dangerous nature would prudently allow, which was not within two miles, cleared two boats of their lines & apparatus, and with suitable instruments for flinching took them on shore. With the first incision we made the oil spring out in streams so that we poured it by buckets full into the boats & then loaded them with about two tons of blubber besides. ['Flinching on shore' *in margin*] We put the oil in casks as it came on board, and plugging up the scuppers made off the blubber at the same time, dispatching the boats as emptied. By the time we had gotten 5 boats loads on

---

[1] In *Account of the Arctic Regions* (pp. 131–2), Scoresby noted that one of the young birds that was taken on board 'was very lively, and grew rapidly; but having taken a fancy to a cake of white lead, with which the surgeon was finishing a drawing, he was poisoned'.

[2] Described and illustrated by Scoresby in *Account of the Arctic Regions*, I, p.544, and II, Plate XVI, Fig. 10. The Latin name still survives.

[3] Transcript error: 'sizes' intended?

[4] In the *Account* (p. 132), Scoresby named several species of seaweed (see also Appendix V in volume I of the *Account*), and in the preceding paragraph (p. 131) he identified the birds observed during the shore visit.

[5] Note in margin: '*There was a harpoon & piece of line attached to it, appeared to have belonged to one of the fishers of the Elbe.'

board, a breeze of wind arose at South, the ['**Saturday 25 July** Lat. [*blank space*] Lon. [*blank space*] Var. SSW to SbE to SW & W' *in margin*] sky became overcast, rainclouds appeared, and a fresh gale of wind with heavy rain, succeeded. The sixth boat had much difficulty in reaching the ship, & the sea having become considerable the boats were unable to reach the place where the fish & men were unless they could be carried to windward & by this time the ship was 5 or 6 miles to leeward. Immediately that the boats were cleared we took them up, and having drifted into 13 fathoms water instantly made sail to attempt to beat up to the men. This took us 6 or 7 hours in effecting, when having gained a <u>weatherly</u> situation we reached between rocks to the S. & N. within about ¾ of a mile of the shore and then dispatched two boats which returned with all the absentees in about an hour and a half. Stood out to sea.*¹

The wind subsided in the evening & veered to the W. & NW.

Sunday 26 July
NW to NbW. Calm
At 8 am. blowing a fresh breeze at NbW we stood in with the land seeing a practicability of bringing off the rest of the fish[.] I reluctantly, being Sabbath day sent the boats on shore to attempt it, least by an increase of sea or worse weather, or westerly winds we might be prevented altogether from getting it – besides the oil was constantly oozing from it & rendering it every hour less valuable. Much difficulty occurred in coming at the under part of the blubber but it was at length accomplished and other five boats' loadings procured. Thus was this arduous operation completed. ['We were howe' *deleted*] Our first spell occupied us near 40 hours, the second, 18. So wearied were the men on the first occasion that some fell asleep in the boats & one man actually slept as he stood upon his feet upon deck, after the watch was set!*² Our fatigue & anxiety, however, was well repaid, for the fish ['produc' *deleted*] filled us 16 casks of blubber containing 40 butts or 20 tons capacity, & probably capable of producing 12 or 13 tons of oil.³

['Sea horse killed. Blowing: food: &c.' *in margin*] We saw several seahorses, in the water but none on shore. One we killed. Its stomach was filled with shrimps, a kind of craw fish, and some other substances. The sea horse in breathing seems to blow like a narwhale. It swims fast. Pays little ['notice' *deleted*] regard to a boat except as an object of curiosity; and when wounded boldly attacks it or at least its companions, which ofttimes drive their tusks through the boat.

---

¹ Pencilled note in margin: '*During these operations men slept standing'.

² Note in margin: '*Our anxiety was considerable during these operations as we navigated a rocky shore which had never been surveyed, & of the charts which had been made I had no copy. Rocks were seen 1¼ miles from the shore & others at smaller distances. The lead was our only guide & this where the rocks are frequently surrounded with deep water, was but an unsafe dependence. We were mercifully preserved.'

³ In the *Account of the Arctic Regions*, I (p. 132) Scoresby omitted these quantities, and instead mentioned that the whale was 'a prize to us of the value of about 400 *l*'. That is consistent with the average price of whale oil, £38 per ton in 1818, quoted by Scoresby in volume II, p. 410 of the same.

Monday 27 July
SW to S. to SSW

The weather being uncommonly fine & wind moderate from the SW to S. afforded me an opportunity of surveying the coast & examining its products whilst the objects of the voyage were not neglected. Stood in for the land in the morning & reached into King's Bay. This place, alike with those situations we had recently navigated, I was also unacquainted ['Entered King's Bay' *in margin*] with. We kept the lead continually going but though we were within ¼ of a mile of the shore on both sides of the bay we never once struck soundings with 50 or 60 fathoms of line. Sometimes we were becalmed beneath the lee of a high mountain lying to the South or SSW of us, at others we had a fresh breeze of wind. I sent a boat to each side of the bay & landed myself on a point consisting of <u>marble rocks</u>. A hut was erected where ['Description of this Bay & shores & products' *in margin*] we landed which appeared to have been inhabited within a few weeks. The shore rose with a gentle slope about 200 yards from the beach & then an immense precipice appeared. The rocks thereof were all a kind of marble, which effervesced with an acid; veined white, reddish brown and ['purple' *deleted*] bluish grey. These like all the former rocks were full of fractures so that it was difficult to find a solid mass above 5 or 6 inches square & a few pieces more than half that size. On the sloping bank was a bog, and some soil which affording fine specimens of the dif*ferent* plants produced in the country, several of them in full blossom. The heaths, & mosses were various. ['At' *deleted*] Towards the sea edge the ['rocks' *deleted*] stones were ['extremely rough and' *deleted*] in ['a' *deleted*] small angular fragments scarcely two ounces in weight. At the margin of the sea the rocks were still full of cracks in every direction: they were chiefly a kind of marble but some pieces of rolled granite appeared.

['Curious cave' *in margin*] A curious cave excited our attention by the sea edge. It was formed in the solid rock over which was a very regular though natural arch. We rowed into it with the boat & found it terminating after running inland about 30 or 40 yards. We could not reach the bottom at the head of the cave with an oar 16 feet long. We found a fine specimen of rhomboidal calcareous spar in the cave, but nothing else which was curious. Saw ['some' *deleted*] several sea horses, some of which we shot but they also sunk & escaped us. I returned on board after a short absence, meaning to put to sea as the weather looked very threatening. Rain clouds appeared; the sun [evaded?] in an haze, and the mountains were deeply capped with clouds. Along the shore we saw a number of perforated rocks & some mountains in the bay exhibited precipices on their sides of ['some' *deleted*] a thousand[1] of feet perpendicular or upwards having the appearance of regular columns. They had quite a basaltic look, but probably they were marble rocks with indentations & blackish perpendicular veins which gave them to [*sic*] columnar aspect.

King's Bay is a capacious inlet. It extends SEbS & NWbN about 10 miles inland. The shore is bold, we were about ⅔'s way to the head, but found no anchoring place.

---

[1] Originally 'thousands', 's' deleted.

It has long been resorted to by the Russian hunters & used to be one of English W. F*ishin*g stations.

['Fineness of weather near the shore' *in margin*] It is worthy of remark that since our arrival ['upon' *deleted*] in the immediate vicinity of the coast we have scarcely had a foggy day & in general the weather has been really pleasant & mild. E.rly winds have prevailed & not westerly as are usual near the ice. We have frequently observed the fog to hang over the ocean but a few leagues distant from us to the westward.

Took the boats on board at 9 Pm. and steered NWbW out of the bay. Rain commenced with an increase of wind, which in a few hours blew so hard a storm that we had all ['**Tuesday 28 July** Lat. 79.10 Lon 7°10′E SSW to WSW.' *in margin*] hands to call to reduce the sails. Steered to the W^d under the three close reefed topsails.

The storm subsided in the forenoon. A fog followed the rain. Tacked in the evening & stood in towards the shore.

Wednesday 29 July Lat. 78.40 Lon. 6°5′E
SSW to E to SW
Fresh breeze in the morning with thick W^r. Clear in the forenoon and moderate wind. About noon the wind freshened rapidly; the barometer having fallen greatly (to 29.38) indeed very uncommonly for the season we called all hands to reduce sails: put the ship under a snug sail: but in the evening the wind blew so hard that we had to rouze[1] them again, expecting every sea to lose some of the boats, as the waist & chains boats were repeatedly in the water, the former quite lifted from the tackles. Took the waistboats in & secured the others by lashings to the Davits. Wore the ship with her head to the SE & lay too under close reef'd maintopsail & mizen stay sail: all other sails stowed. The sea was tremendous: but we were mercifully preserved from any accident. In the morning ['**Thursday 30 July** Lat. 78.48 Lon 6½°E SSW. to W. & N.' *in margin*] an amendment took place & in the course of the day fine weather was restored. Steered to the W^d to make the ice.

I forgot to register in my remarks on King's Bay that I ['Bearing of Foreland from King's Bay: by ☉'s Azimuth' *in margin*] took an azimuth of the sun when it was directly <u>over</u> the North end of the Foreland & the ship was in the very center of King's Bay, which of course gave me the true bearing of the Foreland from the Bay which was S68°W & N68°E: the var*iatio*n ship's head SEbE or ESE was 14W. Probably the true var*iatio*n was much greater: though this does not materially differ from Capt. Phipps' Observation in 177.:[2] At the same time the SW ['or NW' *deleted*] p^t of the bay (the low land) projected to the NW beyond the line of the N. end of the Foreland but only about 5°[E?]. So that the true bearing of the SW p^t from the N end of the Foreland will still be the same within a small fraction of a degree; but the bearing of the middle of the entrance of the bay will be 3 or 4° more northerly.

---

[1] Possibly 'rouse', but *OED* does include 'rouze' as an obsolete variant spelling.
[2] *Sic*; presumably 1773.

Friday 31 July Lat 78.18 Lon. 4°30′E
Calm. N.
Chiefly calm & clear weather. The Middle Hook of the Foreland was rendered visible when not above 2 or 3 minutes of alt. above the horizon by the reflection of the West sun from its sloping hills, which shone with a metallic brightness. Saw 3 razor backs, pursued them to the SW. A breeze of wind from the N^d allowed us to steer WbN towards the ice, designing to give it another visit before we left the country and also to take on board a quantity of fresh water.

Saturday 1 August. Lat 78.0 Lon. 1°0′E Bar 30.00 Ther. 34°34°32°& 30
N. NNW. NNE
Gentle breezes of wind cloudy weather, with showers of hail like, ['snow' *deleted*] or prismatical snow. Saw ice about 8 am.; steered along the north side of a stream until 4 pm. & then passed through a slack place to the south side, where the ice had left a quantity of brash ice among which we sent our boats to procure a stock of water. We took in 6 boats' load and then made sail to the SSW^d on our homeward passage: intending however to course the ice along near as far as Iceland should the wind permit; as there are instances on record of the Dutch having fished on the northern shores of this island after the fishery on the Coasts of Spitzbergen had terminated.

Sunday 2^d August Lat. 76.40+ Lon. 1°30′E Bar. 30.10 Therm. 34. 34. 38
NNE to NW
Fresh or light variable winds. Steered SSW until 10 Am. At 7 passed a stream of ice & at 10 steered SW & in the evening hauled by the wind SWbW or WSW. Fine clear weather. No ice.

Monday 3^d August Lat. 75.14+ Lon. 1°10′E Bar. 30.10 Ther, 32.34.33.
NW to W. Var.
Light variable winds. Pursued our course to the SW^d. Saw neither ice nor ships, or any living creature excepting a few birds. People employed in various useful work.

Tuesday 4 August Lat. 74.40+ Lon. 1°50′E Bar. 30.00 Ther. 33, 34. 33
WbN. W
A fresh breeze of wind with fine w^r urged us to the S^d but prevented us from getting towards the west. Made considerable progress by the wind.

Wednesday 5 August Lat 72.25 Long. 3°40′E Bar 29.90 Therm. 36. 38, 35.
W. WbS Calm. E.rly
The wind fell to calm in the morning: the weather continued fine, but cloudy. Made some advance to the SSW & S. In the evening a light breeze fair. Steered SW. Saw several puffins & arctic gulls.

Thursday 6 August Lat 71.58 Lon. 2°.40′E. Bar. 29.70 Therm. 34 to 36.
ENE to [NNE?]
Light variable winds, rather more wind at night; heavy SE swell. Steering under all
sails SWbW to SWbS. In the night, which ['was' *deleted*] showed twilight, passed a
vessel steering to the E^d. Cleaning the ship with all hands.

Manifest of the Cargo, of the ship Fame of Whitby, Foreign built, burthen per
British register 370 58/94 Tons, William Scoresby Jn^r Master, sailed from Liverpool
to Greenland, and from thence bound for Whitby. To Wit.

One hundred forty leaguers & Twelve puncheons	Containing three hundred twenty six butts of blubber of half a ton each, and fourteen butts of krang and inferior blubber

Three tons and a half of whale finns.
11 Seal skins.

The produce of eight whales, eleven seals, [' three unicorns' *deleted*] one sea horse [skin
cut up for ship use], and three unicorns.

Greenland seas 2^d August 1818.   Willm Scoresby Jnr[1]

Friday 7 August Lat 69°40′ Lon. 2°E. Bar 29.70 Therm. 36° 40°. Bar: 10 pm. 29.82
NE to N, NW & WbN
Fresh to light breezes, fine cloudy weather: course SW or SWbS. velocity 4 to 7 knots.
Several arctic gulls about & fulmars. People variously employed: mechanics industri-
ously engaged, enlarging gun-room, fitting hatches & fastenings, building new
harpoon chest, & new fore hatch ladder & purchase blocks for discharging;
armourer straightening & cleaning fishing utensils, and making bolts & bars for the
hatches, &c. &c. &c. Dusk about 10 pm.

Saturday 8 August Lat 68°57′+ Long. 1°40′E Bar 29.72 Therm. 46 to 52
W to SSW, var. Calm.
Light winds or calm, cloudy, showers of rain in the morning, fine clear weather
about mid-day. Turned all the men's beds, ['&' *deleted*] bedding, ['&' *deleted*]
chests, and clothing upon deck & exposed them to the sun & air; cleaned the
half deck out & cleaned & fumigated every cabin throughout the place. They
were put down in the evening much sweetened, and the men's lodgings much
improved. Courses SW to SE, also NW or WNW. The therm. which was yesterday
36 rose at noon to 52; a variation of 16° in about 24 hours. The weather felt
hot.

---

[1] Note the date on the manifest, four days before the journal entry.

Sunday 9 August Lat. 67.54 Lon. 1°20'E Bar. 29.84 Ther. 44°, 46.
ENE to NNE
Moderate or fresh breezes of wind, showers of rain. Course steered SWbW to SWbS
to suit the position of the studding sail, which we had constantly set on both sides. In
the night stars were first visible, since the month of April. The colour of the sea was
green, on Saturday it was blue without any tinge of yellow whatever. This change of
colour in the sea of the ocean from azure blue (nearly) to greenish blue was more
decided than I have ever before observed it.

Monday 10 August Lat. 66.8 Long. 0°36'E Bar. 29.96 Therm. 48–50.
NNW to WbN
Though the weather was cloudy in the morning, yet the barometer being high, we
washed the whale lines and suspended them across various spars lashed from rigging
to rigging and from mast to mast, to dry. The wind continued moderate, but fair until
noon, it then veered to the W^d and became rather scant. Lat by double altitude 66°8'
Longitude by chronometer 0°11' or 36'E. Course in the evening [*blank space*]

Tuesday 11 August Lat 64.27 Lon. 2°50'E Bar. 30.00 Ther. 52°
SWbW var.
Fresh breezes cloudy weather, showers in the evening. The weather bearing an
unfavourable appearance, took the whale lines down, though not quite dry & coyled
them in the gun room, about 2–4 Pm. Tacked and stood an hour to the NNW but
finding the direction unfavourable tacked again. General course SbE to SSW. Velocity
4 to 6 knots. Saw Puffins.

Wednesday 12 August Lat 62°57½'+ Lon. 5°10'E. Bar. 30.26 Ther. 54, 56.
WNW, W. NW: var.
Fresh breezes, showery weather. Steering under all sails close hauled by the wind from
SW to S. & latterly more westerly. About noon the haze clearing we saw the coast of
Norway, extending from the SE to SSW, the nearest land about 30 miles distant:
Many of the higher hills bore wreaths of snow even at this advanced season of the
year.

Thursday 13 August Lat. 62°0'+ Long. 5°E Bar. 30.30 Ther. 56 to 52.
NW: Calm. WNW to NW
Light variable winds from the NW & W, sometimes calm: The wind blowing nearly
from Shetland obliged us to keep our reach towards the SW. At noon a high Island,
being the southernmost land in sight bore SSE distant apparently 7–10 leagues.
People employed scouring the boats &c.

Friday 14 August. Lat. 60°34'14"+ Long.2°6'E Skerries W10S = 83 miles. Fair Island
W29S:=116'
WNW to N. & NN E
Light to fresh breezes. The wind northering early in the morning permitted us to
shape a course for Shetland. Set every sail in the ship, five studding sails, royals, &

stay sails; besides the usual square sails, mizen, & jibs. Velocity at 10 Am. 9 knots; At noon only 6 being less wind. Sun set by the chronometer at 7ʰ59′ pm. amplitude by compass on the after midship binnacle N30°W & on the Fife rail[1] near the main mast N34°W Lat. 60.10. When ['Magnetic anomaly' *in margin*] the ship steered WbN the sun was ahead at "3.40′" pm. whereas by the supposed var*iation* 2¼[2] pts. it ought only to have been at W¼S. It appears therefore that a great attraction from the ship prevails producing an error of a point of the compass on a West course. The Sun's True alt. being … ° the var*iation* by binnacle compass appears to be [*blank space*] W. This account[3] for the ship being considerably (near 20′) to the eastward of her reckoning though the reckoning was kept with 3 pts var*iation* being an allowance of above ½ [a?] p*oint* for the attraction of the ship. In the day's work from yesterday noon to that of today, the lat. according to courses steered did not appear to be so far south as that by observation by 20′: hence in correcting for the long. supposing the distances to be correct an allowance of about a point besides good allowance for leeway &c. was found necessary to bring the course & lat. correct.

At sun set, the sky being very clear in the West & NW, we ['Shetlandmen left us' *in margin*] got sight of Hang cliff, bearing WNW dist*ant* probably 40′ as it was not visible lower down than the main top. At 11 the land being visible from the deck, the weather fine & likely to continue, barometer being high, the 12 Shetlandmen, one of whom had been sick most of the voyage, left us in 2 boats, with 12 oars, 2 piggings one compass, a quantity of provision, water, and spirits. We immediately changed our course to SWbS: our velocity was then reduced to 3 knots p hour. All sails set.

Saturday 15 August Lat. 59.16+ Long. 0°30′W. Bar. 30.30 Ther. 54–58
NE
Light variable winds but always from the NE to N. Course steered SWbS & SW: velocity 2 to 4 knots. Saw some vessels. Caught above a hundred mackrell. Five or six lines were dragged after the ship at once and frequently three lines hauled up fish at the same moment. Suspended the lines again, got them well dried & coyled them up in coyls of one line each.

Sunday 16 August. Lat. 57.50+ Long. 1°10′W. Bar 30.$\frac{30}{40}$ [*sic*] Ther. 60–64.
NE to E.
Light or moderate ['fine' *deleted*] winds, fine clear weather. Saw MoorMount (near Buchaness[4] at noon bearing W. dist. 30 miles & about 4 pm. the land about Buchaness & Kinnaird Head was in sight & that near Aberdeen at sun set. Course p Compass SWbS: velocity 3 to 4½ knots. Saw several Flemish fishing vessels. The

---

[1] Smyth, *Sailor's Word Book*: 'FIFE-RAILS. Those forming the upper fence of the bulwarks on each side of the quarter-deck and poop in men-of-war. Also the rail round the mainmast, and encircling both it and the pumps …'. Presumably here used in the latter sense, and clearly not an ideal place for a compass reading, because of the iron rails.

[2] There is a ″ sign in this line, beneath 'WbN' in the line above, so that it is possible to read the transcript as '… by the supposed var WbN 2¼ pts, it ought …'

[3] *Sic*: 'accounts' intended?

[4] The parenthesis was not closed.

clouds in the evening threatened wind. Three strata were distinctly visible. ['Modifications and motions of Clouds' *in margin*] The lower one consisting of large dense masses of cloud without any particular shape moved towards the West with a velocity as great as I have generally seen in a storm. The next stratum was of the modification called cirrus. It was beautifully attenuated and streaked with various off shoots. The motion of this was to the south; its velocity likewise considerable. The highest clouds were the cirro-cumulus. They were small, dense, white, & [fleecy?]. They had no motion which was perceptible. Under every possible sail.

Monday 17 August Lat. 55°44′ Long. 1°W. Bar 30.08 Ther. 61–60.
E. NE. ESE
Fresh gales, prevailed after 4 am. with dark cloudy weather, haze, & rain. Carried every sail with increasing hopes of reaching our port by the springs, the highest tide of which is expected to be on the 18th (to-morrow)[.] And, the Fame drawing near 15 f^t water, requires an elevation of tide which does not always occur ['in' *deleted*] even on the springs, but on account of the moon's perigee occurring near the full, a very elevated springs is anticipated. Employed all hands in [***unstowing?] the hold and dragging several casks from aft forward to trim the ship nearer on an even keel being now 2 feet by stern. Saw land through the haze about 2 pm. suppose to be about Holy Island. A great number of Flemish & Yarmouth fishers about us at noon.

Steered SWbS & SSW½W ['all night' *deleted*] in the evening in case of the wind falling & veering to the W^d but on the breeze freshening shaped a course for Whitby SbW.

About 9 Pm. the wind blew very strong at ENE: supposing ourselves near the Yorkshire Coast, took in the stearing sails hauled by the wind & struck soundings in 35 fathoms. Took in top-gallant sails & hauled the courses up & steered SbE & SSE all night with the main yard to the mast. At day break saw land ['**Tuesday 18 August** ENE' *in margin*] under our lee, bore up before the wind & through the showers of Rain which prevailed got sight of Whitby Abbey. Ran down to within a mile of the pier head but too late for tide. Got a pilot on board and immediately made all sail to beat off shore: wind directly upon the land & sea considerable. Lay too on the flood, arranged a signal for our taking the harbour & at 5 Pm. saw the signal displayed from the Ancient Staff on the Cliff, bore up and made sail for the harbour. About 50 yards from the East Pier the ship unfortunately struck and instantly yawed to the SE as if she were running directly upon the [Rock?] – providentially, however, by a prompt manœuvre of the sails & helm she recovered herself to the astonishment of every one & again pointed her bowsprit to the harbourmouth. She continued her course with diminished speed & in a few minutes with in the harbour afloat & out of danger. Had she gone behind the East Pier she must have been wrecked! The sea was heavy & increasing and the nature of the Rock such that there would not have been a hope of her being saved. We hauled her up near the bridge & moved her close to the bank on the W. side of the harbour. She struck very considerably in taking the ground & especially on floating ['**Wednesday 19 Aug^t** ENE' *in margin*] next morning, when the sea & wind were much increased. The tide being good hauled through bridge and grounded on a sandbank. The ship took a great [heel?] and strained considerably, and opened several of her bilge seams. Before the tide fell, however, we had sent down all top gall^t masts, yards, & rigging & struck the top-masts[* * *][1] and removed other top [weight?].

After the cargo was discharged, the ship was put into the graving dock of Messrs Fishburn & Brodrick, and underwent a considerable repair – all the fastenings, underwater, being renewed, the bottom being sheathed & several futtocks that were found broken, replaced with new.

---

[1] The illegible item appears to be the top part of a question-mark, though that makes no sense in the context of the sentence.

Journal for 1820

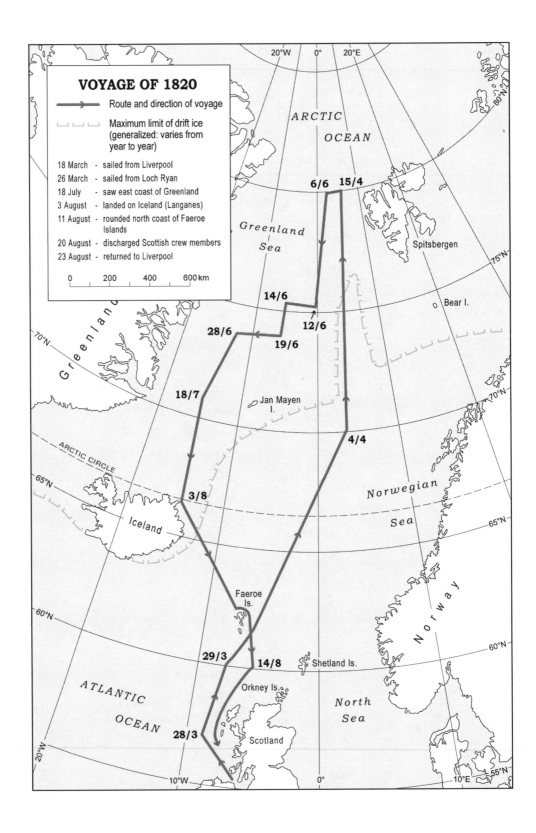

VOYAGE OF 1820

Route and direction of voyage

Maximum limit of drift ice (generalized: varies from year to year)

18 March - sailed from Liverpool
26 March - sailed from Loch Ryan
18 July - saw east coast of Greenland
3 August - landed on Iceland (Langanes)
11 August - rounded north coast of Faeroe Islands
20 August - discharged Scottish crew members
23 August - returned to Liverpool

0   200   400   600 km

ARCTIC OCEAN

Greenland Sea

Spitsbergen

Bear I.

Greenland

Jan Mayen I.

ARCTIC CIRCLE

Iceland

Norwegian Sea

Faeroe Is.

Shetland Is.

Orkney Is.

Scotland

Norway

ATLANTIC OCEAN

North Sea

6/6   15/4

14/6

12/6

28/6   19/6

18/7

4/4

3/8

29/3   14/8

28/3

80°N

75°N

70°N

65°N

60°N

55°N

20°W   0°   20°E

10°E

Journal of a Greenland or Whale Fishing Voyage under Divine Providence in the Ship Baffin of Liverpool by William Scoresby Jun[r], Commander. 1820.

Introduction

Having, in the month of November 1818, contracted with Mess[rs] Hurry and Gibson*,[1] of Liverpool, to join them in a whale fishing concern, I removed, with my family from Whitby to this place, in May of the following year. For some time, Mess[rs] H & G had been on the look-out for a good second-hand vessel; but not meeting with one suitable, for the Greenland Trade, it was at length resolved that a vessel should be built expressly for the purpose. Accordingly, proposals with diff*erent* builders were obtained; and on the ... of June, a contract, with Mess[r] [*sic*] Mottershead and Hays,[2] was executed, in which these gentlemen engaged to build us a ship for the fishing, in every respect complete for the fishery [Hull & Spars][3] and entirely to our own plan and dimensions; for which we were to pay them the sum of ... £ p ton, register, together with an additional [*blank space*] £, for fastening the doubling with copper. ['nails' *deleted*]

JOURNAL of the PROCEEDINGS in BUILDING.

June 25th, 1819 the Keel was laid in 4 pieces; each scarf thereof being fastened with 8 Copper bolts of ⅞ths diameter, driven in ¾ in. holes.

28th. Several floors were placed across, and on **the 3d, July** the stern frame was erected. On **the 6th,** the heel bolts, about 9 in number, of 1⅛ in. copper, the longest 7f[t] 3in. in length, were driven.

July 8. Six after frames erected; **by the 10th,** 4 more; **by the 17th,** 12 more; and **by the 24th,** 10 more. **On the 26th,** 7 frames were erected during the day completing 20 on each side from aft. **On the 27th,** 7 more were erected; **on the 28th,** other 6; and **on the 31st,** 4 more, completing 36 pairs of frames from aft.[4]

August 3. Completed the stern: the two pieces thereof ['bolted' *deleted*] secured together by 4 bolts of ⅞ths. copper: 2 more ['to be' *deleted*] afterwards driven in the

---

[1] Pencil footnote in transcript: '* Copy of Contract, see [***] [***] Journal'.
[2] *Sic*. Actually Mottershead and Hayes (Stewart-Brown, *Liverpool Ships*, p. 132).
[3] Brackets in transcript.
[4] Smyth, *Sailor's Word Book*: 'FRAMES. The bends of timbers constituting the shape of the ship's body – when completed a ship is said to be *in frame*.' See entry for 19 August 1819.

scarf through one of the breast-hooks.[1] The apron[2] was fastened to the stem, together with 4 bow-locks on each side of the stem, and the foremost <u>cant</u>-timbers temporily [*sic*], with iron, which completed the frame of the bow, and was erected on the **4th of August**. At the same time wedged up the fore part of the keel, to give the keel a bend downward in the middle of 6 or 8 inches: which bend it was supposed would become straight, or nearly so, when the ship should be afloat.

August 7th. Erected the last frame of the <u>flat</u>;[3] completed the after and main bodies; also laid across fore-body floors. Employed likewise [checking?] the ['frames' *deleted*] timbers at the feet, dubbing[4] them fair inside and outside, and in levelling the frames.

11th. Middle piece of the kelson put on [board?]; and **on the 12th** the after-piece. **On the 13th** completed the fore-body framing as far letter **H**. or the 8th frame from the flat; and on the next day finished as far as **K**, which [steps?][5] upon the fore-mast floor-ing. Also put up the bow-ribbons or <u>harpings</u>. **On the 18th**, elevated the 3d cant timber, foreward [*sic*], on each side.

August 19th, the 4th cant timber being erected the ship was <u>completely in frame</u>. <u>Size of Timbers</u>. Floorings, ['canted' *deleted*] sided, 11 to 13 inches; 1st futtocks, ... in: 2d futtocks, [*blank space*] in; top-timbers, ... Floorings, depth on the seat, 12 to 18 inches, exclusive of chocks, and at the floorhead ribbon, 11 inches; at the [lithe?] ribbon thickness of timber, in and out, 9 inches; at the main breadth ribbon, ['7 in.;' *deleted*] [upper part of the bends][6] 7 in.; and at the gunwale 5 inches. <u>Cross chocks</u> 4 to 8 feet long. <u>Kelson</u>, middle piece, 48 feet long [English Oak]; after end of it 15 by 18 in. and fore end 14. Quarter timbers 12 inches square.
<u>Number of the Timbers</u>. Stern-post sustains 9 transoms, from the wing-transom downwards, and 3 fashion-timbers on each side. "After-body" frames,[7] 22 pairs, 3 of them farthest aft being cant-timbers; 8½ flats, being all by the same mould; and 10 pairs in the forebody. From chock aft to N° 2, or letter **B**, of the Fore-body, timber and space occupys 2 feet 4 in.; but before this only 2 feet, the frames being all placed close. The after end of the lower piece of the apron butts against floor **G**: Hence the floors **H. J. K.** lay upon the apron.

---

[1] Smyth, *Sailor's Word Book*: 'BREAST-HOOKS. Thick pieces of timber, incurvated into the form of knees, and used to strengthen the fore-part of a ship, where they are placed at different heights, directly across the stem internally ...'.

[2] Smyth, *Sailor's Word Book*: 'APRON, OR STOMACH-PIECE. A strengthening compass timber fayed abaft the lower part of the stem, and above the foremost end of the keel.'

[3] Smyth, *Sailor's Word Book*: s.v. DEAD-FLAT: 'The timber or frame possessing the greatest breadth and capacity in the ship; where several timbers are thrown in, of the same area, the middle one is reckoned a dead-flat, about one-third of the length of the ship from the head.'

[4] Smyth, *Sailor's Word Book*: 'DUBB, To. To smooth and cut off with an adze the superfluous wood.'

[5] Possibly 'stops'.

[6] Here and in next line, brackets in transcript.

[7] There is a line through the text ('frames ... 8½ flats.') but it does not appear to have been intended to strike it out.

21. Employed dubbing the body fair for planking: **on the 23** the garboard strakes, put in.

September 4th. Completed the ['bottom' *deleted*] planking of the bottom and bilges. The flat all of elm, 4 in. thick fastened with [oak?] trenails and copper bolts; the bilge strakes, of elm, excepting where covered by doubling & these of oak, 6 inches thick, 5 in number, all fastened with locust-trenails[1] and copper. Also completed a thick strake above the bilges for the commencement of the doubling and 3 strakes below the [bends?]. Butt-end bolts, of the thick planks 12½ in. long by ¾ in. diameter; all others 10 in. by ⅝. Kelson and floorings previously bolted, each alternate flooring being bolted before the kelson was laid, and the intermediate ones, bolted through the kelson. These bolts 1⅛ in.[2] copper[.]

September 6, the lower strake of the bends put on; and **on the 13th.** the upper strakes finished.

On the 14th, blacking strakes[3] put on: and lower deck stringers, 14 in. broad by 6 in. thick put in, and bolted through every frame. **15**th. took 7 beams on board and **on the 16th and 17** most of the remainder. The beams were spaced, on an average, 5 f^t 3 in. apart, suited to the lengths of the casks, [and?] each secured on the stringer by a <u>dowel</u> besides the bolts.

On the 18th had finished the bends and planed them and the blacking strakes: chocked the top timbers by an extra timber between each frame, &c.; and put up stantion timbers. **On the 22**d [first?] strakes of top-sides put on, and **on the 27th** the 4th & last strake completed, together with 2 upper paint-strakes.

October 2d. The fastenings of the lower deck beams completed: consisting of 2 lodging knees at each end of every beam, secured by 9 or 10, one inch bolts of iron, every bolt clenching[4] into a thick strake laid below the bends, for the upper termination of the doubling. Thus every timber contained 2 bolts and each frame 4. By this time the stern-timbers were also [erected?]; knees of the wing trunnion completed; nose-piece, 18 feet long, and about 18 inches broad put up, and bolted through ['the' *deleted*] all and clenched on the apron within. The bolts [of

---

[1] *Robinia pseudacacia*, the False Acacia or Locust Tree. 'The timber is supposed to unite the qualities of strength and durability to a degree unknown in any other kind of tree, being very hard and close-grained. It has been extensively used for ship-building, being superior for the purpose to American Oak, and is largely used in the construction of the wooden pins called *trenails*, used to fasten the planks to the ribs or timber of ships. Instead of decaying, it acquires an extraordinary degree of hardness with time' (Grieve, *A Modern Herbal*).

[2] There is a question mark inserted above the line, in a different ink, at this point.

[3] Smyth, *Sailor's Word Book*: 'BLACK-STRAKE. The range of plank immediately above the wales in a ship's side; they are always covered with a mixture of tar and lamp-black ...'.

[4] Smyth, *Sailor's Word Book*: 'CLENCH, To. To secure the end of a bolt by burring the point with a hammer.'

copper][1] about the lower deck were 7 feet long! ['of copper!' *deleted*] Also several breast [hooks?] fitted.

By the 18th of October, the upper deck beams, carlings, and knees were all fitted and fastened, and water-ways laid. Stern-timbers and "timber foot transom" fitted and fastened: 'tween-decks ceiled, leaving two air holes. Considerable progress made also in the fortifications.

On the 19th began to lay the deck: finished **on the 23.** Employed for this purpose 3 in. Dantzic Deals,[2] fastening them with copper nails. **By the 30**[th] the Cabin-Deck of 2½ in. deals was laid & caulked: "channel-bends" bolted; 'tween-decks ceiling planed; deck caulked; head & cut-water, excepting figure got up and bolted, &c.

November 3[d] Rough-tree rails in progress: covering boards caulked; head-knees in progress; deadeye & chain plates ['bolte' *deleted*] fixed, &c. Staple knees in 'tween-decks fitted and bolted.

December 1. Ceiling of the hold finished; also cat-heads, comings of hatches, sails, taffrail rail [*sic*]; – Wind lass, capsterns, tafrail, cabin, seamen's cabins &c. in progress.
On the 20th, the caulking of the main skin was completed: **on the 23** water, to height of some feet was thrown into the ship by a forcing pump and every leak discovered, stopped.

27th. Commenced <u>doubling</u> from stem to stern. The strakes of the doubling were allowed to range upward, foreward and aft according to the natural direction of straight plank, and not by the direction of the ribbons: thus crossing obliquely the planks of the main skin, rendering it more secure and making an arch, ['contrary to the' *deleted*] in support of the sheer of the ship, having a great power in preventing the ship from "<u>hugging</u>".[3] The doubling was filled in from the bilges to the bends, into a thick strake above the former and below the latter, it was received so as to admit of the best caulking. It was 3 inches thick forward, [2½?] in. amidships, and 2 in. aft. It was fastened with copper nails and bolts; the former, 6½ to the lb. were 4½ in. long aft, 5 in. amidships, and 5½ foreward: thus being of the greatest length not to

---

[1] Brackets in transcript.

[2] This term does not appear in *OED* until the Supplement, where it is defined as 'used ... chiefly to designate kinds of timber grown in that [Danzig, now Gdansk] district, *Dantzig deal, fir, oak.*' The timber citations in *OED* are from the second half of the 19th century, but 'Dantzic deals of two inches and an half thick, well nailed and caulked' appear in W. Barnard's 1779 paper to the Royal Society 'An Account of a Method for the safe Removal', *Phil. Trans. R.S.L.*, 70, 1780, pp. 100–108.

[3] Because 'hugging', i.e. the ability of a ship to sail close to the wind, is an advantage, it is probable that this is a transcription error for 'hogging'. Smyth, *Sailor's Word Book*: 'HOGGED ... it implies that the two ends of a ship's decks droop lower than the midship part, consequently that her keel and bottom are so strained as to curve upwards.'

prick through the main-skin. The bolts were 9 or 10 inches long, weighing 1 lb each. A nail was put at every foot horizontal distance; and a bolt in every butt end, and also at every 3ᵈ intermediate frame, or every 7 feet distance. Between the doubling and main-skin, was placed a sheathing of flanel [*sic*] dipped in tar and tallow. The doubling consisted of 12 strakes, in midships, and a kent strake at each end, extending from the thick planks above the bilge to the stem foreward, and to the stern post aft. The after kent consisted of a broad elm plank, 12 or 13 feet long; and was fastened on each side, at the lower edge, with 9 bolts, besides nails. The kent strake foreward consisted of the lowest piece of trebling or ice ['knees' *deleted*] piece, and was well bolted to the timbers and plank. These kent pieces being thus well secured, admit of hard caulking beneath & prevent the access of water, upward beneath the doubling. All this work of doubling, excepting the fitting of the kent pieces, was accomplished in 6 days by 4 men and 12 apprentices; being only 8 hands on a side! The doubling [termines?] forward, below, at the 5 feet mark; abaft at 7 feet.

About the 8ᵗʰ of January, 1820; The doubling was all dressed fair, and partly caulked; Seamen's cabins finished; line room deck laid; two capstern's [*sic*], windlass, companion, ['&c. finished' *deleted*] fife-rail, boat's davits, &c. completed.

On the 20ᵗʰ. Commenced putting in ice-pieces about the stern[1] & trebling to the middle of the forechains.

January 28ᵗʰ 1820. Shipped the <u>rudder</u>; the braces on which were in the positions following. Height of the upper edge of each brace on the stern post, measured from the bottom of the <u>main-keel</u>. 1st Brace 22 inches [lower edge 18½]² 2ⁿᵈ brace [without a pin] 3 feet 8 in.; 3ᵈ 5 ft. 5½ in; 4th 8 ft 1¾ in; 5th 10 ft. 9¾in; ['6th' *deleted*]³ 6th, 13 ft. 5¼; 7th [counter brace] 18 feet 5¾ in. The pin of the 2ᵈ brace was fitted on the rudder but afterwards removed, that, in the case of all the braces being carried away, this gudgeon would doubtless be left, and would serve as the lower [band?] of a new rudder. To prevent any danger of leakage from the nails of the 3 lower braces drawing, being fastened on a single skin, these gudgeons were secured by screw bolts, not ['penetrating' *deleted*] piercing the plank entirely through by half an inch; so that should the whole be torn away, there would not, probibly [*sic*], be any leak in consequence of such an accident. Besides all these bands, the <u>rudder</u> and <u>stern post</u> had a further security in 4 heavy iron **KNEES** [5 in. solid in the throat] extending across the stern post and 12 or 14 inches beyond, having the position of the rudder when hard over, so as to support it & the stern post in case of a 'stern-board'. The lowest pair of knees was placed [*blank space*]ft [*blank space*]in. from the bottom of the <u>false</u> keel and the upper pair [upper edge] at the [*blank space*]feet mark. The rudder was built particularly large below; but very light & narrow at the water's edge.

[1] Possibly 'stem'.

[2] These and next two pairs of brackets in transcript.

[3] This deletion appears to have been made because it was at the end of a line and would therefore have been separated from the sixth measurement.

The <u>fortifications</u> were now likewise finished. They consist of the following parts. The breast-hooks as usual in all ships, five in number, are 12 in. square, and about 12 feet in length, and are placed 12 inches asunder. All the breast hooks are extended by an horizontal timber applied to each end, and every space is filled up with 4 similar timbers (a little lighter), while the horizontal ranges of timber of a similar kind are placed beneath the lowest of the breast hooks. These altogether form a solid bed of timber, extending from the hold beams downward to the foot of the apron, and occupying the whole interior of the bows to the distance of 17 feet on each side of the stem. This part of the fortifications interacts, in the direction of its timbers, the square frames and cant-timbers of the bows nearly at right angles, and each hook, intermediate timber and pointer [as the extension of the hooks is called] is bolted with copper into every frame which it intersects. Across the horizontal range of the fortifications are placed 7 riders, extending from the hold beams down to the lowest pointer; one rider is in the centre, corresponding in position, with the stem, another crosses the ends of all the pointers, and two more on each side are placed at equal intervals between those in the extremes and that in midships. [Near?] about the centre of the circle, of which the [bows?] at the height of the hold beams are arcs, is fixed a square perpendicular timber called a <u>King-Post</u>, of the diameter of 18 or 19 inches each side, and extending from one of the hold beams to the kelson. This post is convex on the forepart, presenting an arch towards the [stem?], and receives the interior ends of the [shores?], twenty-eight in number, fixed against the sides. Four of these shores [which are about 6 or 8 inches square] proceed to each rider, on to each extremity and two to intermediate positions. The king-post is supported abaft by two beams, of 12 inches square, one 2½ feet, the other 5 feet below the hold beams, which are securely fastened by knees to the timbers in the bows. As the king-post occupies a central position, with regards to the bows of the ship, the shores being set in close order between it and every rider, become radii of the circle of which the water line of the bows forms the circumference. Hence whenever a blow is received on any part of the bow, the shock must be communicated by the shores directly to the king-post, and from there dispersed throughout every part of the fortifications with which it is connected.

---

14 February. The bowsprit was put in. All the fortifications internal and external, and all the work needful to be done on the stocks were now accomplished. The launch was also laid, and every arrangement for launching in a state of forwardness, so as to take place on the following day.

15. Febr. Tuesday. The morning was fine and the wind moderate. The <u>Baffin</u> being the first Greenland ship ever built in Liverpool,[1] it excited a good deal of interest during the building; and this interest seemed to be augmented at the present time. In

---

[1] If Scoresby meant that the *Baffin* was purpose-built for Greenland Sea whaling, this may be true. However, Credland (*Hull Whaling Trade*, p. 125) noted that the *Mercury*, a bark of 346 tons, was 'Built Liverpool 1814. First reg[istered] Hull 1819, from Liverpool'; she sailed in both the Greenland Sea and Davis Strait until 1827.

consequence of this, together with the inviting day the concourse of people that assembled to witness the launch was immense. A platform erected on one side for the accommodation of the ladies was completely crowded; as was indeed every part of the premises that could command any tolerable view of the ship. As the ship was to be projected over a high quay, the <u>launch</u> was run several yards into the river, supported by posts and the whole kept down by two or three heavy [guns?]. Notwithstanding every precaution, however, some of the supports [worked?] loose, and occasioned some alarm with the builders. At 11h50' am. the retarding shores were struck off and the ship instantly started, and with a velocity that increased much beyond the usual rate, which was extremely fortunate, flew along the slides and cleared the quay, though the exterior part of the launch gave way the moment the weight came upon it. It was a beautiful sight. My friend Dr Traill was on board. Mr Robert Hurry performed the baptismal ceremony of breaking a bottle of wine over the head of our harponeer on the prow, ['and of' *deleted*] while with the best energy of lungs he invoked "Success to the <u>Baffin</u>." This name, it is almost needless to say was chosen in honour of the memory of our long neglected navigator of the same name; whose ['ingenuity' *deleted*] hardihood, skill, and perseverance, in crossing the Atlantic and navigating & discovering the circuit of Baffin's Bay in a vessel of only 55 tons burthen, can not be too greatly estimated.

As soon as the ship was fairly afloat she became our property & not till then; as such I immediately proceeded on board to take possession & was not a little gratified by the waving of hands & kerchiefs on shore and by the handsome manner in which I was received by the people on board.

The Queen's Dock being quite full, where we had intended to take up our moorings for the outfit, we were obliged to go into Salthouse Dock,[1] which being very crowded we found so difficult of access that we did not enter the gates until near an hour after high-water[.]

16 February. This being the day appointed for the funeral of our excellent old King, George III, was a holiday in all departments of business. The Baffin was however moved, and placed alongside the quay near the Gates. Above two feet water was found to have leaked into the ship in the course of 22 hours.

17th An unfavourable day. No work done.

18th. The lower masts put in: and tops and caps elevated into their places.

19th. Saturday. The rigging put over the lower mast heads: and top masts pointed through the Caps.

21. Monday. Stowed 20 Casks in the hold, agreeable to plan arranged before the beams were laid.

---

[1] The location of these 18th-century docks is described in Stewart-Brown, *Liverpool Ships.*

22. Stowed 30 casks: filled those adjoining the Kelson with water; and trimmed twenty tons of shingle and stone ballast in amongst them.

23 February: Wednesday. No suitable Casks being in readiness, nothing was done in the hold. Leak diminished.

24. Stowed a good many Casks. Leak diminished to about 8 inches per day.

25th. Continued stowing Casks. The riggers put up top-gallant masts & placed yards across.

26th. Stowed and filled with water several more casks.

28th. Monday. Received on board and stowed in the 2ᵈ tier of the after hold, 8 casks of beer.

29th. Received 7 [Carts?] of coals.

1 March. No work done. 2d March Nothing done.

3d. – Received 3 carts of coals, making our stock about 20 tons.

4th. – Received on board the Cambouse:¹ filled 5 Casks with fresh water.

7th. (Tuesday) 7 Casks of beef, salted in Ireland under inspection, received from the warehouse of Hurry & Gibson.

8ᵗʰ. Received 150 bushels of potatoes. Also a Chain Cable from Brown & Logan; [***]² iron, weighing (exclusive of shackles and joinings) 4 tons 1 cwt. 3 q. 10 lb.

9. – Received sundry beef, pork, rice. &c.

10. – Received cheese, bread, 10 casks & 7 bags (in locker) – herrings – salt fish – earthenware – tinware – marine barometer & sundry other stores.

11. Saturday. Mustered the crew at this time engaged being the amount required by law: viz. 42 men & boys. Paid advance money to the principal officers, and the rest of the people ['not' *deleted*] promissary [*sic*] notes payable after the sailing of the ship. Received on board the remainder of the beer making a total of 20 casks, or ten tons. Also one anchor, which was stocked & taken on board. –

---

¹ Possibly 'Cambruse'. See journal entry for 30 March 1820.
² Numerals, ending '/8'.

JOURNAL

Saturday 18 March 1820
NW NNW

As the tides were rapidly diminishing in height, so that two days, perhaps longer stay in the Salthouse Dock would have detained us during the neaps, we made preparation for hauling into the River ['sailing' *deleted*]; and though the wind was not fair, but directly contrary, as the weather was fine, with indications of a continuance, we determined, should our principal and essential officers be on board, to put to sea.

Having received the fourth new boat from Mottershead & [Hays?] with two belonging of late to the Fame, that were purchased of my Father, ['together' *deleted*] and one [a spare of?] boat of the James's in lieu of a pattern boat[1] ['from' *deleted*] ordered from Hull which had not come to hand. – together with all the ['requisite' *deleted*] completion of our requisite stores for the fishery, &c. – we hauled to the gates at ['12½' *deleted*] half past twelve and entered the gut[2] about one pm. Warping out of the gut to one of the buoys in the river, we fastened to it until the sails should be set. The tide having turned before our arrangements were completed, so that the ship swung forcibly round, broke our warp ['to the' *deleted*] attached to the buoy in consequence of which, in spite of every exertion with the Sails and the dropping of an anchor, the ship ran against the quay with her [stern?].[3] Though no damage was sustained and though we got clear of the quay in a short time, yet this inauspicious accident considerably annoyed and dispirited us. We now made sail and began to work down the channel.

On mustering the crew we found our cooper and four others, one linemanager and three seamen were absent; notwithstanding which, as we expected we might replace them at Loch Ryan, we beat out of the channel to windward of the Floating light and brought up on the turning of the tide. In the course of this navigation, the river being crowed [*sic*] with shipping, we were twice run on board of and once fell foul of a brig[4] – but fortunately no serious consequence ensued. At 8 Pm. the pilot left us, taking along with him my dispatches to Mrs S. & Messrs H & G.

Sunday 19 March
Calm. NW. to ENE. NNE

A light breeze springing up on the turn of the tide we weighed at 1¼ am. and ['tacked about' *deleted*] worked to windward until 5, when a fair wind commencing we stretched to the NNW for the Isle of Man.

The day was beautifully fine and mild. All hands were called at 10 am. to engage in services suitable the Sabbath. They were assembled ['upon' *deleted*] on the deck for worship: after a selection of the Church Prayers, not meeting with the Sermon I

---

[1] The term 'pattern boat' is fairly clearly written, but is not in either Smyth or *OED*.
[2] Smyth, *Sailor's Word Book*: 'A somewhat coarse term for the main part of a strait or channel.'
[3] Possibly 'stem'.
[4] Smyth, *Sailor's Word Book*, defined 'to run down a vessel' as 'To pass over, into, or foul her by running against her end-on, so as to jeopardize her.' Similarly 'a ship ran foul of us' implied that the ship 'entangled herself among our rigging'.

wished for I gave them a brief address from – Galatians V. v. 19–21[1] – 1st. the intimation of text, That there is such a place as Heaven: – 2d the intimation of the context – That there is such a place as Hell: – 3d the nature of the works that necessarily led to the punishment of the latter: and 4th the practical means of avoiding the one and attaining the other. – The most serious and pleasing attention was manifested during the whole of the service.

In the afternoon I again read the prayers together with a ['sermon' *deleted*] discourse out of Burder's Village Sermons.[2]

At [8?] pm. we were mid-way between the Calf of Man and Anglesey, and sight of the two lights on the Calf[3] and those on Point Linas[4] and the Skerries.[5] Reached to the Westward until 11 pm. and then tacked.

Monday 20 March Lat. 54°10′+ Lon. 5°W.
NWbW Calm. W.
Still fine weather & light winds or calm. Barometer 30.30. All hands were employed all day in putting the ship into order – securing the rigging against the friction of the rails, &c. At 7 PM. the weather became cloudy: the light of the point of Ayr[6] (a beautiful [***][7] illumination with changes of colour) was seen an hour after sunset but afterwards disappeared. At 11½ Pm. saw [**Tuesday 21 March** W. NW. var. SW W. NNW' *in margin*] the New Light,[8] near Strangford bearing about WbN: steered NbW, instead ['beaching' *deleted*] of NbE, up the North Channel, allowing two points for the influence of a leeward tide from 7 pm. until past mid-night.

At 2½ am, saw the Copeland light bearing NWbW. Continued our NbW course until daybreak when the Mull of Galloway was seen a few miles to leeward of us. At 8 am. bore up for Loch Ryan, rounded the ['light house on' *deleted*] Point of Corsil,[9]

---

[1] In the Authorized Version: 'Now the works of the flesh are manifest, which are these; Adultery, fornication, uncleanness, lasciviousness,/Idolatry, witchcraft, hatred, variance, emulations, wrath, strife, seditions, heresies,/Envyings, murders, drunkenness, revellings, and such like: of the which I tell you before, as I have also told you in time past, that they which do such things shall not inherit the kingdom of God.'

[2] Used on other occasions by Scoresby (see entry for 25 April 1813 of these *Journals*).

[3] The Upper and Lower lighthouses on the Calf of Man were both built by Robert Stevenson and first lit in 1818. They are now disused, having been replaced by a modern lighthouse on the Calf and by another on Chicken Rock. The source for these and similar details in other notes is Trethewey & Forand, *Lighthouse Encyclopaedia*. Notes about lighthouses mentioned on earlier voyages are not repeated here.

[4] Undoubtedly in the same location as Point Lynas or Elian Point lighthouse, on the northeast coast of Anglesey, east of Amlwch. However, *Lighthouse Encyclopaedia* gives the date of the present structure as 1835, and does not mention an earlier light.

[5] The Skerries is an island three miles off the northwest coast of Anglesey. There has been a light there since about 1717, rebuilt or improved at later dates, including 1759 and 1804.

[6] The Point of Ayre lighthouse on the northern tip of the Isle of Man, first lit in 1819.

[7] Probably 'revolving', but if so, it is misspelled as 'revoling'.

[8] Possibly the Phennick Point lighthouse near Ardglass, Co. Down. Although *Lighthouse Encyclopaedia* gives no details, it appears that the original structure, built about 1813, was blown down in 1838.

[9] Corsewall Point; Robert Stevenson's lighthouse there was first lit in 1817.

and ['entered the Loch' *deleted*] proceeded up the Loch by the middle of the entrance. A ship was observed coming out, which we found to be the Lady Forbes of Liverpool. We laid too on passing her for the purpose of sending a harpoon gun on board, which we had brought out for her. After this we proceeded to the Kern[1] and anchored about two cables lengths from the east shore abreast of the southernmost house in the village in 7 fathoms water.

I now procured a boat with 4 men to take me up to Stranraer for the purpose of engaging hands to replace those who had run. The distance of Stranraer from the anchorage is about 5 miles. On landing I applied to the usual agent M[r] Angus and after some trouble obtained 4 men, accustomed to boats and sloops but not seamen, at 35/- per month with fish money & boat money the same as our seamen and line-managers.

Having joined the Capt. of a Norwegian vessel at dinner in an inn, I accidentally learned that M[r] Gordon[2] the inventor of the patent portable gas lamp was resident in Stranraer being collector of the customs for the post. Accompanied by Rob[t] Hurry I waited on him and on introducing myself received a very cordial welcome. To my surprise he informed that Capt. Ross[3] was then in ['the town' *deleted*] Stranraer, being a native of the town & having a house in it. He invited Capt. Ross to his house, where I met him in the evening. The similarity of our pursuits and habits: the mutual interest we both felt in the polar Discoveries – soon produced[4] the familiarity of old acquaintance. Before I left the town I accompanied Capt. Ross to his house where he showed me some splendid M.S. maps ['of' *deleted*] being his own drawings, of Baffin's Bay and neighbouring regions. He presented me with a pamphlet containing a description of his deep sea clams,[5] and other instruments – also some engravings, from his drawings, of maps of particular situations in Baffin's Bay, &c.

About half past nine we set out for the ship: the night was boisterous and rainy, and the passage not only uncomfortable but dangerous. We were under sail during some very heavy squalls. The sea was considerable: the boat rolled heavily & shipped

---

[1] Cairnryan village, on the east shore of Loch Ryan. In Sinclair's first *Statistical Account* (1791–99), the entry for the parish of Inch includes the statement that 'The Cairn is the only considerable village in the parish, and contains 130 souls' (Vol. 3, p. 137).

[2] The catalogues of the National Library of Scotland and the British Library include items from the 1820s concerning the formation (actual or proposed) of Edinburgh, London and Provincial Portable Gas Companies. In regard to the last of these, the British Library's item is a 'Report of a meeting of the subscribers to Mr. David Gordon's Plan for forming a Provincial Portable Gas Company, held 15th December, 1824'.

[3] Later Admiral Sir John Ross (1777–1856), who was born in the parish of Inch, adjacent to Stranraer. See Jackson, 'Three Puzzles', pp. 14–17.

[4] Possibly 'procured'.

[5] Ross, *A Description of the Deep Sea Clamms, Hydraphorus, and Marine Artificial Horizon, invented by Captain J. Ross, R.N.*', London, 1819. In Smyth, *Sailor's Word Book*, one definition of a 'clam' is 'a kind of forceps used for bringing up specimens of the bottom in sounding'. In *OED*, a 'hydrophore' is 'an instrument for procuring specimens of water from any desired depth, in a river, lake, or ocean', but the earliest citation is 1842. There is an illustration of Ross's artificial horizon, now in the Stranraer Museum, at www.futuremuseum.co.uk/Default.aspx?Id=174&mode=object&item=2157.

so much water, that with the quantity of rain that fell I was very wet & uncomfortable. We did not reach the ship until mid-night. The Lady Forbes we found had put back & brought up near us.

Wednesday 22 March Loch Ryan
NbW. var. NW. W. SW.
Blowing strong all night & occasionally with intervals of variable light winds. In the morning the wind was moderate. About noon Capt. Ross, agreeable to appointment made the day preceding, came on board the Baffin in his sailing boat: but we were disappointed in the company of Mr Gordon. Capt. Ross brought with him a model of his deep sea clam for the inspection of our armourer, and presented me with a copy of the second edition of his voyage into Baffin's Bay.[1] ['We had di' *deleted*] Soon after dinner he left the ship, having to make his way to Stranraer against the wind. In the evening the wind veered to the SW and blew strong with heavy rain. We purposed to get under weigh ['**Thursday 23 March** W. Var. NW. to NNE.' *in margin*] at day light; but the wind having veered to WbN and the weather being excessively bad we ['lay still' *deleted*] remained at our anchorage.

About 10 in the forenoon, blowing hard and very rainy, the James of Liverpool, bound for Greenland, came into the Loch and likewise anchored near us. The day continued, throughout, very stormy with ['thick' *deleted*] heavy showers of rain. Two small vessels came in and anchored between us & the east shore. All hands employed, since our arrival here, in preparing the fishing tackling; &c. &c. Barometer 29.00.

Friday 24 March
NNE Var. S.erly NEbN
The storm abated in the morning & the weather became clear and tolerably fine. Landed at Stranraerer [*sic*] with my letters and papers for M^rs S & Messrs Hurry & Gibson. Dined at 4 with Capt. Ross. Returned on board at 9 & 11 pm. In the course of the evening we had calms & variable winds with showers of rain and hail. Strong showers and heavy squalls during the night from the NE.

Saturday 25 March
NNE NbW
Strong gales in the morning: clear weather. Two sloops arrived in the Loch.

Sunday 26 March
SW.erly W. Calm. SW
Towards day light the wind veered to the SW^d and much rain fell. The heavy fall of rain which accompanied the wind on its change and its abating some hours afterwards is a circumstance that often occurs after a continuance ['Rain falls on a shift of wind; observation on this fact' *in margin*] of winds, especially gales from one[2] quarter. Hence though the morning was stormy & thick I ventured to predict that the rain

---

[1] Ross, *A Voyage of Discovery*, 2nd edn, 2 vols, 1819.
[2] 'any particular' written above the two preceding words, but no insertion point.

would abate shortly being the immediate and necessary effect of the change of wind. Hence also in the polar regions when foggy weather has been prevalent for many days in consequence of Southerly winds, on a change to the N. or NW the fog does not often clear away until some hours after the change has taken place.

We prepared for sea about 8 am. Just before we started I was informed by Capt. Robertson of the Lady Forbes, that a letter for me was at the post office at the Kern. A boat was immediately dispatched & to my great gratification and surprise I received from the hand of a friend (Mr Laurence Frost) intelligence of the birth of a son which had taken place on the 21st inst*ant*, and of the welfare of both the child and the mother.[1] I hastily acknowledged the gratifying news to Mrs S. and then proceeded to sea.

Loch Ryan is a safe and commodious ['anchor' *deleted*] harbour. ['Description of Loch Ryan' *in margin*] The usual anchorage is near the village of Kern, about 3 miles up the Loch: The ground is tough and affords secure fastening. The tide, however, is some annoyance, running with a velocity of 2 or 3 knots. The best depth is in 7 fathoms opposite the [inn?] or highest house in the Kern. Large vessels however may go up above the scar a shoal that lays on the west side of the Loch and extends two-thirds across towards the Kern. The point of the Kern under which the ships lay (as a seaward point) is low but steep to [back?]. Some rocks lay off the inner part of the Point of Corsil a considerable distance and other off Finnart on the E. side, a cables length or two from the shore. The soundings being regular and very gradual afford every assistance for the safe navigation of the Loch.

Sailed at 9 am.: rounded the point of Corsil at 9¼ am. being preceded by the James and Lady Forbes: found the wind scant at sea. At 2 pm. reached near the Mull of Cantire when we were obliged to tack. Calm weather in the afternoon: at 8 Pm. had a breeze from the SW^d, under which we steered NW for the leeward side of Rathlin[2] Island. At 9 Pm. the Mull of Cantire light (a low indifferent light) bore due north distance 2¼ leagues.

Monday 27 March Lat. 56.9+ Lon. 7°34′W
SW to WbN.
We had a beautiful moonlight night: sailed on a course NWbN p Compass until 6 am. when Inishterhol Light on the coast of Ireland bore WSW dist*ant* 12 miles. From hence we shaped a course, N. for the westward of Barra He*a*d to give a good birth to the Skerrivore rocks extending to the SW^d 15 or 16 miles from Tiri Island.[3] At Noon

---

[1] Cordelia Stamp's *Scoresby Family* states (p. 26) that this son, Henry, was 'born and buried' in 1820, though the journal entry for 23 August 1820 suggests that he survived at least until that date. There is no reference to this birth in the biographies of William Scoresby by Scoresby-Jackson and by Tom and Cordelia Stamp.

[2] The 't' is not crossed, so could be read as 'Rachlin'.

[3] In her book on *Lighthouse Stevensons*, Bella Bathurst devoted a whole chapter to Skerryvore. She noted that there had been demands for a light on the reef since the late eighteenth century, and quoted Robert Stevenson's report in 1834: 'The Rocks of Skerrivore lie 12 miles South of the Island of Tyrii ... This Reef forms a very great Bar to the Navigation of the outer passage of the Highlands ... This reef has long been the terror of the Mariner, but the erection of a Light House upon Skerrivore would at once change its Character and render it a rallying point of the Shipping which frequents these seas.'

we were in latitude by observation 56°9. The wind now increased to a hard gale and became so westerly and scant that we had to proceed on a reach to the NbW. The sea was tremendously heavy; but the ship, contrary to our hopes, sustained her canvas (two treble reefed topsails and close reefed [***]) admirably, and was uncommonly <u>lively</u>. The wind being scant rendered it dangerous attempting to go to windward of the Lewises; and Barra Head not being seen before ['Strong flashes of Lightning to the E^d. Barometer 29.30' *in margin*] night made it too hazardous to run for the opening of the [Manch?].¹ To be as safe as possible therefore under the existing difficulties and hazards, we wore at 8 pm. when we conceived we were the length of Barra Head; Reached to the S^d until 2 am. and then wore ['**Tuesday 28 March** Lat. 57°16' Lon 8°42'W. WbN WSW SW: WSW' *in margin*] to the N^d. Soon afterwards the wind began to abate and veered more the southward on which we made sail to the NWbN & on discovering Barra Head at 6 am. 15 miles off to the E½S. we steered North, per Compass, along the west side of the Hebrides; keeping well to the westward to guard against the danger and inconvenience of a westerly wind. In the afternoon we had again a strong gale of wind with occasional heavy rain[,] applied rolling tackles to the topsail yards. At 2 steered NNE. At 4 got sight of the island of St Kilda, and at 6 passed the west side of it at the distance of 4 or 5 miles. Moderate wind about sun set, with an increase toward mid-night. Course now shaped NE.

Wednesday 29 March Lat. 59°45' indiff*eren*t obs*ervation* acct. 60.² Long. 7°31'W. SWbW to SWbS WSW

A progressive increase of wind took place in the course of the night so that in the forenoon it blew a very heavy storm. About noon the scene around us had a most sublime aspect, while the ship scudded with a velocity of 10 knots before the tempestuous ['Reflections' *in margin*] blast, the sea³ might be said to be mountains high – wave after wave followed us in rapid and varied succession: breaking and roaring along each side of the vessel and ['Description of a Storm.' *in margin*] occasionally throwing their sprays over the deck: the heavens were shrouded in a murky density; – the horizon was intercepted and the lower atmosphere obscured by the scum of the breaking waters; – the wind falling with striking violence on the sails occasioned a quivering in the masts and produced in the squalls a most prodigious velocity in the vessel. The scene was sublime. The horrific appearance of the tumultuous waters elevated into peaks and hills so high as to reach 10 degrees above the horizon⁴ of an angle when observed from our quarter deck, was not a little aided by the gloom of the atmosphere – suddenly, however, on the breaking through of the

---

¹ Clearly the Minch, between the Outer Hebrides and the Scottish mainland, is what was meant, but the transcript cannot be read as 'Minch'. As in 1818, Scoresby chose to sail to the west of the Outer Hebrides, and even to the west of St Kilda (57°50'N 8°30'W).

² Originally '60.07' but minutes deleted.

³ At this point there are several illegible deletions, as though Scoresby was groping for (and eventually finding) the best description.

⁴ There are lines in the text here that suggest that 'above the horizon' should be moved to follow 'of an angle'.

sun, with equatorial splendour, the aspect of the picture was changed, cheerfulness succeeded to despondence and ['pleasing' *deleted*] sensations ['were communicated' *deleted*] of a pleasing nature were communicated and took the place of the gloomy ideas suggested by the former scenery ['in all its danger and' *deleted*] replete with sublimity and danger.

Our course was NE until 10 am. when we hauled out ENE½E to ['Lightning in the Northern quarter. Bar. 29.10' *in margin*] give a berth to the Faroe Islands towards which we were rapidly approaching. Velocity from Mid-night 8 to 10½ or 11 knots. The night was stormy; but beautifully moonlight. The influence of ['**Thursday 30 March** WSW. W. NW.' *in margin*] the moon in expelling dense vapours and ['and' *deleted*] its power in breaking ['Excellent adaptation of the ship' *in margin*] through dense strata of clouds, were strikingly exemplified.

At day light changed our course to NE: the storm ranged with augmented violence; yet such was the delightful adaptation of the Baffin, that she surmounted the most powerful surges, and ['during' *deleted*] notwithstanding the dangerous nature of the navigation in scudding during a tremendous sea, scarcely received a spray on board. The dark light had been put in as a safe guard to the cabin windows, but the precaution was found to be needless.

At noon an observation of the sun's altitude gave us 61°32′ for the latitude which was fully a degree to the southward of what we had expected. During the 24 hours the distance run by the Log ['NW' *in margin*] was 214 miles [46 feet being allowed p knot for a glass of 20 seconds]; the mean course steered, corrected for variation was NEbN, yet the difference of latitude obtained was only about 107 miles instead of ['about 160' *deleted*] above 170. As the ship steered with uncommon and even remarked accuracy the loss of latitude [here?] was entirely to be attributed to an excess of easting gained above what was intended. On correcting the reckoning on this supposition, an influence of "deviation" or attraction on the binnacle compass, amounting to 2 points, on an E or W course, was discovered!

In the afternoon the wind veered towards the North.

['Reflections on Providence' *in margin*] In the most common concerns of life, in persons who have the ['fear of' *deleted*] God before them, numerous gracious interpositions of Divine Providence may be discovered, wherin their welfare and safety have been preserved by evident and clear ['interpo' *deleted*] Providences: But in the concerns of a seaman these interpositions bear a more decided and striking and even gracious character. I speak from experience. About 1 pm. while I was admiring the excellent properties of our vessel – her buoyance – liveliness – dryness – and superiority of construction I was suddenly roused to a different train of ideas by being told that the ship was on fire! Merciful God! how I started. The storm yet raged – the sea yet ['Ship on Fire!' *in margin*] foamed around us and the wind still hurled on our rigging! Where was our refuge? I flew to the spot.[*1] The deck under the Cabouse[2] was ['on fire' *deleted*] burning: the boards were ['almost through' *deleted*] almost

---

[1] Note in margin: '*The place was filled with smoke and the vapour of water.'

[2] Smyth, *Sailor's Word Book*: 'CABOOSE, OR CAMBOOSE. The cook-room of kitchen of merchantmen on deck … It is generally furnished with cast-iron apparatus for cooking.'

consumed, and spouts of fire were seen descending among the coals. Water! water! was the general cry. Hand along water! Water being brought: the fire in the hearth was quenched – the hearth was removed – the sheet iron on which it stood was torn up and water applied to the glowing planks. ['Mercifully' [?] *deleted*] Providentially the fire had not begun to blaze, or in a few moments we might have been involved in a ['serious destruction [?]' *deleted*] dangerous, awful and ruinous conflagration! For the whole compartment was intolerably hot and dry and must have fed a flame with the most destructive energy: while the immediate vicinity of 20 tons of coals must have augmented the power and strength of this powerful element. Providentially the discovery was made in time –and only just in time – the fire was quenched and the danger we trust, for the time, overcome.

The burnt part of the deck was cut away and replaced with new plank – the iron casing was reapplied – and the Cabouse, raised on blocks 5 inches above its former position, was then restored to its place. The accident arose from the feet of the cabouse being too short. They were only 3 inches in length; in consequence of which ['Lightning: Bar. 29.70' *in margin*] the heat of the furnace was communicated in [***] to the platform on which it stood. Lightning at 11 pm. in the western quarter.

Friday 31 March Lat 63°12' Lon. 0°39'W Bar. 29.25
Calm: SE. S. W. SW.
Calm about mid-night and until 2 am. A breeze from the SE^d then sprung up and increased progressively to noon, accompan*i*ed with heavy rain. It then blew a fresh gale. Our course was NNE p compass velocity at mid-day 10 knots. This course applying the deviation (near ½ p^t) easterly and variation 2¼ westerly makes a due course of N¼E. The rain abated about 2 pm & the sky cleared on the wind shifting suddenly to the westward. Set top gall*ant* sails. Last evening we were surrounded by vast ['flocks' *deleted*] numbers of Fulmars, and also observed several Dolphins ['Herrings' *in margin*] [Delphinus deductor of Dr Traill].[1] Hence we concluded that herrings were plentiful in the neighbourhood.

['At 5^h52'59" Pm Long 49'½ W. Chron*o*meter Slow – 4'39" Gaining daily 12'4.' *in margin*] At 5^h51'38" pm by Chron*o*meter [4'39" Slow] alt. sun's [upper?] limb 5°5': latitude 63°57'; hence apparent time 5.48.50 and true time 5.52.59. Longitude 49'30"W.

Fine clear weather in the evening: the Aurora-Borealis in ['Aur. Borealis Barometer 29.30' *in margin*] considerable streams. Velocity of the ship at mid-night was 7 knots.

Saturday 1 April Lat. 65°19'+ Lon. 37'W Aur. Bor. Barom 29.14
SSW to SSE
Course NNE all day: velocity 8 knots down to 1. Wind a fresh breeze to calm at midnight, True course suppose N¼E. All hands being summoned in the forenoon, cables were unbend and the best bower hauled partly on deck to dry, the morning being fine & [clear?] but showers of rain occurred about 11 am. & continued occasionally throughout the day. Aurora Bor. again considerable in the N. at 9 Pm.

---

[1] These and following brackets in main text (except '[upper?]') are in transcript.

Sunday 2ᵈ April Lat 66°53′+ Lon. 0°18′W. Bar. noon. 29.53
Calm. WNW NWbN N.
Calm for two hours. Fresh breezes about 3 am: had occasion to reef top-sails. Continued a NNE cruise until the veering of the wind towards the North diverted us towards the NE. All hands were summoned to public worship at 8 am. & as many as could get in attended in my cabin at 11. After prayers [Church of England service modified and abridged][1] I gave them an address on the Third Commandment. The attention manifested was pleasing. God grant that these imperfect services may be blessed & rendered profitable to a dissolute and thoughtless crew.

In the evening a moderate breeze prevailed from the North.

Monday 3ᵈ April Lat 67°53′ Lon. 1.20E
SW Werly
The morning of the 3ᵈ was fine and clear and the wind fair. Our fishing apparatus not being in a very favourable state and our rigging being slack & the mast in consequence insecure, all hands were called at 8 Am [***] these various and important operations. The main rigging was first set up: each shroud was tightened by measure[2] and the dead eye[3] brought down 4 inches. The mizen rigging admitted of 9½ inches and the mizen top mast backstays of 10 inches. The insecurity of this mast was so apparent that we had a tackle upon it to act against the stay as a support in place of rigging. The gammoning[4] of the bowsprit was then set up, and 3 inches of the strap gained. The bobstays and bowsprit shrouds came down 5 or 6 inches and the foretopmast stays about 10 inches. While each mast was undergoing these operations the sails upon it were all taken in.

The cable being dried was stowed in a snug coyl in the forepart of the tier and space made for the ice ropes abaft it.

A heavy and long continued shower of rain occurred about noon; but the evening was fine and clear.

['Aurora Borealis described.' *in margin*] At 9 Pm. the aurora borealis appeared with peculiar brilliancy. It ['first appeared' *deleted*] was first seen in the north: then extended ['by' *deleted*] in a luminous arch across the zenith ['to the' *deleted*] almost to the southern horizon. A [***] aurora next sprung up and filled the whole of the heavens to the eastward of the zenith, while only a few luminous specks were visible to the westward. The eastern aurora were grey and obscure and exhibited little motion: but the arch extending across the zenith showed an uncommon playfulness of figure and variety of form. Sometimes it exhibited a luminous edge towards the west, in some places concentrated into a fervid brilliancy and stretched from ['North' *deleted*] NE to ['South' *deleted*] SW with a ['[waved?]' *deleted*] rectilinear, or now &

---

[1] Brackets in transcript.

[2] Possibly 'measuring'.

[3] Layton, *Dictionary*: 'Deadeye. Hard wooden block, pierced with holes, fitted in lower end of shroud to take lanyard for setting up.' There is also a lengthy definition in Smyth, *Sailor's Word Book*.

[4] Smyth, *Sailor's Word Book*: 'Seven or eight turns of a rope-lashing passed alternately over the bowsprit and through a large hole in the cut-water, the better to support the stays of the foremast ...'.

then, with a slightly waved course: but each extremity of the band was curved upward. The rays were a little oblique to the position of the arch; but were ['Aurora Borealis. Bar. 29.70: Wind W.erly. Temp. about 38°" *in margin*] generally parallel and in a N & S. direction. At one time they extended sideways against the wind: at another in a contrary direction: now they shot forward numerous luminous pencils then shrunk into obscurity or dispersed into a mere vapour. The colour was yellowish white and greyish white. All the stars of the 4th magnitude were visible through the meteor even in its most vivid exhalations. The ursa major was at one time encircled with such a characteristic blazonry of light – that the bear seemed to spring into figure, and to be shaking his shaggy limbs, as if in contempt of the less distinguished constellations around him. The pleides [*sic*] were almost obscured in the light produced by the aurora: though venus and some of the superior stars, shone with becoming splendour. I was not sensible that the [shooting?] of the aurora was accompanied by any noise: the turbulence, indeed of the waters prevented slight sounds from being heard.

Tuesday 4th April Lat. 70°26′ Lon. 3°30′E
WSW. SW
Steered NEbN [or allowing deviation][1] NE½N all night. Velocity ['5 or' *deleted*] [8?] knots, sometimes more.

Fine weather throughout the 4th: generally clear with a fresh breeze of wind. Summoned all hands again at 8 am. to complete the operations commenced the preceding day. The carpenters finished 2 of the whaleboats, and completed their arrangements for coyling lines when it should be necessary.

About 4 in the afternoon a most melancholy accident happened. The Carpenter, Thomas Harrison, being in the main chains about to ship one of the boat's skeeds, lost his hold and fell along with the ['A man overboard!' *in margin*] skeed into the water. The velocity of the ship being 5 or 6 knots, he was astern in a few seconds, and before I could reach the deck on the alarming cry of "a Man overboard", he was beyond the limits of immediate aid. The ship was instantly hauled to the wind and every possible exertion made to get a boat down. The stern boat was the only one at all capable of being dispatched: its lashings were cut and after a considerable delay among its fastenings it was got into the water, manned, and furnished ['Carpenter drowned!' *in margin*] with oars. These operations were not effected in less than, I dare say, 10 minutes: meanwhile our[2] unhappy comrade supported himself on the skeed and was every now and then seen conspicuously elevated in the water. Our hopes of his safety became now great – the boat rapidly neared him – the vigour of the rowers seemed to increase – he now ['reared his head above the waves,' *deleted*] exerted the remaining powers of animation, reared his head above the waves, relinquished his enervated grasp, and then sank to rise to no more! Poor unfortunate shipmate, thy fate has been a melancholy one – thy death unexpected and premature: may the deep impression made on my mind by this distressing Providence be long ere it be

[1] Brackets in transcript.
[2] This word replaces a deletion, possibly 'he'.

erased; and may its effect on the hearts of all the anxious [panting?] spectators be such as shall render the dispensation a blessing to some.

The boat hovered for some time about the place – the crew picked up the skeed to which he had so long clung, and his hat floating buoyant by the spot, and then returned with saddened features to the ship. Many eyes that refused a tear to the [tossing?] of a tempest – to the crashing of masts and yards – to the stranding of a vessel – emitted a shower of briny drops to the fate of poor Harrison! This distressing event so operated on my mind that every sound made me start; and every voice heard in the course of a disturbed night, impressed me with the fear of another man overboard, and occasioned a most painful palpitation.

The sea being considerable when the Carpenter fell overboard the boat on attempting to hoist her up with the jerk of the sea broke the rings and fell adrift: we hoisted out another boat to pick her up, took her in upon deck & the whaleboat at the quarter. Course NEbN: velocity about mid-night 9 knots. Blowing strong.

Wednesday 5 April Lat 72°46+ Lon. 5°E
EbN
Blowing strong in the night: moderate through the day. Cloudy weather: sometimes clear. Spliced ['harpoons' *deleted*] foregangers to harpoons and made various preparations for the fishery.

At 4ʰ53′22″ (app*arent* time) longitude by chronometer 6°25′E. ['at 4ʰ53′ pm. Long 6°25′E+ Therm*ome*ter 34¹–32°° *in margin*] This being considerably to the eastward of our reckoning we changed our course to NbE¼E, expecting with 2 points ['[deviation?]' *deleted*] var. W. and ¼ point deviation E to make a due north course. Velocity 9 to 4 knots.

Thursday 6 April Lat. 74°6′ Long. 6°25′E Therm: 32°-30°-30°
Variable SWbS Calm. Eerly.
Calm in the forenoon: at 10 am. a breeze of wind from the Eᵈ sprang up and increased to a fresh gale. Steered by the wind to the Northward. Snow in the afternoon.

All the harpooners dined with me, when I took occasion to give them my advice, with numbers of regulations, for conducting the fishery. My remarks consisted of …. articles, of which an abstract may be hereafter given. This being the anniversary of the birth of my Dear Mʳˢ S. Jʳ; due remembrance and honour was done to the occasion.

Friday 7 April Lat. 75°40′ Lon. 5°12′E Bar. 29.60 Ther. 30°, 32°, 29°.
EbN: E ESE, SE
The wind becoming favourable in the morning we steered NEbN, expecting, if it should be an open sea of which there is every appearance, that that course would lead us to the Northward between the main western ice and Spitzbergen. At 2 Pm. the wind having increased to a heavy gale – the sea being cross and high – and the weather thick with fog – I thought it not prudent to run but hauled to the wind

¹ Possibly '30'.

(ENE), and ['Slight Aur. Borealis in the evening' *in margin*] reduced sails to two close reefed top sails, & sent down top-gall*ant* yards. Notwithstanding the heaviness of the swell the ship was dry & easy.

Saturday 8 April Lat. 76°40 Long. 5°26′E Bar. 29.70 Ther. 30°-29°-28°.
SE SbE
Blowing hard all night with fog, or snow. Twilight throughout the night. At 9 am. ['being' *deleted*] the wind having moderated and the sea having a little subsided, we set reefed courses and stay-sail, and steered NE½N, or NNE course, true;–

At 2 Pm. saw a small piece of ice; imagining it to have come from the land pack steered NNE. In the evening passed amidst some streams and numerous detached pieces of ice. The sea being heavy & ['Made the Ice' *in margin*] the weather frequently thick with snow, tacked at 8 pm. and stood by the wind out to sea. At mid-night cleared all the ice. Saw two ships, both under lofty sail, reaching to ['the' *deleted*] seaward. Many roches, ['snow' *deleted*] kittywakes, fulmars, &c. seen. Passed two pieces of drift wood. Ship under close reefed topsails & reefed courses.

Sunday 9 April Lat. 77°0′ Lon. 4°0′E Bar. 29.60 Ther,. 32, 30, 28.
SbE to EbS. EbN
Moderate or light breezes with foggy or snowy weather. [Stood?] to the SW & W^d until 8 am. then tacked and steered NNE. Our courses during the night having given us a considerable distance of westing I apprehended, should the ice we made be the land ice, that our now steering NNE would lead us clear of it ['and' *deleted*] on the west side. About 4 am. there was an appearance of land bearing NE: a ship passed us under all sails.

With the assistance of a Sermon by Revd G. Young,[1] from Matthew VIII: 24–26v,[2] in which I adopted some alterations and additions, I attempted to improve the melancholy death of our comrade, the Carpenter: the sailors were numerous in their attendance and appeared very attentive.

Saw no ice until 7 Pm. when we got sight of 2 or 3 pieces; afterwards saw a detached piece occasionally.

Monday 10 April Lat. 78°16′ Lon. 2°33′E Ther. 28, 20, 16, 10 Bar. 29.70
E. Calm. NE
Calm at 4 am. afterwards a breeze sprung up at NE which soon increased to a gale, and obliged us to treble reef the topsails, &c. All hands had previously been called to coyl lines; as such two boats were removed from the 'tween-decks, and one

---

[1] Presumably the Rev. George Young, minister of the New Presbyterian church in Whitby, and author of *History of Whitby* (1817).

[2] 'And, behold, there arose a great tempest in the sea, insomuch that the ship was covered with the waves: but he was asleep. / And his disciples came to him and awoke him, saying, Lord, save us: we perish. / And he saith unto them, Why are ye fearful, O ye of little faith? Then he arose, and rebuked the winds and the sea; and there was a great calm.'

suspended at each quarter: three others stood on the main deck. One of the officers declaring he saw land at 3 am. bearing NE distant 8 or 10 leagues, I was led to believe that the ice around us must be the land ice; we therefore reached to the westward. At 8½ am. passed through some streams of heavy ice, into an opening in which were small patches & detached pieces. At 11½ Am. being very thick with snow & frost rime & meeting with much ice we wore and dodged under three topsails and fore t. stay sail having the main top sail aback. Wore usually every three hours. In the evening the frost rime was intensely thick. From the deck we sometimes could not see a ship's length, but from the masthead, ice could be discerned at the distance of half a mile. The navigation amongst ice of which we knew not the situation was in consequence very critical and even dangerous. A heavy SE swell. Saw several narwhals.

At 4 Am. thermometer 28°, at 10 am. 16° frost rime began to appear; at 4 pm. 12 at 6, 10°.

Coyled four boats' lines.

Tuesday 11 April Lat 78°26 Long. 1°10′E Temp. 8 am. 10° 12 = 8. 2 pm = 6, masthead 3;[1] 11 pm = 5. Bar. 29.90
NE – N NNW

The frost rime having subsided considerably in the morning, and the wind blowing less forcibly, we made sail at 8 am and stretched by the wind to the NW^d and at 10 am. fell into a clear space of water, where was some swell, communicating apparently with the sea and extending greatly to the northward. At 1½ Pm. we fell into newly formed and forming bay ice, and at 3 reached the edge of body of heavy & bay ice intermixed, which was so compact as to ['tinge[?]' *deleted*] reflect into the atmosphere the lucid appearance called <u>ice blink</u>. This ice blink extended from SW or SSW to NE. Here, seeing nothing to induce our stay, we tacked and on standing to the E^d fell in with the John of Greenock, commanded by my brother in law, ['Capt' *deleted*] Mr Jackson. Capt. J. took tea with us. He sailed on the 22^d ult; has caught nothing. Under favour of a N.erly breeze we now stood to the ENE & NE. Calm some time in the night. Two or 3 ships seen.

The temperature was as low as 5°;[2] and at the mast head 3. Frost rime was prevalent all the day. ['Two or three' *deleted*] It is a little curious that ['Variableness of temp. within short distances.' *in margin*] while we yesterday had a temp. of 10° and most intense frost rime, in the John [of Greenock],[3] ['when' *deleted*] though only 50 or 60 miles to the SE^d of us they never had the temp. below 24° and had no appearance whatever of frost rime; but on the contrary experienced a fine and agreeable day! During the greatest cold, the cabin windows were embossed with variegated feathers of ice, ⅛ of an inch thick; the rigging was ['Effects of Frost.' *in margin*] clothed completely with a double fringe of frost, collected on different tacks & the

---

[1] Scoresby's punctuation suggests that the deck temperature of 6° and the masthead temperature of 3° were both measured at 2 p.m.

[2] Or '6°': one was altered to the other, but the intended value is uncertain.

[3] Brackets in transcript.

sails that had been furled, or reefed, on being unfurled or the reefs let out, retained every wrinkle, even in a brisk breeze and were so uneven in their surface during a day or two, that they resembled sheets of lead that had been rolled up, and were as difficult to extend!

Wednesday 12 April Lat 78°45′+ Long 1°50′E Temp. 4 am = 4½°; at 8 = 8°; at 4 pm = 18 & at 6 = 20°, being a rise of 15½° in 14 hours. Bar 9 pm. 29.60.
Calm NW, W, W, SW
The morning though cold was remarkably fine: the frost rime was not visible for some hours and the sun shone with brilliancy. Stood to the NE until we approached a considerably body of ice somewhat slack, and followed its margin to the E. & SE until 2 Pm. when we observed an open sea to the ENE. Steered in that direction under a brisk sail and a fresh breeze of wind, hauled more to the E^d or N^d, occasionally as we were directed by streams of ice that we now and then met with. At 7 Pm. blowing very fresh and seeing some cetaceous animals that we took to be mysticete, we hauled under[1] a stream of ice and lay too. But at 10 the wind having moderated & nothing seen we bore away under easy sail towards the NE. Eight or ten ships seen during the day. Snow showers at night.

Thursday 13 April Lat. 79°46 Lon 4°30′E. Therm. 8 am = 14°; Noon 12 8 pm 7, 11, 3°; 12 Zero! Bar. 29.90
WSW. to NW; N. NE. Var.
Light winds during the night. Pursued at [sic] NE course, seen a few detached pieces of ice, until 2 pm. when we had to bear up for a stream. The ice then lay ENE, with a strong blink as far as NE. The wind then veered to NE & blew fresh. Worked up into a bight of the main ice, [***] open pack, and lay too during the night, the weather being very thick with frost rime. At mid-night the temperature was as low as zero!

Friday 14 April Lat 79°40′ Lon. 5°E. Temp. 4 am = 0!; 7 am, 5°; 12 = 16°; 4 pm, 20; 5 pm. 26°. Bar. 30.00.
NE, ENE. Var. S.erly
The frost rime having cleared, and snow showers (beautiful crystals) which had been prevalent throughout the night having partly abated, we made sail at 7 am. not having seen a single whale, and running out of the bight reached to the SE^d in an open sea & with a moderate wind until the afternoon. The temperature which at 4 am. was zero gradually rose as per margin as the day advanced, and at 4 Pm. had risen 20°, in 12 hours. This remarkable rise of the thermometer ['suggest' *deleted*] indicated a Southerly wind, and I predicted confidently such a wind 2 or 3 hours before it reached us. About this time, or rather from 2 pm. until 5 pm. we had a considerable fall of snow, which (also indicative of a S. wind) sometimes cleared to the southward. At 4½ Pm. the wind subsided to almost a calm: ['Appearances on a change of wind: Thermometer predicts the change' *in margin*]

---

[1] Possibly 'across'.

the sails fluttered with variable breezes, and in a few minutes, a strong luminousness appeared to the S^d the snow soon abated, the thermometer rapidly rose to 26 and a strong wind from the SSW sprang up & presently increased to a fresh gale. The remarkable increase of temperature during a NE wind, ['showed that' *deleted*] with the fall of snow accompanying it, showed that in the higher regions of the atmosphere a southerly wind had for sometime blown, which being surcharged with moisture, deposited a profusion of crystals of snow, on assimilating into the northerly breeze. The Phoenix had two boats out after a whale: Passed the Volunteer, fished. John & Phoenix in C^o. Saw the Land, bearing SSE to ESE.

Saturday 15 April Lat 79.57+ Long. 6°20′E 4 pm. 80°5. Ther. 27. 24. 26. Bar. 29.83 & 29.46
SW to South SE, S.
Having made a long stretch into the land ice, consisting of streams of bay and heavy ice intermixed, until the Headland bore EbS distant 20 miles, we tacked & lay too; but seeing no whales, as the weather was clear though rather windy, we wished to improve the opportunity for searching a still more northern quarter. As such we made the best of our energy out of the ice, then steered NNW. At 10 am. the wind having increased to a fresh gale, and ice, apparently a crowded body, appearing to the NE, N, NW, & WNW of us, with a strong ice blink from WNW, north about to E, we hauled by the wind to the W^d. The wind still increasing and finding ourselves near the lee ice in a deep bight, we carried a brisk sail. At noon wore & stretched to the E^d until 4 Pm. when the wind having moderated & veered to the SSE or SE we tacked and hauled the courses up to wait for the John, which ship with the Volunteer kept us Company. At this time it was thick with snow. Wind moderate.

About 7 pm. a strong gale suddenly sprang up at S. accompanied with ['snow' *deleted*] much snow or mist, and in a few minutes blew a dismal gale. We had broken the hold out for some bread – had the decks [lumbered?] with provision casks, and such an additional weight on the lee side that it threw the ship down almost with her gunwale in the water. It was about two hours before the hold was secured and the sails close reefed. Under 2 close reefed topsails & courses we then steered to the W^d. At 9 Pm. fell in with a stream of heavy ice: the pieces drifted rapidly & were enveloped in broken water; we passed among a great number of dangerous pieces and at 9¼ Pm. fell into more sea room. The gale being in the very ['**Sunday 16 April** Lat. 79.50 Lon. 6°30′E Ther. 10 am, 28° 1 pm. 18: 9 pm. 21 Bar 29.49 & 29.23' *in margin*] worst quarter for our safety, we were obliged to carry as much sail as possible to keep off the lee pack. About 2 am. fell in with a stream of ice, wore; reached four hours to the eastward and then wore again. Somewhat clearer towards morning: John in C^o.

In the forenoon the wind abated: At noon, a fresh gale from the N^d suddenly commenced. The temperature almost immediately fell 10 degrees, and frost rime began to appear. Very thick at night & blowing, occasionally very hard. ['In the morning intervals of snow moderate weather' *deleted*.]

Monday 17 April Lat. 79.40 Lon 6°E Therm. 11, 9, 8. Bar. 29.13
NE
Fresh gales all day with snow showers and intensely thick frost rime. Dodging about the same spot among detached pieces of ice, and streams on the western reach, under 3 close reefed topsails & fore top staysail. John in Company.

Tuesday 18 April Lat. 79°25′ Lon. 5°20′E Therm. 9 am: 10 noon 9; 11 pm 6 Bar. 29.30
NE
Plying as above but with a ['retrograde' *deleted*] motion to the southward, the wind still blowing strong. Standing 4 or 6 hours on each tack, and alternately making the western streams. Generally so thick of frost rime that we could not see above two ship's lengths and sometimes scarcely more than one. The John parted Company.

Wednesday 19 April Lat. 79°10′ Lon. 4°55′E Therm. 3°, 3°, 3°, 10 pm 1° Bar. 29.50: 29.65
NE
The weather still intensely thick with frost rime, though the sun frequently broke through and shone with some brilliancy. Blowing fresh generally; but sometimes a strong gale. Towards night we had a very hard gale. Meeting with many pieces of heavy ice and occasionally streams the navigation was extremely dangerous. Happily, however, we avoided all the ice.

Thursday 20 April Lat.78°50′ Lon. 4°30′E Therm. 5, 5, 5, 4 Bar. 29.65+ 29.75.
NE
Very severe weather: cold and tempestuous. The navigation became more and more dangerous. Struck a hard blow against a heavy piece of ice, which woke me out of a sound sleep, and induced me to ['run' *deleted*] jump up and run on deck: the ice was then close under the lee fore chains: a formidable adjustment of the sails and helm [carried?] us clear of it without any accident.

Falling in with much ice during the day, the sea being considerable and the frost rime astonishingly thick, we traversed a sort of lake amidst surrounding streams and patches of ice, in which we had got miserably involved, with much danger and anxiety. In the evening the Sea was crowded with clumps of ice, as well as other masses, which ['having little drift' *deleted*] being deep in the water and having little drift, intimated that a considerable body of ice was to leeward of us. This gave me no little alarm: we set all the sail we could carry, consisting of three close reefed topsails and courses, with the foretop m. stay sail, and endeavoured to beat to windward. We fell in with ice on each hand at no great distance and doubted not but it was continuous to leeward of us. Being able to see much further at the mast head than on deck, I spent about two hours in the crow's nest where the temperature was about zero.

At 10 Pm. the barometer began to rise and we anticipated with much [pleasure?] a speedy change of weather. Showers of snow.

Friday 21 April Lat 78°50' Lon. 4°20'E Therm. 8°, 6°. 5°. Bar. 29.84. NE N.

Fresh gales, squally, with snow and frost rime, in the former part of the day; the latter part moderate gales.

The preceding five days, have been a continuous series of the most disagreeable and trying weather that occurs in the arctic regions. During [four?] days the frost rime has been so thick that generally we could not see, from the deck, a distance of 200 yards, sometimes not 50, and never half a mile. During this period it ['has been' *deleted*] was continually stormy, not always blowing ['Singular effects of Cold!' *in margin*] heavy ['certainly' *deleted*] but sometimes a hard gale. During this interval the thermometer ['has' *deleted*] was never ['been' *deleted*] above 11°, the average temperature ['was' *and* 'has' *deleted*] being 6¼°. The constant prevalence of such a degree of cold, accompanied by storms, frost rime, snow and a considerable sea, produced singular and disagreeable effects. ['By the help' *deleted*] With the advantage of a[1] hot air stove in the cabin, indeed, the temperature through the day was generally kept up as high as 45°, or 50°; though the stream of cold air rushing down the companion, the door of which, ['for' *deleted*] on account of smoke, we were obliged to keep open, gave a chilling sensation when the cabin was at the warmest; yet in other parts of the ship, even in the steerage, intense frost prevailed, ice formed in the mate's bed cabin, and water instantly froze when left in the chill atmosphere. The ship, hull and rigging, was completely white with the adhesion of the frost rime, and every rope appeared ['like a clumsy white' *deleted*] as if covered with a clumsy fringe. The bows, channel bends,[2] and quarters of the ship were loaded with ice and the decks covered with the same to a considerable thickness. The bowsprit shrouds and bobstays, sustained immense pear shaped masses, altogether many tons in weight; and the head, timbers sails, and [figure?] were consolidated into an irregular compact mass. The weight of ice was such that it brought the ship down by the head several inches and completely changed her trim.*[3] Some of the sailors suffered no little from the severity of the exposure, many (which is not usual) were affected with colds: the mate on taking off his shoes found his stockings frozen to the leather, and crystals of ice, arising from previous perspiration, enveloping his feet!!

[*At this point the normal structure of the journal is interrupted, with half a page being devoted to the following table, after which the structure and the entry for 21 April are resumed.*]

---

[1] Originally 'an'; 'n' deleted.

[2] See also journal entry for 27 April 1820. Smyth, *Sailor's Word Book* s.v. WALES: '… Strong planks extending all along the outward timbers on a ship's side, a little above her water-line; they are synonymous with *bends* … The channel-wale is below the lower-deck ports …'.

[3] Note in margin: '* The rudder was obliged to be repeatedly freed from ice or it would have been frozen immoveable: and the [pumps?] were required to be kept in almost constant [flow?], or they would have frozen solid and burst.'

Distribution of the Baffin's Crew into Watches, &c.

Captain's Watch	Mate's Watch	Specksioneer's Watch
Thomas Forster, Harp[r]	William Lloyd, M & Harp[r]	Thomas Murray, H.
Christopher Bennington B.	Thomas Atkinson, B.	Samuel Chambers, B.
Thomas Sargeant,[1] Line.	William Williams, Li.	Charles Morrison, Li.
Thomas Janion, S.	John Wright, Seam[n]	John O'Neill, Seam[n]
John Wilson, – S.	Thomas Selvey. appr.	John Thompson, ½ S.
John Neale, ½ S.	Thomas Murtha, ½ S.	John Beaton ½ S.
Thomas Page, Harp[r]	John Nattiass, Harp[r]	Thomas Baldes, Harp.
William Carr, Boats[n]	Isaac Wilson, Boats[n]	Richard Simpkin, B.
Alexander Flet, Line[r]	James Wells, Linem[r]	Matt[w] Swinburne, Li.
James Linland, Lan.	John Edwards, S.	Robert Poster, S.
Thomas Smith, Seam.	William Thompson, S.[2]	Don Donovon, S.
Robert Phelp, ½ S.	William Brown, ½ S.	Morris Williams, Carp[r]
Extra	*Extra*	*Extra*
Alexander Martin, ½ S.	Henry Sheridan, App.	James Thorburne, ½S.
Thomas Shaw App.	James Frost, App.	John Keogh.
15. Peter Jevons, Appr.	30. Robert Hurry.	45. Robert Kennedy.

Also, No. 46, Will[m] Nivison, Surgeon: 47, Tho[s] Lashley, Cook: 48 Dav[d] Vadone Stew[d]; & 49 W.S. Junior, Com[r].

The frost rime continued throughout the day, though not so thick as formerly. Finding the ship enveloped by streams of heavy ice, in which were many remarkable pieces and some <u>bergs</u>, the water clear and no whales seen, we made sail in the evening and stood to the eastward all night: passed numerous streams and at 7 am. fell into what appeared ['**Saturday 22 April** Lat. 78°55′ Lon. 6°00′E[3] Therm. 2 am. 8; 8 am. 18, 18. Saw Land. Bar. 29.89 N. NE. SEbS: NEbE' *in margin*] to be an arm of the sea. Then plyed along the exterior of the sea stream towards the NE & ENE.

The wind during the day blew a moderate breeze, sometimes fresh, and was very variable. It shifted suddenly from NE to SEbS and gradually veered back again to the NE. Much snow fell occasionally especially on the changing of the wind. Saw 3 or 4 ships; but no appearance of ['**Sunday 23 April** Lat. 79°5 Long. 6°40′ E Therm. 10, 6, 12, 9 Bar. 29.91 NE NNE' *in margin*] whales. Blowing fresh in the night with thick frost rime: about 9 am, found ourselves deeply involved amidst streams and patches of ice, where, from the intensity of the frost there was a great risk of getting frozen up. As such we ran out ['into' *deleted*] to the southward, into a more open situation & then lay too. In the evening spoke the Ebor with 2 fish close in with the Headland!

---

[1] Originally 'Seargent'; 'e' deleted.
[2] Originally '½ S'; '½' deleted.
[3] Apparently corrected; this appears to be the revised value of the longitude.

Monday 24 April Lat. 79°0 Long. 6°E Therm. 6°, 5°, 4°, 2°: Bar. 29.92
NNE

Fresh gales of wind with thick frost rime and snow showers. Lay too most of the night & day, that is, stood backward & forward, with the main yard aback. Lost, therefore, but little ground. We should have proceeded to the N^d but the formation of bay ice, intimating a risk of being frozen we ['lay too' *deleted*] preferred remaining to the southward of the ice streams. <u>Saw a whale!</u>

When I retired to rest the preceding evening there was no bay ice to be seen; but when I arose the sea was almost covered with extensive streams of cake ice and sludge. These streams lay NNE & SSW, principally, or in the direction of the wind. In some of them the ice had already gained such a consistence that the ship almost stopped in passing through them. Their formation seemed little impeded notwithstanding the force of ['Frost rime over bay ice. Its appearance.' *in margin*] the wind and a strong wind lipper. I observed that amidst the most extensive streams of bay ice, the windward edge of which we could not discern, that frost rime skimmed along the surface, though not so thickly as on the water. The frost rime resembled the smoking of a pond of warm water from a steam engine, during cold weather. The rime exactly resembled the vapour of steam [&?] appeared in streaks and patches with intervals between.

The water here is very green and turbid. On examining a portion ['Animalcules in the sea.' *in margin*] with a microscope I observed several new animalcules. One appeared of this form [*very small sketch inserted in text*]; it was $\frac{1}{4000}$ of an inch diameter; it advanced by a steady motion of $\frac{1}{150}$th of an inch in a second. Two or 3 occurred in almost every drop of water! The second kind was longer; it was of this form [*very small sketch inserted in text*], transparent; had an irregular rolling motion of about $\frac{1}{100}$th of an inch in a second; its diameter was $\frac{1}{800}$th of an inch. Each drop appeared to contain one of this kind. The third species was the 350th of an inch in length being of a conical form, [*very small sketch inserted in text*]. It advanced with a steady motion, thick end first & passed through the $\frac{1}{150}$th of an inch per second.

Besides ['Singular minuteness; a comparison!' *in margin*] these animalcules there were numerous minute [medusae?] before described. These little creatures require 1½ or 2 minutes to move an inch.*[1] of the smallest kind a row of 48,000 would only extend a foot in length! The army which Bonaparte took into Russia estimated at

[1] Note in margin: '*at the latter rate they would be 25 days 4 hours & at the former 33 days 13 h. 2′ in moving a nautical mile or 6040 feet. The frigate bird it is said could circumnavigate the pole at the equator in 8 days: these animalcules, in still water, could not accomplish the same in less than (at the quickest rate or an inch in 1¼ minutes) 1480 years 303 days.' In the published version of these calculations (see note to journal entry for 31 July 1820) some revisions were made. Movement was altered to 'an inch in three minutes' and the published text continued (p. 113): 'At this rate, they would require 151 days to travel a nautical mile. The Condur [*sic*], it is generally believed, could fly round the globe at the equator, assisted by a favourable gale, in about a week; these animalcules, in still water, could not accomplish the same distance in less than 8935 years!'

500,000 men, would have ['required' *deleted*] extended in a double row, or two men abreast, with 2 fᵗ 3 in. space only for a pair of men, a distance of 106 miles: the same number of these animalcules of the smallest kind arranged in rows would only reach 5 feet 2½ inches! A whale requires a sea, an ocean to sport in; ['one of' *deleted*] a hundred of these creatures could [sport?] for their ease in a single drop of water![1]

Tuesday 25 April Lat. 78°45′ Lon. [6°?]E. Ther. 2, 1, 1, –1 Bar. 30.07. 4pm 0: 9 pm.10: 12pm. 18!
NNE

Wind a strong gale; intense frost and thick frost rime. Standing too & fro under two top sails, the main one generally being aback, and wearing every two hours. Streams and loose pieces of ice around us; the bay ice diminishing on account of the strength of the wind and increase of the sea.

The fixed thermometer at noon, sun shining ['bright' *deleted*] through the frost rime, indicated a temperature of 1°, and two thermometers placed to windward of the ship & partly clear of the radiation from the vessel sank to –1 and –2°. The former, however, on examining the thermometer was found to be most correct. On trying the effect of some freezing mixtures I found that snow & salt*[2] equal parts, cooled down to 2° and then ['combine' *deleted*] mixed, provided a cold of –9°; this was with the proved thermometer; the other therm. marked –10½°. My muriate of lime[3] was bad and did not answer the purpose. The above experiment was suggested by my surgeon Mʳ Nivison.

In freezing some freshwater for obtaining ice for pounding, it being in a large shallow vessel, smoked and emitted rime while in the act of ['Artificial frost rime' *in margin*] freezing, as if it had been hot. This shows that the difference of the temp. of the air & water is the only cause of frost rime and that it is not owing to the vapour thrown into the air by the curling, and topping of the waves.

['Sailors frost bit.' *in margin*] During the intense frost of this day, several of our sailors had their cheeks frost bitten: but by a timely application of snow with friction the benumbed parts were restored. When the thermometer on ['Cabin 70° or 80° warmer than the air!!' *in margin*] deck was at zero, the temperature of the Cabin was 74°!

Fell in with much ice at 3 pm.; saw a large heavy stream wore & stood to the Eᵈ. during 2 hours in troublesome and somewhat dangerous ice; then fell into a better navigation. at 9 pm. the wind suddenly abated, and veered about mid-night to ENE. Soon afterwards, however, the storm ['**Wednesday 26 April** Lat. 78°37′+ Lon 5°0′E Temp. 12, 14, 16 Bar.30.35+ ENE. NNE: NE.' *in margin*] recommenced with augmented severity and blew during the day <u>a hard gale</u>. The became [*sic*] heavy;

---

[1] In the published version (p. 114) this sentence became: 'A whale requires a sea, an ocean, to sport in; about a hundred and fifty millions of the animalcules would have abundant room in a tumbler of water.'

[2] Note in margin: '*[pounded?] ice and salt produced a cold ⅓ of a degree lower.'

[3] Calcium chloride CaCl₂. Scoresby was presumably aware of the paper by Walker, 'On the Production of Artificial Cold' (*Philosophical Transactions of the Royal Society of London*, 91, 1801, pp. 120–38).

many heavy pieces of ice being around us, and some of them drifting at the rate of 2 miles per hour, we traversed the sea with much anxiety and some hazard. Happily, however, the weather was pretty clear and as we could see the Dangers at a considerable distance the hazard was much diminished.

As we drifted to the southward the temperature of the air became gradually higher & the frost rime at length disappeared. From the 17th until today ['Average temperature during 10 days = 5°.3!!' *in margin*] (10 days) frost rime has been almost perpetual & so thick, generally, that we could not see, from the decks, above 200 yards, sometimes not 50. The mean temp. during these 10 days was (by thermometer hanging in the binnacle) 7°.5 from which deducting 2° the effect of radiation from the ship reduces the average temperature to 5°.5! Yet such has been the effect of habit, that when ['yesterday' *deleted*] blowing a gale of wind on the 25th with a temp. of zero, I felt <u>not the least inconvenience</u> from the Cold when on deck. My additional clothing was only a coat. ['and' *deleted*] mitts, and gaiters. Such was the effect of use, that on the rising of the thermometer to 16°, the air ['Saw the Land' *in margin*] felt comfortably mild! – Detached pieces of ice around us.

At mid-night still blowing a very strong gale with high sea.

Thursday 27 April Lat. 78°10′ Lon. 5°10′E Therm. 16. 16. 16 Bar 30.35 NE: ENE N.
The wind moderated towards morning and showers of haze or snow occurred. The ship being so loaded with ice as to resemble an ice berg we ran to the SW^d & W. in the forenoon to seek for shelter from the sea, in some bay of the land ice, the west side of which we coasted, that we might get the ice removed. At [10 am?] we fell in with a point of ice, hauled around it & hoisted out a boat and detached many tons of ice from the bows, head, channelbends and sides. At 6 Pm. the snow having cleared away, we found we were in a lee bight, ice extending ['from' *deleted*] almost all round us. Made sail and began to ply to the N^d out of it. The ice here we found very close and remarkably heavy.

Friday 28 April Lat. 78.0 Long. 5°E Ther. 18.18.17 Bar. 30.35 N. SE Var NE
Light variable winds in the morning: fresh gales with strong squalls towards noon & snow showers. The sea becoming again very considerable so that ice rapidly generated about the bows we took shelter in sinuosity of the ice on the east side of the bight. At 5 pm. the wind having moderated we made sail and stretched to the westward until 2 am. when we again fell in with the western ['**Saturday 29 April** Lat. 78°9′34″+ Lon. 4°20′E. Therm 10° 10° 12°: B. 30.22 NE to NNE' *in margin*] ice. Stood off & on until the forenoon, and then entered the skirt of the ice in a slack place in search of whales, but none, except a white whale, was seen. The ice was generally close and heavy but in the interior I observed large spaces of water. The wind now blew a fresh breeze and was accompanied with snow; frost rime, slightly, also moving along the surface of the water. At noon stood off to the eastward, designing to examine the land ice. In the evening little wind: at 11 pm. saw ice to leeward, and about 4 am. ['**Sunday 30 April** Lat. 78°48′+ Long. 7°30′E Ther. 16° 18° 20° Bar 30.18 NNW.

N. Calm. Var.' *in margin*] rounded a point which seemed to be the eastern extremity of the bight out of which we have been plying since Thursday evening. Saw a ship.

During the ['forenoon we' *deleted*] day we stood to the NE having moderate winds & fine clear weather, the first fine day of some weeks. Thousands of roches (alca alle)[1] about us, producing a perpetual noise with [their?] chattering or ar-r-r-rat-et-it. The sea was very turbid and of an olive green colour, containing many medusae and [squellie?]

Saw Charles Island, or the Foreland, in the evening bearing SE dist*ant* perhaps 20 miles. Calm in the evening: Sea covered with a pellicle of ice.

Monday 1 May Ther. 24. 21. 19. Bar. 30.30
Var. SW. S.
Calm weather in the morning with snow.

This being a day usually distinguished by the whale-fishers [1 May][2] was celebrated by our crew with remarkable spirit. The proceeding commenced immediately after mid-night by suspending a garland in the rigging composed of hoops decorated with ribbons and surmounted by a representation of Neptune with emblems of the fishery,)[3] from the main-top-gall*ant* stay.

A sailor then strongly metamorphosed with a garb studiously extravagant was heard to hail the ship, ordering the main yard to be braced aback and a rope given for his boat, and immediately afterwards the odd figure, representing Neptune, and accompanied by <u>his wife</u>, a barber, & his mate, ascended the deck by the bows. All hands were now summoned by this ['[***] self' *deleted*] assumed marine potentate; and each individual passing before him received from the barber ['a' *deleted*] distinguishing patches of black and white upon his face. His marine majesty then went below ['Humours of May-Day.' *in margin*] and entered into a division screened off from the 'tween-decks and ordered the hands that were <u>not free</u> of the Greenland seas to come one at a time before him. They were constrained to go, and each submitted to his humourous interrogatories and to the coarse operation of shaving. As the non-free man entered he was received with seaman-like courtesy by his majesty and had opportunity given him of surveying the wondrous beings before whom he was convened. Neptune appeared with proper dignity. His face was masked his back hunched – his legs bandied & as thick as his body. His head was covered with a huge wig – his body by a cloak and belt. His barber, who was prepared to ['shave' *deleted*] perform the shaving operation was clothed in white nankeen[4] & formed a singular contrast to his ['brother' *deleted*] brethren around him. His lather was a mixture of soot, grease, tar, and various filt [*sic*] scraped up for the occasion – his brush was a tar brush – his razor a piece of iron hasping. The lathering now commenced – questions were proposed by Neptune – & if the unlucky ['wight' *deleted*] fellow happened to

[1] The Little Auk (*Alle alle*). In *Account of the Arctic Regions*, I, p. 528, Scoresby termed it 'ALCA *alle*. The Little Auk, or Roach'.

[2] Brackets in transcript.

[3] This parenthesis appears to be a transcription error; the remainder of the sentence is enclosed in brackets in pencil; these seem unnecessary, and are omitted here.

[4] Smyth, *Sailor's Word Book*: s.v. 'NANKIN. A light fawn-coloured or white cotton cloth.'

give an answer, the brush invariably penetrated to his throat & filled his mouth with its superabundant juices. The shaving was not very delicate.

Such of the people as were decent, well-behaved – and orderly characters were passed without suffering much inconvenience: – but two who had shipped themselves as seamen & proved landmen, and those of the most worthless kind, were shaven with vast deliberation and coarseness, and passed through two or three courses of the operation. These were*¹ hypocrites – having two characters and two faces: the false face they tried to remove by scraping that the true might be conspicuous.

The shaving being concluded and all hands made free, a sort of rude masquerade commenced. The characters were not numerous, but they were pretty well sustained and not a little grotesque. The people were then marshalled on deck, and marching round, caused the air to resound with their loud & repeated huzzas! The marching was followed by dancing: for want of more melodious instruments, frying-pans, kettles, tubs, and suchlike articles were substituted, and if a judgement of their effort might be formed from the energy and spirit of the dancers, they must have formed a most stimulating harmony. <u>Taste is every thing! What's one man's meat is another's poison</u>. The filthy process of daubing one another's faces with nastiness and the coarse operation of scraping it off with an iron hoop – were to the sailors most amusing recreations; while the strange mixture of harsh sounds to which they danced² seemed to form a charming concert in their refined ears! [But enough of such folly!³

The sea freezing rapidly about us, we found it necessary to remove to some other situation to prevent our complete detention. Accordingly on a breeze springing up about 9 am. we steered to the westward, finding ourselves within 20⁴ miles of the land: The Foreland [N end] bearing S5°E [Compass] Dist. 20', at noon, & Middle Hook or land to the Southᵈ S.5°W.

We have long observed the Baffin to be in a bad trim, being too much by the stern and very 'tender'.⁵ To remedy these inconveniences as much as possible we spent 14 hours this day, in filling water in the fore-hold, in the lower and middle tiers of casks, and in sending down the Mizen top-mast, yards, and sails, and fixing in place of them a light pole for setting the gaff top-sail. After these operations were complete we found great alteration for the better. – Several ships seen.

At 9 pm. we approached the western ice, wind a fresh breeze, ['**Tuesday 2 May** Lat. 79°37+ Long. 6°E. Therm. 21. 24. 27 Bar 30.40 S. SW. S.' *in margin*] weather fine and clear. Ran a few miles to the ENE and then began to ply back again, observing ships near us in pursuit of whales and one engaged in flensing. In forenoon we dispatched two boats, for the first time, after a whale but they never came near it. The day was beautifully fine: the [even*ing*?] cloudy & more windy.

Many ships [20 or 30 sail] passed us during this and the preceding day running to the NE or Eᵈ.

¹ Pencilled insertion in margin: '*stated to be'.
² This phrase, 'to which they danced', was a replacement for an illegible deletion.
³ The bracket was not closed.
⁴ Overwritten on '30'.
⁵ Layton, *Dictionary*: 'Said of a vessel having small righting moment; so being easily moved from her position of equilibrium, and slow in returning to it.'

['(Sea very turbid.) Birds show open water & leave places where the sea is freezing' *in margin*] It is worthy of remark that ['when' *deleted*] though 1000's of roches & other birds were about us on Sunday, as soon as the sea began to freeze, they began to leave us in large flocks: all proceeding to the SW & W^d & pointing <u>out to us</u> the direction where there was no freezing going on.

Wednesday 3 May Lat. 79°45′ Long. 6°E Therm. 25, 20. Bar 30.40
S. SSW. SSE. S.
This was a fine day: the weather was clear and mild & the wind moderate. Several whales having been seen around us in the preceding day in the opening of the bight that lay to the NNW of us, we lay too during the night & this morning ran into the bight & found shelter by hauling to the W^d, from the sea: but after examining the opening during 6 or 8 hours and seeing nothing we left the place & ['Sea very turbid' *in margin*] began to ply to the SW^d. – The Land in sight from E to SE. Dist. 50′.

Thursday 4th May Lat. 79°50+ Long. 5°50′E Therm. 22. 27. 20. Bar. 30.28
S. SSE
Under all sails made the best of our way to the WSW or SW along the edge of the pack lying to the NW^d of us. At 6 pm. passed a vessel flensing. Other vessels seemed to be hunting whales, but we saw none. The day was delightfully fine: the wind a moderate or light breeze. ['19 sail in sight' *in margin*] In the night ran down into a bight among some loose ice, as far as the pack edge, where two ['vessel' *deleted*] ships struck fish, but we saw none.

Friday 5 May Lat. 79°20′ Long. 5°30′E. Therm. 24.26.26. Bar 30.09 25 sail in sight
SSE SE. E.
The morning was thick, with snow: the wind a fresh breeze. Entered a large collection of open ice, in a SW.erly direction, through which we passed after 6 hours sailing and entered an arm of the sea, having streams of ice ['all' *deleted*] around us and a close pack to the W^d and NW. Capt. [M***][1] of the Neptune came on board. He is yet without fish.

In the evening saw two whales. Had 4 boats in pursuit in competition with others of the Neptune & Cato: many of the boats came extremely near but none of them succeeded. Lay too or beat to windward during the night, near the pack edge. Two whales were ['**Saturday 6 May** Lat. 79°0′ Long.5°E Therm 20°. 22°. 21° Bar 30.02 ENE' *in margin*] struck by the people of two ships near us; but both escaped into the pack. In the night a fresh gale of wind; cloudy weather.

Fresh gales with cloudy weather. Made sail in the morning & plyed along the pack edge, generally at a little distance, towards the loose ice we passed yesterday, for the benefit of shelter.

The [Exmouth?] killed a large fish near us; to the assistance of which ship we sent a boat.

[1] Presumably Martin Munroe of Hull, master of the ill-fated *Clapham* (see entry for 15 May 1815 of these *Journals*), and of the *Neptune* from 1816 to 1823.

In the evening we reached the loose ice and lay too. The Lady Forbes was seen to the E^d fast to a fish: we made sail towards her to afford some assistance; but falling in with a whale by the way we proceeded in pursuit of it. The Lady Forbes' fish escaped.

Sunday 7 May Lat. 78°45 Long. 4°50'E Therm. 17. 18. 19. 21 Bar. 29.94 46 sail in sight.
ENE
Blowing fresh all night: weather cloudy, but <u>perpetually clear over the pack</u>, and has been for 2 or 3 days. Lay too most of the day being the Sabbath. In the evening run a little before the wind; spoke the Lady Forbes & the James, both without fish & then lay too. In the morning 46 sail were in sight; but at night most of them had gone out of sight.

Monday 8 May Lat. 78°35' Long. 3°30'E. Therm. 18° 22° Bar 29.90
NE: NNE
Blowing strong in the morning with snow showers: in the evening more moderate; cloudy. Heavy Southerly swell. At 8 am. made sail, (having dodged during the night) and stood to the NW through a great quantity of heavy and bay ice, until we reached the pack ice at noon. Near it we lay too and soon afterwards saw a fish: sent 4 boats in pursuit. Running two or three miles to leeward we saw two more whales near the pack, both of which narrowly escaped us. The pack which on Saturday was perfectly solid, today was varied with several openings in the interior; but owing to the strength of the swell, the heavy ice was forced close up against it & rendered the edge very close. The ice being crowded where we ['lay' *deleted*] navigated during the day we could not avoid all the pieces: one heavy piece was [forced?][1] to windward against the ship and hit her a hard blow. The sea roared upon it dismally. In the night stood out to the E^d to the seaward edge of the loose ice. Lay too.

Tuesday 9 May Lat. 78°30' Long 4°E. Therm. 22° 23° 23 Bar. 29.84
S.erly. Calm: Var.
Light variable winds or calm. Thick snow occasionally. The southerly swell continued all day. The sky was dark and threatening in the quarter from whence the swell proceeded; but bright towards the E. There seemed to be a conflict between the S.ern and E.ern winds. In the evening the bright sky to the E. increased until at midnight, almost the whole heavens was clear. Saw numbers of narwals [*sic*] & one whale. The Neptune killed a fish near us: 18 sail in sight.

Wednesday 10 May Lat. 78°34 Long. 3½°E. Therm 24. 22. 18 Bar. 29.67
Calm: NE NNE
A fresh breeze sprang up about 2 am. Lay by the edge of the ice until 8 am. then made sail and stood to the E^d to endeavour to get through the loose ice ['around us' *deleted*] almost surrounding us, and then to increase our latitude: we found however the ice too compact. Tacked and stood to the W^d. Weather hazy or showery.

[1] Possibly 'passed'.

During the afternoon we plyed to the NE amongst much ice, until we reached the edge of the main pack about 8 pm. From this pack the borders were rapidly separating. Afterwards we stood to the E.ward, ['close by' *deleted*] close hauled by the wind, among streams, patches, and drift pieces of ice, until 11 pm. when having reached a commodious opening & having seen a whale in it, we lay too and dodged during the night. Wind a fresh gale with almost constant snow.

Thursday 11 May Lat. 78°44′ Long. 3°50′E Therm. 18° 19° 18° Bar. 29.90 NNE

Fresh gales or strong breezes: snow showers. About 7 am. the ['specksioneer' *deleted*] second mate in attempting to pass a stream of heavy ice, injudiciously took a narrow opening where the pieces were in the act of closing, and struck the ship against the opposing ice with dreadful violence. The shock was terrible. More water being found in the ship than usual we were afraid she had been stove; but finding no appearance of damage on examination, inside or outside and less water, nearly the same as usual, afterwards occurring in the hold, we hoped that our fears were groundless.

Beat to windward among open, sometimes crowded, ice from 7 am. to 4 pm. excepting when we occasionally lay too, to pursue some whales that were seen. At 4 reached to the eastward through some more awkward ice and entered a spacious opening having the appearance of an arm of the sea about 6 pm. Here we saw several whales and had boats repeatedly in pursuit; but without success. Worked to windward during the night; Seeing fish occasionally.

Friday 12 May Lat. 79°0′ Long. 4°0′E Therm. 12. 14. 15 Bar 29.90 15 sail in sight. NNE

A fresh breeze prevailed in the morning with showers of snow. By this time we had reached the windward pack and now made considerable progress to the NE, passing through a good deal of bay & heavy ice intermixed. At 11 am. on the lee side of a large opening, terminating to windward in a close pack & floes of ice, we saw some whales. Were in pursuit with from 2 to 6 boats during 6 or 7 hours; but could not make a capture. In the evening stood into a quantity of bay ice & then returned into a windward opening formed by bay floes and heavy ice; yet saw no fish. Ran therefore to leeward, where we had seen in [*sic*] the fish above, as far as an extensive patch of ice. Then returned to windward.

Saturday 13 May Lat. 78. 50 Long. 3°55′E Therm 15.15.15. Bar. 30.00 NNE N.

Fresh breezes with snow showers. At the borders of a patch of ice as we returned to windward we fell in with a fish: two boats being sent in pursuit one of the Harponeers succeeded in striking it. It immediately made its appearance and was chased by ship and boats for

['Thoˢ Murray **M** = 12T Nº 1: 9′ 4 bone' *in margin*]

about an hour, when the mate succeeded in striking a second harpoon. It was struck at 8 am. and killed at 10½. Moored the ship to a small bay floe, and after clearing the hold for a flens-gut, [***] kenting tackle and specktackles, &c. &c. began to flens about 4 pm. The flensing was finished by about 8½ pm. but it was past mid-night before all was cleared away, sails set, and ship under way. Above 20 sail in sight.

Sunday 14 May Lat. 78°40′ Long.3°56′[1] Therm. 12.13.10 Bar. 30.10
NNE & N.
Fresh gales: cloudy weather with some little snow & light frost rime. The ice setting round us having obliged us to cast off, we plyed a few miles to the ['E[d] &' *deleted*] NE. and dodged in a large opening clear of loose pieces. In the afternoon we made sail and began to ply towards the NE in much water and surrounded by patches & streams of bay & heavy ice, with a pack, a few miles distant to the N[d2] of us. Some ships about us were in pursuit of fish.

Monday 15 May Lat. 78°50 Long 3°E Ther. 12°12° 12° Bar. 30.10
NNE
Fresh gales with thick snow showers and some appearance, occasionally, of frost rime; but most generally nothing like this vapour. Throughout the night, and until noon we beat to windward under a smart sail, amidst large patches of bay & heavy ice with a solid pack on the NW and N. of us, and during most of the day a pack also to the SE of us, affording a narrow navigation between the two. Having worked close up to the pack edge where were no whales, the water indeed having changed its appearance from turbid green to transparent blue; at the same time bay ice annoying us on every hand and forming rapidly round about us – we bore up and returned to the SW[d]. Shortly afterwards some of the ships in C° [9 sail][3] followed our example. We proceeded as much to the S[d] as practicable and at 8 pm. passed the southern point of the <u>East pack</u>. Here we saw two ice bergs, one of them ['30 or' *deleted*] about 40 or 50 feet high had a perpendicular edge and bluish-grey shining ['like marble' *deleted*] surface, like marble. Here we saw a fish, but did not pursue it on account of the badness of the situation. Hauled a little to the W[d] into a large opening and dodged during the night.

Thursday 16 May Lat. 78.25 Long 3°W Ther. 10. 12. 14 Bar. 30.10
NNE NE
In the morning, (the wind still blowing fresh with thick snow showers or frost rime in the night) stood into ['close ice' *deleted*] rank ice to the eastward & SE, with the view of getting further to the N[d] after making a circuit round the ['ice' *deleted*] more crowded ice; but falling into a <u>clear blue sea</u>, where there was no hope of fish we hauled to the NW[d] and stretched some hours by the wind until we reached the pack edge. The same blue sea prevailing, we returned to the SE and about 8 pm began to ply to windward. Much ice and some ships about us.

---

[1] *Sic*; '50' intended?
[2] Originally 'NW[d]'; 'W' deleted.
[3] Brackets in transcript.

Wednesday 17 May Lat. 78°20 3°20'E Ther. 16. 18. 19 Bar. 30.00
NE ENE E. ESE
Fresh to moderate breezes, thick snow showers. In the morning made a long stretch to the SE^d and then finding good room among the ice, began to beat at windward. The navigation was often troublesome on account of the great quantity of heavy ice that lay all round us. At mid-night finding ourselves involved in much ice, bore away to the S^d sometimes by the wind at others ['**Thursday 18 May** Lat. 77.37+ Long. 4°30'E Ther. 26. 26 Bar. 29.93 E. SE. E NE. Var.' *in margin*] a little off the wind, making during the night (till 8 am) about a SbE course by compass & a progress of 20 or 30 miles. Passed several ships plying to windward. The ice was less crowded as we proceeded; but still a considerable quantity occurred: At 2 pm. finding the sea bluer than ever tacked & stood to N^d. Beat to windward among open patches during the afternoon & evening. Delightful weather.

Friday 19 May Lat. 78°10' Long. 4°20'E Ther. 22. 22. 21 B. 29.80
NE. N. NbW. N.
Fresh breezes with considerable showers of snow. About 7 am. we found further plying to windward impracticable on account of the vast quantity of heavy ice about us. Proceeded therefore to the ENE. E. & ESE in the clearest leads; but found the navigation often very intricate and hazardous; frequently having but one channel in which we could go, and that crooked, narrow & obstructive. Three ships in sight & partly in C°. Passed a number of small floes and a vast body of heavy ice. In the evening wind light breeze: made all sail still to the ENE, and at 10 pm. were interrupted by a compact body of ice, which proved to be a sea stream.

Saturday 20 May Lat 78°54' Long. 6°50'E Ther. 23. 26. 23 Bar. 29.70
S. to E. NEbE
Lay too part of the night, the wind being very light, and took on board some fresh water ice. In the morning, the weather was clear & fine the wind southerly. Observed an opening to the NE and passing through it, found ourselves at sea. Steered to the NNE along the edge of the ice. Fitted up the blubber cutting apparatus[1] and made off the fish in the forehold. The cutter answered admirably; dividing the blubber into regular pieces as fast as two hands could supply the <u>hopper</u>. 22 casks were filled with blubber; capacity 32 butts. In the evening tacked for ice. land in sight from SE to E dist*ant* 50' to 60'.

---

[1] This appears to be the first time that Scoresby used the 'excellent apparatus for cutting blubber' that he described in *Account of the Arctic Regions*, II, pp. 309–10. It is illustrated in Plate XXII in that volume. The description suggests that Scoresby had seen it used, presumably on another whaler, before 1820, had therefore equipped the *Baffin* with the device, and felt confident enough to state in the *Account of the Arctic Regions* (p. 309) that it 'promises in a few years to supersede the use of the speck-trough and its cumbrous appendages'. Scoresby's optimism was, however, premature. More than half a century later, the traditional, labour-intensive and tedious process was still the norm (see Markham's 1873 account in *Whaling Cruise*, pp. 59–61, and Ross, *Arctic Whalers*, pp. 209–10).

Sunday 21 May Lat. 79.15+ Long. 6°E Ther. 22. 22. 20. Bar. 29.55
NE
The wind increased to a fresh gale during the day & was attended with showers of snow. Stood off and on by the ice throughout the day; in the evening made a long stretch to the W^d where we fell in with some considerable floes. 3 or 4 ships in sight.

Monday 22 May Lat. 79.35 Long. 5°0'E Ther. 28. 20. 16 Bar. 29.95
N. to E.
A fine morning, clear and ['warm' *deleted*] temperate. At the edge of

['John Nattpass F.   3T N° 2 = 2.8 F.

Thos Forster   Narwhal.' *in margin*]

a large floe, or aggregation of floes, forming part of the main body of ice, we saw several whales during the day, & no ship latterly being near us, we had excellent chances, but did not succeed until 10 pm. when a small fish was struck and killed. Before this a strong gale of wind had commenced. Killed also a female narwhal, 12 feet in length.

Tuesday 23 May Lat. 79.20 Long. 4°20'E Ther. 16°14: 12 Bar 29.83
E. NE
Flensed the whale, under shelter of an attached floe, and dodged near the same until noon. Spoke the Lady Forbes with 2 fish, 125 butts of blubber. James, clean. Finding the fish very scarce and not being able to get hold of any, we made sail about 6 pm. & steered to the SW^d, 4 or 5 miles and the hauled up NW, into a deep bight, bounded by Floes on the

['Willm Lloyd F.   6T N° 3 = 6.6' *in margin*]

N. & S. and by a ['large' *deleted*] thin field, or the main western body of ice, on the W. Here we saw a great number of whales, sent all the boats in pursuit and struck & killed one. Made fast to the ice to flens, and after allowing the boats a considerable trial for other fish, without success, accounted probably by the formation of bay ice which made thick about us, we recalled them. 10 ships in sight.

Wednesday 24 May Lat. 79.10 Long. 4°E. Ther. 16. 16. 20 B. 30.15
NE. N. Var.
Light breeze, inclinable to calm towards night with fine clear weather. As soon as I arose, finding the opening of the floes increasing and the bay ice falling to leeward from the floe edge, we cast off and stood as far to the NW^d

['Tho. Page   N° 4: = 4'6

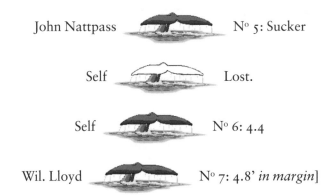

John Nattpass   N° 5: Sucker

Self   Lost.

Self   N° 6: 4.4

Wil. Lloyd   N° 7: 4.8' *in margin*]

as we could get, and obtained a clear situation free from any incumbrance from bay ice or interference from any other ships, for a while at least, where were a vast number of fish. Made "a loose fall", and soon succeeded in striking two. After these were killed I went away myself struck two fish (one of them got loose), struck the second harpoon into another and killed it. Thus four were killed about 10 pm. Began to flens: Several ships had now collected round us. New bay ice began again to annoy us. Made fast to the western field.

Thursday 25 May Lat. 79°5′ Long. 4°E Ther. 21: 24: Bar. 30.25
N. NW. Var.
Light airs, inclinable to calm all day. Continued moored to the field: While employed flensing, another fish was struck: it was soon killed and was flensed in course. About 1 pm. I again went out to try to entangle another whale

['Thos Forster   N° 8 = 5.10

Self   ' *in margin*]

and after about 3 hours watching struck, with a heave, a large fish. It took from my boat, in spite of all endeavours to arrest its flight, 18 or 19 lines: after which, it having gained shelter in a body of bay ice, &c. we united another line to the running line, by which the harpoon was at length drawn. This event occasioned us a vast labour, without any profit but the contrary: a second harpoon having been struck & with about half a line attached to it, lost, along with the fish; being the whole of the lines in the boat. Several ships around us most of them fishing: 26 sail in sight. Took the lines to the ship at 10 pm. & began to heave them in by the capstern.

Friday 26 May Lat. 79°10′ Long. 4°E Ther. 28. 28. Bar. 29.93
SW.erly S. SSE
Soon after the lines were wholly reclaimed, a breeze of wind sprang up and blew almost directly towards the ice: we had some difficulty & had to make great exertion before we could cast the ['vessel' *deleted*] ship off and get under way. Beat to windward in a clear

opening to the W^d of where we entered the floes with an increasing breeze. About 4 pm. spoke the Venerable, Capt. Bennet, with 15 fish about 100 tons of oil. This appears to be one of the best fished ships in the Country. Many of her fish have been obtained in the past week. It is probable that near 120 fish have been killed around the field, from where we unmoored, during the last 4 or 5 days. In the evening the wind increased to a strong gale and was attended with thick snow. We attempted to get out to sea, lest we should be closed in: but the obscurity of the weather preventing us, we were obliged to lay too about mid-night, under the lee of a light floe. Several ships near us.

On comparing chronometers with Mr Bennet, found my Chronometer ['Rate of Chronometers' in margin] 9′26″ slow of ['Green' deleted] Mr Bennett's [sic] or, if his be correct, so much [behind?] mean time at Greenwich: & by a lunar observation of M^r B's 4′22″ still more slow.

Saturday 27 May Lat. 79°20 Long. 4°0′E Ther. 31. 24. Bar. 29.34+ 6 pm 29.50
SSE SW to W. to NNW.
It continuing blowing hard & snowing thick until 6 am: the wind then moderated & the snow somewhat abated. As our blubber was already wasting & we were anxious to avoid working on the Sabbath, we made fast to a light floe at 8 am. & cleared the hold for making off. When the casks in the lower hold were all broken out as far as wanted & emptied of their contents of water, the wind veered to the NW & began to blow very hard, directly on the face of the ice to which we were moored. The situation of the hold rendered any immediate removal impracticable: but as soon as the ground tier casks were nearly filled we attempted to get under way. The strength of the wind & position of ice, however, rendered casting the ship off utterly impracticable. A large floe appeared to be setting to leeward & came within 300 fathoms of us & threatened us with detention, if not danger; providentially, however, we were beyond its influence & it passed us to the E^d ['above 50 sail in sight!' in margin] though threatening us for several hours. About mid-night, after some exertion we got the ship off the ice and under sail. Lay too, until the blubber was all made. Owing to the detention received from the ice, we were driven, much against our inclination, some hours into the Sabbath, with our operations. On this occasion 37 Casks were filled, of the capacity of 71 butts, besides 5 Casks well advanced not included. Wind more moderate.

Sunday 28 May Ther. 24. 22 Bar. 29.90
NW.erly N.erly Calm.
Light airs & variable; or calm all day. Traversed an opening of the ice bounded by streams without altering materially our position. Saw 1 whale: several ships about us: Lat. 79°20′ Long 4°20′E.

Monday 29 May Lat. 79.25 Lon. 4°50′E Ther. 24 26. Bar 29.90
Var. SSW.
Calm or light variable winds until about 4 pm. when a moderate breeze, accompanied by hazy weather, arose. Seeing no whales run[1] to the NNW among open ice, until 4 am. when we reached the main ice, being here a pack. Lay too.

---

[1] Probably a transcription error for 'ran'.

Tuesday 30 May Lat. 79°35′ Long. 3°50′E Ther. 29. 30. 26 Bar. 29.95
SSW: Calm Var.
Calm a few hours, afterwards a small breeze with haze or snow. 30 ships about us: but no fish; several unicorns seen & a seahorse. Sailed about 20 miles to the ENE^d: much water to the SE of us & much ice to the NW^d.

Wednesday 31 May Lat. 79°55′ Long. 4°E Ther. 26 .27.21 Bar 30.10
N. NE
Moderate or fresh breezes: fine weather. About 4 am. passed into the sea, through a sea-stream & beat from thence along the ice towards the NE. About 10 pm. perceiving an opening in the interior where there were ships fishing; repassed the sea stream & worked up to the NW among loose ice, until we reached a floe about 10 am.

Thursday 1 June Lat. 79.55 Long. 3°30′E
Var. Calm.
Joined the Fame[1] with 7 fish, 45 tons oil: & John 8 fish, 26 tons; all well. Calm the rest of the day: visited my Father. Many ships about us. Barometer found broken. Ther. 25°25°.

Friday 2 June Lat. 80.5 Long. 3°20′E
SSW
Having a commanding breeze of wind, sometimes blowing fresh worked into an opening among the floes and had good chances for 2 fish: but both escaped us. Several ships took fish near us. We made every exertion; sent boats into every crack & opening without success. About 60 sail of ships in sight. Therm. 26. 27.26.

Saturday 3 June Lat. 80.15 Long. 3°50′E Therm. 28. 30. 32
W SW
Light or fresh breezes: showery. Steered a few miles to the ENE, having seen some fish passing that way, & fell in with 4 or 5. The boats came very near two of them. Spoke the Mars, stove, 2 fish.[2] In the night lay too under a floe.

Sunday 4 June Lat. 80°17′+ Long. 3°50′E
SSW
Strong breezes. Worked a few miles to windward in the night. Lay too most of the day. In the evening reached to the SE^d in C° of the Fame, John & Mars. Therm. 32. 34. 32.

---

[1] After his 1818 voyage in the *Fame*, Scoresby had yielded full ownership of the vessel to his father. Because of her draught and size, the elder Scoresby sailed her from Hull, instead of Whitby, from 1819 until 1823, when the ship was destroyed by fire in Orkney. The record of the 1820 voyage is included in Dellenbaugh's *Seven Log-Books*. See Introduction, p. xxi.
[2] In 1816 and 1817 the new ship *Mars* had been commanded by William Scoresby, Senior, though Lubbock (*Arctic Whalers*, p. 204) incorrectly named his son as the commander of the 1817 voyage. In 1820 it was captained by Johnson, who moved from the *Aimwell* in 1818.

Monday 5 June Lat. 80°26′+ Long. 4°E. Therm. 31. 31.[1] 28.
W. NW. NNW

Moderate breezes: fine weather. Steered 8 or 10 miles to the NE^d & then hauled in to the [W^d?] under the lee of a huge field, into a deep bight on the NE side of which the ice trended to the SE^d. Seeing no fish, after some hours search proceeded to the S^d passed a sea stream & entered the northern water. Steered along the ice to the SW^d. John, Fame, &c. in C°.

Tuesday 6 June Lat. 79°40′ Long. 3°50′E Ther. 27. 29. 28.
Calm. NE. ESE

A fresh breeze of wind sprang up in the forenoon – steered to the SW. Found a body of open ice lying to the E^d of us, and extending, apparently, in with the land. In the afternoon proceeded to the W^d & in the evening towards the NW. About 6 pm. reached the edge of a large [fine?] field. Several ships in sight; but no fish. The weather was foggy to the E^d: but at the ['Partial fog.' *in margin*] field & to the N^d of it perfectly clear.

Wednesday 7 June Lat. 79°25′ Long. 2°20E Therm. 28. 30.
E. ENE

Blowing fresh with clear weather while we remained at the field: thick with snow or fog to the E^d. Seeing no fish, excepting one that was taken by a brig, the water being a bad colour, & having met with no success of several days, I became wishful to examine the ice of lower latitudes. Accordingly at 9 am. made sail to the SE^d doubled a point of ice & then pursued a devious navigation towards the SW. W. S. &c. among much loose ice, patches & floes. Left about 40 sail of ships in sight in the ice: six followed us.

In the afternoon fell in with very cross & compact ice; thick snow prevailing rendered our navigation difficult & hazardous; we however turned in various directions from WNW to SE & sometimes beat to windward. In the evening, having made about a SW or SWbS course, found more room. Passed the Lady Forbes, which for some hours accompanied us in our run & then separated to the W^d.

Thursday 8 June Lat. 77°30′ Long. 2°E Ther. 30. 32. 30
ENE

Still blowing a fresh gale with thick & almost constant snow. About 4 am. fell into very rank ice: hauled up to the SE but found ourselves involved in the midst of a heavy close patch. In a small opening into which we penetrated at 6 am. we made several tacks & then found more room to the eastward. At 9 am. discovered the sea very near us and at 10 am. passed the sea-stream. Steered from point to point, along the ice, about W. or WSW: passed 3 or 4 vessels, plying to windward, part of them followed us. At 10 pm. observed ice to the eastward of us: hauled up by the wind but could not weather it.

---

[1] Possibly '37'.

Friday 9 June Lat. 76°40' Long. 1°00'E Ther. 31. 32.
ENE
Saw 3 or 4 ships working out of the same bight further to the W^d. One point of ice appeared beyond another as we plyed to windward [weather tolerably clear][1] the ice continuous, heavy & compact, so that we did not weather the extreme point until 10 pm. The wind was then light: steered S. SW. &c. according to the trending of the ice. Blue sea. 1000's of seals on the ice.

Saturday 10 June Lat. 76°10' Long. 2°50'E
ENE, Var.
Light variable winds or calm, made some little progress to the WSW. Saw ice occasionally. 3 or 4 ships seen. Many seals. Blue Sea. Therm. 33. 33. 32.

Sunday 11 June Lat 76°6'+ Long. 2°E
NW. Var.
Light winds or calm. Beating to the W^d but making little way. Passed a forign [*sic*] brig: appeared very deep. Sea blue. Fine weather. SE swell. Therm. 32. 32. 32.

Monday 12 June Lat. 75.49+ Long 10'W. Therm. 33.33.32.
E to SE
Light variable winds ['all' *deleted*] most of this day, occasionally calm: fog or snow showers. Steered NW and NWbN in an open sea, never having seen any ice until midnight, when a stream appeared to the NW^d. Advanced about 45 miles.

Tuesday 13 June Lat. 75°47'+ Long. 3°W Therm. 34. 30. 29
Var. WSW
A breeze at WSW having sprung up early in the morning, hauled by the wind to the NW. About 8 am approached the ice within 2 or 3 miles, and lay along the weather side of an extensive [range?] of streams &c. until noon: then tacked at the pack edge. 12 sail in sight, most of them steering to the SE^d: one ship, the Albion sent a boat on board. He[2] has 2 fish; has been here about nearly a month & caught nothing & has not seen a fish of a week & has never been able to get into the ice. Wishes to accompany us if we can get in. Observing by the blink, which was very fine (of which I took a sketch affording a good map of the principal positions)[3] I think that there was water

---

[1] Brackets in transcript.

[2] Richard Wallis Humphrey, in his first year in command (Credland, *Hull Whaling Trade*, p. 137).

[3] In his *Life* of William Scoresby, Scoresby-Jackson noted this sketch and quoted (p. 158) the following description: 'This appearance of the ICE-BLINK occurred on the 13th of June 1820, in latitude 76° north. The sky aloft was covered with dense, uniform hazy cloud, excepting a portion near the bottom, where it seemed to be repelled. The upper white blink refers to ice about six miles distant being beyond the horizon; the narrow, yellowish portions refer to floes and compact ice; the lowest yellow blink, which in brightness and colour resembled the moon, was the reflection of a field, at the distance of thirty miles, to which, directed by the blink, we made way in the *Baffin*, through the channels of water represented in the sky by bluish grey streaks. The FIELD we found to be a sheet of ice 150 miles in circumference.' This sketch could not be traced in the current inventory of the Scoresby Papers.

in extensive lakes in the interior, a [floe?], a few miles in, and very large and heavy field, at some leagues distance, [proved to be 30 miles off][1] and that an opening seemed to be breaking out a little to windward, – ['Fine ice blinks, afford most accurate pictures of the ice 30 miles off!' *in margin*] we worked up 3 or 4 miles & on approaching the edge of the ice found that we could ['get in' *deleted*] penetrate by boring. Accordingly we put the ship into it & in about half an hour had forced our way through among the closest pieces & gained sailing room. By a variety of [crooked?] channels we reached the edge of the floe marked out by the blink & steered along it to the NNE, then doubling its northern extremity hauled round it, in plenty of water, to the NW. This was at 6 pm. From hence we steered NWbN, N. & occasionally NNE, making a [NbW?] course towards the northern part of the field depicted by the blink. At 7 pm. we fell in with a barrier of ice, through which we made way in intricate channels, and ['then' *deleted*] at 8 reached the edge of the field. We sailed along it ['Immense field.' *in margin*] NNE, 12 miles; N, 4 miles, NNW, 8 miles, & were still far from its ['western' *deleted*] north termination. The weather then becoming thick & stormy & heavy floes appearing close to leeward we tacked & lay too or dodged during the night. Killed a bear but it sank. The Albion in C°. – Sea very blue & transparent. No fish:

Wednesday 14 June Lat. 76°4′+ Long. 6°W. Therm. 29. 30. 32
WSW
Still blowing strong, foggy in the night, clear in the morning. As soon as we could discover our situation, we made sail and plied to the westward of the field to the very head of a deep bight where we were surrounded, excepting in one point of the compass, with floes or fields. No fish was seen nor any prospect of any from the clearness of the water. At 1 pm. ran out of the bight; traced the edge of the field to the N & then to the E^d & S^d, and finally left it in the evening and reached to the S^d towards the place where we entered the ice: six or eight ships were seen plying towards us. Foggy in the night.

Thursday 15 June Lat. 75.36+ Long. 4°20′W Therm. 30. 33. 32.
W. NW. N. Var.
Light variable breezes: occasionally calm. Advanced a few miles towards the SW, among crowded ice and floes. No fish seen but several narwhals.

Friday 16 June Lat. 75.7+ Long. 4°W Therm. 33. 38. 33
SE. S. SW. var.
The calm weather continued with fog or snow showers. Perceiving no intimation of advantage in staying in this location, we made all sail & with the assistance of 2 boats, towing & clearing the way for the ship, proceeded through extremely rank ice towards the SE where we observed an opening. Having reached this & gained its SE.ern boundary, we saw the sea, to the SE & S. of us, at the distance of 3 or 4 miles. Again we entered an intricate navigation; but by means of 3 boats, towing, & making

[1] Brackets in transcript, as an insertion above the line of text.

an ['passage' *deleted*] opening between the pieces of ice, we soon accomplished a passage through it. Having a breeze of wind in the evening stood to the southward. Killed a large seal. 11 ships in sight.

Saturday 17 June Lat. 74.42+ Long. 4°W.
SW. W. WNW
A gentle breeze with fog showers or snow all day. Stood 8 hours to the S^d, then returned by the wind to the edge of the ice. Albion & others in Company. Therm. 30. 33. 32.

Sunday 18 June Last 74.7+ Long. 7°W Therm. 32. 33
var. E NE.
Having been disappointed in our expectation of finding whales, in latitude 76°, where they usually occur at this season, we made the best of our way to the SW^d meaning to attempt to approach the <u>West Land</u>, if we should still fail in meeting the objects of our search. In the afternoon fell in with a ship making off & at the same time, entered a narrow stream of deep green coloured water. These promising appearances induced us to lay too.

Monday 19 June Lat 73.51+ Long. 7°W Therm. 34. 35. 34
NNE. NE. N. Var.
Light winds during the whole 24 hours. The Captain of the ship mentioned above as having been seen making off came on board the Baffin in the forenoon and informed us he had captured 6 large fish, in latitude 74° within a few miles of the place where we now lay, and that he continued to meet with fish so long as he remained within the skirts of the ice. This vessel is the Bremen of Bremen, Capt. .....; His present cargo, including above 2000 seals he estimates at 160 English tons of oil! This is perhaps the largest cargo that has been taken to Bremen or any of the neighbouring ports, this 20 or 30 years past or more. – This important intelligence induced us immediately to enter the ice though exceedingly crowded, and penetrate as far as possible to the NW. We passed the edge at 2 pm. & about 5 were obliged to tack for an impervious pack. Plied with all sail to the N^d & observed vessels to N & NW fishing & flensing. There was no possibility, however, of effecting a passage to the NW, therefore continued beating to windward, as well as the intricate nature of the navigation would permit. About 8 pm. saw a whale & shortly afterwards another: sent all the boats in pursuit. These leading to windward, the boats followed & some of them entered an arm of the sea ['**Tuesday 20 June** Lat. 74°0′ Long. 7°50′W Therm. 33. 34 NNE N.' *in margin*] to the N. of us, where a considerable number of whales were observed. None however we entangled. Being foggy occasionally we had much anxiety & difficulty in making our way through this ice; but at 4 am. succeeded in reaching an arm of the sea being the S. side of a deep bight, so that in our arduous navigation we found that we had merely worked through a point of ice. Here were several ships; and as we beat to windward in a stream of green water, we saw several whales. Our boats being continually in pursuit, at length succeeded in entangling one. It ran

['John Nattrass F.  N° 9 = 12.2' *in margin*]

wildly about and appeared 3 times before it was again struck. In an hour and 20 minutes it died. It was taken alongside at 12 o'clock & after clearing a flens-gut & allowing dinner to the men the flensing was performed; the ship drifting meanwile [*sic*] with topsails clewed down.

In the killing of this fish it rose beneath one of the boats, forced the keel upwards until the planks on each side ['swelle' *deleted*] burst out, gave the boatsteerer a toss in the air, threw the harponeer on his back, and cut, by means of an oar, the cheek[1] of one of the rowers completely through into the orbit of the eye.

Owing to the conduct of a sailor of the name of John Wright, who insulted the mate, challenged the officers to fight and raised a complete ferment in the ship, the flensing was protracted above six hours. This impudent man refusing to hold his peace, or go below or to the mast-head out of the way so that the flensing might proceed obliged me to threaten him with confinement by irons or shackles: ['this so enraged him' *deleted*] previously, however, he had used most insulting & gross language to myself, so that for the ['Mutinous sailor!' *in margin*] sake of keeping up a proper command I ordered him to be lashed down to a ring bolt and his hands, which became extremely mischievous to be tied behind him. Though I never spoke a passionate word to him, he not only abused me but threw whatever came in his way at me attempted to strike me and threatened my life. Such mutinous conduct required prompt and firm measures; particularly as I found that there were four or five more unprincipled men who were inclined to take his part against the officers and even against myself. As such I ordered a pair of hand-cuffs to me[2] made, and secured him from doing any serious mischief for the moment: though in a few minutes after he was allowed to go below I was told that he was free from his shackles. This being the case [the lock securing the bolt of the shackles having been broken by some of his abettors] I was under the necessity of ordering other shackles, which I rivetted on his wrists. The malignity, savageness, blasphemies, and shocking conduct of this man, exceeded any thing I ever before witnessed. I was happily, however, preserved from anger or passion, & perhaps my coolness & indifference to what he said might tend to irritate him the more.

After the flensing was finished, made sail & began to ply to windward.

Wednesday 21 June Lat. 74°5' Long. 8°W. Therm. 34. 35. 33
NE.erly SE. var SSW
Light or moderate & variable breezes. Clear, warm weather great part of the day: foggy in the evening. Having worked up to the NE side of the opening, made a stretch into some very crowded ice on a northerly course, where we met with a considerable number of large fish: and though we had boats often in pursuit & sometimes very near to fish, we did not succeed. Several ships killed fish about us. About 23 sail in sight.

---

[1] Could be read as 'chest', but 'cheek' clearly is more probable in context.
[2] *Sic*; 'be' presumably intended.

Thursday 22 June Lat. 73.55′ Long. 8°20′W Therm: 34. 38. 34.
SSW. WSW

About 2 am. all the principal officers being accidentally on deck, were called into the cabin to consider the conduct of John Wright, and to take measures for preventing, as far as possible, any injury being done to the voyage, that is, as regards its prosperity from his influence & example. The persons present were Wm Lloyd, Chief Mate; Thos Murray, Specksioneer; Thos Forster, Second mate; Thos Blades, Thos Page, & John Natrass, harponeers; Willm Nevison, surgeon; Robert Hurry, gentleman; and myself. It was found on investigation, ['that it' *deleted*] & could be attested on oath by at least some three, of the council, that every article of the following summary is strictly true.

That the said John Wright having unprovoked, bred a disturbance in the ship, so as completely to suspend the flensing of a fish, to the great disadvantage of the voyage was requested by the Captain to cease his quarreling – then, to go below; – then, to go to the mast-head: to all of which he answered severally he would not – ['but' *deleted*] & at length he would be damned first. That there being no means of getting him away without constraint, he was secured by rope, on which he threatened the life of the Captain & chief mate; – twice attempted to strike the former; – called out, ['in' *deleted*] repeatedly in words to this effect – a. "if two or three like myself ['will' *deleted*] would stand by me I would take the ship from you all, and you [the Captain] should not be the long there" that he would have blood for supper; that he would rejoice to drink the Captain's blood and other mutinous expressions and conduct, besides the most horrid blasphemies and the most gross and extravagant insults. That some among the crew showing a disposition to support him, ['He was' *deleted*] it was unanimously agreed that the lives of the Captain & principal officers were ['considered' *deleted*] unsafe, and that there was a danger of a mutiny; and as such, the said John Wright could not without great risk, to the personal safety of the officers, be set at liberty.

This Wright, it appears, was long in the navy, in the situation of boatswain's mate: he is truly the most shocking blasphemer, and the grossest blackguard, I ever met with; and at the same time ['one of' *deleted*] the most queroulous [*sic*], overbearing, and savage character.[1]

The fog continued till about 2 am. & then cleared away, on a moderate breeze springing up, on which almost all the fish seen during the day, having been moving

---

[1] The Scoresby Papers in Whitby Museum contain a separate document (WHITM:SCO1290) that is a record of this meeting ('Council' as it is described in the document) and on which the journal entry is based. It is rather stronger in tone, however: whereas the journal states that Wright could not without great risk be set at liberty, the document records that '... it was <u>unanimously resolved</u> That the said John Wright must be secured by irons in the most effectual manner'. On the reverse of the document is a listing of those who could attest to specific mutinous behaviour by Wright, e.g. 'Threatened the life of the mate: Self; Hurry; Murray; Sec^d mate of Mercury' and '"He would have blood for supper": Lloyd; Hurry; Page.' Also of interest, because Scoresby did not include this material in his journal, is the following: 'Ill disposed men in the ship, Swinburn; Porter; Morrison; Lashley?; Wm Thomas; James Wells. Write [*sic*] says he has 14 or 15 on his side & if he had a few more he would make us all march overboard'.

briskly towards the SW & WSW we proceeded with all dispatch in plying to windward. About 11 Am. we reached the[1] windward edge of the opening: the ice to the
WSW being rather slack, we continued to beat to windward all the day, though the
navigation was uncommonly intricate and troublesome. Occasionally saw fish; but
about 9 Pm. saw a considerable number; sent all the boats away in pursuit & at 11¼
Pm. one of them made a successful

['John Natrass **M.**   N° 10 = 10.0' *in margin*]

['**Friday 23 June** Lat. 73°50' Long. 8°40'W Therm. 37.33 WSW: W.' *in margin*]
attack and struck a whale. It was attacked with some vigour and killed within the
hour. Made the ship fast to a piece of ice; cleared a flens-gut & then took the fish in.
Saw no fish, scarcely, while we were flensing but just as we concluded 4 or 5
appeared. We were not successful in the pursuit. A thick fog then commencing, our
further fishing, at least at any distance, was prevented. Previously the weather had
been most delightful. During the 24 hours, the sun was never shrouded in a cloud. –
Sea blue here: but green a little to the NE of all the ships to leeward of us: 3 or 4 not
far distant.

At 9 pm. the weather being foggy, began to clear the main-hold for making
off.

Saturday 24 June Lat. 73.55 Long. 8°0'W Therm. 40. 36.
W. SW
Fresh breezes; foggy occasionally but most generally cloudy. Employed all day in
making off; ship made fast to two pieces of ice. In the evening 15 sail in sight, chiefly
to the W^d & NW^d of us. At 9 pm. finished making off, having filled 44 casks with
blubber = 87 butts. Caught 3 bears. Saw one whale.

Sunday 25 June Lat 73.48' Long. 8°0'W
SW to S. & SE
Moderate breezes ['chiefly foggy weather' *deleted*] sometimes foggy; but chiefly clear.
In the evening a heavy fall of rain. Being Sabbath day, lay moored to the ice. Some
ships passed us. Therm. 40. 38.

Monday 26 June Lat. 73.30' Long. 8°20'W Therm. 41. 38. 33
SE to E
Foggy all the day: wind moderate; a fresh breeze in the night. Cast off about 9
am. the fish having totally disappeared since Friday, and steered to the WSW &
SW, meaning afterwards to go to the NW, the course followed by most of the fish
seen. But finding the ice more and more crowded & the weather intensely thick,
we lay too as well as we could about 4 pm. & at mid-night made fast. Saw no
fish.

[1] At this point 'Spent 13 hours in the crow's nest' is pencilled in the margin.

Tuesday 27 June Lat 73.39 Long. 9°W Therm. 37. 33. 33
E to NE
Blowing fresh with thick fog in the morning: nevertheless cast off and began to ply to
the N^d among very crowded ice. In the afternoon being somewhat clearer, made a
stretch of 12 or 14′

['Thomas Page   F. N° 11 = 9.1' *in margin*]

to NWbN, and at 8 pm. fell in with a fish. On its second appearance it lay fully 5 minutes, and affording an excellent opportunity to our boats was struck. It was soon
killed: made fast to flens. Another fish which rose near the ship ['was' *deleted*] escaped
by the bad management of one of the harponeers. At mid-night totally clear weather:
wind moderate. 7 sail in sight. A large floe near us to the N^d. Very rank ice all round.

Wednesday 28 June Lat. 73°30′ Long. 10°W. corr^d <u>11.50</u>W Therm. 40 - 42 - 40 -37
NNE Calm. NW. Var.
Light airs or calm: frequently thick fog. At 10 am. cast off and attempted to make
our way to the NW or W. the course followed by all the fish seen of late; but finding
the ice very cross and wind failing us we again made fast. In the evening a gentle
breeze springing up, cast off and after some difficulty reached a small opening to the
['Curious appearance of Ships & ice.' *in margin*] NE leading to greater spaces of
water to the N^d of us. Here we plyed up a narrow channel & with the assistance of a
boat towing worked through a channel not above 3 ship's lengths wide, and got into
sufficient room. Saw several fish during the day & had some good chances but did
not succeed in a capture. Killed 3 bears.

    In the evening, from 6 to 12 o'clock a singular refractive appearance was observed: in
['Tar melting in the rigging & water running in streams off the ice' *in margin*] which
some ships beyond the horizon were brought within it & had their masts shortened,
others had their mast [*sic*] increased to twice their ordinary length, & some had inverted
images, as dark & distant as the ships themselves, joined mast-head to mast-head &
others had, two distinct images above them, both inverted with the reflection of ['19 sail
in sight' *in margin*] the ice in one or two strata at an elevation of 10 to 15′ of altitude as
seen from the mast-head & measured with a quadrant. For particulars see Sketch-Book.[1]

Thursday 29 June Lat. 73.24+ Long. by Chrono*mete*r 10°20′30″W Therm. 40. 41.
37
NE. NW. W. Var.
Calm or gentle breezes. Plying to the N^d during the morning. Saw several whales;
some had narrow escapes, even 5 or 6. About 10 am. one was happily

['Thos Blades F.   N° 12 = 11.1' *in margin*]

struck and very soon subdued. Made fast to a large piece of ice & flensed it.

---

[1] This sketch-book does not appear to be among the Scoresby Papers.

In flensing, the armourer was struck by a capstern bar and driven down the companion & it is feared considerably hurt.

As soon as the fish was flensed (having a fresh breeze of wind & clear weather,) we cast off and stood to the westward. 3 or 4 hours through loose ice until we reached the edge of a chain of floes running WSW & ENE. Here having tolerable room, plyed to windward, and saw fish occasionally.

Friday 30 June Lat. 73°15 Long. 11°10′W. Therm. 34. 33. 33
W. WSW
It blew strong in the night & during the forenoon, & became a little foggy about noon: seeing several fish about the edge of a floe, we sent boats in pursuit, though the floe was not a sound one. Had some good chances; but succeeded not. At 6 pm. made fast to the floe and ['began' *deleted*] cleared the after-hold for making off, keeping 2 boats on watch.

Saturday 1 July Lat 73°15′ Long. 11°10′W Therm. 38. 35. 30
WSW. Var. SW. SSW.
Wind a light or moderate breeze, mostly foggy. Spoke the Albion with 4 fish, James [Liverpool][1] 5 = 45 t. Mars 4 = 40 t. [Shannon?],[2] 7 = 115 t: The chain of the floes is in this place separated so as to admit a navigation to the westward: one ship has been, we were informed, to the West Land, but having seen no fish returned hither. Saw scarcely a fish during the day, but some hundreds of narwals.

['Made off 59 Casks of blubber = 85 butts; allowing 5 butts for casks indifferently filled.' *in margin*] At 6 pm. having finished making off, & the wind having veered so as to blow along the ice, we cast off & lay too until mid-night, by which time every thing was put in order.

Sunday 2 July Lat. 73°10′ Long 11°W. Therm. 38°. 32°. 35
SSW. Var. Calm.
Light winds or calm with fog or rain. Clear for a few hours in the middle of the day. Having worked into the loose ice in the night we fell in with a great number fish in the forenoon. A boat was lowered when I was in bed: but being Sabbath Day, recalled when I arose and no other dispatched during the day. One ship flensing near us. In the evening made fast to the floe from whence we had unloosed on Saturday: in [ev^g?] narwals about us & occasionally a whale. The Albion has killed 2 fish here since Friday.[3]

---

[1] Brackets in transcript.

[2] Probably the Hull vessel commanded from 1814 to 1821 by Robert Kelah or Keilah (Credland, *Hull Whaling Trade*, p. 137).

[3] In his 'Sabbaths in the Arctic Regions', pp. 3–136 in *Memorials of the Sea*, Scoresby used the 1820 voyage, and especially the month of July, as the 'Indications of a Providential Blessing, in connection with Sabbath forbearance' (p. 35). He began by noting that several of the harpooners 'were, in the early part of the voyage, very much dissatisfied with the rule. They considered it a great hardship that, whilst other ships took advantage of the seven days of the week … they should be restricted to six …

Monday 3 July Lat. 73°5 Long 11°W. Therm. 40. 38
S.erly Calm
Nearly calm all day with thick fog. At 1 am. having a very light air of wind & believing the fish to be amongst the loose ice to the E^d of us cast off and proceeded in that direction. A continuance of calm, however, & fog prevented our entering the ice. Saw an old bear with two cubs, feeding them with a piece of whale tongue on a bit of ice, sent a boat to them, killed the mother (which sank) and took the two cubs alive. At mid-night lay too off the edge of the loose ice. Some ships occasionally in sight to the W^d of us. No fish seen.

Tuesday 4 July Lat. 73.0 Long. 10½W. Therm. 34. 34. 33
NE
Having a gentle breeze of wind, with an attenuation of the fog, below, now and then entered the loose ice and proceeded 12 miles towards the ESE: there saw 3 fish: pursued them without success. Spoke the Mercury[1] with 23 fish, 180 tons oil!

Wednesday 5 July Lat 72.56 Long 11°W. Therm. 38. 37.
Calm SSW to SE
Calm until 8 am. with thick fog: a light breeze of wind then springing up, we stood to the W^d into a thick patch of ice and fell in with two fish: one of them we struck & were successful

['Thos Page F.   N° 13 = 10.6.' *in margin*]

in killing. Made fast to a small floe to flens.

When the jaw bones are removed from the carcase of the whale, it sometimes, not infrequently indeed, floats at the surface.. For several days we have traversed water (blue & transparent) on the surface of which floated a large quantity of a brownish coloured substance, that I imagine is the [dung?] of the whale & if so the sea hereabout ['must have' *deleted*], recently, ['bee' *deleted*] must have been swarming with fish.

The early and middle part of the fishery … having proved very unproductive, our principles, towards the conclusion of the season were put to a severe test, when, for three successive Sundays, a considerable number of fine whales most invitingly appeared around us …

On the first occasion, during the night, in neglect or forgetfulness of the general order, a boat had been sent off in pursuit; but it was recalled when I arose … and none afterwards permitted to be lowered, though an unusual number of fish, from time to time, were in view' (pp. 36–7). Scoresby then noted that on the following Wednesday (5 July), 'whilst the fog was yet exceedingly dense' the capture of a 'fine fish' was 'unexpectedly successful.' See Introduction, p. xxvi.

[1] Probably the Hull whaler commanded from 1820 to 1823 by William Jackson (Credland, *Hull Whaling Trade*, p. 137). See note to Scoresby's journal entry for 15 February 1820. In *Arctic Whalers*, pp. 215 & 218, Lubbock noted that 'The year 1820 was the most successful in the whole of the Hull fishing records' and listed the *Mercury* as the vessel with the largest cargo of that port: 24 whales, yielding 540 butts or 300 tons of oil. There is clearly an inconsistency in the reported yields, if this was the same *Mercury*.

Thursday 6 July Lat. 72°50′ Long. 11°W. Therm^r 37 - 40 - 35.
Var. Calm. SE.
Light variable breezes or calm. About 6 am. being clear weather, cast off & stood to the SW^d until we reached the edge of the same floe to which we moored on the 30th June. The sea ['swarmin' *deleted*] being almost covered, ['almost' *deleted*] in some places with fulmars ['Beautiful animals [See Sketch Book]' *in margin*] we examined the water & found it swarming with white insects of the crustaceous kind. They occurred at every 6 inches interval, were about ½ an inch long, and of the same kind apparently, though greatly larger, as that represented in plate 16 fig. 15 of my "acct. of the Arctic Regions." They are extremely beautiful when examined through the microscope. The tail appears ['actually to be' *deleted*] as if composed of 10 [***] feathers & resembles the tail of a bird. The horns which are longer than the [body?] animal are used in springing forward. ['Saw West Land!' *in margin*] At their extremity are two collateral fibres ['like' *deleted*] feathered on one side, which are [moveable?]. The whole [horn?] is capable of great flexure.

A breeze of wind, with rain, having sprung up in the evening we ['stood' *deleted*] ran to the NW. on the N. side of the floe, and passed through a large quantity of very crowded ice ['**Friday 7 July** Lat. 72°58′ Long. 12°W. Therm. 35. 36. 35. SE to EbS. to W.'[1] *in margin*] beyond it. At 2 am. came to another floe where we saw 3 or 4 fish. Losing them we proceeded onward to the lee side of the floe and dodged in an opening among loose ice until mid-day. About 10 pm. last evening, I think I saw the West Land, bearing NW p Comp.

Several fish were seen in the opening where we dodged, but all running to the N^d.

At noon made sail to the NNW falling into very open ice with floes, leaving to appearance a free navigation to the W. Land. Coming on thick at 2 pm. hauled up NNE. In the afternoon saw 2 fish: made fast in the evening & began to make off.

Saturday 8 July Lat.73°10′ Long. 12°30′W. Therm. 35 - 33 - 32
W. WSW
Blowing fresh with foggy weather. About 10 am. finished making off having filled 25 casks [or 46 butts] with blubber. This completed the 2^d tier fore and aft excepting two beer butts, together with 20 casks in the third tier, main hold.

Cast off: saw 2 fish: stood to the NW saw no more. Sea green for first time since the 25 June. Watered off a floe. Plyed to windward in the night:

Sunday 9 July Lat. 73°0′ Long. 12°W.
WSW. SSW
Strong breezes with fog or rain. Occasionally partially clear. Saw 10 ships. Lay too under the lee of a large floe, where 2 or 3 fish were seen: but being Sabbath we did not lower a boat. In the evening stood to the W^d. – Therm. 34 - 35 - 33.[2]

---

[1] Possibly (and more logically) 'N'.

[2] 'The next Lord's day, though fish were astir, was a day of sanctified and happy repose' (*Memorials of the Sea*, p. 37). Scoresby then elaborated on his journal record of 11 July to link the success of that day, despite great danger to the ship, to the previous Sunday's observance. See Introduction, p. xxvi.

Monday 10 July Lat 72°40′ Long. 12°10′W. Therm. 33 - 33 - 31
SW to WNW to WSW

Fresh breezes with thick fog in general; tolerably clear for an hour or two. Beat to windward all night under a brisk sail. In the forenoon saw two fish, one of which offered us a flattering chance of success; but it escaped us. Taking a long stretch to the SW & South in the afternoon we fell into very blue water, crowded ice, ['and' *deleted*] without fish. Tacked & in the first good opening dodged – the weather amazingly thick. Saw a large <u>she</u> bear with two cubs: killed the former which sank & took the cubs alive.

Tuesday 11 July Lat. 72°30′ Long. 12°30′W Therm. 33. 34. 33
WSW: SW

Strong gales: clear weather for a few hours in the morning, afterwards thick with fog or rain. Making a stretch to the NW^d about 4 am. we fell in with, at the edge of a large floe, a number of whales. Three boats being out in pursuit, about 8 am. a fall was called, and the fish, under two harpoons soon killed. The wind laying rather on the ice, we could not make fast but dodged for the fish until it should be cleared of the floe. But before this was well accomplished another was struck. This for want of boats, one having the fish in tow, 2 others being without lines & a fourth having her lines hanging out, had nearly

['Thos Page **M.**   N° 14 = 11.5' *in margin*]

escaped us. For want of necessary force indeed she[1] kept us some hours, and ran out two boats lines from the first fast boat – the end of which was then taken to a hummock & the harpoon drawn. Out of the 2^d fast boat 10 lines were taken out & the end in the hand of the harpooner, when the fish was arrested by the lances of the other boats. She was at length killed at the distance of 2 miles from the other fish, between some large heavy pieces of ice & the floe. As we could not get near with the ship we dodged near the floe edge, trying first however every direction to get to the weathermost fish, during some hours very thick fog. At length, about 6 Pm., the fog cleared during about 15 minutes, in which happy interval we got sight of all the boats: got the last killed fish in tow & while we drifted to

['John Natrass **M.**   N° 15 = 9.8' *in margin*]

leeward sent the boats to get the other fast[2] clear, it having drifted into the ice. This was just accomplished as we reached them & the other fish also taken in tow. Three boats were now dispatched to get the lines in 24 of which = 5760 yards in length were hanging by the ice! Meanwhile we continued to drift to leeward, meaning to endeavour to moor to the leeside of the floe that the boats might be able to find us in the thick. But the weather was again intensely thick, the wind blowing a gale, the ship

---

[1] Note that both fish caught on this date were recorded in the margin of the journal as males.
[2] *Sic*; 'fish' intended?

among floes & heavy loose ice & owing to the two fish almost unmanageable. In this state we fell in with a small floe under our lee & in attempting to wear clear of it, the ship, after every exertion on our part & slacking the warps by which the fish were held did not clear it above half a breadth! My anxiety at this moment was extreme. If we made fast to any loose piece of ice – the boats would lose us: if we contended to reach the floe we might fall in with ice under our lee (as we could not see 100 fathoms,) and be under the necessity of cast the fish adrift. This might be the means of losing one or both of the fish & endangering the people as well as the ship. Trusting, turning to Almighty God for direction, to whom I looked with prayer and hope, we were most Providentially directed, having fallen in with the edge of the floe near a leeward point & drifting safely along it, selected a place for mooring, cast the fish adrift as near it as we could bring them & then made fast.[1] Thanks to God for his mercies.

Wednesday 12 July Lat. 72.25 Long. 12°35′W Therm. 35 - 36 - 35
W. Var.
Wind more moderate: fog still very thick. In the course of the morning ['all' *deleted*] the boats found their way to the ship and brought with them the whole of the lines and other apparatus left suspended by the ice. Began to flens about 4 am. The people being fatigued and not a little indolent – they were a dismal time in flensing. One of the fish, the first struck was so swollen before it was flensed, that the blood had begun to penetrate & discolour the lower part of the blubber. Saw a black coloured bird, supposed to be a <u>raven</u>.[2]

Thursday 13 July Lat. 72. 20 Long. 12°40′W. Therm. 34 - 36. 35
Var. SE. SSE
Light variable breezes. About 2 am. the weather having cleared, cast off & ran to the SW[3] along the edge of the floe with a view to proceed round it in search of the run of fish out of which we procured our two last. A fog setting in again however interrupted us for several hours. About 4 Pm. the fog again dispersed partially. Stood to the W^d along the edge of the floe, where it was ['defended' *deleted*] pretty closely encompassed by smaller floes and drift ice. About 7 Pm. having fallen into a vein of green water, swarming with medusæ and insects, we fell in with a number of fish in pursuit of which we sent six boats. The Mary & Eliz. in C° together with the Phoenix

---

[1] Scoresby expanded on this sentence in *Memorials of the Sea*, pp. 40–41. 'Whilst the topsails were kept shivering, in order to diminish as much as possible the leeward pressure of the wind, and to give time for what was essential to be done, a convenient place for mooring was sought out, and an ice anchor dexterously fixed, but with every effort and possible despatch the ship had fallen too far to leeward. In a moment the encumbering fish were cast adrift (the ends of the hawsers being dropped into a boat with a single hand to secure them) and, then, by the prompt management of the sails we fetched just within range of the desired spot, and happily effected a mooring ...
    The ship being well secured to the floe, all the remaining boats were sent out to tow up the whales ...'.
[2] Scoresby did not include the Common Raven (*Corvus corax*) in his list of birds in *Account of the Arctic Regions*, I, pp. 527–38, but the bird's extensive range includes high arctic latitudes.
[3] Possibly 'NW'.

had also several boats in chase. The former killed a fish. In the night, fog returned with uncommon obscurity. The loose ice & smaller floes setting rapidly up rendered our stay dangerous, yet ['**Friday 14 July** Therm. 35–40 SE to SW' *in margin*] we continued plying about in the most open part until 4 am. when the mate having heard a fish blowing, went out in pursuit & struck it. The Phoenix's boat "bent-on" & the Mary & Eliz. ['boats' *deleted*] people struck 2ᵈ & 3ᵈ harpoons & killed it, saying they mistook it for a loose fish & were not satisfied until every possible & desirable proof was given them that our harpoon was yet fast to it. It was then of consequence relinquished as our prize. The contention respecting it occasioned

['William Lloyd **M.**   Nº 16 = 11.9' *in margin*]

an unfortunate delay, during which the fish and boats were beset by some large sheets of ice setting against the floe. They remained enclosed some hours: but at length about 11 Am. by great exertion, were enabled in a slight slacking of the ice, to escape with the fish. After we got it along-side we ran to the NNW into an open space of water, to avoid the further dangers of the ice around the floe. Began to flens at 12½ Pm; finished at 4. At 6 having discovered a detached piece of heavy ice made the ship fast, meaning if the weather & ice were favourable to commence making-off as soon as the people should have obtained a little rest.

Foggy throughout the day: Light or moderate winds. 3 sail in sight.

Saturday 15 July Lat. Long.¹
WSW
Moderate breezes: thick weather in the morning in the evening clear & warm. Commenced making off at 5 am. Completed the third tier after-hold; also the fore-hold, excepting 3 casks, which 3 casks not being able to finish them before mid-night ['Curious reflection of Atm. See 17 July' *in margin*] were left for a future occasion. 9 sail in sight. Curious reflection of ice & water: see accᵗ of this phenomenon on 17 July: – Therm. 37 - 40.

Sunday 16 July Lat. Long. Therm. 44 - 48.
WSW. W. SW.
Light breezes, beautifully clear weather, sun hot: distant objects strangely² affected by the reflection & refraction of the fog banks. A quantity of blubber which lay on deck all day, exposed to the sun, was almost dissolved. A great quantity of oil was lost. Several fish seen near us: but being Sabbath were not pursued.³ Several ships in sight.

¹ The entries for latitude and longitude were left blank for this and the next two days.
² Possibly 'strongly'.
³ 'A day of sweet and welcome repose was the succeeding Sabbath … . Several whales sported around us; but, as far as we were concerned, they were allowed a Sabbath-day's privilege to sport unmolested.
  The men were now accustomed to look for a blessing on Sabbath observances. And within the succeeding week … the blessing was realized' (*Memorials of the Sea*, pp. 41–2).

Monday 17 July Lat. Long. Therm. 40 - 45 - 48
SW. W. E. Var. SW. Calm. SW

Light variable breezes: most delightful weather: momentarily a fog arose but was immediately dispersed. Re-commenced making off as soon as the ['day' *deleted*] Sabbath was past. Completed the fore-hold: and at 7 Pm. the main hold also. Procured the assistance of the Cooper of the James[1] [Capt. Quickfall] who was of imminent service to us. Stowed 5 or 6 casks in the 'tween-decks & filled them: afterwards having to wait for casks, set the watch. E & W wind suddenly alternated 4 or 5 times.

The singular appearances, produced by distant fog banks, by the refraction & ['Singular atmospheric reflection & refraction' *in margin*] reflection of objects near the horizon, have been prevalent during three days almost continually. The ice on the horizon, in one two or three horizontal strata, was reflected at the ['the' *deleted*] altitude as seen from the deck, of 10 to 30 minutes[2] from the verge of the sea; and where water occurred on the horizon, a horizontal ['darkish' *deleted*] blackish grey [streak?], was seen undulating [with?] waves running to leeward, apparently the reflection of the water disturbed by the wind-lipper. In some places the reflected ice was in narrow streaks: in others in broad bold patches, resembling cliffs of white marble, of the basaltic structure. Sometimes the phenomenon extending through half of the circumference of the horizon: at others appeared in detached spots in various quarters. Seen from the deck, the images of distant ships appeared in the air, while the ships themselves were beyond the reach of vision. Some ships had their masts uncommonly extended in height, or compressed almost into nothing: others had ['reflected' *deleted*] inverted images joined to their mast heads. Hummocks of ice, here & there were reared into obelisks: and every remarkable or prominent object was either magnified or distorted. These appearances were not very striking when viewed with the naked eye: but when magnified by a common telescope, they presented a varied scene of interesting imagery.[3]

[1] The Whitby *James*, not the *James* of Liverpool mentioned in the journal entry for 19 August, 1820 (Lubbock, *Arctic Whalers*, p. 229).

[2] Presumably a slip of the pen: 'degrees' intended?

[3] In his *Life* of William Scoresby, Scoresby-Jackson included (at p. 159) a reproduction of Scoresby's sketch of a 'Curious Atmospheric Phenomenon' and quoted Scoresby's comments on the reverse of the sketch: 'During the month of July 1820, the weather being often foggy, with a bright sun sometimes shining at the height of the day, some extraordinary coronæ were observed from the mast-head. These occurred opposite to the sun, the centre of all the circles being in a line drawn from the sun through the eye of the observer. On one occasion [represented in the sketch] four coloured luminous circles were observed. The exterior one might be 20° in diameter; it exhibited all the colours of the spectrum. The next, a little within it, was of a whitish grey colour; the third was only 4° or 5° in diameter, and though it exhibited the colours of the spectrum, these colours were not very brilliant; the fourth was extremely beautiful and brilliant; the interior colour was yellow, then orange, red, violet, &c. The colours of the whole three coronæ were, I think, in the same order; but of this I am not very certain. Indeed, on reflection, I suspect that the second circle must have been in the reverse order of the first; the first and fourth being the same: the third was not coloured. In the midst of these beautiful coronæ I observed my own shadow – the head surrounded by a glory. All the coronæ were evidently produced by the fog; my shadow was impressed on the surface of the sea.' As Scoresby-Jackson noted, Scoresby referred again to this observation, in the course of a longer commentary on optical phenomena, in his *Journal of a Voyage to the Northern Whale-Fishery* (1823, pp. 274–84).

Tuesday 18 July Lat. 71°20′+ Long at 5ʰ53′10″ [am?] by Chronometer: 14°5′W. Diff. of Long. of <u>West Land</u> bearing due W. 2°20′ consequently its Longitude 16°25′W Therm. 30ᵗ 41 - 42
SW. SSW

By the way of obtaining further assistance from the cooper of the James, we were obliged to follow her motions: accordingly about 1 Am. ['got' *deleted*] made sail & cast loose from the ice and proceeded through some rank ice and between ['several' *deleted*] floes to the NW into a large opening, extending apparently in a winding direction to the very shore of W. Greenland.² In passing through this crowded ice, I was astonished ['Bay ice formed!' *in margin*] to find the water covered with a pellicle of bay ice, perhaps ¼ of an inch thick, which had apparently frozen during the night, though the sun does not set & though the temperature during the day has generally been as high as 40° or 42°.³

The West Land [Greenland]⁴ was in sight and bold; extending from W to NNW per ['appearance of West Greenland & effect of refraction' *in margin*] Compass: the nearest part bearing WNW apparently 40 miles distant. Of this coast I [took any?] eye draught:⁵ and a sketch of the land as distorted by the influence of a tremulous transparent vapour which could be seen at a distance, with a telescope, floating along the surface of the Sea. The various changes in the form of the hills were extremely interesting and often beautiful. Obelisks, monuments, towers, spires, ['castles' *deleted*] ramparts, turrets and basaltic cliffs were frequently represented in clear and distinct forms. – This coast very much resembles that of Spitzbergen, though it is less burdened with snow. It appears high land and of a very irregular mountainous surface.⁶

A moderate breeze of wind prevailed throughout the day & clear weather until about 5 pm. a thick fog then set in & continued to the end of the 24 hours. Observed 2 or 3 ships flensing to leeward: saw 2 or 3 fish: pursued them to windward. When

---

¹ Followed by what may be a query ('?').

² In modern terminology, this would of course be the eastern shore of Greenland.

³ Scoresby had evidently entered the East Greenland Current, responsible for transporting more than 90 per cent of the ice exported from the Arctic Ocean. The surface layer, to about 150 metres depth, is cold polar water with a temperature between 0°C. and the freezing point of sea-water (Gyory, Mariano and Ryan, 'The East Greenland Current'). The formation of an overnight ice cover is therefore not surprising, but Scoresby was more accustomed to conditions in the warm, northward-flowing, Spitsbergen Current. See journal entry for 9 July 1817.

⁴ Bracket in transcript.

⁵ If this reading ('I took any eye draught') is correct, it is presumably equivalent to the modern phrase 'I made a mental image'. Although *OED* devotes an unusual amount of space to 'draught', the term 'eye draught' is not mentioned.

⁶ This is the foot of a page, but beneath it, below a drawn line, is the following note: 'Correction of the Longitude of W. Greenland – Longitude of ship corrected by new rate obtained Augᵗ 11 & 12, being 4. 42″ gaining daily: 17°32′15″W
    Diff. Long. of ship –   2°10
Corrected Long. of E. Coast of W. Greenland in Lat. 71°20′N = <u>19.42.15</u>′
This correction was noted in the journal entry for 12 August 1820. The actual longitude of the coast at that latitude is approximately 21°36′W, a difference of about 37.3 nautical miles from Scoresby's corrected value.

the fog commenced dodged by the edge of a floe. The coopers having prepared casks nearly sufficient for the blubber; set all hands to work to make-off the remnant ['off' *deleted*] in casks stowed between the beams under and about the main hatch way forming a fourth tier. At mid-night all the casks being filled that were ready & yet blubber remained, set the watch.

Wednesday 19 July Lat. 71°16′ Long. 14°40′W Therm. 32. 31
SW: SE. var. Calm
Light airs or calm: foggy all day. About 3 a.m. while our making-off was drawing to a conclusion, a fish arose close by the ship, and was pursued by the mate. The fog being thick he was in a few minutes out of sight of the ship. While we were preparing to send a boat to ['his assistance' *deleted*] accompany him, we were rejoiced by the cry of "a fall". The noise of the people in the fast boat, pointed out to the rest of the crew their position: the first boat was just in time to save the lines of the fish. The blowing

['Willm Lloyd F. N° 17 = 10^ft 2^in' *in margin*]

of the fish was at length heard & directed by the sound the boats gave chase and happily found her, struck 4 more harpoons, and soon killed her. This fish being calculated to fill all our casks, the boats towed it on board with flags flying, in token of a "full ship" – thanks to God for all his Mercies![1]

Flensed the fish made fast to a small piece of ice: kept the lips and kent entire.

Thursday 20 July Lat 71°12′ Long. 15°W. Therm. 6 am. 31°. 34.
Var. SW.
The ice to which we moored being too small to hold the ship cast off about 4 am on the springing up of a fresh breeze of wind & made fast to a large floe. As we

---

[1] Many years later, in his *Memorials of the Sea*, Scoresby elaborated on this capture, and used it as another example of 'unusual success, closely following upon special self-denial in remembrance of the Sabbath day' (p. 43):

'We were employed in "making-off" … when a fine stout whale rose close by the ship. As quickly as the lumbered state of the decks and disposition of the crew would permit, a boat was dropped to pursue it. Being a thick fog at the time, the boat was in a few moments out of sight. But before we had arranged for the dispatch of a companion for their assistance and security, the usual alarm of a successful pursuit, – "a fall! a fall!" – resounded through the calm atmosphere from the lips of our absent people. The noise of the lines in "the fast boat," as they were dragged out under the resistance of several turns round the stem, served as a guide to the assistance now yielded; and one of the boats fortunately got up with fresh resources, just in time to save the lines, and to preserve the connection with the entangled whale. The distinctness with which sounds are transmitted through a calm atmosphere across the unruffled surface of an interglacial sea enabled the boats to pursue the chase through the resounding only of its own excited respirations, so that in brief space four additional harpoons were struck, and the vast animal soon yielded its life to the skilfully-plied lances of its pursuers … . In token of the happy circumstance of the attainment of a complete cargo, or "a full ship," the important prize was towed by all of the boats in a line, with flags flying, and constant animated cheers, till they arrived alongside' (pp. 42–3).

approached it we found the James flensing a fish that they had just picked up dead. This makes her cargo about 95 tons of oil.

Having started all the bread into a temporary compartment in the store-room, the coopers trimmed the casks for blubber¹ & also finished setting up strakes. These casks were therefore put below & formed a fifth tier immediately before the main-mast; and part of the crew began to fill them with blubber. All the casks that now remain to be trimmed are a few beer ['casks' *deleted*] & provision casks.

Blowing strong with thick fog until noon when the sky cleared for a short interval and enabled us to discover our position. Found the floe ['turn' *deleted*] wheeling to the NW (against the sun) at the rate of perhaps ¼ of a mile per hour: several floes to the W [&?] SSW, & NE: but much open water to the S. & North.

The sea here is somewhat shallow, compared with the usual fishing stations in this region. The harpoon by which our last fish was entangled having drawn went to the bottom & brought up some coralines² and two animals with numerous jointed arms and branches, the .... [*sic*]

A large piece of ice having set up against us forced us from the floe, ['and' *deleted*] but afforded us an opportunity of making fast to it. Continued making off.

Friday 21 July Lat. 71°15′ Long. 15°W. Therm. 33 - 34
SW to WNW

Strong gales with thick weather most of the day. The piece of ice to which the ship was fastened driving towards a lee-floe, we were obliged to cast off and make sail. Lay too for some time & then dodged under the lee of a floe, where was a considerable opening. The dangerous nature of the ice, ['owing' *deleted*] in this quarter owing to its magnitude, various setting, and the foggy weather, was the occasion of much anxiety of mind on my part which, with the numerous operations connected with the fishery, in which we have of late been engaged, has occupied so much of my attention, that during the last 8 or 9 days I have never slept more than 4 hours at a time, and often only 1 or 2; and have seldom obtained above 5 hours rest in the 24.

In the evening called all hands, made the ship fast to a floe, stowed the lips & kent of the last fish in bulk, between the beams in the 'tween decks, cleared the gun-room of all the store casks, emptying the pease, oatmeal, rice, &c. into various vessels and lockers, so that almost every cask in the ship, excepting [irish?] provision barrels, ale barrels, and 4 beer casks, were obtained for taking blubber, ['and' *deleted*] stowed in the 'tween decks, and in the course of the night filled. Calm at mid-night. Ice setting up to the floe, forced us off, made fast to a detached piece of ice.

---

¹ *OED* includes a 1725 citation from Daniel Defoe, '71 Casks ... which their coopers assisted us to trim, season and fit up' as an example of 'trim' in the sense of 'To put into proper condition for some purpose or use.'

² *OED*: 'Coralline ... A name given originally to organisms thought to resemble or be of the nature of coral, but of more minute size, less firm texture, etc. ... the name is no longer a term of Zoology ...'.

Saturday 22 July Lat. 71.10 Long. 15°10'W Therm. 37.33
Var. SW

Having filled all the casks we could command, amounting to 50 in the 'tween decks (2 lips & kent in bulk) we cast off in the morning, being able to see a mile occasionally, and with a moderate breeze of wind beat towards the SW. in search of another fish. In the night thick fog: lay too. 6 ships occasionally seen.

Sunday 23 July Lat. 71°5 Long 15°20'W. Therm 35. 37
SW.erly: S. SE. ENE

Light variable breezes: generally thick fog. Dodged during the day. Having taken a trip to the mast head about 7 Pm. to ascertain the position of the ['ship' *deleted*] ice around us, during a short interval of clear weather, I discovered a large dead fish a little to the SE of us. A boat was dispatched to endeavour to take possession of it as other ships were near; but others being sent from the Mary & Elizabeth, though at a greater distance, out-pulled ours and gained the prize! Observed several floes about us & much loose ice: but towards the NE & E. a considerable clear opening, towards which we plied on the wind freshening accompanied by fog & rain. A whale came up alongside the ship!

Monday 24 July Lat. 70°55' Long. 16°W. Therm. 34. 34. 33
ENE, NEbE

The wind continued to increase during the night, attended with heavy rain & in the morning blew a ['hard' *deleted*] gale & in the afternoon reduced us to close reefed top sails. We should have been tempted to take advantage of this wind to proceed homeward had we been out of the ice; but its present violence & the crowded ice lying in the way rendered such an attempt ['at' *deleted*] now too hazardous. Dodged among loose ice & floes. 4 ships near us. Much rain fell.

Tuesday 25 July Lat. 70°48' Long. 16°50'W. Therm. 34.35.34
NEbE NNE

The wind having moderated during the night, we sent a boat a floe[1] with some barrels for water, from which we filled, all our empty casks, about 600 gallons, for a stock for the passage home. After which, being able to see about a mile, we made sail and steered to the SSE amid floes and open ice. The rain which had generally prevailed during 36 or 40 hours now abated & was succeeded by a dense fog, in which we soon got bewildered in the mazes of numerous floes and large collections of heavy drift ice. One floe we passed presented a <u>tongue</u>, estimated at 30 feet under water at its upper surface, probably 40 or 50 deep altogether! Finding any further advance to the SE or SSE prevented by a chain of floes, we worked out to the N^d and made fast to a ['large' *deleted*] heavy detached piece of ice. Saw a razor back. No ships in sight.

---

[1] Possibly 'sent about a floe'.

Wednesday 26 July Lat. 70°40′ Long. 16°W. Therm. 34. 35. 34
NEbE
A moderate breeze of wind prevailed during the night, (which was gloomy, and near 12 o'clock very dusky twilight) accompanied with thick weather from fog or heavy rain. About 9 am. the extent of vision might be a furlong: cast off & after the stretch to the NNW, stood to the SSE during an hour: but the wind having freshened and the fog having become so intensely thick that we could not see 100 yards, sometimes scarcely 50, we soon again got involved amid the floes, where for some time we navigated in great uncertainty & danger. At 2pm. fell under the lee of a large heavy floe, where, after searching to the leeward for any dangerous ice, we dodged. Heavy rains occasionally occurred; yet the ['fog' *deleted*] thickness continued without the least ['alteration' *deleted*] attenuation, which is not a little uncommon.

In the evening strong gales with rain or fog: at mid-night rather clearer: saw 2 ships to the NE^d ['of us' *deleted*].

Thursday 27 July Lat. 70°36′ Long. 16°10′W.¹ Therm. 36. 37.
ENE: SE NE: E. Var.
In the morning, after several sudden changes of wind, and much rain, (which with the motion of the "scud" towards the WNW intimated a SE.erly wind at sea) the storm again abated; but the weather continued so remarkably and ['continual' *deleted*] constantly thick that we were unable to penetrate the mazes of the chain of floes lying to the E^d of us.

While the ship lay moored to a floe during 2 or 3 hours in the evening, I took to the ice my magnetical instrument which I propose to name an ['Experiment with my new magnetic Instrument' *in margin*] Elkusmosometer*,² or measurer of attraction, for the purpose of trying an experiment on the magnetical dip. The iron bar used in the Exp^t was heated red hot & cooled in an E&W position to [free?] it from magnetism, yet on trial it was found to be slightly magnetized. One end presented to the Compass needle on the brass Table, was void of attraction when the nearest end was depressed at any angle of 17°20 with the horizon: the other end at an ∠ of 10°40′. On shifting the ends of the bar, the moveable plane slipped down so as to give a slight jerk to the bar on which, its poles were found to be changed; one end now having no ['Its extreme delicacy' *in margin*] attraction at 23°40′ the other at 4°30: After a short interval a third experiment was made when the ∠'s of no attraction were 19° & 8°40. Had the bar remained in the mag. equator it is presumed that it would have soon lost the little magnetism that it had acquired. This great effect of a slight shock of the bar on a piece of wood, in reversing its poles, shows the extreme delicacy of the instrument, and its almost infinite superiority over any other for detecting ['the' *deleted*] minute portions of magnetism in iron. It would be of admirable use in trying the exp*erime*nt of magnetising iron by the violet rays of light,

---

¹ '17.30?' added, apparently at a later date and in pencil.
² Note in margin: '*Magnetimeter.'

See Edinb. Phil. Journal. N° 2: p.242.[1] The means of the above three experiments very nearly coincide: viz

$$\frac{17°20 + 10°40}{2} = 14°0°; \frac{23.40 + 4.30}{2} = 14°10'; \frac{19°0 + 8°40}{2} = 13.50:$$

General mean 14°0'–90° = 76°0' = Magnetic Dip.

Friday 28 July Lat. 70.34+ Long. 16°20'W. Ther. 35 - 40
E. NE var.

Light variable breezes or calm with fog: in the afternoon & about mid-day so clear that we could sometimes see 4 miles. Joined C^o with the Mary & Eliz. of Hull Capt. Weldon,[2] who having but 80–90 tons of oil, furnished us with some shakes and the use of his cooper for taking up our blubber in bulk.

['Sea like mustard! See July 31 1820' *in margin*] What little progress we made was towards the E. where we thought there was a break in the chain of floes. In the evening, having a breeze at W. entered the floes, steering S. SSE & SE generally but sometimes diverted by the appearance of floes.

Saturday 29 July Lat. 70°28' Long. 15°50'W. Therm. 40 - 43.
W.erly Var. Calm. NNE

Light variable breezes or calms during the first 18 or 20 hours of the day: in the evening a moderate wind sprang up from the NNE. The fog continued intensely thick most of the night & until near mid-day when it cleared away & was succeeded by a warm sunshining day. During the fog we were much perplexed by occasional floes that we met with & particularly by a heavy field that we saw about 2am. The edge lay NNE & SSW: proceeded ['Progress through the ice: tremendously heavy field; and dangerous nature of the Sea stream.' *in margin*] at a slow rate to the S^d amid numerous floes & much loose ice. When the fog dispersed we discovered that notwithstanding the intensity of the ['fog' *deleted*] thickness and the consequent uncertainty of the navigation, & the dangerous motions of the ice urged[3] strong winds and currents we had been directed by that beneficent Being to whom I looked especially & fervently for assistance & guidance, as correctly and as safely as if the weather had been clear & perhaps more so: having penetrated a chain of floes in which we could discover no opening & having well advanced towards the southern extreme of a heavy field, which stretched to an unknown distance to the N^d without opening or even fissure. Perceiving now that the southern boundary of the field was not above 3 miles distant & that slack ice for some distance beyond would permit a considerable advance towards the South or SbE, during a temporary calm we "called all Hands" & placed 6 boats ahead of the ship & ['towed' *deleted*] "towed her" forward at the

[1] Scoresby was referring to the anonymous article, 'Account of the Experiments of Morichini', pp. 239–43. It concerned a debate on whether needles could be magnetized by the violet rays of the solar spectrum; this appeared to be possible on the basis of Italian experiments, but under 'a more northern, and less serene sky, the experiment has been unsuccessful' (p. 240).

[2] Henry Wheldon, according to Credland, *Hull Whaling Trade*, Appendix 3. This was his only voyage as master of a Hull whaler.

[3] *Sic*; 'by' omitted?

rate of 1 or 1½ knots. At 6 Pm. passed the SW.ern corner of the field, which we found tremendously heavy: hummocks appeared in numerous places, consisting of heavy ['Heavy ice!' *in margin*] & extensive masses of ice, 30 or 40 feet above the level of the water: & we could observe "tongues" on the margin 20 or 30 feet deep, so that in some places, there is no doubt, the ice must have been upwards of 50 feet thick, perhaps near 100! From the SE ['east' *deleted*] corner of this field another chain of floes extended to an unknown distance to the S^d through which we ['made a p' *deleted*] effected our passage in an intricate channel: we then came to loose ice, with small floes here and there, but nothing to impede our progress to the S^d. Steered therefore SSE or within a point or two of this course with a freshening breeze & still clear weather until our velocity ['at [***]' *deleted*] increased to 5 or 6 knots. At mid-night we were cheered by a glimpse of the <u>Sea</u> or at least an arm of it, ['**Sunday 30 July** Lat 69°55' Long. 15°W. Therm 34. 35. 43.[1] NNE. NEbE. to NbE.' *in margin*] extending from SE to SSE. We advanced towards it: but as we came near, we found the ice heavier and more & more crowded until the safe navigation, hitherto enjoyed, was interrupted by a dangerous sea stream, the exterior ice of which could be seen, ['by' *deleted*] with the aid of a telescope, to be in a violent state of commotion. The [foreground?][2] of the ship being torn off by a blow received in the ['Narrative of our progress in passing a dangerous Sea Stream.' *in margin*] early part of the voyage, and the keel projecting now in front without any defence, appeared liable to be ['torn off' *deleted*] struck off by a very slight blow from a tongue of ice: which danger, became very appalling, when we had the prospect of being obliged to force through a sea stream of heavy ice & in a swell, where numerous pieces appeared having tongues projecting from their corners, of 10 to 20 or 30 feet deep! This circumstance ['induced me to' *deleted*] made me shrink from the attempt to pass the stream, notwithstanding our anxiety to escape, until the wind, which now blew strong, had abated, the sea had fallen, or at least a better prospect of a safe egress had appeared: but the Mary & Elizabeth, which had closely followed us since Friday having "taken the ice", I was induced, though almost against prudence, to advance in the openings which she had made. Commending myself, therefore, to the protection of that God, who is a present help in time of trouble & danger, and looking to Him for ['guidance' *deleted*] his infallible influences to guide & direct me, I ordered all hands to attend the sails, and followed the ['Mary' *deleted*] track of the leading ship. In this way we proceeded safely until we approached the edge within ['Narrative continued.' *in margin*] 2 or 3 pieces of ice, when the Mary & Elizabeth escaped out of a narrow & dangerous opening, ['that was imposs' *deleted*] which two minutes after was absolutely unnavigable. I was alarmed with the view of her danger, notwithstanding the advantage afforded by the opening, the sea roaring & breaking upon tremendous lumps of ice within a yard or two of her lee. To ['attempt to' *deleted*] follow was impossible and to attempt to force through the heavy interposing masses, ['when in

---

[1] There is a transposition sign around the latter values, suggesting that the correct sequence is '34.43.35'.

[2] This may be a transcription error for 'forefoot' (see Smyth, *Sailor's Word Book*); however the term is repeated again in the transcript, in the final paragraph of the 1820 journal.

violent' *deleted*] averaging 13,000 tons in weight, when in violent ['con' *deleted*] agitation, would have been ['madness' *deleted*] a degree of temerity, in which it would not have been reasonable to look for the blessing of Providence: – we, therefore, as the only means of avoiding the threatening danger, instantly grappled the nearest piece of ice with a warp astern, and dragging it some distance to leeward, by the force of a gale of wind, through a chain of heavy lumps of ice, where there was ['a little' *deleted*] shelter from the swell, made fast to a heavy mass until I should be able to decide on the best mode of proceeding. The succeeding hours, for a length of time was a season of vast anxiety; and had it not been for the confidence I felt in all my ways being under the Direction of a Merciful God, whose assistance on the outset of this attempt I had fervently invoked, I should have been in the greatest distress and terror. The wind freshened to a gale, rain began to descend in torrents, the sea rolled upon the ice and reveled[1] its effects to us even when not observing it, by its ['horrid roaring' *deleted*] sublime & terrible roaring. We had now three alternatives: to attempt to return to the westward by boring through the pieces interposing which were heavy & numerous, and which could not be accomplished without some danger, – to remain stationary to try the event of more favourable weather, where there was a risk of the sea breaking in upon us & exposing us to the most dangerous kind of situation, – or to "bore" to leeward by a small piece of ice astern where we might be sheltered, apparently, from the sea, but would drive into a close pack & get beset. The second alternative appeared the least objectionable and was adopted for the time being; to be persevered in or rejected as circumstances should justify. In an hour or two, however, the piece of ice to which we moored, being passed by the smaller masses, brought us within a piece or two of the sea, yet without any chance of escaping, and exposed us to a little swell. Hence it was prudent to remove; took hold of a small piece of ice cast off from the larger, and forced to leeward until we again found ourselves sheltered & then again secured hold of the largest piece of ice that came near.

As the day advanced the weather became finer, and the wind happily abated and veered from NEbE towards the N: but the piece of ice we had more to [*sic*] drifting too far to leeward, carried us beyond some openings that occasionally broke out, through which there was a prospect of escaping had we been further to windward. After Divine Service, in the usual manner, had ['Narrative Concluded' *in margin*] been performed in our humble way, we warped the ship to windward, a distance of 500 or 600 yards, by whale lines affixed to a heavy large[2] piece of ice, & obtained a situation about 10[3] Pm. where we could take sail. ['The wind being now moderate,' *deleted*] What ice was formerly the sea edge being now sheltered by a sea stream, a mile distant, that had formed out of a point of ice which had been turned round by the swell, now became quiescent, when, the wind having moderated, the weather being fine & the ice somewhat slack afforded a prospect of our escaping. We

---

[1] *Sic*; 'revealed' presumably intended.
[2] A transposition sign is around the last two words, indicating that the text should be read as 'large heavy'.
[3] Overwritten on '9'.

therefore set our sails, placed three boats at the tow rope to assist the ship in difficult passages where she ['was' *deleted*] would be required to sail within 5 points of the wind, or make very sudden turns, we cast off, and again commending myself ['Escaped out of the Ice.' *in margin*] to God, we proceeded ['in' *deleted*] with the most admirable success, through the various windings, and difficulties without touching a single piece of ice of the least consequence, and on reaching the newly formed sea stream, I fortunately discovered a tolerably safe channel, through which at 11½ Pm. we escaped to sea without either undergoing any particular hazard or happening the least accident. Thanks be to God!

Five boats being dispatched for ['obtaining' *deleted*] fresh water ice, obtained a considerable quantity, which, with the fresh water procured on Tuesday last & frequently replenished since, was considered a sufficient stock for the homeward passage: then concluding the day with the Evening Liturgy and a sermon from Burder's Village Discourses, together with other duties related to the Sabbath – we made sail to the South to get clear of the ice.

Monday 31 July Lat. 69°40′+ Long. 14°35′W. Therm. 43 - 47.
NE: var. Calm.
Not wishing to interrupt the narrative of our proceedings through the ice I omitted, for the first convenience [*sic*] place, the mention of curious currents observed in passing through the floes; and singular appearance of the sea in the same situation, where it was more discoloured by a substance having the resemblance[1] of mustard! The currents appeared to be superficial, not affecting the ship or the heavy ice; but causing the thin ice & small pieces to flow towards the north at the rate of upwards of a mile an hour & bringing numerous pieces in contact with the ship that seemed to be many yards clear of her.

['Examination of a mustard coloured sea water' *in margin*] The yellowish green or mustard coloured water was still more singular. It occurred in small patches or in [waving?] streaks & was very abundant during 18 hours sailing on Friday evening & Saturday morning [28ᵗʰ & 29ᵗʰ July]. When the ship passed any of this water, the substance that discoloured it ['was like' *deleted*] appeared about the surface & near the surface ['(not at any depth)' *deleted*] (being quite superficial) like as if large quantities of fine mustard or flowers of sulphur[2] had been thrown into the sea. Suspecting it to be of an animal nature, a quantity of the yellow water procured and on being examined by a microscope, was found to consist of animalcules, in immense numbers of a yellowish or yellowish green colour. The larger proportion consisting of a coloured ([lemon?] yellow) crystalline [***] substance of a globular form[3] appeared

---

[1] Marginal note at this point, enclosed in brackets: 'See Edin. Phil. Journal to which an accᵗ of these phen. were given.' A later hand, probably Scoresby's own, has added, in pencil, 'Vol. IV (Nᵒ 7) p. 111'. This refers to Scoresby's article entitled 'Observations on the Currents', published in that issue (pp. 111–14, January 1821) of the *Edinburgh Philosophical Journal*, which combined his observations on this date with those made earlier in the voyage, on 24 April 1820.

[2] Sulphur in powdered form.

[3] A small sketch follows, within brackets.

to possess little motion; but a part amounting to about a fifth of the whole [[*small sketch*] See fig. 18 pl. XVI of "Account of the Arctic Regions[1]] were in continual action. Some advancing by a slighty [*sic*] waving motion at the rate of $\frac{1}{180}$th of an inch in a second and others spinning ['Strange number of anamalcules!' *in margin*] round with great velocity, gave great interest & liveliness to the examination. But what afforded the most astonishment was the numbers of these little creatures. In a ['single' *deleted*] drop of water, examined by a power of 28.224[2] [magnified superficies] there were 50 in number in each square of the micrometer glass $\frac{1}{840}$th of an inch in diameter & as the drop occupied a circle on a glass, of 26 ['squares' *deleted*] divisions of the micrometer glass in diameter, equal in area to a square of 23 divisions each side, there must have been in a single drop of the water, taken accidentally from the surface of the sea & in a place by no means the most discoloured $23 \times 23 \times 50 = 26{,}450$! Hence reckoning 60 drops to a dram, there would be a number in a gallon water, exceeding that of the population of the whole globe! How insignificant, in number, is man! What a conception does it give to the lower and minuteness of creation, when we think of 26,000 animals obtaining subsistence, and moving at their ease without hindrance to one another in a single drop of water!! The diameter of the largest of these animals was only $\frac{1}{2000}$ of an inch![3]

We had not been long steering to the southward before the wind died away & left us becalmed within a mile of a point of ice, on which a heavy swell was rolling: this obliged us to summon all hands to tow the ship off. With the aid of a little breeze this was soon effected & at the distance of 4 or 5 miles we were again becalmed. The day being fine & clear, made off the remnant of blubber in the casks furnished us by the Mary and Eliz*abet*h; it filled 5½ casks = 9 butts. Also suspended jaw-bones in the rigging; sent up fore royal mast, &c. &c.

The sea here was swarming with medusæ, shrimps, & other aquatic insects: several razor backs about. ['Much' *deleted*] Many pieces of drift wood seen.

In the evening got an angular distance between the ⊕[4] and ☽: on which however I had not great dependence as the altitude of the sun was only 1°13′ consequently[5] highly influenced by refraction. For the time, however, I had fortunately obtained an altitude at 7½ pm., which could be depended on. This distance gave 15°35′15″W for the longitude; while the altitude obtained at 7½ Pm. gave only 10°52′45″W, differing 4°42′30″ or 18′15″. From which the chronometer would appear to be 1′43″ fast only;

---

[1] Marginal note. Closing inverted commas omitted.

[2] '28,224' in the *Edinburgh Philosophical Journal* version.

[3] '... and many only the $\frac{1}{4000}$th' in the published version.

[4] *Sic*; not '☉'.

[5] Marginal note: 'Long: lun. obs.   15. 35. 15
            Chron^r   10. 52. 45
add to prec^g Obs^n   4. 42. 30
Distance of the edge of the ice 6′.'

allowing no rate! This compared with remark inserted May 26th, on Capt. Bennets Chronometer, receives additional support. Calm during 20 hours.¹

Tuesday 1 August Lat. 69°.0' Long. 15°32'W
S to SEbE
A breeze sprang up at 2 am. which ['accom' *deleted*] increased before mid-night to a strong gale, accompanied with rain or fog and a heavy southerly swell. Steered a little off the wind, WSW to SW, and made a progress of 2 to 5 knots. The lee boats frequently touching the water, took the lines out of them, washed them and coyled them partly on the quarter deck & partly in the cable tier, then secured the boats by lashing them to the tops of the davits; by which they were out of reach of the waves.

Wednesday 2 August Lat. 67°43'+ Long. 14°50'W.
E to SSE
Blowing strong with heavy head sea, and much rain. Proceeded under a brisk sail to the SSW or SbW, with the hope of weathering Iceland; but the wind veering to the S^d, set aside the expectation. At noon [Longaness?] [NE corner of Iceland]² bore (due course) [SW?] or SW¾S by compass, distance 75': that is according to our position determined by lunar observation & the position of Longaness, as given by Henderson in his "Iceland" in the drawing of the map of which Island, he was assisted by recent Danish surveys, laying the extremity of this promontory down in lat. 66°29' long. 14°40'W.

Thursday 3 August By acc^t &c. Lat. 66°26'+ Long 15°52'W. By Henderson's chart Long. 15°15'W
S to ESE var.
Fresh gales with fog and rain. The night being rather dark & believing ourselves to be near land stood to the E^d from mid-night till 2 am, then tacking proceeded to the SW^d. At 11 am. saw land, at SW toWSW; and about 1 pm, the fog clearing to leeward, showed us land very distinctly from SW to WNW. Shortly afterwards, the fog left the windward side, and exposed ['land' *deleted*] a point of land jutting into the sea from SW to SEbS, at the distance only of 3 or 4 miles. From the circumstance of the fog being generally thick over this point while there was a clear sky to the SW^d and W^d, I felt some confidence that it was the narrow head-land of Langaness & received the fog immediately from the sea. ['If so' *deleted*] And this opinion was corroborated by the form of the land, a deep bight being to the SW, corresponding

¹ The Scoresby Papers in Whitby contain a manifest for the voyage (WHITM:SCO646.1) in the same general format as those included in the journals of previous voyages. Addressed to 'Messrs N Hurry & Gibson' it is dated 'Greenland Seas, 31st July 1820' and lists 'Two hundred forty leagers Sixty puncheons Three Barrels in all, three hundred three casks, containing five hundred and fifteen butts of blubber of half a ton each' together with 'Eight tons of whale-fins, not packed One seal skin. Five bear skins. Three bears', these 'being the produce of Animals taken in the Greenland Seas, consisting of Seventeen <u>Whales</u>, one <u>Seal</u>, eight <u>Bears</u>.'
² Brackets in transcript

with Thissilsfiord,[1] and a headland to the WNW, agreeing in position with Rauderness.[2] If so the accuracy of my lunar observation becomes pleasingly attested, the position of the ship on Henderson's map being within 4 leagues of her apparent position by the land! From an observation of the latitude [not very good] I should imagine that Langaness was laid down, 4 or 6 miles more northerly than it really is.[3] Bent chain cable.

['Landed in Iceland.' *in margin*][4] At 2 pm. struck soundings in 20 fathoms rocky bottom; ['about' *deleted*] and at 2½ pm. Langaness at EbS & Rauderness at NWbW p compass, tacked in 14 fathoms water, about a mile from shore. Wishing for some fresh stock made a signal for a boat, but none attempted to come off. At 6 pm being within ¼ of a mile of a hamlet, lowered a boat in which I proceeded to the shore and landed on steep beach formed of large rounded stones, where was some surf. As we approached several people were seen watching us by the side of the hamlet, on waving our hats they ran down to meet us & just reached the water's edge as the boat struck the ground. They received us by taking off their hats and bowing, and unexpectedly, though not a little agreeably, by offering their hands, in place of saluting[5] us, a custom, in ['some' *deleted*] most parts of Iceland, which by its generality must often be very disgusting. At first, we could comprehend nothing that they said; but in a very short time, dissimilar as the English & Icelandic languages are in the general, we found our intercourse more easy, agreeable, and satisfactory.[6]

On reaching the hamlet, we were surrounded by all its inmates, consisting of a female, three men, and 4 or 5 children. I caused a small bag of bread to be emptied into the hut, on which the woman sized the hand of the person who carried it in, and kissed it with the greatest expression of joy & gratitude; but on being informed by the older peasant that I was the Captain, she ran up to me seized my hand, and kissed ['my hand' *deleted*] it with such fervour & joy that, knowing the custom of the place, I could not resist offering her a salute. This was indeed no great trial, as she was a fair ['woman' *deleted*] good looking woman, and though strangely attired by no means so dirty in her appearance as I had anticipated.

---

[1] Thistilfjördhur (Þistilfjörður in Icelandic characters), the deep bay on the north side of the Langanes peninsula.

[2] The Melrakkasléta peninsula but not shown as such on Henderson's map.

[3] Scoresby was broadly correct. The map in Henderson's *Iceland* shows the Langanes peninsula extending to 66°30′N, whereas modern maps put the cape at 66°23′N, a difference of 7 nautical miles. Scoresby's spelling of 'Langaness' (and later in the account of the volcano of 'Krabla') follow Henderson, whose extensive journeys in Iceland did not extend to the peninsula.

[4] On each of the later pages devoted to the lengthy entry for this day, 'Iceland.' is noted in the margin. In *Memorials of the Sea*, there is an expanded account of this visit, 'A Glance at Iceland', originally published in the annual *Winter's Wreaths* about 1828.

[5] 'Both at meeting and parting, an affectionate kiss on the mouth, without distinction of rank, age or sex, is the only mode of salutation known in Iceland, except sometimes in the immediate vicinity of the factories …' (Henderson, *Iceland*, p. 55).

[6] 'Though at our first meeting we were not aware that our languages had anything in common … we soon found that the dialects of Yorkshire and Scotland afford numbers of words exactly according with the Gothic language of Iceland' (*Memorials of the Sea*, p. 198).

I now made them understand I wanted a sheep or two, and some fresh fish; but the fish being somewhat stale it was neglected & while the[1] ['proceeded' *deleted*] children proceeded in chase of the lambs, I obtained leave to examine the hamlet; for so the hut might be called from its numerous ramifications. Its form was that of a cross, consisting of four huts so arranged, & closely combined in the roofs, so as to require only one entrance. I observed only two holes in the roof, which served as windows and one of them also for a chimney. The sides were [boards?] & earth; the roof covered with green sods, the floors damp earth. The interior was very dark and smelt so ['dis' *deleted*] strong of grease, from a large heap of kitty wakes & other smaller sea birds [called by them "lums" or "looms]"] on the first entrance, ['and a tub of' *deleted*] a large quantity of sea birds hanging from the roof of the interior that appeared to be ['roasted' *deleted*] dried, and a tub of "traan" or oil, from the liver of fish, that even I a whalefisher and accustomed to oil found it necessary to make a speedy retreat. The roasted birds with dried fish [seem?] to be their principal stores of provision; that of ['flesh' *deleted*] fresh fish being uncertain from the exposed nature of the Coast; and that of flesh being only very occasional. The former, with the milk of ['goats and probably some kind of meal' *deleted*] cows or [***] seemed to be their general food. The first or entrance hut contained the heap of birds and in it a girl of 9 or 10 years, was employed churning in a wooden vessel resembling a chimney can; the left hut formed their kitchen & had a fire of drift wood, &c; the right hand hut was their sleeping apartment, containing a long bench covered with hay, &c. without any clothing that appeared; and the hinder hut seemed applied to various uses. Connected with the dwelling hut were two little huts with distinct entrances; one of which was a ware-room, and contained all their stockings, mitts, flocks, sheep skins, ['&c.' *deleted*] and other articles of like nature intended for trade. These they immediately offered in barter: and a hammer I carried for obtaining mineralogical specimens, ['seeming' *deleted*] being to them a desideratum they immediately offered 5 pairs of stockings for it & obtained it. They expressed a great wish for handkerchiefs & shirts ["sarks"]. I pointed to the ship & invited the whole family on board, desiring them to bring 2 lambs with them & they should have their desire.

The dress of the male peasants consisted of a coarse jacket, a woolen shirt, breeches, stockings, & ['skin [***]' *deleted*] a piece of skin bound ['like a [***]' *deleted*] over each foot as shoes, together with a wretched hat or cap. The woman had a cloth ['jacke' *deleted*] or flannel jacket, ['a sort guernsey frock' *deleted*] which only met in part before, a sort of guernsey frock, in place of shift and all other superior garments, a large thick petticoat of wadmel[2] & stockings & shoes similar to those of the men. She was without cap or hat. The dress of the children [the girls][3] was similar but torn & dirty. The youngest girl [6 or 7 years old] was delicate & appeared sickly; the elder girl, however, was active, cheerful, and robust. From the porous texture of the shoes [***] by these people, their feet must be almost continuously wet.

---

[1] Originally 'they'; 'y' deleted.
[2] '... a white woollen cloth, of native growth and manufacture, called *wadmel*' (*Memorials of the Sea*, p. 189).
[3] These and the next brackets in transcript.

We were treated by the peasants with a quantity of butter milk, in a wooden can.

Interesting as it was to land in this singular country; this was probably one of the least curious tracts, ['to which our st' *deleted*] in a mineralogical view, to which our steps could have been directed. The ['stones' *deleted*] rocks about were all broken and detached; and the beach was composed of large rolled masses. Some of these were of the trap kind & one mass appeared to be vesicular lava; in general however, there was no signs [*sic*] of the action of volcanic fire. A little to the eastward, however, we observed a most interesting spot, which I intended to visit but the recurrence of the fog & variable wind rendered the attempt imprudent. It consisted of a splendid range of high, and apparently regular, basaltic columns, in a perpendicular position. In point of height they appeared superior, and in regularity & beauty equal to any thing of the kind in the north of Ireland. The view from the ship at the distance of near 2 miles, through a good telescope, was striking, bold, and beautiful.

The uncertain state of the weather; the strength of the wind & our ignorance of the nature of the coast as to hidden dangers, induced me to make a very short stay on the shore; which prevented us travelling to such a distance as might have made our visit, in a mineralogical way, of some importance.

The grass was cut around the hamlet & seemed likely to afford a good crop of hay, but the extent of the pasture was very limited. Two or three other huts lay scattered about the beach – none however of equal appearance to that we visited.

Leaving those harmless & apparently contented people, we proceeded to our boat: she was fast aground, and there seemed some danger of getting her safely off: with great care, however, we all re-embarked without accident and arrived without any other adventure at the ship.

In a few minutes afterwards we observed a boat push off from the beach and the Iceland family embark in it. Notwithstanding the mutual civilities that had passed they approached the ship with some caution, and it was not until a second attempt that they succeeded in getting alongside. The passengers were the principal peasant, his wife, the female formerly mentioned, their son a fine lad of about 20, and a relation, more aged than the rest; and their cargo consisted of two lambs, & a quantity of mitts & stockings.

I received them at the gangway and endeavoured to dissipate the timidity that the sight of 50 men [crowding?] the decks seemed to have upon them & after some stay upon deck took them into the cabin. Their first attention was directed to traffic: a shirt was the price they put on the lamb, & a shirt & [***] purchased a ['small' *deleted*] sheep. Both of them were of a very small kind. Three shirts; 3 or 4 handkerchiefs, a pocket knife, and some other little articles purchased all they had. In addition to our share of the barter, I gave them a small bottle of rum [this the woman took charge of & having no pocket, placed it in the sleeve of her jacket under the arm];[1] some pens & ink; a little bread, &c. After each exchange, being entirely to their satisfaction, the woman eagerly seized my hand & kissed it with great fervency; and after each little present repeated the same action with every expression of delight and gratitude. Though they seemed highly to admire the plates, knives & forks, and various

[1] Brackets in transcript.

utensils about them, they never initiated any request for them, after their articles of trade were expended. In such a class of people, indeed, I never saw any individuals, among strangers, ['less' *deleted*] so little craving or so evidently satisfied. After I had given them some ham & bread, with ale, &c., I showed them my 'state-room': they expressed more surprise at this [so different from their sleeping apartment] than any thing that was shown them: The female especially ['[***]' *deleted*] examined with ['much' *deleted*] great marks of astonishment the furniture of the bed, a chest of drawers, and a book case. Agreeable with the remark of former travellers I found these people, [insulated?][1] & desolate as they appeared, well acquainted with the use of the pen: one of the men wrote his name (only indifferently) but the woman put down the names of herself, her son & her husband, with great readiness and even with some degree of neatness. I gave them in return my name with the name of the ship, her ['ports &c.' *deleted*] port, &c. with which they seemed highly pleased & particularly as my christian name corresponded with that of the youth who accompanied them.[2] The weather having set in foggy, our visitors began to prepare for their departure; before, however, they arose from the table the woman kissed my hand with great warmth & distinctly pronounced the word "thank" or ['thanks' *deleted*] "tank": each of ['the other' *deleted*] her companions taking my hand, rising, and [having?] made use of the same expression & then proceeded on deck. At parting they all again shook hands: the female came up to me with ['much' *deleted*] great expression of gratitude & affection in her countenance, took my hand & fervently kissed it: then pointing to her hamlet made me understand how rejoiced she should be to see me there, tendered the parting salute which I did not decline, and left me with the usual ['indication?' *deleted*] invocation of the Divine blessing, highly pleased with her conduct and the warmth and gratitude of every action. The youth before he left the ship sought out the lambs, went up to them with expressions of affection in his countenance, kissed them several times with fervour, and cast a longing, mournful eye towards them as he withdrew to the boat! As soon as they pushed off from the ship, we ['made sail' *deleted*] directed them towards their hamlet & made sail toward the Sea.

I considered my self happy in the opportunity of giving the[3] inhabitants of this remote region a favourable impression as to the character of my country. British sailors, of all others, are perhaps the most careless of this. Some from levity others from burden of disposition, too often throw off all restraint in a foreign country, and ['giving themselves' *deleted*] assuming to themselves an imperious superiority, afford a degrading specimen of the inhabitants of the country to which they belong. And as people in general are more apt to form their opinions of the character of any ['peop'

---

[1] 'isolated' intended?

[2] In *Memorials of the Sea*, Scoresby quoted Henderson on the high standard of literacy throughout Iceland, and added (p. 196), in the present context, that 'The writing utensils proved so attractive as to overcome that delicate self-denial which, in regard to other things, they had so strikingly evinced. It was clear that our female acquaintance was anxious to possess them. I therefore presented her with the ink-bottle, pens, and a little paper, which she received with the liveliest expression of thankfulness.'

[3] Originally 'these'; 'se' deleted.

deleted] national from a few individual ['instances?' *deleted*] examples, than from an enlarged view of the inhabitants, – the misconduct of a single ship's company has a tendency to degrade the national character in general among the people with whom they associate. Hence it becomes the duty of every one, who possesses the least spark of patriotism, independent of the claim all strangers have to our civilities, to afford by his example, such a specimen of national character as he would wish his ['own' *deleted*] personal character to be considered.

The dress of the female peasant was improved when she visited us to what it was when we saw her on shore. It ['was' *deleted*] now consisted, in addition to the jacket shift and petticoat <u>of wadmel</u>, of a striped apron with a coloured border, of the same; a handkerchief about the neck, and a blue cap with a pointed top hanging down on one side, terminated by a little various coloured tassel, and a pair of mitts. This it seems is the general dress of the peasantry throughout the island.

The occupations of these families, about ['this' *deleted*] Langaness, seems [*sic*] to be fishing, (in which it would appear the women sometimes embark from their expertness in rowing,) manufacturing stockings & mitts, ['caps' *deleted*] & dressing skins. For their necessities they also attend to the cultivation of grass; The grass was already cut; but not dried; also to manufacture of butter, &c. They had sheep, cows, and horses among them. On the whole, the situation was not a little barren and wretched. It [***], however, from its peninsular situation that it affords a bad specimen of the country in general, and is much more subject to fogs and rain than the districts in the interior or lying farther to the southward.

We had but a slight view of the inland country. For a short time indeed, the interior was unshrouded by fog, and the appearance of Krabla,[1] afforded associations of the mighty powers of the volcanoes, and recalled ideas of the descriptions of the devastations & wonders performed by the[2] subterranean furnaces. Little snow was seen on the land: only here and there a patch on the sides of the hills: in many places near the shore a refreshing verdure was observed.

Friday 4 August Lat. 66.27 Long. 14°48W
ESE. SE to ENE
Thick fog or rain prevailing during the night & day, we stood off and on until about 3 Pm. when supposing we should be able to double Langaness we kept our stretch to the S^d & E^d. In the evening the wind freshened to a gale. Steered SSE.

Saturday 5 August Lat. 65°49 Long. 13°27′W
ENE to SE & SSE
It blew very hard about 2 am, so as to reduce us to treble reefed topsails & close reefed foresail & even under this sail, owing to a heavy head sea the ship pitched so

---

[1] Krafla, at 65°44N 16°47′W, is about 120 km (75 miles) southwest of the eastern tip of the Langanes peninsula. Possibly over 800m above sea-level in Scoresby's day, it is now at 650m (2133 ft). Krafla was active between 1724 and 1746, and again between 1975 and 1984. It is the site of a geothermal power station.

[2] Originally 'their'; 'ir' deleted.

hard as sometimes to dip the cabin windows almost underwater. The weather at the same time being thick & darkish, the wind dead on the shore, and a great uncertainty prevailing as to the situation & form of the coasts I was obliged to keep the deck all night. We carried as much sail as possible; and as soon as the wind abated, which it did about 5 or 6 am. we immediately made sail as briskly as it had been taken in. Rain persisted until the wind moderate [*sic*] & was then succeeded by a thick fog. Sounding during the continuance of the fog in 90, 85, 95, 110, &c. fathoms water. At 10 am. the ship breaking off to SbW, a course not calculated we believed to take us clear of the land, and being fearful of getting near the shore during the intensity of the fog, with little wind & heavy swell, tacked. Stood to the NE^d until 4 Pm. & again tacked. The weather becoming somewhat cleared stood to the SW^d until 10 pm: again coming in thick wore and stood off to the E^d.

6 August Sunday Lat. 65°44′ Long. 13°23′W.
SSE SE: var to ENE
Fresh breezes with thick fog or rain the forepart; latter part light airs, rainy, cloudy or foggy. Sounded at noon in 75 fath*om*s water. In the evening Iceland in sight from SbW to NbW, the nearest part 15′ or 20′ distant. Steered SSW, SW, to SSE, from 4 pm. till mid-night. While the atmosphere was dark & ['**Monday 7 August** Lat 65°12′+ Long. 12.13 W NE to N. to WbN & N.' *in margin*] foggy at sea, or obscured by a dense haze, over the land appeared to be a clear sunshine: what clouds occurred in that quarter were ['resplendent' *deleted*] extensive masses of cumuli, which compared with the obscurity in other quarters appeared resplendent and beautiful. The same appearance occurred when we were onshore: Langaness was shrouded in fog while the land to leeward [to the W^d] was ['clear of' *deleted*] free from any clouds excepting distant cumuli: which afforded an idea ['of' *deleted*] that the weather in the interior was <u>sunny</u> and warm.

The wind was fair most of the day; but being generally light, we had advanced at noon only 48 miles towards the SE^d. All hands employed scrubbing the ship. Rain in the afternoon.

Tuesday 8 August Lat. 64°27′ Long. 11°25′W.
SW. S. SE.
A fresh breeze came on in the morning; in the afternoon it increased to a strong gale. A heavy head sea coming on at the same time, the lee cabin windows were repeatedly underwater. Rain fell almost the whole day. Toward mid-night the wind abated: but the sea contin*u*ed.

Wednesday 9 August Lat 64°3′ Long. 11°54′W
E.erly. NE. N. to NW & W.
The night was dismally obscure: a thick fog in addition to the darkness occasioned by the absence of the sun prevented us seeing two ship's lengths, and was the occasion of much anxiety; the island of Enkhuysen, a rock low & white, lying 50 or 60′ from Iceland being supposed to be within a league or two of our position! Sea tremendously heavy.

A fair breeze sprang up at 4 am. proceeded to the SSE & afterwards SSW making sail as the head sea subsided; on which we went from 1 to 9 knots. Rain almost all day: strong squalls in the evening reduced us to treble reefed topsails.

The mutinous spirit observed among our crew on the 20th June has for some days past reappeared. When I am on deck, myself, indeed, my orders are obeyed, but often ['Mutinous spirit of the crew.' *in margin*] when I am below, the command [*sic*] of the officers are not only unattended to but answered by some insulting language. The officers from a [feeling &?] delicacy refusing to name any of the agressors [*sic*] prevents me taking proper measures with them. The quantity of water in the ship being small I deemed it necessary to order a cask of about 45 gallons, ['to serve' *deleted*] with an equal quantity of beer to serve 2 days. This allowance of a gallon a day per man (water & beer) has <u>not been sufficient</u>, and grumbling & threatening has [*sic*] been the consequence. Wright, the ['offen' *deleted*] principal offender on the 20th of June, has been heard repeating his former threats of revenge on myself & officers & others have threatened every individual who supported me against his mutinous conduct. These circumstances with various shocking expressions occasionally overheard by the officers, and suspicious consultations & conversations, ['among' *deleted*] with watchings & listenings, among the infected party – rendered the safety of the ship without great care & superior protection, extremely precarious. The officers [harponeers] having dined with me, expressed unanimously, their serious apprehensions, that the bad party might have some design of endeavouring to seize the ship and convey her & ['Characters of some of the crew.' *in margin*] her valuable cargo to a foreign country. Such an act ['among' *deleted*] with an ordinary crew would be out of the question: but from the known character of many of our ship mates the most dreadful outrages, had they the opportunity, could scarcely excite surprise. For it is hardly to be credited how many really bad characters have met together. One man [William Williams] was a little time ago taken among the crew of a pirate in the West Indies. The pirate after committing numerous depredations and cruelties and taking ['A pirate!' *in margin*] property to the value of some hundreds of thousand pounds, whereby the crew were wholly enriched, was intended to make but one or two more captures & then to proceed to some distant port and <u>enjoy</u> their ill-gotten wealth. Being in a creek of one of the West Indies islands resting, the Peake Frigate, somewhat disguised, appeared in the offing: this vessel they mistook for a slave ship that was daily expected & for which they were on the watch. As such they instantly put to sea, by no means in ['order for' *deleted*] a trim for any hard service, and got so near before they discovered their mistake, that being embayed at the ['same' *deleted*] time, it was impossible for them to escape. The Captain of the Peake ordered the pirates to strike or he would sink them: the master of the pirate swore he would never strike – he might fire & be d—d. According to preconcerted plan, the steward of the pirate, hardened by his diabolical profession so as to be insensible to the state that awaited him, went below & deliberately setting fire to the magazine blew himself ['into eternity' *deleted*] and many comrades into eternity and the vessel's stern in the air!! The crew consisted of 105 men, 32 of them were killed by the explosion or drowned, and 73 were picked up by the boats of the frigate. On trial, 62 were executed in the West Indies, and Williams with 10 others, after lying several months in prison, were released from it appearing that they were ['inve' *deleted*] trapanned[1] into the pirate, and from want of evidence [though they had been some months' aboard of her] that they had shared in any of the spoils. This evidence could not be obtained from the sufferers: an oath of <u>honour</u> they had taken having its influence on such hardened and hopeless wretches. The wealth on board the pirate it seems was very great: individuals among the sailors who had been in her during the whole cruise having 1500£ due to them; the officers of course immense sums. A [branch?] of the crew of the pirate, had shortly before seperated themselves with the consent of the rest. The Captain not having specie at the time for paying their prize money made up the deficiency by capturing a small vessel & presenting it & its cargo to them. They departed and steered for some obscure port or creek little known to any navigators but themselves; where sheltered by the woods they could remain undiscovered in the most vigilant search. As they proceeded they fell in with a fine valuable schooner, laid her alongside & [carried?] her: the crew they put into their little vessel & after ['[***]' *deleted*] taking everything out of her of any value ['to them' *deleted*] released them, naming the schooner in reference to that transaction, the "Exchange". In this superior vessel, they also became pirates and augmented their former cruises by repeated depradations on the defenceless traders. After the destruction of the <u>parent</u> pirate, the concealment of the Exchange was revealed and the vessel was found and secured.

After Williams' acquittal, he had the assurance to ask the Admiral ['[Lord Cochrane]' *deleted*] Sir Home Popham[2] for some money or clothes, in both of which articles he either ['Some adventures of a Pirate!' *in margin*] was or pretended to be deficient. The hardihood of this request, after his narrow escape from death, so surprised ['Lord Cochrane' *deleted*] Sir Home that he not only refused it, but ['about' *deleted*] observed – "You are a case-hardened villain, and deserve hanging as well as ever any fellow in England did". Was not the former part of this remark verified in the very circumstance of his telling my mate the fact? Surely if he had had the least shadow of delicacy or ['fear of' *deleted*] value for a good name, he would not voluntarily have made this communication![3] Williams, though open as to many of his communications, was very guarded on some points. On it being observed to him that of course he would get a share of their booty – he replied: "aye – that's what they wanted to know: if they could have proved that I had taken a single dollar they would have condemned me". In relation of ['many' *deleted*] anecdotes of their piracies – he usually said at such a time <u>they</u> took such a vessel: but forgetting himself occasionally he would say and such another vessel <u>we</u> also took. In these anecdotes he always denies their having shed any blood after capture: but in several relations where he represented the vessels having been plundered & destroyed he involved himself in difficulty as to the fate of the crews. Their conduct was often very daring: on the coast of africa they observed a vessel supposed to be of some value, in the opening of a port

---

[1] *OED* considers 'trappan' an obsolete form of 'trepan': 'To lure, inveigle (*into* or *to* a place, course of action, etc. *to do* something, etc.)'

[2] From 1817 to 1820, Rear-Admiral Sir Hume Popham (1762–1820) was commander-in-chief of Jamaica. See entry in *Oxford Dictionary of National Biography*.

[3] There are pencilled brackets around this sentence in the transcript.

where there was a fort. They stood in; ['boldly' *deleted*] but their appearance being suspicious a gun was fired at them on which the pirate hoisting Spanish Colours ['and' *deleted*] stood boldly into the fort. This removing the suspicion – the brig proceeded to sea & as soon as ever she was beyond the reach of the guns of the fort, the pirate gave chase, came up with her and took her. As the vessel was of some value to the proprietors who resided at the port close by which she was taken, the pirates offered to ransom her for 15,000 dollars: and to enforce their demand, they sent part of the crew on shore in the brig's boat (detaining the supercargo & principal officers) assuring them that if they did not return with the required ransom before 11 o'clock in the evening the prisoners would be strangled and the boat destroyed. The ransom was paid at 9 o'clock. Williams mentioned one circumstance which showed in a striking view the sanguinary disposition of the Captain. The Captain had received some serious injury from a Spaniard, effected however, I believe by an accident, & meditated revenge. In one of the West India Islands he heard of a relation of the person by whom he had suffered, got access to him, and invited him on board of his vessel. The gentleman not suspecting the character he was to be entertained by unfortunately went. After dinner, no less to his surprise than horror he was unceremoniously told to prepare for death, and in a very little time he was beheaded!

During the time Williams was on board the pirate, he, with another of the crew, an american, concerted a plan of escape, each loaded with the spoils of their cruize. The vessel lay in a creek: the sentinel over the treasure was asleep & only Williams & his companion on the watch. Their misfortune was the want of a boat, those belonging to the vessel being secured upon the deck – no boat or raft appproached within hail during the night, so that their designs were frustrated. The treasure they proposed to have taken was half a hundred weight of gold apiece, or more if they found the carriage of it practicable. This they ['prop' *deleted*] intended, in the first instance, to have buried in the earth, & to have withdrawn it at their convenience.

From the habits of Williams his character may be easily inferred: and the worst character than can be drawn ['will' *deleted*] would not be belied by his physiognomy.

Besides this dangerous character and the no less dangerous John Wright, who [*sic*] mutinous conduct on the 20 June has already been alluded to in the transactions of this day, there is another who has been lately engaged in a plundering expedition in South America, where at Valperazo[1] alone he obtained 4000£ sterling; a fourth who had been a boatswain's mate, of the lowest order in the navy; two others whose history I know not; a ['sixth' *deleted*] seventh, T. Lashley, formerly harpooner in the Greenland Trade, whose character for secret mischief & prompting others to disorderly acts is notorious, and an eighth who stripped in the case of Wright to fight anyone who should pretend to ['detain him' *deleted*] secure him by either ropes or irons. The extent of wickedness to which the first four named have attained, and the ['utter?' *deleted*] degree of subjucation of every feeling of compassion or decency have reached an height which would scarcely be credited. Porter, the 4th person mentioned in this catalogue, was informed while we were on fishing stations by the crew of a

---

[1] This place name, presumably the modern Valparaiso, appears to have been inserted later in pencil.

Whitby vessel, that one of his sisters was dead: on his return to his own vessel (for he had received the intelligence when in the boat) he exclaimed to some of his comrades – "Oh – d—me! one of my b—ing sisters is dead"!!

With such a crew, had they the ascendancy, what might not be dreaded?

To provide against any surprise, the principal officers were cautioned to be always on their guard and to inform me of the first appearance of any disorderly or suspicious proceeding. For my own part I armed myself with a pistol and a cutlass & placed both within my reach when in bed. The mate also furnished himself with a similar means of defence and secured all the cutlasses lying about the 'tween decks that he could obtain. One or two however that he had seen, before he could deposit a quantity he had gathered together, were removed when he returned to take them away![1]

I sat up till mid-night & then commending myself to the protection of Him who neither slumbers nor sleeps, obtained a comfortable repose.[2]

Thursday 10 August Lat. 62°7' Long. 7°37'W
W. to SW & SSW: W.
Fresh breezes with rain or thick fog in the morning: in the ['evening' *deleted*] afternoon heavy squalls with showers; in the evening and night blowing a hard gale. The Sea was latterly very tumultuous: the ship ['rolled' *deleted*] pitched heavily & in dipping abaft broke almost all the squares in one of the cabin windows. At noon made the Farroe islands, and at 1 pm. tacked close in with Myginess,[3] the NW.ern

---

[1] In Scoresby-Jackson's *Life* of William Scoresby, he commented (p. 157) on the voyage of 1820 that 'Few circumstances of interest occurred during this voyage', and made no mention of these incidents involving Wright and other potential mutineers.

[2] Among the pages of this lengthy entry for 9 August 1820 is a loose sheet, apparently added by Scoresby some years later. The text is as follows: '<u>Mem</u>. There is no frigate called the Peak, the vessel alluded to must be the <u>Pique</u>, 42, which was stationed in the West Indies from April 1816 to September 1818. By the Navy List for March 1816, this ship was at Portsmouth; by the next List she was on the Jamaica Station under the command of Capt. James H. Tait. Capt. Tait I presume was superceded by Capt. Mackellar who by the List of June 1817 had taken command of the Pique. This ship continued under his Command on the same station till September 1818, but in December she stands in the list at Deptford.

In the Naval Chronicle for 1818, Vol. 40 p. 99, mention is made of a vessel called the Alice which was plundered by pirates, and it is stated that one of the crew of the Alice named <u>Williams</u> deserted into the pirate. This is rather a singular circumstance but whether or not it be the same I cannot determine.

In the "Courier" for 24 July 1822, there is an account of some dreadful cruelties practiced by pirates in a speech by Mr Canning.

The fate of the four principal disorderly characters in the crew of the Baffin is not a little extraordinary, if [we?] may credit the reports circulated among some of my old crew in Liverpool. Williams, it is said, was imprisoned in America for stealing, Porter was one of four who rose against their Captain & took ['comman' *deleted*] charge of a brig from Liverpool to America (homeward bound) but on the appearance of a man of war on taking his oath not to 'impeach', he was released; Wright knocked his Captain down on the deck on a voyage to the West Indies & suffered for his mutiny it is said & another was imprisoned for a robbery between Liverpool and Manchester: and all these extraordinary results occurred within 12 months!!'

[3] Mykines, 62°8'N 7°38'W.

island of the group, which we could not weather: at 10 pm. wore, being to windward of the same, & stood to the N^d finding we could not weather the rest of the chain.

In the afternoon we had an auction of the wearing apparel & tools of Thos Harrison, our late Carpenter. Everything sold very well. Finding an empty bottle in his chest I ordered 2 glasses of rum to be put into it & then offered it for sale: it fetched 3^s/6^d, and on promising the same quantity the following day, the price given was 4^s6^d! The buyer Robt Porter, named above. The crew also entered into a subscription for the benefit of the widow.

My longitude by account this day was 9°46'W: that given by the chart from Danish surveys 7°37'W. The difference is to be attributed to the anomalies of our compasses: ['not' *deleted*] sufficient deviation not having been allowed on the SE.erly courses.

Friday 11 August Lat. [*blank space*] Long. [*blank space*]
W. NW
A hard gale prevailed during the night accompanied with rain & a heavy sea. Stood to the N^d until 4 am & to the S^d until 8 am. being then near the land wore. Finding ourselves considerably to leeward of Myginess with no hope of weathering it during the gale, we bore up to the E^d intending to attempt the channel between ['Stromroe?' *deleted*] Ostroe & Kalsoe; but ere we had run 6 miles heavy rain commenced & the weather became so thick that we could not see a quarter of a mile.[1] Presuming on the accuracy of the Danish surveys of these islands, the known boldness of the coasts, – a good lookout – and above all on the Protection of a Kind Providence – we continued our course for some time after the weather became thick, until observing a darkness through the mist indicating the close proximity of land we lay too. A shower passing us the prospect was extended to a mile; and suddenly a tremendous precipice appeared to leeward within ¼ of a mile of us. The sea broke with fury against its base & rose to the height, in some places, of near 100 feet. The partial observation of the summit of the cliff, which could just be discovered peeping above the clouds at an angle of 10 or 15° elevation – the blackness of the rock – the magnitude & elevation of the precipice, ['<u>Faroe</u>: Sublime precipices, &c.' *in margin*] which must have been upwards of 2000 feet perpendicular*[2] – the foaming of the waters – the raging of the storm – the universal gloom & obscurity around us – and the threatening of danger, though only apparent, to the vessel: – altogether formed one of the ['sublimest' *deleted*] most sublime pictures I ever witnessed. The scene was truly awful & grand.

The atmosphere having partially cleared we again bore away, and the wind having moderated a little made all sail, for the channel. But as we approached the apparent position of the opening the obscurity ['was such' *deleted*] became so great, that we could not with any degree of prudence attempt the passage. Proceeding to the eastward, therefore, we came to the Northeastern Cape about 5 pm. Here being another

---

[1] Scoresby appears to have intended to take the channel between Eysturoy and Kalsoy. It is not surprising that he quickly abandoned this plan and chose instead to pass north and then east of the Faroes.

[2] Note in margin: '*The inhabitants state this precipice at 2400 feet.' The inhabitants did not exaggerate; Cape Enniberg, the most northerly point of the Faroes, is a vertical cliff rising 754 m (2474 feet) above the sea.

majestic precipice we were becalmed under its lee & found the ship from 5½ to 7½ Pm. going astern by the influence of the tide. After having various short puffs of wind from the W, NW & N, we at length got clear of the islands of Fugloe & [Swinor?]¹ and made the best of our way to the SW.

['Character of the Land' *in margin*] The northern face of the Faroe Islands abounds with huge perpendicular cliffs, in some parts imperfectly columnar – rearing their proud crests over the ocean 1000 to 2000 fᵗ height & defying the ['rage' *deleted*] ravages of time & the rage of the elements; for from the deepness of the water close by the cliffs it would appear that there has not been a waste of many fathoms since the creation! In one place I observed a column, on a point of land separated from the cliff extending like an obelisk. It might be 30 feet in diameter & 300 or 400 feet high. In some places a where [*sic*] there was sloping ground, principally in the E & W. sides of the islands, a green sward relieved the picture & presented an agreeable contrast to the blackness of the cliffs. Here and there were rills of water & in some parts small cascades tumbling from ['the' *deleted*] great² elevations. There appeared to be streaks of ice in two or three ravines. Some of the sloping grounds were regularly furrowed as if they had been plowed.

['Inaccuracies of the Charts.' *in margin*] From the courses we steered along these islands it would seem that Kornoe lies far to the Nᵈ & Fugloe more to the Sᵈ than the positions in which they appear in the Charts. From the calm we experienced under Fugloe at 2 miles distant, it is probable the channels cannot easily be passed but with a wind well aft, from the calms that are likely to prevail in the midst.

Saturday 12 August Lat. 61.15 Long. 5°45′³
NW to W.
Moderate or fresh breezes: nearly calm in the evening. The morning being very gloomy & threatening rain we neglected getting the lines suspended for drying otherwise we might have secured them from further risk from being exposed to constant wet; for the day became clear & warm. This ['is' *deleted*] was in fact the first fine day we have had since the 17th or 18th of July, excepting the first day after our escape from the ice! Tarred part of the main rigging. In the evening, at sun-set, Suderoe,⁴ the most southern of the Faroe islands, was distinctly visible from the deck at the distance of 40 miles. All hands on allowance of water, 2 quarts p man p day.

Having ['taking?' *deleted*] taken an alt. of the sun [30°58 True] on Friday at 9ʰ14′57″ p. Chron*o*meter, Myngeness ['Rate of Chronometer Corrected. [See cover of Naut. Alm. 1820.]' *in margin*] [lat. by Danish surveys 62°3′ long. 7°25′W] at SWbS by compass (S. true) distance 7′, I found the Chronometer 5′49″ fast: – And by an alt. taken this day, 12 August, 37°19′ [true], at 10ʰ12′40″am. by chrnmʳ; latitude of ship by the bearing of Suderoe [due W] being 61.16 and long. 5°45′W. the chronometer appeared to be 5′42″ fast; difference only 7″. Hence the chronometer obtains a new rate of 4′42″, gaining, having been 4′39″ slow on the 31 March. This new rate

¹ Fugloy and Svinoy.
² Originally 'greatest'; 'est' deleted.
³ Clearly this a west longitude, though for once this is not stated.
⁴ Suðeroy.

applied to the ['Longitude' *deleted*] observations made in sight of W. Greenland gives the long. of the ship [July 18] 17°32'W: + diff long of land 2°10'W, makes the <u>West Land</u>, or the E. Coast of W. Greenland in lat. 71°20, in longitude 19°42'W.

Sunday 13 August Lat.60.27 Long. 6°8'W.
SbE. S SW. W.
Blowing fresh with strong squalls, variable winds, and much rain. In consequence of adverse winds and almost constant head sea our progress was not very considerable. The forepart steered to the SW & W the latter part to the S^d.

Monday 14 August Lat 59°40' Long 6°50'W.
W. SSW. W.
Light breezes with hazy weather or rain in the morning, fresh breezes towards noon, & in the evening strong gales which reduced us to a less sail. Courses steered WSW to WbN, NW, velocity seldom exceeding 3 knots. Saw a brig standing to the W^d.

   When near the Ferroe Islands, I noticed, what indeed is very common in mountainous countries, that when the lower clouds – (called by the sailors ["<u>carry</u>"?] or "<u>scud</u>", which ['Theory of Clouds' *in margin*] is seen flying ['in' *deleted*] with vast velocity in gales of wind) had a great speed in the open air, ['those in' *deleted*] the tops of all the higher hills were covered by a [*illegible word deleted*] cap of similar cloud, which rested motionless notwithstanding the force of the wind. As the cloud itself cannot possibly maintain the position without passing to windward with a velocity equal to that of the wind, its fixedness is to be attributed to progressive deposition or formation on one hand and equal solution & dispersion on the other. From the state of electricity perhaps it is of the elevated peaks, air, otherwise transparent, when it comes in contact with the hill or [*illegible word deleted*] within range of the electric atmosphere, becomes obscure from the deposition of moisture; this obscurity continues until the air passes beyond the sphere of the electric action, and then is immediately re-dissolved & disappears. In this way we may account for the apparent suspension of clouds, [without?] the [***] of [***] vapour as light as air; by supposing the cloud to maintain its form & position merely by continual condensation on the upper & solution on the lower part. The [resting?] of clouds on hills, as above observed, in boisterous weather, is in confirmation of this opinion, as is also ['that' *deleted*] the fact that in fogs (or in the [midst?] of a cloud which is the same thing), the vapour is continually descending, however slowly.[1]

Tuesday 15 August Lat. 59°6' Long. 6°33'W.
W. WSW WNW
Strong gales with considerable showers of rain, most of the day. At mid-night being near the Barra & Rona, by Chronometer & the night very dark & stormy, we wore

---

[1] What would now be termed 'orographic clouds' have nothing to do with atmospheric electricity. But Scoresby was close to an accurate explanation: as air rises over a hill or mountain, it may be cooled below its dew-point, so that condensation occurs. Then as the air descends on the lee side, the air is warmed again so condensation ceases.

& stood to the NNW until day light then to the SbW till 9 am. then to the NW^d again. About 10, the atmosphere clearing a little we discovered, the Barra Island [*small sketch inserted in line*] bearing ESE dist*ant* 10 or 12 miles. From the position of the Barra, I find the chronometer about 30' too far east in longitude, or the Barra laid down too far to the W^d. The Barra is a conspicuous isl*and* visible 20'–25' off the ['Bar' *deleted*] Rona is low & not so easily discovered.[1] At [1?] pm. more moderate, tacked, lay SW. At mid-night blowing hard again.

Wednesday 16 August Lat. 58°38'+ Long. 6°18'W.
W. NNW. W.
Fresh gales with strong squalls in showers of rain. Stood off from 12 to 3 am. & in[2] ['until' *deleted*] [to the SSW][3] until 11 am. being then within 2 miles of the Butt of the Lewis, bearing SE, wore & stood off until 3 Pm. & again wore. The wind moderating a little made sail. Stood off again in the night.

The Butt of the Lewis is rather low land, but is rendered conspicuous by the hills a little inland of it. The Coast is pretty & bold, and what dangers there are, are clearly exhibited by the almost incessant swell.

Some additional observations on Faroe, recalled by reading an acc*oun*t of these ['Feroe. [*sic*] additional observations' *in margin*] islands occur to me.[4]

At the NW. extremity of Osteroe, near our position when the weather cleared, I observed two large detached rocks, one of them in particular having something of the human form – these are about 240 feet high & are called by the natives <u>Risin</u> and <u>Kiedlingen</u>, or giant & giantess. Near Andifiord, a village on E or NE side of the same island, is a remarkable stone a few feet from the shore, 24 feet in length, 18 in breadth & 6 to 12 feet above water besides a considerable depth below which is so poised [not being fixed in the ground] that whenever there is any swell it vibrates backward & forward several inches,[5] ['accompanie' *deleted*] The motion is accompanied some-times by a creaking noise & is so easily produced that it can be sensibly moved <u>by hand</u>. The Faroe Isl*and*s are 22 in number of which 17 are inhabited & contain about 5000 souls. The <u>Greater Di'mon</u>[6] one of the smaller islands [2½ by [½?] a mile in diameter][7] is inhabited by one family & is remarkable on acc*oun*t of its precipitous sides & the voluntary imprisonment, as it were, of its inhabitants. It is only accessible in two places & in these only one person can ascend at a time. When the clergyman

---

[1] Scoresby was referring to the islands of North Rona and Sula Sgeir, the latter then also known as 'Barra' (see note to journal entry of 13 April 1818). However it is North Rona that is higher and much larger than Sula Sgeir.

[2] I.e. presumably meaning 'stood in'.

[3] Brackets in transcript.

[4] Scoresby was basing the following notes on the lengthy account of the Faroes by Landt published in 1810. From the map in that account it is clear that 'Osteroe' and 'Stronroe' are the modern Eysturoy and Streymoy respectively. What Scoresby describes as the village of Andifiord is the modern Oyndarfjørður; his descriptions of Risin and Kiedlingen, and the rocking stone, (the Rinkesteen) closely follow Landt, *Feroe*, pp. 40–41.

[5] These appear to be closing quotation marks, but there are no opening ones.

[6] Stóra Dimun.

[7] Brackets in transcript throughout this paragraph.

visits it, which is perhaps only once a year, ['it is nec' *deleted*] he is hauled out of the boat by a rope & hoisted up the cliff![1] There is no accommodation for a boat in the island, so that the people ['are' *deleted*] would be doomed to perpetual imprisonment, if ['none of' *deleted*] some of their neighbours ['should' *deleted*] did not occasionally visit them[.] The island swarms with birds. The number of birds which resort to these islands is almost incredible. In some places they darken the air in their flight drown the noise of the billows with their cries. One particular employment of the people is catching the birds in the cliffs. The occupation is dangerous – but its importance & the great success of the fowlers encourages the risk. According to Landt, they are sometimes let down from cliffs ['[precipices' *deleted*] by ropes 200 or 300 fathoms in length [Descrip. of the Faroe Islands] p. 337, – swing themselves into hollows 30 or 40 feet from the perpendicular [p. 339] & with assistance from below 100 or 120 feet! [p. 339]. In these hollows & ['clif' *deleted*] ledges of the cliffs the fowler will catch 200, 300, or even 400 puffins & other birds in an afternoon. [p. 338] The apparatus used in catching the birds is a sort of net stretched on the end of a pole, in the meshes of which ['the heads of' *deleted*] the birds [***] their heads & entangle themselves.

I observed several caves in passing along the coast:– some of these it appears are very extensive & affording retreat to numbers of seals become[2] the field of warfare on the species from the inhabitants, who kill numbers of them occasionally by entering the caves [***] with their boats. Basaltic columns are abundant around the islands, according to Landt: he mentions a pillar 60 feet in length in Osteroe, which having fallen into a gulley rests with its two ends on opposite sides; so as to form a ['natural' *deleted*] bridge [39] (This must be greenstone?)

Most of the harbours in Feroe are exposed to tremendous squalls in the winter time; though from the clean bottom, good shelter of islands & headlands, & accommodations for mooring several of them are very good retreats. the coast though in general bold is not so safe perhaps as is too generally reported:– the sound between Osteroe & Stronroe is represented by Landt as particularly dangerous for vessels[3] & even some of the ['larger' *deleted*] wider channels are ['liable' *deleted*] subject to calms, squalls, and currents, which render them rather unsafe to strangers.

Thursday 17 August Lat. 58°20′ Long. 6°30′W.
W to WNW.
Moderate or fresh breezes; rain in the morning & showers during the day. Suspended all the whale lines ['about' *deleted*] on spars extended from the main mast to the

---

[1] There is still no ferry service to the island, but clergy and others can use the regular helicopter service.

[2] Originally 'becomes'; 's' deleted

[3] 'Near the village of Stromnæs ... the Sound between Stromoe and Osteroe ... though in general from about half a mile to a mile and a quarter in breadth, becomes so narrow that its width scarcely exceeds half a cable-length. In this narrow sound there are many sunken rocks, that great skill and caution are necessary to pass through it even with a large boat; and ... the sea flows with such rapidity for about the length of a cable, in the narrowest part, that ... in going against the current eight or ten men are necessary to row the boat ...' (Landt, *Feroe*, p. 43).

mizen-mast. In the evening showers threatening coyled them below only partially dried. Stood off & on between the Butt of the Lewis & Galleon Head.[1] The wind being too scant to lead through within the Lewis & the sea being pretty [smooth?] we had no inducement to bear up & try the Mansh.[2]

Friday 18 August Lat. 58°29′ Long. 7°W.
WNW. NW. N. NE.
Light airs or calm the forepart: in the evening a moderate breeze increasing towards mid-night; fine weather during the day, occasional[3] showers. In the evening having a fair wind steered WbS & at 8 pm. Galleon Head bore SSW & the Flamen Islands NWbW½W.[4] Dried off & coyled away 10 or 11 lines. Caught between 20 & 30 cod & coal fish. Many of the latter were [hooked?] near the surface of the water where they were in chase of herring & mackerel. In one of them 5 herrings were found. They were often seen leaping out of the water. Numbers of solan geese [gannets][5] flying about & picking up herrings about us & perhaps mackerel. The fish afforded all hands an agreeable treat after 5 months subsistence on salt provision.

Saturday 19 August Lat. 57°5′+ Long. 7°40′W.
E. NE. NNE.
Fresh breezes, occasional showers, fine weather. At day light, still steering WbS [one point allowed for deviation of the compass [*a closing* ']' *deleted*] otherwise the course would have been WSW][6] St Kilda was discovered bearing about NNW. [Nearing?] Barra Head, which promontory we passed at 3 pm.[7] From hence we steered SbW till mid night, when considering ourselves well clear of the Skerrivore, dangerous rocks lying a great distance from land hauled up SbE & SSE. Passed the James of Liverpool.[8]

Sunday 20 August Lat 55.14 Long 5°35′W
N. NE. E.
Fresh to light breezes, sometimes nearly calm. Saw Inhisterhul light at 2 am. At 4 the Point of the Runs,[9] Mull of Kinoe,[10] Mull of Cantire, Rathlin H^d & the No. coast of Ireland in sight. At noon were partly becalmed under Cantire. The light here is low &

---

[1] Gallan Head, on the west coast of Lewis, in the same latitude as Stornoway.

[2] I.e. the alternative route, east of the Outer Hebrides through the Minch offered no advantages.

[3] Originally 'occasionally'; 'ly' deleted.

[4] The Flannan Islands, about 15 miles west of, and visible from, Gallan Head.

[5] Brackets in transcript.

[6] Brackets in transcript.

[7] Barra Head, on the island of Berneray, is the southern tip of the Outer Hebrides.

[8] Capt. Nesbitt (Lubbock, *Arctic Whalers*, p. 218).

[9] Rinns Point, the southwest tip of the island of Islay. On Joseph Huddart's 1794 'new chart of the West coast of Scotland from the Mull of Galloway to Dunan Point in Sky', the Rinns of Islay (i.e. the western peninsula of the island) is shown as 'The Runs'.

[10] What are now known as the Oa peninsula and the Mull of Oa on the south coast of Islay were shown on Huddart's 1794 chart as 'The Oe' and the 'Mull of Kin-oe'.

indifferent being situate about ⅓ up the cliff & on the W. side of the point, so that vessels at all to the E^d cannot see it. A valuable addition to lighthouses would be the erection of one on the Skerrivore, or rocks near it. Some of these rocks it appears are above water. A light on one of them would exhibit the danger of the blind rocks lying 2 or 3 miles without [to the SSW due]¹ and others several miles within [to the NNE.] Ships would then be able to make bold with the middle & N. part of the channel & many losses on the N. coast of Ireland might probably be prevented. At 8 pm. being near Port Patrick hoisted a signal for a boat & fired a musket, whereby a conveyance was obtained & our 4 men procured at Loch Ryan, <u>landed</u>. Steered along the land for an hour & then proceeded SbW½W for the Calf of Man. Tide setting to leeward. James far to the W^d of us.

Monday 21 August Lat. 54°0′ Long. 4°40′W
E. SE. E. NE. to E.
Moderate breezes, fine weather. At 2 am. [Copeland?] light at NNW & [New?] light at WbN.² At 11 am. passed the Calf of Man, in which are two good lights, one elevated a little above the other. The lights in a line show, I believe the position of a low rock above water, called the Chicken, lying at some distance from the Calf.

Since our approach to the British Coast the following observations for the longitude & regulation of the Chronometer have been obtained. The bearings are all <u>true</u> course, not magnetic – the latitudes & longs. from Steele's Chart of the N. of Britain, the time p Chronometer, no rate allowed.

						Lat.	Long.
1. Aug. 16. Wed. Butt Lewis EbN,5′:	☉'s True Alt. = 3°22½′	Time Chr. 7^h37′50″ pm	58°28′.6	2′1 W.
2. —— 19. Sat . Barra H^d.	E.	2′ ☉	—— 33.22 ——	3.45.0 pm	56. 48′	7°37′W
3. —— 21. Mon. Calf of Man SSE½E 3 ☉	——	40. 59 ——	10.18.30 am	54. 5	4. 46.

Having a fair wind during 3 or 4 hours in the afternoon, & blowing fresh made good progress towards the SEbS [the direct course to [SW?] buoy]; but the wind scanting about 6 PM. found Great Orme's Head, somewhat on the lee bow. At 8½ Pm. a pilot boat being seen hoisted a light & had the happiness in a few minutes of a Liverpool Pilot on deck; on which, though he could give me no account of my dearest connexions, I could enjoy a comfortable repose. Tacked at midnight.

Tuesday 22 August Lat. 53°39′+ Long. [*blank space*]
E to NE ENE
Blowing strong all night with considerable sea: stood off & on, near Great Orme's Head until 11 am. having then a favourable wind tacked and steered by the wind to the ESE. At 4 pm. being sight of Bidston lighthouse, made Mess H & G private signal, being blue Peter at the main & a ball at larboard top Galant yard arm: also the Baffin's signal, consisting of a triangular fishing [***] at the fore. At 8 pm. brought up near the NE buoy, the tide being too late to go through the channel. A shoal laid

¹ These and following brackets in transcript.
² See entry for 20 March 1820.

down in the charts about 4 miles NE of *Great* Orme's Head, with only 3 fath*om*s water, does not appear to exist. The James anchored in the course of the night.

Wednesday 23 August
ENE
Early in the morning, we prepared to get under weigh and as soon as the flow of the tide was sufficient to take us over the shallows we were under sail. The morning was calm & beautifully fine. Several boats were hoisted ['our stores were so far expended that we were out of tea, sugar, coffee, [coals?], water, ale, beer, &c.' *in margin*] out and ['preceded' *deleted*] towed the ship up the channel. Before we reached the lock, a boat, in which we found were several of our friends, particular Mess. Hurry, Gibson, &c., approached the ship. With ['great [prudence?] and' *deleted*] his [wonted?] thoughtfulness, Mr Hurry called out, the moment he was within hail – "All's well at home" – a piece of intelligence which in the want of news for 5 months, was most important & gratifying. The individual welfare of my Dear Wife and Children, and of our dearest friends was speedily confirmed; and our friends were not a little rejoiced to find us in health & so well provided with the essentials of a good cargo: while Mr Hurry had the additional gratification of meeting his Son under every circumstance of health and satisfaction. – Our boats towed us across the river, and by the help of a steam boat which opportunely came up at the moment of high water, we accomplished a safe entrance into the Queen's Dock. After our friends, who assembled on board to congratulate us on our safe arrival & great success (the Baffin having brought the greatest cargo ever imported from Greenland into Liverpool) had quitted us, I proceeded homeward & had the happiness of realizing the accuracy of Mr Hurry's intelligence in ['the' *deleted*] meeting my affectionate wife & children in excellent health. Thanks be to God for all his goodness.

As soon as the Cargo was discharged, the ship, being very leaky and the <u>fore-ground</u> ['being' *deleted*] evidently damaged by the ice, was put into the graving dock. The <u>nose-piece</u>, on examination, (or <u>false stem</u>,) was found to be cut completely through where it was 12 inches broad and 9 inches thick, at the five[1] feet mark, and all the portion below carried away, so that the front of the keel projected above a foot beyond the stem in a most unprotected and dangerous state. We found additional reason to be grateful for our safety, under the circumstances in which we found the keel. A very slight blow might have dislodged the keel and sunk the ship. The injured portion of the nose piece was removed, along with a few of the ice plates, and a new piece of oak fitted into the ['place' *deleted*] vacant space. A doubling of 2¼ in. oak plank was also applied from the former doubling terminating at the 5 feet mark, down to the keel and extending 15 or 20 feet along the bottom of the ship. This with several additional oak ice plates formed an improved security against a blow on the stem or bows at a great depth. A portion of a seam was found not caulked, which appeared to have occasioned great part of the leakage.

[1] Appears to be written over 'four'.

APPENDIX

The Building of Arctic Whalers

Fred M. Walker

Introduction

In 1819, the placing of an order for a wooden whaling ship with an up-and-coming Liverpool shipbuilder marked a small turning point in the history of whale ship construction. To some in this northwestern city it appeared that a branch of ship-building which had not been seen on the Mersey for many years might be re-established. Through the skill of the shipbuilders and the meticulous oversight of Captain William Scoresby, a fine vessel was planned, built and safely launched, and the investors made aware of the high standards of their ship. Just as important, we in the early twenty-first century have as result a rare and excellent historic report on state-of-the-art specialist shipbuilding in Britain two centuries ago.

In the past few decades, through assiduous research and the reorganization of archives, not only in Britain but elsewhere, information on seventeenth-, eighteenth- and nineteenth-century sailing ships has become available widely, although in most cases pertaining only to naval and military craft. Scoresby's diaries are refreshing in that they take us to the sharp end of commercial shipbuilding, a subject rarely described, and only recently becoming an area of research interest. The small collection of Scoresby's diaries, sketches and records, among the important shipping archives held by the Whitby Literary and Philosophical Society, are of considerable importance as they give an unique overview of whaling ship design and construction as seen through the objective eyes of a young master mariner and trained scientist.

Whaling has been carried out worldwide since time immemorial, and in the years of the Hanseatic League, between say the thirteenth and the eighteenth centuries, Arctic whaling rose to become a major European industry. At first it was a special preserve of the Dutch and later the Scandinavians, especially the twin kingdoms of Denmark and Norway with their long association with Iceland and Greenland. The British sailing fleets from England and Scotland were slow starters, becoming involved in the late sixteenth and early seventeenth centuries, but increasing in importance over the years until, in the late eighteenth century, their annual harvest was large and they were accepted as Europe's real business leaders. From the late eighteenth until the late nineteenth century, immortalized by historians and writers as the 'heroic period', the British whaling fleet operated from a dozen ports. In the peak years following the end of the Napoleonic Wars, as many as 150 vessels made their way to the Arctic whaling grounds, but these numbers rose and fell over the years for a variety of reasons including the risk of being captured during years of conflict with France and the United States. Indeed 1830 was a particularly black year when 19 ships (21 per cent) were lost out of a fleet of 91 British ships operating west of Greenland and in addition 21 vessels (23 per cent) returned home 'clean', or without any whales in their holds.[1] To indicate the severity of losses in the nineteenth century, the port of Dundee could claim a total fleet of just over 80 vessels, of which at least 59 were lost at sea for one reason or another. While numbers are unknown the crew losses may have reached 500 persons.[2] The British were to outlast all other nations in this demanding trade, but eventually the number of British whaling ports fell away and the fleets downsized. At the start of the First World War, Dundee was the last British whaling port with only a few vessels earning meagre returns. By then, the commercial outlook was bleak; stocks of whales in the northern seas had been over-exploited, a situation exacerbated by a steadily diminishing demand for whale oil and baleen.

The British fleets had a wide range of home ports, some like Peterhead operated for many years, others were short-lived. The fleets tended to be known as either English or Scottish as this described their main crew recruiting areas; such nomenclature is found still in the modern fishing industry and has been traditional for centuries. However, all ships flew the Red Ensign, were subject to British law, and all 'Greenlanders', as the men were known, shared a common bond of loyalty. These bonds were strengthened by intermarriage, and also by the lifestyle and high levels of superstition of the whalemen. In alphabetic order, the whaling ports included Aberdeen, Berwick-on-Tweed, Dundee, Greenock, Hull, King's Lynn, Kirkcaldy, Kirkwall, Leith, Liverpool, London, Newcastle, Montrose, Peterhead, Scarborough and Whitby. Stornoway was used by many Scottish ships as a port of call, both outward and inward for enlisting and discharging crew members. Of the whale ports, the most productive were probably Dundee, Hull and Peterhead.

Initially almost all whalers were sailing ships of fairly standard forms, but in all cases with special features added either during construction or as modifications put in place when they were purchased from other trades. Such changes were essential for the hard voyages to the north and as often as not included the strengthening of the hull, the increase in storage capacity for consumables and the simplification of the sailing rig. In the early part of the seventeenth century many were built or purchased second-hand from Denmark, Norway, Holland and even Finland – countries with an established record in the industry. The purchase of ships from the Maritime Provinces of Canada and 'Down East' USA began in the early years of the nineteenth century and continued until the 1880s. It was inevitable that a few of these North American products would join the ranks of the Greenland ships especially as the North American shipyards exported a surprising number of ships to the UK and at a time when North American whalers and their trade were held in esteem.

The Early Nineteenth-century British Shipyard
In the early nineteenth century, all shipbuilders worked in timber. Basically the yards were of two types. The large production units akin to the great naval dockyards of the south of England or the large shipyards of the Thames which built for the

[1] Lubbock, *Arctic Whalers*, pp. 278.
[2] Watson, *Dundee Whalers*, pp. 184–7.

Honorable East India Company and a few other prestigious clients. The other yards were small industrial units, to be found all round the British coasts and far removed in scale and style from even the smallest shipbuilder of the early twenty-first century. Ships were built of timber throughout, with hulls fastened by large wooden dowels called treenails (also known as trenails or trunnels) of dense, tough and fibrous hardwood. The only metallic parts of construction would be nails, dumps,[1] bolts and other hull fasteners, as well as fittings like rudder gudgeon of iron and sometimes copper. Once assembled, the hull would be made watertight by caulking, a process whereby the seams were packed with fibrous material such as oakum which is hemp based fibre, usually obtained from picked-out old rope (the horrendous task once assigned to convicts). The underside of the hull would then be given a coat of some material like tar or perhaps a simple and early paint preparation.

The first properly constructed iron ship was launched in 1819, and it was some years before even a handful of shipyards became dedicated to this new form of construction.[2] Iron whaling ships were few in number, as experience showed that anything but the highest quality of iron could shatter under impact with ice or surface wreckage in cold conditions, wrecking the ship's watertight integrity and rendering her unseaworthy. An example of this was the Dundee steam whaler *River Tay* which sank on her maiden voyage in 1868 after striking ice. Tried and tested timber hulls were to remain in vogue until the very end as their massive timbers, oversize floors and frames, and generous scantlings[3] were large enough to ensure piercing of the hull by ice unlikely. As Scoresby had discovered in the *Esk* in 1816, the massive timber construction of seasoned shipbuilding timbers (with a specific gravity akin to that of sea water) would ensure that hulls remained afloat even when the ship was flooded internally, provided weather conditions were reasonable.

All small nineteenth-century shipyards were unsophisticated and nowadays would be described as 'undercapitalized'. Their efficient operation depended on five main factors:

1. Good quality labour backed by dedicated supervision.
2. Ample quantities of high quality timber supplies.
3. Suitable ground on which to build the ship.
4. Three or four items of specialist shipbuilding equipment.
5. Close attention to traditional building methods.

Labour Supply

It is remarkable how quickly a small team can prepare the material for hull construction, erect the frames and finally plank the hull and decks. Most yards were under the direction of the owner who might well be the master shipwright with a team of from half a dozen to a score of men and boys in his employ, of whom many might

[1] Dumps are bolts with slightly tapered points, usually driven 'blind' into wood and then the head is clenched.

[2] Walker, 'Early Iron Shipbuilding'.

[3] The scantling is the official and regulated dimension of each structural part of a ship's hull. In modern practice (21st century) such dimensions are laid down in the Rules of Lloyd's Register or similar classification societies.

be itinerant tradesmen moving round the coast as job opportunities arose, and all of whom understood the simple international conventions in wooden ship construction. Despite limited access and space in a small ship hull, a well-trained and motivated team of shipwrights could achieve high output, provided each journeyman was allowed some freedom of manoeuvre, and provided he had an understanding of timber construction. A case in point is the Aberdeen shipyard of Alexander Hall and Company, which for many years produced several high-quality ships per year: some whalers, some sealers and a large number of the world-famous Aberdeen tea clippers. This work was carried out by a total workforce seldom exceeding twenty persons and yet their building rate of one ship every six to seven weeks was not regarded in the industry as anything special.[1]

Timber and Materiel Supplies

Timber might arrive on horse- or ox-drawn transporters and, in some cases, by water, delivered by barge or coasting vessel. Just a few yards had lumber delivered straight from the forests, being floated downstream as in the case of the River Spey shipyards on the Moray Firth.[2] This lumber would be sawn, or in some cases hewn, into planks, and if time was available then stored for seasoning, an exercise in stock control which was costly. It goes without saying, the best quality of shipbuilding timber should be stored in airy conditions for up to two years, during which time certain types (like oak) can loose as much as 50 per cent of the original grown weight and can then be incorporated in the hull with some expectation of giving long service. However 'green', or unseasoned, timber is not always risky to use, and many ships built with great speed have continued in service for unexpectedly long periods.

Many shipbuilding sites had log-ponds where lumber, and in particular mast and spar material, was stored in sea water. This allowed very slow maturation and obviated any twisting or bending of the spar owing to poor shoring on land or uneven drying out. Such ponds can be seen at the Chatham Historic Dockyard, and also on the south bank of the River Clyde, east of Port Glasgow, where nineteenth-century pens are still just visible.

The normal timbers used in most shipyards varied slightly, dependent on whether the yard was sited in England or Scotland, and might include:

Oak *Quercus robur*. Durable heavy timber for keels and for frames.
Larch *Larix decidua*. Strong timber most suited to hull planking.
Ash *Fraxinus excelsior*. Shock resistant, suitable for spars.
Rock elm *Ulmus thomasii*. Tough and abrasive resistant, used on keels.
Douglas fir *Pseudotsuga taxifolia*. Often used for decking (also known as Oregon pine).
Elm (various). Wych/Scotch elm preferred to Dutch or English elm.
Locust *Robinia pseudoacacia*. Dense durable timber used for treenail fasteners.

As the nineteenth century progressed and as British (especially English) supplies became stretched, the United Kingdom increased imports from Scandinavia and the

---

[1] This is based on my private research on the fleet list and particulars of Alexander Hall & Co., shipbuilders of Aberdeen, between 1811 and 1958.
[2] Skelton, *Speybuilt*, p. 5 *et seq.*

Baltic as well as starting to purchase timber from India and Burma, from North America and West Africa. More exotic timbers like mahogany, Sitka spruce, American firs and pines, pitch pine and opepe therefore began to appear on the British market.

Other materials required in the shipyard would include:

Oakum: the unravelled fibres of old rope and similar hemp-based materials, used to caulk (fill any gaps) between the seams of hull planking to ensure watertightness.

Iron: for hull fittings, fasteners, nails, dumps and spikes.

Copper: for a variety of purposes, including bolts and hull fasteners; hull sheathing (the practice of sheathing the below waterline hull of a ship with thin sheets of copper or other metal) was becoming commonplace at the beginning of the nineteenth century, having been pioneered by the Admiralty for the large British Navy (around 700 ships) then almost all on continental blockade. The purpose was twofold, first to prevent growth of weed on the ship's bottom, thereby keeping resistance to motion low, and secondly to prevent infection of the wood by ship-boring parasites such as gribble or the teredo worm. Few whaling ships had this luxury as arctic conditions were not conducive to weed or borers and secondly such plating would be vulnerable to damage from ice floes.

Hardwood: for hull treenails. Long dowels or pegs driven through very tight holes in adjoining timbers ensure a tight fit. In the case of the *Baffin*, the choice of timber was locust.

Stockholm tar: Tar imported mostly from the Baltic for use on underwater hull coatings and for laying on top of caulked seams of deck planking.

Hemp, cordage, blocks etc.: All ropes and fittings for rigging.

Canvas: Sails – this work sometimes completed on site but most often contracted out.

Ironwork fittings: all blacksmith work for the ship including anchor stocks. Some shipyards had a blacksmith on site, others had contractual arrangements with local journeymen.

Most of the main supply items for the new rigged ship would be owners' supply and would include bosun's stores, supplies of sail and cordage, compasses, charts and consumable stores.

Land

The layout of shipyards varies according to local topography, but three criteria have to be met; as shipbuilding is first and foremost an assembly business, there has to be ample ground for storage and in particular for the storage of long lengths of lumber and of 'grown timber'.[1] Furthermore, the construction site for the ship, otherwise known as the building berth, must be stable ground, well compacted and free of any liability of ground slippage when point loads are applied. Ground upon which ships have been built for many years is likely to be settled and offer little likelihood of

---

[1] Grown timber is the name given by shipbuilders to specially selected pieces of timber which have an unusual shape, and can be selected for use as knees, brackets and so on, where their natural curved grain confers great strength.

movement. The berth usually has a slope which will allow the ship to slide into the water, and this declivity is anywhere between 1 in 10 and 1 in 20. Finally there has to be ample water for the ship to float away from the berth and a position where the vessel can be secured to a quay or at least a pontoon while final outfitting takes place afloat. The outfitting berth might well 'dry-out' at low tide, and usually this was not regarded as a problem, especially as most early nineteenth-century ships were built to take the ground when repairs were needed.

Tools

It was a matter of pride for journeymen that they would have more than an adequate set of professional heavy-duty wood working tools – and all in perfect condition. The apprentices would try to emulate their seniors and accumulate the best set of implements that they could afford from meagre wages. Such tool sets would include the obligatory measuring rules, saws, chisels, hammers, axes, punches, and the one very special tool of the shipwrights – the adze. The shipyard might well supply the long two-handed saws used for cutting the lumber into planks over the saw pit, a trench over which tree trunks were positioned before being sawn. During this task the senior man would work on top, with his less fortunate assistant working below in the fast-falling sawdust. Where shipyards were on low ground, or where the underlying watertable was high, then the wet and dangerous saw pit would be exchanged for a rack which could hold the tree trunk well above the ground. While sawing planks is hard work, it is not soul-destroying provided the saws are well maintained; teams could get great satisfaction from producing a load of planks which would be used to cover a significant part of the hull or the weather decks.

At the beginning of the nineteenth century, most shipyards bent planks using steam, supplied in a steam box. This is a long narrow receptacle with a door at one end through which the plank is offered for heating and then removed when close to a temperature of 100° C. The box is heated by passing steam from a steam generator, often an item akin to a large kettle. At the required temperature, the plank (which has been carefully cut and bevelled) is taken out by a team of men wearing protective leathers and placed on the ship and bent into the final shape before being secured. On cooling the plank will retain this new form.

Most shipyards had a variety of other tools. Some like hull moulds (which were used to define cross-sectional shape) were fairly sophisticated, and all yards had need of a screive board on which sections of the ship would be drawn at full scale and from which key templates would be prepared for construction.

Where Were British Shipyards Sited?

Until the mid-nineteenth century, the preponderance of larger British shipyards was in southern England. The build-up of the Royal Dockyards in Portsmouth, Devonport, Chatham, Woolwich, Sheerness and elsewhere ensured there was a supply of well trained skilled labour in the south, which was a clear benefit to these regions. However there were small shipyards placed all round the British coasts, and in particular large groupings of them on the River Wear at Sunderland as well as the Yorkshire coast at Whitby, Scarborough and other ports.

Many ships of the whaling fleet of Whitby were built in Yorkshire, but with the decline in the Whitby Greenland trade, British-built new construction tended to be ordered from some of the newer shipbuilding areas and in particular the shipbuilders of eastern Scotland. The ports of Dundee and Aberdeen were to establish themselves as the greatest builders of wooden whalers and sealers of all time, and the company of Alexander Stephen and Sons, founded in Burghead in 1750, and later in Aberdeen, Arbroath, Dundee, and finally at two different shipyards in Glasgow, was one of the most prominent.[1] Another household name was that of Alexander Hall and Company of Aberdeen, which founded in 1790, became renowned for clipper ships as well as whalers and sealers. Stephen's yard in Dundee produced more than twenty-five whalers and sealers in the nineteenth century and Hall's of Aberdeen produced at least six with others coming from other shipyards in the port.[2]

At the time of the building of the *Baffin*, the Clyde shipyards (which one hundred years later would be building one quarter of the world's ships) were in an embryo state and, with the notable exception of Alexander Stephen's shipyard, few whaling ships were produced there.

The Builders of the *Baffin*

With the order for the *Baffin*, the fairly insignificant Liverpool shipyard of Mottershead & Hayes was to ensure a small place in history. Records of this yard are sparse, but recent studies indicate a shipyard which started operating around 1815, and was to produce slightly more than fifty ships in a period of about ten years. The names of several other yards in the locality included 'Mottershead', thereby indicating that this family, while minor in Liverpool terms, was incorporated in a local shipbuilding dynasty.

Liverpool shipbuilding had reached its zenith by 1799 and most yards were to disappear by the end of the nineteenth century when all shipbuilding sites on the north of the Mersey were bought up and the land used in the construction of the magnificent dock system. When the *Baffin* was built, Liverpool shipbuilders were in decline and they had become a disparate collection of small organizations – all working in wood. A few years later, on the opposite side of the Mersey at Birkenhead, the Lairds were among the early pioneers of building in iron and later in steel, and their great shipyard, renamed Cammell, Laird, was to dominate the port in terms of shipbuilding, repairing and engineering right up until the mid-1980s.

The known record of ships built at the yard of Mottershead and Hayes is incorrect as it describes their largest vessel of being around 190 tons, much less than the Builder's Old Measurement (BOM) tonnage of the *Baffin* which was 322.[3] Records of that period are notorious for inaccuracy, with matters even as important as main dimensions and tonnages being open to question. However, one can rest assured in the knowledge that the technical particulars of the *Baffin* are correct as they were

---

[1] See Carvel, *Stephen of Linthouse*.

[2] This is based on my private research on the fleet list and particulars of Alexander Hall & Co., shipbuilders of Aberdeen, between 1811 and 1958.

[3] Van Driel, *Tonnage Measurement*, p. 12.

carefully recorded by William Scoresby, someone with no reason to exaggerate or mis-quantify. The choice of a shipyard is influenced always by a series of factors, foremost of which are price and confirmed delivery date. It is not known how William Scoresby came into contact with Mottershead and Hayes as Liverpool had almost no tradition of building whalers, and the Liverpool contribution to the annual British fleet for Greenland was always insignificant.[1] However, as Scoresby's new partners were from Liverpool, there would be a clear advantage in building provided the quoted price was attractive.

Basil Lubbock in his *Arctic Whalers*[2] mentions the figure of £9,500 as the agreed cost price, which translates into nearly £30 per ton – an extraordinarily high figure in the 1820s when Alex. Hall & Co of Aberdeen were building (admittedly smaller) ships for just under £10 per ton. Again early records of this nature are scanty, but in his book *Merchant Sailing Ships 1815–1850*, David R. MacGregor gives the cost breakdown of *Baffin*, and this indicates the extras required in the full and final fit-out of the ship for sea.[3] Here the cost per ton of hull and spars comes to £16, an acceptable figure when one takes into consideration the construction of a whaler with heavy scantlings and the unusual feature of fortifications:[4]

Hull and spars @ £16 / ton on 321″ tons	...	5,144
Copper	...	56
Sails, cable and equipment	...	1,543
Casks, barrels etc	...	867
Boats	...	119
Smithwork	...	150
Blockmaker	...	112
Anchors	...	72
Other costs	...	5
Total disbursement	...	£ 8,068

This indicates that Mottershead and Hayes charged close on two-thirds of the total cost for construction, and the remaining third was for outfitting and equipping to the owners' account.

It is assumed that the shipyard was near Baffin Street,[5] within a short distance of King's Dock, Salthouse Dock and Queen's Dock on the north side of the Mersey.

---

[1] An unidentified document in my possession conflicts with Scoresby's entry for 15 February 1820 as follows: 'The *William* was the first Greenlandman (oil trade) launched in Liverpool from Sutton's Yard in 1775. She continued in this trade until 1822 when she was sold and placed in the King's Dock as a floating Chapel for Seamen. In 1850 she was condemned and broken up.'

[2] Lubbock, *Arctic Whalers*, p. 45.

[3] Figures given by MacGregor are credited to the Scoresby papers at Mystic Seaport, Connecticut.

[4] Lubbock, *Arctic Whalers*; MacGregor, *Merchant Sailing Ships*, p. 182, and my own research on the fleet list and particulars of Alexander Hall & Co., shipbuilders of Aberdeen, between 1811 and 1958.

[5] It is possible that the street was named after the ship.

The Role of the Superintendent within the Shipyard

The *Baffin* was a first in several respects as it is a certainty that no whaler built before 1819 had been subjected to such intense design study, nor to such close scrutiny while under construction. This came about when Captain William Scoresby accepted the responsibility of acting as superintendent for the owners of *Baffin*, a task to which he brought the unique qualifications of experience in seafaring and whaling, endorsed by the distinction of being a Fellow of the Royal Society of Edinburgh. His maturity of thought in matters maritime and man-management must have been helpful to all parties in the shipyard, and it is certain that he was in a position to stand his ground on matters both practical and theoretical. Often in the nineteenth century, young men spent short periods at one of the ancient universities in Scotland, Edinburgh in Scoresby's case, and this introduced him to disciplined scientific reasoning.

Based on the assumed size of ships built and annual yard output, it is likely that Mottershead and Hayes employed somewhere between one dozen and twenty persons. In many similar yards, the lead would be given by the two managing owners, with most likely one in charge of sales and administration (prosaically known as the counting house) and the other in charge of operations including boat- and shipbuilding. In 1820, the shipyard is unlikely to have submitted work to any external inspectors such as the Board of Trade or associations like Lloyd's Register of Shipping, then a young organization enduring growing pains. The contract for construction is likely to have been a hand-written letter of perhaps three or four pages indicating the requirements for the ship, her main dimensions, any special features, and a synopsis of the price and the schedule of payments. A great deal had to be taken for granted, but this was acceptable as ship construction was fairly standard; disagreements if and when they arose would be centred on quality of material or standards of workmanship. It is here that the benefit of a conscientious owners' representative came to the fore, as regular on the spot inspections tended to keep the shipbuilding staff alive to their responsibilities and gently remind the shipbuilding principals of their legal obligations. The careful inspections of a courteous superintendent ensured agreements are honoured, standards upheld, and – of equal importance – the details and particulars of the ship were recorded for future reference. There is little likelihood that any major plans for the ship were drawn up, instead she would have been built almost by entirely by eye, by experienced shipbuilders, to the overall dimensions agreed between the proprietors and Captain Scoresby. Scoresby's work would have been a continuous task of watching and recording progress, ordering stores, agreeing to the arrangement of spars and rigging and procuring suitable sets of sails. The ordering process is likely to have included purchase and invigilation of build (or conversion from secondhand material) of the whaling boats, which incidentally seem to have been remarkably inexpensive.

Scoresby's notebooks give one a clear sense of his dedication to the ship and the trade, as well as demonstrating his understanding of whaling. The science of naval architecture was in its infancy at the beginning of the nineteenth century, and the overall design of ships was influenced by the experience and 'feel for the job' of the master shipwright. Examples of this would include the stability of the ship for which no easily applied calculations were available at that time, but the ballasting would be carried out in the shipyard once the vessel was afloat, and continued until the ship was brought to a depth in the water and having 'stiffness' acceptable to the master shipwright and the master designate – both men with years of experience. This was of particular importance as the safety of a whaling ship depended on being able to remain upright in high wind conditions when the vessel had ice on deck and in the rigging, a situation understood by every officer and crewman aboard.

In the case of the *Baffin*, the owners held two trump cards. First, William Scoresby was a young, enthusiastic commander backed with great experience and endowed with the trained mind of a scientist. Secondly, the shipyard, having built several ships, would also be employing shipwrights of all ages, with the probability that several of them had experience in working elsewhere and understood the unwritten international conventions adopted in practical shipbuilding. In modern days, it is normal for ship-owners to maintain a team of professionals to invigilate the design and construction of a ship. Such inspectors often are known as superintendents or sometimes inspectors and more formally as the 'owners' representative'; a title underlining the ultimate authority vested in the person on the building site. William Scoresby must rate as one of the earliest 'owners' representatives', and through his meticulous record-keeping set a worthy example for all superintendents to follow. Not only did he record all matters, but he witnessed key events in the construction, kept a diary, noted defects and formally agreed to changes in construction, as well as keeping the interests of the ship-owners and their crew to the fore. He would inspect all timber, especially the spars for the rigging, check the quality of workmanship including the effectiveness of the hull fastenings, and may even have requested hose testing or similar checking of items that have to be watertight. It is recognized in a well-run shipyard, that positive co-operation between the shipyard officials and the superintendent can lead to reduced costs and to real customer satisfaction. Occasionally, the reverse is true when the two parties do not see eye to eye and try to outsmart one another. Happily this was not the case, as the diaries of William Scoresby the master-designate give no indication of disharmony.

The Principles of Wooden Ship Construction
From earliest times there have been three major forms of ship construction using natural materials. The first is the carving of a hull from a solid tree trunk to make what has become known as the dug-out canoe, a structure that is more complex than many would suppose. However, owing to limitations in size and carrying capacity it has never become a universal type. The second form of construction comes by forming a skeletal framework for a small ship using timber and other natural fibrous materials. This framework is covered then with animal skin, canvas or similar materials which are made waterproof by applications of oil, paint or bitumen. As with the log-boat, this form of construction suffers from lack of strength, size and carrying capacity.

The third form of construction is that of a timber skeletal form which is covered by closely fitted strips of timber or planks giving a light, flexible and strong hull. This system has been in vogue for close on two thousand years with one of the earliest existing examples being that of the fourth-century Nydam Boat discovered in the bog-lands of southern Jutland, and regarded as one of the forerunners of the Viking ships which in turn were true precursors of the wooden planked ship. The *Baffin* is an excellent example of an early nineteenth-century planked wooden ship with high cargo capacity and considerable strength.

Planked wooden hulls have several limitations: The two main ones are limitation in overall length (which rarely exceeds 75 metres) and the inherent required thickness of frames, floors and planking which reduces the bale or carrying capacity of the ship. The overall related dimensions of structural parts are given the collective name of scantlings, which in the case of a Greenland ship will be well above norm.

The main components of a skeletal hull include:

Keel: This is the lowest continuous-strength member of the ship, and can be described as the backbone. It should be manufactured from the minimum possible pieces of wood, each of which must be accurately scarfed together and bolted securely. See Figs 3, 4 and 5.

False keel: This is a sacrificial timber bolted or spiked on to the underside of the keel. The purpose is to save the keel from damage in the event of the ship running aground or striking some underwater obstruction.

Frames: These are the 'ribs' of the ship and lie at right angles to the keel. Being shaped in complex manners, they are made up of sawn timbers bolted together. The lower parts which cross the keel are known as floors, and the upper parts which support the side shell are known as futtocks. See Figs 2 and 6.

Floors: See 'Frames' above.

Futtocks: See 'Frames' above.

Keelson: This is another longitudinal member which is above the floors and when bolted through to the main keel ensures that the lower structure is squared off and locked securely.

Sternpost: A key member of the structure, being the near vertical post around which the stern is constructed and the rudder is hung.

Stem: Another near vertical post, being the principal timber in the bow structure and which incorporates the 'cut-water'.

Stemson: An internal partner to strengthen the stem.

Breasthooks: Horizontal brackets which confer enormous strength to the complete fore end hull structure.

Deadwoods: Fabricated timber structures placed in the 'elbow' of the stem and keel at the fore end and between the sternpost and keel at the aft end of the ship. These are designed to increase longitudinal rigidity.

Beams: The timbers which support deck and other structures and which in normal circumstances lie across the ship joining the port and starboard sides of each frame. Deck beams support the deck planking.

Planking: The timber sheathing covering the hull and attached to the floors, frames and futtocks – and the deck planking laid on the beams. These skins of timber are caulked to be watertight, that is the seams are packed with cotton or oakum and after being hammered tight, a watertight material such as Stockholm tar is applied.

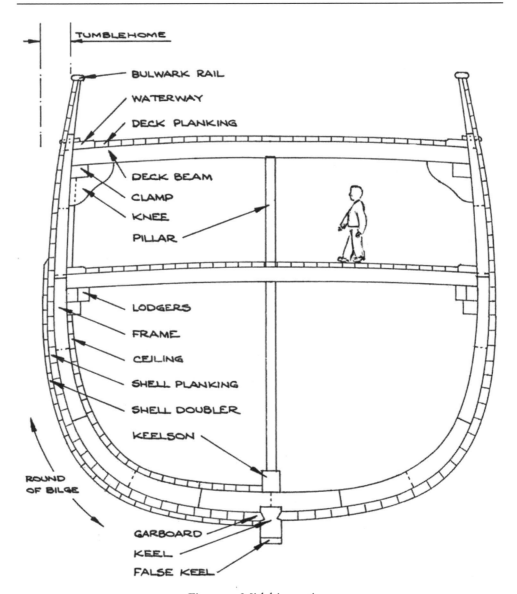

Figure 2. Midship section.
This is a conjectural drawing showing the main structural items in the mid-part of a whaling ship.
No fortifications are shown as their position on the *Baffin* is unknown.

Planking strakes: The lines of planking running from bow to stern. It is usual in
  wooden ships for the planks to increase in width towards midships in order to
  maintain the same number of strakes. Strakes are numbered from the keel
  upwards, often using letters, i.e. A, B, C, D and so on, until the top or sheerstrake.
Garboard strake: The bottom strake (or A strake) fitted into the keel and adjoining
  the next up or B strake.

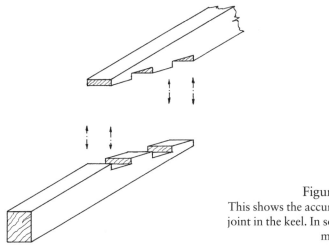

Figure 3. Keel scarf.
This shows the accurate and carefully manufactured joint in the keel. In some naval ships this can be even more intricate.

Knees: Triangular pieces of natural timber placed vertically between the futtocks and the deck beams, known as hanging knees, and those which are horizontal between beams and side stringers, which are known as lodging knees.

Fortifications: These are timbers supplied to confer additional strength on a ship which continuously runs the risk of being embayed and then crushed in ice. Fortifications take various forms; some are simple doubling, partnering or 'sistering' of timbers, while others are the more radical approach of fitting diagonal braces and similar strength members throughout.

Longitudinal timbers: are multifarious and include: shelves and clamps, partners, waterways, bulwark rail etc.

The Construction of the *Baffin*

The Journal of Construction runs from 25 June 1819 with the entry: 'The keel was laid in four pieces; each scarf thereof being fastened with 8 copper bolts of 7/8ths diameter driven in 3/4 in holes'. The Journal ends 37 weeks and 2 days (or 261 calendar days) later on 11 March 1820 with a report on crew payments and the

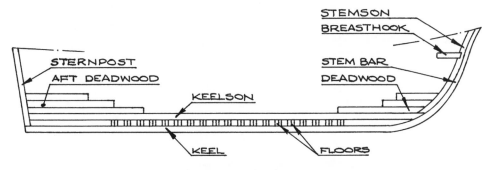

Figure 4. Longitudinal structure.
A longitudinal view of the keel, stem and sternpost.

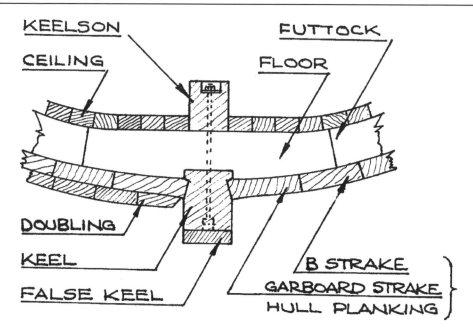

Figure 5. Keel.
Structure showing how the floors are locked between keel and keelson.

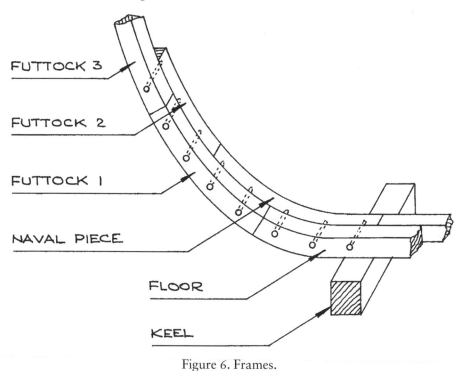

Figure 6. Frames.
Another conjectural drawing showing a probable method of manufacturing the frames from a
series of alternate sawn timbers bolted through.

delivery and shipping of a vital spare anchor. The building progress is shown below with days numbered (seven to the week) as per the calendar

Day	Date	Work completed
1	25 June	The keel is laid using four pieces of timber, all scarfed and bolted together with 7/8″ diameter copper bolts.[1]
4	28 June	Several floors laid across the keel.
9	3 July	Stern frame erected.[2]
12	6 July	Heel bolts driven.
14	8 July	Six after frames erected.[3]
37	31 July	Two frames erected bringing the total to thirty each side from aft.
41	4 August	Erected stem.[4]
44	7 August	Erected last flat frame – completing the framing in the aft end and in the parallel mid body. Commenced laying floors in fore end.[5]
50	13 August	Laid main keelson.
72	4 September	Completed planking on bottom of ship and on turn of bilge.[6]
90	22 September	First strake of topside planking.[7]
108	10 October	Completion (?) of upper deck beams and carlings.[8]
121	23 October	Water-testing of the hull. An unusual entry in Scoresby's Diary – 'as the caulking of the main skin was completed, water to a height of some feet was thrown into the ship by a forcing pump and every leak discovered and stopped'.[9]
128	30 October	Weather deck completed and caulked.
160	1 December	Completion of hold ceiling.[10]

[1] The keel should be formed using as few pieces of timber as possible – in this case four – which are joined by a complex scarf designed to maintain continuity of strength.

[2] This is a key part of the structure from which the rudder is hung.

[3] Frames are too large to be made from one piece of timber, and therefore are constructed of several pieces bolted together and manufactured so that the outer face offers the hull shape at that point and is cut to the necessary bevel.

[4] Once the stem and stern frame are erected, deadwoods are installed to ensure the ends of the ship are rigid.

[5] Once all the frames have been erected, then the vessel is described as being in-frame.

[6] This indicates all shell planks under the ship and up to the round of bilge are fitted.

[7] Any staging (the shipyard term for scaffolding) would be quite primitive and expected safety items like toe-boards and handrails would be non-existent.

[8] These are the transverse beams (one to each frame) supporting the decks. The carlings are small fore and aft timbers fitted for strength.

[9] This is an unusual practice, but has much to recommend it. The lower hull is filled with water to enable leaks to be seen and rectified. The weight of water involved would be considerable, placing a stress on both ship and supports. Also, unless the ship was built on a horizontal plane, the water would not test all parts of the hull equally.

[10] This is the inner lining of the hold, designed to prevent weights driving from the inside on to the shell planking. In addition the ceiling confers additional strength on hull structure.

186	20 December	Caulking of main hull complete.
193	27 December	Commenced doubling stem to stern.[1]
195	5 January	Commenced caulking of hull doubling.[2]
210	20 January	Ship rudder.[3]
235	14 February	Fortifications complete. Bowsprit shipped. Launch arrangements complete.[4]
236	15 February	Launch of the *Baffin*.
237	16 February	Public Holiday for the funeral of HM King George III.
239	18 February	Lower masts shipped.
240	19 February	Rigging commenced.[5]
242	21 February	Commenced stowing ship.

Launching of the *Baffin*

The narrative of the launching of the *Baffin* is thin. Around the early nineteenth century, most shipyards in Britain had commenced to launch ships stern-first, and on reflection, this appears the most probable method for *Baffin*. The most likely scenario is that, during the last few weeks of construction, two fixed rails would have been laid under the hull, on either side of the centre line and about one-third of the ship's beam apart. These rails would have an upward-facing surface on which the cradle supporting the ship would slide and, to prevent movement, they would be firmly secured by shores.

Occasionally one of the rails might be below the keel and the other on one side, and the ship weighted to ensure it did not topple on the free side. The fixed rails would be greased with a proven mixture of oils and greases before the cradle would be run in and positioned under the ship. It would be fitted closely to the vessel and the cradle and ship connected by wedges driven tightly home. Safety dogs would be fitted to ensure the ship did not slide away prematurely – however, this was unlikely as most launches in small yards required help of tow-lines pulled by windlasses powered by men.

The ship would move fairly slowly to the water, but would gain some speed at the end of the ways and should slide into the water without touching the ground. The hull afloat would be checked for leaks and structural damage, and if lying badly in the water would be temporarily ballasted to keep it upright.

No mention is made of celebrations or of a naming ceremony, but undoubtedly the ship would be dressed with flags, and indeed Scoresby's papers describe the design of

---

[1] This is the fitting of thinner sheets of timber on the outside of the hull planking below the water-line. The purpose is to protect the hull planking by acting as a sacrificial timber in the event of a collision or grounding.

[2] At this stage any ice-plates, that is iron plates to protect the stem, would be bolted on.

[3] The rudder would be firmly secured until the launch was completed safely.

[4] The fortifications are sundry timbers placed in key positions to strengthen the ship well beyond the norm of an ordinary trading vessel. Many timber sections on the *Baffin* were possibly as much as twice the size of cargo ships.

[5] The speed with which a ship can be rigged is surprising. However, many parts will have been prefabricated elsewhere and the masts and spars will be almost complete.

Baffin's house flag, a pennant with horizontal bands of red, blue and red. Food and drink was normal at launches in those years, often in the form of a party held later in the day for the shipbuilders, their families, the owners and their guests. 'Success to the ship!' or 'The New Rigged Ship!' would be an inevitable toast.

Sometime between the launch and the maiden voyage, the ownership of the vessel would be transferred from shipyard to the whalers. The timing of this would be in the contract and dependent on transfer of all monies owed, less any agreed retentions. From launch onwards William Scoresby would be very much more in charge.

Some Comments on the Design of the *Baffin* and Whale Ships

The Ship's Particulars

Scoresby's papers record the dimensions of the *Baffin* as:

Length aloft – an archaic description of length overall	103'-11"	31.67m
Breadth	26'-3"	8.00m
Depth in Hold at forepart of hatch	19'-0"	5.79m
Depth in 'tween decks	6'-7" & 6'-8"	2.00m
Length of keel (for tonnage)	82'-0"	24.99m
Rake forward	21'-7"	6.58m
Rake aft	4"	0.10m
Tonnage (BOM)	321 87/94	

There are no technical records for the *Baffin*, but the full load displacement can be estimated by assuming a full load working draft and applying a probable block coefficient. Assuming a draft as the ship returns to port of 16'-0" (that is 4.88 metres) and a block coefficient of 0.7, then the displacement (or complete mass of the ship) is:

$$\text{Block Coefficient} \quad \frac{\text{Displacement in cubic metres}}{\text{Length on WL} \times \text{Breadth} \times \text{Draft}}$$

$$0.7 \quad = \frac{\text{Displacement in cubic metres}}{\text{Ca } 31.0 \times 8.0 \times 4.88}$$

$$\text{Displacement} = 0.7 \times 31.0 \times 8.0 \times 4.88 = 847$$

As a cubic metre of fresh water has a mass equivalent to 1 tonne (or metric ton), it follows that a cubic metre of sea water (S.G. = 1.025) must have a mass of 1.025 tonnes. Hence the displacement will be of the order of 847 × 1.025, which is 868 tonnes – significantly different from the BOM of nearly 322 tons.

The Principle of Tonnage

Since earliest times Tonnage has been a means of describing the comparative size of ships, and of finding an impartial means of levying charges on ships according to their size and earning capacity. Tonnage is computed on two bases: the first is measurement, or an algorithm based on the size and thereby the carrying capacity of a ship. The second is for scientific purposes and is the mass or 'weight' of the vessel or equivalent to the mass of water displaced.[1]

Before looking at the system in use at the time of construction of the *Baffin*, it may be helpful to examine the principles established at the beginning of the twenty-first century.

Tonnage based on the capacity of a ship: Here the enclosed spaces of the ship are measured accurately, and this figure converted to a number representing Gross Tonnage, where 2.83 cubic metres (or 100 cubic feet) represent one ton. While Gross Tonnage is therefore an indication of the total internal capacity of the ship in question, it does not reflect the cargo-carrying capacity, which is known as Net Tonnage. Here the total enclosed capacity is reduced by a deduction for all 'non-earning' spaces such as engine room, crew accommodation, bunkers, stores, navigational wheelhouse and so on.

Total capacity of ship in cubic metres divided by 2.83 gives	Gross Tons
Total capacity of machinery spaces, crew accommodation, bunkers, wheelhouse, stores etc. divided by 2.83	Tonnage deduction
Net figure on which most dues are paid	Net Tonnage

Needless to say there are many variations on this theme, with specialized tonnages computed for situations like the transit of the Suez or the Panama Canals.

Tonnage based on the ship's mass or 'weight of water displaced': This tonnage figure is based on the geometry and hence the displacement of the underwater hull, which changes as the ship's draft increases. The volume of the hull displaces its own mass of water, an amount which is known as Displacement, and which is defined in modern times in tonnes (or metric tons). This tonnage is made of:

The mass of the hull and fittings but without cargo, fuel etc.	Lightweight
Stores, cargo, crew and effects, fuel etc.	Deadweight
Full total is known as	Displacement

Displacement tonnages are of key importance to naval architects in their design calculations, and deadweight tonnages are vital to those persons responsible for the commercial operation of ships, as they must guarantee the ability of a vessel to uplift an agreed amount of cargo.

Tonnage at the Beginning of the Nineteenth Century

At the time of construction of the *Baffin*, ship's tonnage was based on a simpler and empirical rule known as Builder's Old Measurement (BOM), which was introduced in the United Kingdom by an Act of Parliament in 1720, and remained in force until

---

[1] See Van Driel, *Tonnage Measurement*.

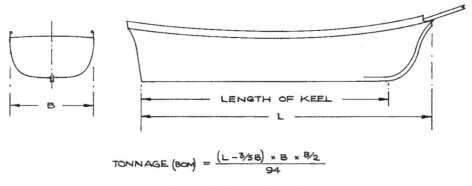

$$\text{TONNAGE (BOM)} = \frac{(L - 3/5B) \times B \times B/2}{94}$$

Figure 7. Tonnage formula.
The formula in use at the time of building of the *Baffin*. It can be seen that this was inadequate as it ignored the depth of the ship which directly affected cargo-carrying capacity.

1835. See Fig. 7. While inexact, BOM was accepted worldwide as a rough and ready, but fairly accurate, means of comparing ship sizes. It was calculated using the under-noted formula, with all dimensions being given in imperial feet.

BOM tonnage: $\dfrac{(\text{Length of keel}) \times (\text{Breadth}) \times (1/2 \text{ of Breadth})}{94}$

As can be seen, this measurement takes no account of the depth of hold of a ship and hence shallow-hulled vessels were penalized with this formula. A further problem arose in that while the breadth of a ship could be measured at almost any time, the length of keel could be more difficult to obtain as it can be measured only when the ship is docked or standing free for inspection on a slipway or hard. Consequently a compromise formula had to be adopted in which an approximation for length of keel could be inserted using the known overall length and the breadth as follows:

BOM tonnage $\dfrac{(\text{Length overall} - 60\% \text{ Breadth}) \times (\text{Breadth}) \times (1/2 \text{ of Breadth})}{94}$

Scoresby's Tonnage Enigma

The tonnage of the *Baffin* is given in Scoresby's notebook (SCO597) as 321 87/94 tons.

Based on the 'admeasurements' quoted by Scoresby in the notebook, the tonnage can be worked out as:

$$(82.00 \times 26.25 \times 13.25) \times 1/94 = 300 \ 52/94 \text{ tons}$$

Using the second or approximate formula, the tonnage is:

$$(103.92 - 3/5 \times 26.25) \times (26.25) \times (13.125) \times 1/94 = 323 \ 15/94 \text{ tons}$$

This latter figure compares most satisfactorily with that Scoresby gives in his note-book. The problem is that it is strange for a higher tonnage to be quoted when clearly the lower figure (upon which harbour dues, pilotage and other costs are based) can be not only be justified but proved by measurement on the shipyard slipway.

One possible explanation is that the lower figure of marginally over 300 tons is too close to the British Government Whaling Bounty payment for comfort. It is possible that Scoresby decided to use the higher figure which is incontrovertible and which freed him from the accusation of rule-bending, as the maximum bounty was based on a BOM of 300 tons. This freedom from suspicion was gained on an increase of 23 tons or less than 8 per cent. Another possibility is that the ship was afloat when it was examined by an independent officer, and the latter rule had to be applied.

The *Baffin* is recorded in both the Underwriters' and also the shipowners' editions of Lloyd's Register for 1820–21. This indicates the ship must have been inspected or surveyed during her construction or immediately after. Her master is noted as 'Scorisby' (*sic*) and the owners as 'Hurry & C' in one case and 'N. Hurry' in the other, the tonnage is shown as 321, and she is noted as having iron cables. The ship is shown as A1 for operation between Liverpool and Greenland.

Factors Affecting the Design of the *Baffin*

The design of whaling ships was a fairly routine matter, and when William Scoresby became involved in 1820, he did not have to start with a clean sheet of paper, as the role of these vessels was understood and many hundreds had been produced in the previous century. During his time at sea, he had had time to consider and assess this dangerous trade and this would stand him in good stead during the exciting period of construction. The matters he would take into consideration included:

Good Range of Stability. All ships require high levels of inherent stability, that is the ability of the ship to return to an upright condition once pushed over at an angle by wind, movement of weight aboard or severe sea conditions. At the time of construction of *Baffin*, such qualities came through a mixture of good luck and the experience of the shipbuilder, as the theory of ship stability was only then in process of being formulated and no simple method of calculating this existed. Fortunately, builders and seafarers had a feel for a stiff ship, one that resisted overturning, and they knew how to use ballast low down in the hull for safety.

Whalers were difficult for several reasons. Their hull shape was more rounded than other cargo carriers as it was found that a rounded mid-section enabled a ship to move upwards in a close pack and avoid becoming beset by ice. However, in Arctic gales the decks and rigging could become covered with ice, making the vessel top-heavy and ready to roll over. Many, many good ships and their crews were lost in these conditions.

In modern days, through careful calculation, the 'condition' of a ship can be predicted for every state of loading and operation. This advantage was not available to William Scoresby, and he had to consider the *Baffin* in several situations, such as the northwards journey with the ship carrying stores, empty casks and so on and the return voyage to the UK with the ship (hopefully) laden with blubber and baleen. The most difficult condition aboard might well be the return voyage with the ship 'clean' or without whale products and with the stores near depleted. Most ships would have a small amount of ballast, possibly shingle or sand, carefully gathered in one spot and secured with tarpaulins and lashings. There is every likelihood that this material could remain in position for the active life of the ship. However all cautious captains would be prepared to carry additional ballast, especially when the ship was light in the water – this could be additional shingle, or general cargo or perhaps water stored in empty casks.

Hull Strength. The *Baffin* was built to withstand severe mechanical shock, such as collision with ice, wreckage or underwater reefs. The external underwater hull was covered with boarding, known as doubling, placed to save the main timbers from severe damage, and for similar reasons the keel had a lower appendage known as the false keel or, in some countries, the slipper, fitted as a sacrificial timber.

The most important strengthening had the quirky name of fortifications. These took several forms, such as an overall increase in the scantlings (see p. 215, note 3) of the vessel and the addition of a greater than usual number of knees, brackets and clamps. In several ships the fortifications include the fitting of diagonal timber columns across the ship, giving massive transverse strength. Such fittings are seen to this day on the restored Arctic exploration ship *Fram* in Oslo, where massive (300 by 300mm or one foot square) baulks of timber help to ensure that she retains her shape when nipped by ice. Ice protection plates were fitted on either side of the stem in way of the waterline, protecting the timber hull at the cutwater.

Sailing Characteristics. While the whaling fleet did not need the ultimate racing speed of tea clippers, it was helpful to run a ship with a fair turn of speed to reduce the time required between Britain and the whaling ground and back. For this, good spreads of canvas were helpful, and Scoresby's sketches show the fitting of stun-sails which were additional sails placed outboard of the main square sails in good weather conditions. While these would assist in fast passages north and again south, they would not be used in the Arctic where handling could impose an unnecessary strain on the crew who were on constant standby to launch their whale boats. In the event of several whale boats being on the water, the deck crew might be halved and then the need was for a ship that was docile and easily handled. When amongst whales, with the whale boats employed on the water, Scoresby would have a ship with a severely depleted crew and would try to keep the ship moving gently by using the staysails and not the square sails. The demands on the deck crew would be kept to a minimum. The masts, spars and rigging had to be suitable for heavy lifts and able to hold and lift parts of whale carcasses.

Accommodation and Storage Space. The ship was designed to carry a crew of around forty in less than luxurious conditions. It is probable that most men had small bunks and lived in a communal forecastle, while the officers were aft in slightly better conditions. The *Baffin* had a 'tween deck or second deck beneath the weather deck. This, with the holds below, allowed for flexible stowage of gear and particularly the large

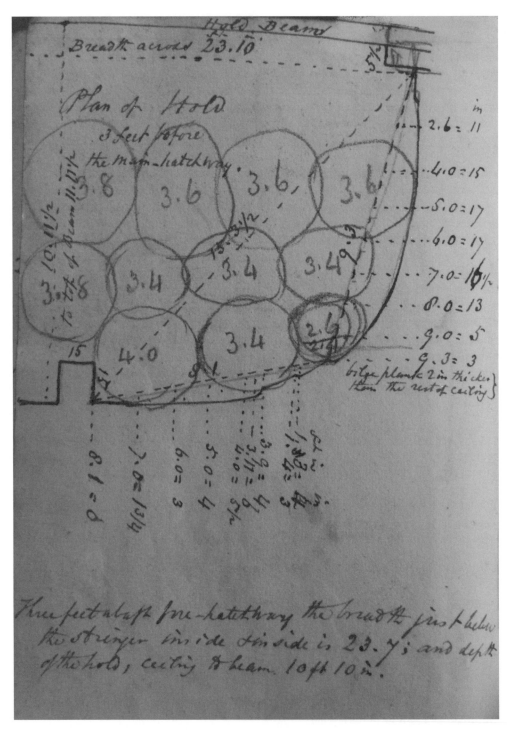

Figure 8. Scoresby's stowage plan for the *Baffin* from his notebook.
Whitby Museum MS SCO597. Photo courtesy of Whitby Museum.

numbers of barrels and casks required for stowage of blubber which had to be taken back home for rendering down. The 'tween deck is unlikely to have had bulkheads and would be a through space serviced by small hatches to the deck above and the holds below. This is a situation that would not be tolerated in today's safety-conscious era. The stores carried would be close to that taken by a sailing ship of the time, with water a valuable commodity. However, when in the ice there were occasions when fresh water could be harvested. It seems remarkable that little thought was given to the problems encountered if a ship was embayed and might have to spend more than a season in Ultima Thule. On the return journey the quantities stowed might be of the order of 200 or 300 tons of whale products. See Fig. 8 for Scoresby's own storage plan of the hold.

Optimum Size of Vessel. It is known that the size of ship exercised William Scoresby's mind. Here are a few pointers to the design philosophy. Owing to the limitations of wooden ship construction, the overall length of the ship could not exceed 75 metres. The ship would have to carry a minimum of about 30 tons of ballast, most usually in the form of shingle. On a return journey, if some twenty 'fish' had been taken, she might load 300 tons or more of animal product. The government bounty for a whale ship stopped at 300 tons BOM. There was a distinct advantage in having a ship which achieved this figure. In Volume 1 of his *Account of the Arctic Regions* (p. 507), following a survey of requirements of whaling ships, Scoresby makes the pragmatic remark that 'it warrants the equipment of vessels of 330 or 340 tons in preference to any smaller dimensions'. This in fact is the BOM tonnage of the *Baffin*!

Works Cited

Allen, Grahame, *Inflation: the Value of the Pound 1750–2002*, Research Paper 03/82, London, House of Commons Library, 1999. Online at www.parliament.uk/commons/lib/research/rp2003/rp03-082.pdf.

Anonymous, 'Account of the Experiments of Morichini, Ridolfi, Firmas, and Gibbs, on the Influence of Light in the developement [*sic*] of Magnetism', *Edinburgh Philosophical Journal*, I, 2, October 1819, pp. 239–43. Online at Google Books.

Barnard, William, 'An Account of a Method for the safe Removal of Ships that have been driven on Shore, and damaged their Bottoms, to places (however distant) for repairing them', *Philosophical Transactions of the Royal Society of London*, 70, 1780, pp. 100–108. Online at JSTOR.

Barrington, Daines, *The Possibility of Approaching the North Pole Asserted*, London, Allman, 1818. (Note: Earlier editions of this book carried different titles. It was originally published in London by Heydinger in 1775, as *The Probability of Reaching the North Pole Discussed*. This version was reprinted in facsimile by Ye Galleon Press, Fairfield, Wash., in 1987. A selection of Barrington's writings, published by White and Nichols in London in 1781 and entitled *Miscellanies*, included the same material but with the more cautious title *The Possibility of Approaching the North Pole Discussed*.)

Barrow, John, *An Auto-biographical Memoir of Sir John Barrow ... including reflections, observations and reminiscences at home and abroad, from early life to advanced age*, London, John Murray, 1847.

[Barrow, John], Review of 'Narrative of a Voyage to Hudson's Bay – by Lieut. Chappell RN', *Quarterly Review*, 18, 35, October 1817, pp. 199–223. Online at British Periodicals Online.

Barrow, Tony, *The Whaling Trade of North-East England*, Sunderland, University of Sunderland Press, 2001.

Bathurst, Bella, *The Lighthouse Stevensons: The Extraordinary Story of the Building of the Scottish Lighthouses by the Ancestors of Robert Louis Stevenson*, London, Harper Collins, 1999.

Beaglehole, J. C., *The Life of Captain James Cook*, The Hakluyt Society, Extra Series 37, London, 1974. Online at www.nzetc.org/tm/scholarly/tei-Bea04Cook.html

Bennet, Abraham, 'Description of a New Electrometer', *Philosophical Transactions of the Royal Society of London*, 77, 1787, pp. 26–34. Online at www.wirksworth.org.uk/BEN-PT-1.htm

Bravo, Michael, 'Geographies of Exploration and Improvement: William Scoresby and Arctic Whaling, 1782–1822', *Journal of Historical Geography*, 32, 3, July 2006, pp. 512–38. Online at Science Direct.

Burder, George, *Village Sermons; or ... plain and short discourses on the principal doctrines of the Gospel; intended for the use of families, Sunday schools, or companies assembled for religious instruction in country villages*, 8 vols, London, RTS, 1838.

Burns, John J.; Montague, J. Jerome; Cowles, Cleveland J., eds, *The Bowhead Whale*, Lawrence, Kansas, Society for Marine Mammalogy, 1993.

Carter, Harold B., *Sir Joseph Banks 1743–1820*, London, British Museum (Natural History), 1988.

Carvel, John L., *Stephen of Linthouse, 1750–1950*, Glasgow, 1950.

Chambers, Neil, ed., *The Letters of Sir Joseph Banks: a Selection, 1768–1820*, London, Imperial College Press, [2000].

Credland, Arthur G., *The Hull Whaling Trade, An Arctic Enterprise*, Beverley, Hutton Press, 1995.

Dellenbaugh, Frederick S., *Seven Log-books concerning the Arctic Voyages of Captain William Scoresby, Senior, of Whitby, England*, 8 vols, New York, The Explorers Club, 1917.

Elton, C. S., 'The Nature and Origin of Soil-Polygons in Spitsbergen', *Quarterly Journal of the Geological Society*, 83, 1927, pp. 163–94. Online at http://jgslegacy.lyell-collection.org/cgi/reprint/83/1–5/163.

Fleming, Fergus, *Barrow's Boys*, London, Granta, 1998.

Gad, Finn, *The History of Greenland*, 3 vols, London, Hurst, 1970–82.

Grieve, Margaret, *A Modern Herbal*, London, Jonathan Cape, 1931. Online at http://www.botanical.com/botanical/mgmh/mgmh.html

Gyory, Joanna; Mariano, Arthur J.; Ryan, Edward H., 'The East Greenland Current', online at http://oceancurrents.rsmas.miami.edu/atlantic/east-greenland.html

Haldiman, Jerrold J. and Tarpley, Raymond J., 'Anatomy and Physiology', in John J. Burns *et al.*, *The Bowhead Whale* (q.v.), pp. 71–156.

Henderson, Ebenezer, *Iceland; or the Journal of a Residence in that Island, during the years 1814 and 1815*, Edinburgh, Oliphant,Waugh & Innes, 2 vols, 1818. Online at Google Books.

Holmes, Frederic L., 'Elementary Analysis and the Origins of Physiological Chemistry', *Isis*, 1, 1963, pp. 50–81. Online at JSTOR.

Howard, Mark, 'Coopers and Casks in the Whaling Trade 1800–1850', *The Mariners Mirror*, 82, 4, 1996, pp. 436–50.

Huddart, Joseph, *A new chart of the West coast of Scotland from the Mull of Galloway to Dunan Point in Sky*, London, Laurie & Whittle, 1794. (Note: The chart was first published in 1781, but the 1794 imprint is the best online version, at http://www.nls.uk/maps/early/coasts.cfm?id=826)

Jackson, C. Ian, 'Three Puzzles from Early Nineteenth Century Arctic Exploration', *The Northern Mariner/Le Marin du Nord*, 17, 3, 2007, pp. 1–17.

Jackson, Gordon, *The British Whaling Trade*, London A. & C. Black, 1978.

Jakobsson, M.; Macnab, R.; Mayer, L.; Anderson, R.; Edwards, M.; Hatzky, J.; Schenke, H. W.; and Johnson, P., 'An Improved Bathymetric Portrayal of the Arctic Ocean: Implications for Ocean Modeling and Geological, Geophysical and Oceanographic Analyses', *Geophysical Research Letters*, 35, 2008, L07602, doi:10.1029/2008GL033520 (online).

Landt, Jørgen, *A Description of the Feroe Islands, containing an account of their situation, climate, and productions, together with the manners and customs of the inhabitants, their trade, etc. translated from the Danish*, London, Longman, Hurst, Rees, and Orme, 1810.

Latta, Thomas A., 'Observations on Ice-Bergs, made during a short Excursion in Spitzbergen', *Edinburgh Philosophical Journal*, 3, 6, October 1820, pp. 237–43.

Layton, Cyril W., *Dictionary of Nautical Words and Terms*, 4th revised edn, Glasgow, Brown, Son & Ferguson, 1994.

Lecky, S.T.S., *"Wrinkles" in Practical Navigation*, London, George Philip & Son, 1881. (Note: There have been many subsequent revised editions, but the 1881 edition was reprinted in facsimile in 2002 by Adamant Media Corporation in its Elibron Classics series.)

Lincoln, Margarette, 'Mutinous Behavior on Voyages to the South Seas and Its Impact on Eighteenth-Century Civil Society', *Eighteenth-Century Life*, 31, 1, 2006, pp. 62–80. Online at ecl.dukejournals.org

Lloyd, C. Christopher, *Mr. Barrow of the Admiralty: A Life of Sir John Barrow, 1764–1848*, London, Collins, 1970.

Lubbock, Basil, *The Arctic Whalers*, Glasgow, Brown, Son & Ferguson, 1937.

MacGregor, David R., *Merchant Sailing Ships, 1815–50*, Conway Maritime Press, London, 1984.

Manby, George W., *Journal of a Voyage to Greenland, in the year 1821. With graphic illustrations*, London, Whittaker, 1822.

Markham, Albert H., *A Whaling Cruise to Baffin's Bay and the Gulf of Boothia, and an Account of the Rescue of the Crew of the "Polaris"*, London, Sampson, Low, Marston, Low & Searle, 1874, online at Google Books.

Martin, Constance, 'William Scoresby (1789-1857) and the Open Polar Sea – Myth and Reality', *Arctic*, 41, 1, 1988, pp. 39–47, online at www.arctic.ucalgary.ca

Montgomery, Hugh, *William Scoresby: Arctic Explorer (1789–1857)*, Edinburgh, History of Medicine and Science Unit, University of Edinburgh, 1982.

Nansen, Fridtjof, *"Farthest North": Being the Record of a Voyage of Exploration of the Ship Fram 1893–6*, 2 vols, London, Constable, 1897.

Narborough, John, *An Account of several late Voyages and Discoveries to the South and North towards the Streights of Magellan, the South Seas, ... also towards Nova Zembla, Greenland or Spitsberg ... By Sir J. Narborough, Captain J. Tasman, Captain J. Wood, and F. Marten of Hamburgh. To which are annexed a large introduction and supplement, giving an account of other navigations to those regions, etc*, London, 1694. Online at Early English Books Online.

Neill, Patrick. *A Tour through Some of the Islands of Orkney and Shetland: with a view chiefly to Objects of Natural History, but including also Occasional Remarks on the State of the Inhabitants, their Husbandry, and Fisheries*, Edinburgh, Constable, 1806. Online at http://gdz.sub.uni-goettingen.de/

Phipps, Constantine John, (Baron Mulgrave), *A Voyage towards the North Pole undertaken by His Majesty's command, 1773*, London, Nourse, 1774.

Raspe, Rudolf E., *Baron Munchausen's narrative of his marvellous travels and* campaigns in Russia ... London, 1785. Online (*The Surprising Adventures of Baron Munchausen*, 1895 edition) at Project Gutenberg.

Ross, John, *A Voyage of Discovery, made under the orders of the Admiralty, in Her Majesty's Ships Isabella and Alexander, for the purpose of exploring Baffin's Bay, and enquiring into the probability of a North-West Passage*. 2nd edn, 2 vols, London, Longman, Hurst, Rees, Orme and Brown, 1819. The first edition had been published in London by John Murray in the same year. Online at Google Books.

Ross, John, *A Description of the Deep Sea Clamms, Hydraphorus, and Marine Artificial Horizon, invented by Captain J. Ross, R.N.*, London, 1819.

Ross, M.J., *Polar Pioneers: A Biography of John and James Clark Ross*, London, McGill-Queen's University Press, 1994.

Ross, W. Gillies, *Arctic Whalers, Icy Seas*, Toronto, Irwin, 1985.

Schell, Donald M. & Saupe, Susan M., 'Feeding and Growth as Indicated by Stable Isotopes', in John J. Burns et al., *The Bowhead Whale* (q.v.), pp. 491–509.

Scoresby, William, *An Account of the Arctic Regions, with a History and Description of the Northern Whale-Fishery*, 2 vols, Edinburgh, Constable, 1820. Online at Google Books. (Facsimile reprint, with an introduction by Alister Hardy, published by David & Charles Reprints, Newton Abbot, 1969.)

Scoresby, William, *Discourses to Seamen*, London, Nisbet, 1831.

Scoresby, William, *Journal of a Voyage to the Northern Whale-Fishery; including researches and discoveries on the eastern coast of West Greenland, made in the summer of 1822, in the ship Baffin of Liverpool*, Edinburgh, Constable, 1823. (Facsimile reprint, Whitby, Caedmon, 1980.)

Scoresby, William, *Memorials of the Sea*, London, Nisbet, 1835. Online at Google Books.

Scoresby, William, 'Observations on the Currents and Animalcules of the Greenland Sea', *Edinburgh Philosophical Journal*, 4, 7, January 1821, pp. 111–14.

Scoresby, William, 'On the Greenland or Polar Ice', *Memoirs of the Wernerian Natural History Society*, 2, pp. 261–338.

Scoresby, William, 'Account of the Seven Icebergs of Spitzbergen', *Edinburgh Philosophical Journal*, II, 4, April 1820, p. 111ff. This is a verbatim extract from *An Account of the Arctic Regions*, I, pp. 101–9.

Scoresby-Jackson, R. E., *The Life of William Scoresby, M.A., D.D., F.R.S.S.L. & E.*, London, Nelson, 1861.

Serreze, Mark C. & Barry, Roger G., *The Arctic Climate System*, Cambridge, Cambridge University Press, 2005.

Sinclair, John, ed., *The Statistical Account of Scotland 1791–1799*, online at http://stat-acc-scot.edina.ac.uk

Skelton, Jim, *Speybuilt: The Story of a Forgotten Industry*, Garmouth, Morayshire, 1994.

Smith, W. E., 'On the Design of the Antarctic Exploration Vessel "Discovery"', *Transactions of the Institution of Naval Architects*, 47, London, 1905, pp. 1–42.

Smyth, William H., *The Sailor's Word Book of 1867; an Alphabetical Digest of Nautical Terms*, London, Blackie, 1867. (Facsimile reprint published by Conway Classics, London, 1991.)

Stamp, Cordelia, *The Scoresby Family*, [Whitby?], n.p., [1989?]

Stamp, Tom and Cordelia, *William Scoresby, Arctic Scientist*, Whitby, Caedmon, [1975?]

Stewart-Brown, Ronald, *Liverpool Ships in the Eighteenth Century: Including the King's Ships Built there with Notes on the Principal Shipwrights*, Liverpool, Liverpool University Press, 1932.

Times Atlas of the World, 7th comprehensive edition, London, Times Books, 1985.

Traill, Thomas S., 'The Thermometer and Pyrometer', *Library of Useful Knowledge: Natural Philosophy*, 2, London, Baldwin & Craddock, 1829–38. Online at Google Books.

Trethewey, Ken and Forand, Michael, eds, *The Lighthouse Encyclopaedia*, 2003 edn, published in compact disc (CD) format by the Lighthouse Society of Great Britain, Torpoint, Cornwall, 2003.

Van Driel, A., *Tonnage Measurement: Historical and Critical Essay*, The Hague, Government Printing Office, 1925.

Walker, Fred M., 'Early Iron Shipbuilding – a Re-appraisal of the *Vulcan* and other Pioneer Vessels', *Transactions of the Institution of Engineers and Shipbuilders in Scotland*, 133, Glasgow, 1994–5, pp. 21–34.

Walker, Richard, 'On the Production of Artificial Cold by Means of Muriate of Lime', *Philosophical Transactions of the Royal Society of London*, 91, 1801, pp. 120–38. Online at JSTOR.

Watson, Norman, *The Dundee Whalers, 1750–1914*, East Linton, Tuckwell Press, 2003.

White, Adam, ed., *A Collection of Documents on Spitzbergen & Greenland, comprising a translation from F. Martens* Voyage to Spitzbergen: *a Translation from Isaac De La Peyrères* Histoire du Groenland: *and God's Power and Providence in the Preservation of Eight Men in Greenland nine Moneths* [sic] *and twelve Dayes*, London, The Hakluyt Society, 1st ser. 18, London, 1855. Online at Google Books. (Facsimile reprint published by University Press of the Pacific, Honolulu, 2003.)

Young, George, *A History of Whitby and Streoneshalh Abbey: with a Statistical Survey of the Vicinity to the Distance of Twenty-five Miles*, 2 vols, Whitby, Clark and Medd, 1817. Online at Google Books. (Reprinted in facsimile by Caedmon of Whitby in 1976.)

Index

Note: As with the preceding volumes of Scoresby's journals, no attempt has been made to index the daily details of navigation, sail-setting, ice distribution or whaling activities. Similarly, there are no entries for William Scoresby, Junior or his crews. References to other ships in the whaling fleet are indexed separately.

aurora borealis, 8–9, 75, 144–6, 148

Baltasound, Shetland, 68–70
Banks, Sir Joseph, xxviii–xxix, xxxi–xxxiii, 46n, 61–2, 70n
Barrow, John, xxvii–xxxv
Beerenberg (volcano, Jan Mayen), 52, 73–6
Board of Longitude, xxxv
Brewster, David, xxxvii
Brodrick, Thomas, xix–xx, xxvi, 125

Cook, Captain James, RN, xxxiii
Cursham, Reverend Thomas, xlin

Faeroes, xxiii, 54, 204–9
Fair Isle, 7, 122
Fishburn, Thomas, xix–xx, xxvi, 125
food consumption by whaling crew, 92–3, 212
Foula, 55

Gibson (N. Hurry's partner), xxv–xxvi, 129, 137, 211
Gordon, David, 139–40
Greenland, east coast of, xxiii, xxviii, 22, 50, 61–2, 179, 184

harpoon gun, 97–8, 100, 102
Holloway, Reverend James T., xxiii, xxvi
Hurry, Nicholas, xxv–xxvi, 129, 137, 211–12
Hurry, Robert (son of Nicholas), 135, 154, 174, 212

icebergs, 25, 163
ice blink, 50, 149, 171
Iceland, 53, 62, 194, 199–200

Jackson, Thomas, xx, 20, 27, 32, 66, 99, 149
James, Professor Robert, xxviin, xxxvn, xxxvi–xxxvii
Jan Mayen island, xix–xx, 51–3, 62, 73, 75–6, 116

Langanes, Iceland, xxiii, 194–200
Latta, Dr Thomas, xxxix–xl, 110n
Lerwick, Shetland, xvii, xx, 7–8

Liverpool, xx–xxiii, xxv–xxvi, xxx, xxxvi, 61, 70
Leslie, Professor John, 18, 48n
Loch Ryan, xxi, xxiii, 137–41

Mackenzie of Coul, Sir George S., xxxvi
Manby, Captain George W., xli
Mayday celebrations, 17, 158–9
Meares, John, xxiii
Moorsom, Richard, 3
Munchausen's travels, 98
Mutiny, threatened, xxii, 173–4, 201–4

Nansen, Fridtjof, xxviii
North Rona & Sula Sgeir islands, 67–8, 207–8
Norway, coast of, 72

Orkney, 55, 67–8

Peggy (Barrow's 1780s whaler), xxx
Phipps, Constantine John (expedition 1773), 98n, 107, 119
Playfair, Professor John, xxxvi

Raffles, Dr Thomas, xxv
Richardson, Christopher, 3
Robinson, Sir Frederick (President, Board of Trade), xxxiv–xxxv
Ross, Sir John, RN, xxi, 139–40
Royal Navy
    arctic exploration by, xxxi–xxxiii
    unemployment in, xxx–xxxi

St Kilda island, xx, 67n, 68, 142, 210
Scientific observations and measurements, Scoresby's,
    arctic mean temperature, xxxviii
    atmospheric electricity, 73–6
    glaciers, xxxix–xl, 109–10
    ice density (specific gravity), 43–4, 80–81
    latitude determination in fog, 42
    magnetism and navigational compass, 15, 22, 30, 123, 143, 188–9
    marine biology and sea colour, 27, 56, 155–6, 179, 192–3

ocean currents in the Greenland Sea, xviii, 18, 27, 41, 47, 192

ocean depth, xviii, 30, 36–8, 104–5

optical phenomena, 176, 182–3

snow and ice crystals, hoar frost, rime, 16, 18, 21, 48, 79, 155, 156

weather systems in the Arctic, 11–12, 150–51

whale oil characteristics, 78, 83, 96

Scoresby, Mrs Mary, xxvii, 8, 63, 137, 141, 147, 212

Scoresby, William, Senior, xix–xx, xxiv–xxv, 19–20, 61, 66

Shetland, xx–xxi, 4, 6–8, 12, 54–5, 68–73, 98, 122–3

Spitsbergen, landing on, xxi, 107, 112–17

Sumburgh Röst, 7

Traill, Thomas S., xxvi, xxxvii, 48n, 135, 144

Wernerian Society, xxvii

Whitby harbour, xxi, xxv, 5, 57, 124–5

Wrangham, Archdeacon Francis, xli

Yeoman, Henry W., 3

Index of Whaling Vessels

Note: As in the earlier volumes, this index includes only those vessels mentioned in Scoresby's journals. Home ports and masters shown in parentheses are based on the contemporary printed lists prepared by Devereux & Lambert ('Oil and Whalebone Factors and Insurance Brokers'), London in 1817 and by Francis Devereux in 1818 and 1820. In cases where vessels of the same name sailed from different ports, there is sometimes uncertainty as to which vessel the journals refer. In each of the three years, the printed lists include 150 to 159 British vessels engaged in whaling in the Greenland Sea and Davis Strait, returning with blubber from 828 whales in 1817, 1208 in 1818 and 1595 in 1820. The *Fame* is indexed for 1820 when captained by William Scoresby, Senior, but not for 1818.

Aimwell (Whitby, Johnston 1817, Baxter 1818 & 1820), 5, 10–12, 31

Ajax (Hull, Stephens 1818) 94

Albion (Hull, Smart 1817, Slingsby 1818, Humphrey 1820), 170–72, 177

Alert (Peterhead, Penny), 33, 36

Anne Marie (Hamburg), 91

Aurora (Hull, Angus Sadler 1817, Griswood[1] 1818, Thomas 1820), 32–3

Bremen (Bremen) 172

British Queen (Newcastle, Beautyman 1817 & 1818, Warham 1820),[2] 45

Cato (Hull, Turnbull), 160

Cherub (Hull, William Jackson 1817 & 1818), 90

Dauntless (London, 1817 Bruce), 21, 25–6, 33–4

Dexterity[3] (Peterhead, Geary 1817 & 1818, Robertson 1820), 21

Ebor (Hull, Lee 1820), 154

Ellen (Kirkwall, Spence), 20

Enterprize[4] (Lynn,[5] Sanderson) 25–6, 32–3

Exmouth (Hull, Thompson 1818 & 1820), 16

Fame (Hull, Scoresby Senior 1820), 137, 168–9

Fortitude (London, Galloway 1817), 21, 25–6

Greenland (Amsterdam, Broerties), 27

Guilder (Hull, Joseph Sadler 1817, Bruce 1818 & 1820), 16

Harmonie (Hamburg), 75

Henrietta (Whitby, Kearsley 1817 & 1818; Aberdeen, Small 1820), 5, 19

[1] Credland, *Hull Whaling Trade*, names Griswood as master of the *Hunter* in 1818, but elsewhere lists that vessel as lost in 1807.

[2] The printed lists have the spellings 'Beautiman' in 1817 and 'Wareham' in 1820; those shown above are based on Barrow, *Whaling Trade of North-East England*.

[3] Another *Dexterity* sailed to the Greenland Sea from Leith in all three years.

[4] Vessels with the same name, but different tonnages, sailed from Peterhead in 1818 and London in 1820.

[5] Kings Lynn was normally abbreviated to 'Lynn' in whaling references.

Ipswich (London, Taylor 1817, Gordon 1818 & 1820[1]), 112

James (Liverpool, Clough 1817 & 1818, Nesbit 1820), xxi, 90, 137, 140–41, 161, 165, 177
James (Whitby, Smith 1817 & 1818, Quickfall 1820[2]), 183, 186
John (Greenock, Jackson), xviii, xix, 17, 19–20, 22, 27, 31–2, 34–6, 38–41, 43, 45, 47, 50–51, 53–4, 90, 94, 99–100, 149, 151–2, 168–9
Juno (Leith, Robertson), 79

Lady Forbes (Liverpool, 1820 Robertson), xxi, 139–41, 161, 165, 169
Leviathan[3] (Newcastle, Preswick 1817), 21, 25, 26
Lion (Liverpool, Hawkins 1817), 21, 25, 26
Lively[4] (Whitby, Baxter[5]), 4, 17, 103
London (Montrose, Brand 1817, Robertson 1818, Cunningham 1820), 94

Manchester I (Hull, Adair 1817, Farrow 1818, Taylor 1820), 45, 47, 49
Mars (Whitby, Scoresby Senior 1817, Johnston 1818 & 1820), xviii, 3–5, 16, 18–24, 29, 31–2, 34–6, 39–40, 168, 177
Mary and Elizabeth (Hull, Cook 1817 & 1818, Wheldon[6] 1820), 181–2, 187, 190, 193

Mercury (Hull, Jackson 1820), 178

Neptune (Aberdeen, Drysdale 1817 & 1818, Ridley 1820), 38
Neptune[7] (Hull, Munroe[8]), 32, 160–61
Nord Stern (Germany?), 23
Norfolk (Berwick, Marshall 1817[9]), 25, 33
North Briton (Hull, John Allan[10]), 94

Perseverance[11] (Peterhead, Milne), 90
Phoenix (Whitby, Dawson), 4, 17, 19, 35, 49, 151, 181–2

Resolution (Peterhead, Suttar 1817 & 1818, Philip 1820), 31, 33
Resolution (Whitby, Kearsley), 5, 7, 94
Rookwood (London, Todd 1817 & 1818[12]), 36

Shannon (Hull, Kielah), 177
Spencer (Montrose, Keith), 45
Superior (Peterhead, Manson), 21, 25–6, 33

Valiant (Whitby, Agar), 5, 7, 45, 103
Venerable (Hull, Bennett), xix, 26, 40–41, 43, 45, 47, 50–51, 53, 54, 167
Volunteer (Whitby, Craig), 4, 20, 151

Walker (Hull, Richard Harrison), 33, 35
William and Ann[13] (Whitby, Stephens 1817 & 1818, Terry 1820), xix, 4

[1] In 1820 the *Ipswich* was listed by Devereux as sailing to Davis Strait.

[2] In 1817 and 1818 the Whitby *James* sailed to Davis Strait. In 1820, however, she joined the Greenland Sea fleet and it is not always clear whether it is to this vessel or the *James* of Liverpool that Scoresby refers in his 1820 journal entries.

[3] Another *Leviathan* sailed to the Greenland Sea in all three years from Hull.

[4] Another *Lively* sailed to the Greenland Sea in all three years from Berwick.

[5] 'Baxter' is also listed by Devereux as the master of the *Aimwell* in 1820.

[6] Spelling is according to Credland; Devereux's is 'Weldon'.

[7] A third *Neptune* sailed to the Greenland Sea from London in 1817 and 1818; in 1820 she went to Davis Strait.

[8] Spelling is Credland's; Devereux's are 'Munro' and 'Monro'.

[9] In 1818 and 1820 the *Norfolk* sailed to Davis Strait.

[10] Or 'Allen', according to both Devereux and Credland.

[11] Another *Perseverance* sailed to the Greenland Sea in all three years from Hull.

[12] In 1820 the *Rookwood* sailed to Davis Strait.

[13] Another *William and Ann* sailed to the Greenland Sea in all three years from Leith.